AMERICAN ANTHROPOLOGY & COMPANY

*Critical Studies in the
History of Anthropology*

SERIES EDITORS
Regna Darnell
Stephen O. Murray

American Anthropology & Company

Historical Explorations

Stephen O. Murray

University of Nebraska Press
Lincoln and London

Library of Congress Cataloging-in-Publication Data

Murray, Stephen O. (1950–)
American anthropology and company : historical
explorations / Stephen O. Murray.
pages cm. — (Critical studies in the history of
anthropology)
Includes bibliographical references and index.
ISBN 978-0-8032-4395-8 (cloth : alk. paper)
1. Anthropology—United States—History.
2. Anthropological linguistics—United States—
History. 3. Sociology—United States—History.
I. Title.
GN17.3.U6M87 2013
301.0973—dc23   2012050027

Set in Lyon Text by Laura Wellington.

In memory of
Robert A. Nisbet (1913–1986)
and Dell H. Hymes (1927–2009),
mentors of vast erudition,
who crossed disciplinary borders
with impunity

Contents

Illustrations

Series Editor's Introduction

REGNA DARNELL

I have known Steve Murray since he was a University of Toronto sociology graduate student starting a network analysis of anthropological linguists. From research on anthropological linguists and linguistics—which culminated in his magisterial 1994 book *Theory Groups and the Study of Language in North America*—and without any institutional support, he branched out to examining other borders of academic anthropology, including the obvious one for a sociologist, sociology, plus (ethno)history, as well as psychological anthropology (in its "culture and personality" guise). Very few readers are familiar with the full disciplinary range of his work. Most of the papers published in this volume have appeared in earlier forms in print, directed to diverse audiences. It seems to me that his method and argument define a unique critical perspective on anthropology as institutionalized for the past century and a quarter in North America. Reflexive bookends at the beginning and end motivate the choice of papers and integrate Murray's preoccupations over his career. Few other historians of anthropology have written broadly enough on the subject for a career perspective to emerge.

Several of the chapters of this book look at histories of central institutions of American anthropology, including its core journals and geographical expansion. Familiar, canonized anthropologist "culture heroes" (Sapir, Kroeber, Lowie, Mead, Boas, Redfield) indeed appear, but they are juxtaposed with the likes of William F. Ogburn and W. I. Thomas, leading figures of American sociology whose history was interwoven with that of anthropology at least until the end of the Second World War. Murray unravels much of the tension behind disciplinary coexistence at major institutions, particularly the Universities of Chicago and California, Berkeley. At Chicago, an anthropology department split off from its august sociology department. At Berkeley, the anthropologists, particularly Alfred Kroeber, effectively opposed the emergence of a department of sociology and relegated the work of demographer Dorothy Swaine Thomas to agricultural economics (thereby also excluding her from histories of sociology, though she was the first female president of the American Sociological Society).

Murray brings critical distance to the emergence of peasant studies as a rebellion against Boasian Native American salvage research; he foregrounds the sociological side of anthropology that attempted to move beyond the isolationism of North America in the interwar years. Murray is inclined to attribute the contemporary approach to urban anthropology and the ethnography of complex societies to Chicago sociologists rather than to the anthropologists in their midst and clearly shares a distaste he reports sociologists had for the pronouncements about "American culture" of 1940s anthropologists who had done little or no research on their own "home" society and culture. Questions of political suppression arise, for example, in the analysis of anthropologists' complicity in World War II Japanese internment and with the long-running martial law on Taiwan by the Kuomintang, purporting to be "the Republic of China." The history of anthropology and associated disciplines does not emerge as uniformly benign, and Murray's work challenges contemporary anthropologists to evaluate where they have come from as part of present practice.

Murray consults archival sources for professional correspondence and the published literature of articles and reviews for cues to anthropologists' networks and frames them in terms of institutional developments and cultural trends that were far from unique to anthropology. He is a tenacious archivist, following individuals and events from institution to institution and integrating widely dispersed sources. Trained as a sociologist, he counts things that can be counted—then tells his readers why the numbers explain what people were up to (citations, numbers of students, book reviews, etc.). He elicited memories and explanations from elders of the "tribes" (disciplines) who are now dead and triangulates these "native views" with archival records and published social science literature.

Murray is skeptical of the stories anthropologists tell about themselves for an audience within the discipline and seeks out alternative explanations and connections, particularly at disciplinary connecting points where cross-fertilization is most likely to occur. He has a way of getting to the point and challenging readers to disagree, but only on the basis of historicist interpretation of concrete evidence. Sloppy generalizations about the history of anthropology annoy him and often stimulate him to undertake research complicating pat explanations.

In addition to ethnological analysis and theorizing, Murray has done (and published in refereed journals) ethnographic work in Latin America and Asia as well as North America, giving his voice an all-too-rare comparative ethnographer resonance. He deploys his insider-outsider status in anthropology to approach the preconceptions the anthropologist takes to the field in his collaboration with Keelung Hong on the latter's native Taiwan and emphasizes the explicit challenges this perspective poses to established anthropological wisdom. Questions are raised at the peripheries that tend to be glossed over at the center. This collection is provocative and needs to be taken seriously as both substantive historiography and methodological caveat for a critical history of anthropology.

Introduction

Collecting some of my writings about research on the history of American anthropology and its social science neighbors (history, linguistics, psychology, and at greatest length, sociology) provides the opportunity to reflect on how they came about and to see some relationships between a range of research projects aiming to answer questions about some things that happened and some that did not but seemingly could have along the relatively unfortified borders of twentieth-century American anthropologies.

Having had no undergraduate sociology or anthropology course but having read books about scientific communities by Herbert Butterfield and Don Price, I wandered into the history of social science stimulated by Thomas Kuhn's (1962) *The Structure of Scientific Revolutions*, which I read in 1972, during the summer after I graduated from college. At the University of Arizona two years later, Keith Basso stimulated my interest in social influences on language use. When my sociologist mentor Robert Nisbet told me he was leaving Arizona and that I needed to find a different PhD program, I migrated to the University of Toronto, intending to do dissertation research about power in spoken interaction, building on the work we did in Keith's seminar.

William Samarin took over my education about sociolinguistics, and I picked up some ideas about ethnohistory from him as well. The summer after my first year in graduate school I attended my first annual meeting of the American Sociological Association—at which I heard some very unimpressive presentations by many of the biggest names in the field. However, I also went to a sociology of science session in which I heard a paper by Nicholas C. Mullins (published in 1975) that provided the model of revolution-making in science that I would test and refine in my doctoral dissertation and one by Harriet Zuckerman (1974, never published, though the main example for it was, as Zuckerman and Lederberg 1986) about how lines of work can be postmature as well as premature, which bore fruits especially evident in chapters 10 and 12 of this volume.

I proposed a dissertation testing the bipartite (functionalist and conflict) Mullins model of group formation and rhetorics of continuity or of making revolutions. I quickly realized that context-free measures of the amount of discontinuity in practices or in theories did not exist and would be essentially contested were any proposed, whereas intercoder reliability about proclaiming continuity or revolution was obtainable. What I proposed eventually became *American Sociolinguistics* (Murray 1998), but the dissertation reached beyond anthropological linguistics to unanthropological linguistics (the purported "Chomskian revolution" in particular: see Murray 1980d) and back through centuries of North American work describing and attempting to explain language(s): what became *Theory Groups in the Study of Language in North America* (Murray 1994b).

The case studies (including theorizing that did not lead to "theory groups") contained a lot of detail, but were being deployed to test Mullins's model. I have included none of this line of work here. Indeed, only two chapters in this collection (2 and 10) deal with linguistic anthropology. Both focus on Edward Sapir's years (1925–31) in the University of Chicago Department of Sociology (of which an anthropology program was a junior partner before becoming a separate department in 1929). I feel that as a linguistic anthropologist (which I sometimes think I am) I am in the Sapir tradition, but am aware that I would probably not have gotten along with him had I been his student or colleague. I feel that opportunities for interdisciplinary integration were missed at Chicago of the late 1920s (for which there is plenty of blame to go around!) and that Sapir was the person there with the knowledge about languages to supplement Chicago sociologists' experiences doing ethnography.

I also think that anthropological research on peasantries by American anthropologists was late, if not fully "postmature." When it *was* done, it was done primarily by students of Robert Redfield at Chicago and those who had studied with Alfred Kroeber at Berkeley. This turn is explicable in expanding the subject matter as the supply of "tribal"/"primitive" people was rapidly waning. Kroeber supervised and encouraged work on peasants, though his own ethnographic work was "salvage anthropology" of severely disrupted California indigenous groups, along with archaeology in Peru and analysis of cultural changes over centuries within large-scale civilizations.

It is difficult not to notice that anthropologists and sociologists who were trained at Berkeley and Chicago loom large and recurrently in my historical explorations (along with those, including Kroeber, Robert Lowie, Margaret Mead, and Sapir, who had been influenced by Franz Boas at Columbia, plus Columbia sociology PhDs such as William Ogburn and Elsie Clews Parsons). In part this focus on those sites is because they were important centers for social science research and theorizing. In part, it is that so much biographical work has been done on Columbia faculty and graduates that I did not see much point in undertaking research on them. Probably another part of the explanation is that very rich archives exist at the Bancroft Library (Berkeley) and the Regenstein Library (Chicago). I have spent a lot of time in both libraries, along with a week's time spent in the Boas Collection of the American Philosophical Society Library in Philadelphia.

Kroeber and Sapir play major roles in the stories told in several chapters, as do W. I. Thomas and his wife, Dorothy Swaine Thomas (who was already named Thomas before marrying him). I see tragic elements in the career (and inept careerism) of Edward Sapir. I see W. I. Thomas as something of a martyr who refused to consider himself a victim—Dorothy Thomas as a tragic heroine who also refused to consider herself a victim. The final two Berkeley-centered chapters can be read as cases of ingratitude by young and ambitious men (Morton Grodzins and Robert Nisbet) to accomplished and senior scholars whose sex made them vulnerable to marginalization (Dorothy Thomas and Margaret Hodgen).

I am not pushing a particular theory (about sexism, theory-group formation, or anything else) in the studies collected here. Most of my research projects were stimulated by doubts about particular claims. (Taking examples other than the historical ones examined in this volume, I was skeptical about the use of weak ties in getting job information or that interruption is a male monopoly in naturally occurring speech.) I think most of the chapters show that developments in (social) science are fitful and far more complicated than simpleminded "just-so" stories like those Derek Freeman and others have told. Zadie Smith wrote that "most of us have complicated back stories, messy histories, multiple narratives" (2009:42), and so do scientific "schools," theories, and methods. Kuhn (1962 and elsewhere) considered social sciences "preparadigmatic" because of dissensus about such basic matters, though I have my doubts about any paradigm commanding the assent of every credentialed participant in any modern scientific field. I am interested in developments in anthropology and other fields but very skeptical of Development (or Evolution) in the singular. My dissertation research convinced me that there are both major continuities across the punctuations of "scientific revolutions" as well as major discontinuities within "normal science." Moreover, "normal science" (and, indeed, all academic disciplines) is often very rancorous, and even seemingly hegemonic theory groups are riven with internal controversies and personal antagonisms, though these may be cloaked in rationalizations of methodology and interpretations of doctrine and data.

Labels—even those such as "Boasian," "Freudian," or "Parsonian," which I sometimes use—often obscure nearly as much as they illuminate. I think that at least some of my work, especially the first four or five chapters in this volume, looks at practices, which to me include recurrent omissions as well as recurrent commissions in what social science practitioners do or did. Having entered the field looking at network clusters rather than genealogies, I wish that history of social science writing focused more on practices, less on pronouncements about affiliations to theoretical paradigms and apostolic successions.

Insofar as cultural anthropologists, linguists, and sociologists are "professionals," their "profession" is as "professors," not as researchers or writers living on fees for service and royalties.[1] Professors often seem more interested in professing to colleagues away from their institutional bases—whether in person or in keyboarding and subsequent publication—than to students at the university. When I speak of their "practices," this includes what they do inside their discipline (and subspecialty) more than what they do within a particular university or other institution. Jockeying for place and for quasi-ownership of particular research domains (places or topics) is a focus of many of these historical explorations. From my dissertation research on anthropological linguistics, my curiosity carried me from that borderland into unanthropological linguistics (see Murray 1994b) and unlinguistic anthropology (most of the chapters herein).

My first interest in Boasian anthropology was stimulated by Claude Lévi-Strauss, who was in the French sociological tradition of Émile Durkheim (and, especially, Durkheim's nephew and collaborator, Marcel

Mauss), as well as in the comparative social theorizing of Charles de Montesquieu and Jean-Jacques Rousseau. I've been tempted to include my first presentation at a professional meeting, "Lévi-Strauss in the State of Nature" (presented in El Paso at what was then called the Rocky Mountain Social Science Association), an honest-to-God structuralist analysis of the "states of nature" in Thomas Hobbes's *Leviathan*, Rousseau's *Social Contract*, and Lévi-Strauss's *Tristes tropiques* (and some articles by him).

My undergraduate background in social theory (in the ornately named major "Justice, Morality, and Constitutional Democracy" at James Madison College) allowed me to do well in the "pretest" that Robert Nisbet gave students on the first day of his social theory class. Nisbet had written two books on Durkheim and found my approach (through Rousseau, Montesquieu, and Durkheim) at least interesting. So, although my research on the history of anthropology followed interest in anthropological linguistics, that interest itself flowed from the French tradition of theorizing about society/ies.

I've already mentioned that I had no undergraduate sociology (or anthropology) courses, but I had read some Max Weber (not least, "Science as a Vocation") and was intrigued by the Weberian base of Berkeley sociologist Jerome Skolnick's (1967) police ethnography *Justice without Trial*. Weber is not viewed by as many anthropologists as having done ethnology as Durkheim, particularly in his last (1910) book, is seen as an ancestor of symbolic anthropology and (in earlier work) as a pioneer of structural analysis and of analysis of phenomena such as suicide with social variables. Durkheim's *Elementary Forms of the Religious Life* (1912) was (among other things) an ethnology of Australian aborigines. Weber's life project was comparative, comparing material on religions and economies; drawing data from historical texts and archival material along very long historical *durées*, Durkheim used then-recent ethnographies by others in *Elementary Forms* and official statistics in *Le suicide* (1897). I was once accused of being a "closet Weberian" but don't think that my comparativist interests were ever closeted. The comparativism among American social science traditions may not seem obviously Weberian, but in examining multiplicities rather than proclaiming a singular evolutionary trajectory, I feel that what I do is Weberian more than Durkheimian (or Marxist). I do not see the history of sociocultural research as teleological, progressing even unsmoothly to one ultimate

Truth (explanatory principle). Anyone seeking a teleological history can find it in Marvin Harris's *The Rise of Anthropological Theory* (1968), which definitely does not focus on practice(s).

This personal contextualization is included to establish that although my path into or toward sociocultural anthropology was through linguistic anthropology, once I arrived there, I had some relevant background. As a historian, I approached the anthropology-sociology border from anthropology, having approached sociocultural anthropology from linguistic anthropology and linguistic anthropology from the Durkheimian/Lévi-Strauss tradition. Perhaps my idiosyncratic peregrinations through social science disciplines did not matter to how I interviewed those with memories of the events and/or scholars in whom I came to be interested or how I worked through archival collections. I certainly learned some things about interpreting texts from my undergraduate (Justice, Morality, and Constitutional Democracy) and graduate (sociology and linguistic anthropology) classes and did some (Weber-influenced) content analysis in a social psychology methods course taught by William Crano at Michigan State. Part of my disillusion with the Arizona sociology program was the unconcern about data gathering I felt was prevalent there: the focus, particularly from Otis Dudley Duncan— my academic genealogy link to Ogburn—was on grinding quantitative data gathered by others; only a decade later did I find out that Duncan shared some of my concerns about the validity of the numbers he taught us to grind (Duncan 1984).

It might seem more-or-less natural that a sociologist who undertook research on anthropologists would take an interest in the sociology-anthropology border regions and that it was from having been a post-doctoral fellow in the Berkeley anthropology department that I would take an interest in earlier interdisciplinary projects and conflicts at Berkeley. Prefiguring an argument I will make in the conclusion, such "commonsense" inferences are misleading. It is from having been a student of Robert Nisbet's at Arizona that I explored the fate of the peculiar department in which he had been a student and junior faculty member. Similarly, my interest in the professional unpopularity of scientists who do popularizing work (chapter 3) came in part through Brandeis (where I've never been, but where Everett Hughes influenced some people who influenced me), in part through having lived in the Arizona-Sonora desert with connections through whom I reached and talked to Edward and

Rosamond Spicer, and in part from one of the theory groups of my dissertation research having been ethnoscience (see Murray 1982). On the other hand, despite my grounding in Freudian conceptions from undergraduate courses, the chapter (6) focusing on Freudian anthropology developed while I was in Berkeley, supposed to be working on linguistic anthropology, but having easy access to George Devereux's PhD dissertation on Mohave sexuality. If I didn't live in the San Francisco Bay Area, I might not have undertaken to write about Berkeley anthropology during the 1950s (that decade I chose because it seems less written about than earlier or later ones there). It was also while I was a Berkeley postdoc that Keelung Hong directed my attention at anthropological (mis) representations of Taiwan (chapter 8), including but not confined to Berkeley ones, with less-compromised work from people at my first alma mater, Michigan State (of whom I had been unaware when I was there).

Topics of Particular Chapters

The chapters within each of the two sections of this book are roughly in chronological order. The expanse of time covered in some of them makes for some temporal backtracking, however.

Divergences among "Boasians" are foci of the first and third chapters. I think that these chapters are concerned with practices in research and inference more than in theorizing. (I see Boas as antitheoretical, though many of his students were not, including Edward Sapir, a major character in the second chapter, one particularly focused on practices and how field practices and assumptions about a singular structure being recoverable from any speaker affected the descriptions and analyses produced.)

As the "salvage" project of American(ist) anthropology waned, some anthropologists got around to studying peasant communities. (Sociologists had been doing both rural and urban community studies for some time, though the 1930s was a "boom time" for community studies in sociology as well as in anthropology.) Anthropologists trained by Kroeber and Lowie at Berkeley were among the anthropologist pioneers of peasant studies (along with those trained at Chicago by Robert Redfield and A. Radcliffe-Brown), as is elaborated in chapter 4.

Chapter 5 shows that a geographic expansion of interest beyond U.S. territory was more gradual and less complete than some have suggested. In addition to expansion of geographic range, increased attention was paid to enculturation in early life, attention encouraged by Freudian assertions about character structures being set in infancy and early childhood. In chapter 6 I look at the dissertation and predissertation fieldwork and training by Kroeber and Lowie of Georges Devereux, who became one of the most orthodox of Freudian anthropologists but was, I show, not one yet at the time of his Berkeley dissertation on the Mohaves.

Chapter 3 is unusually focused on a center of American anthropology research and training (Columbia/Barnard/New York's Museum of Natural History) rather than on anthropology borderlands (linguistic, psychoanalytic, or sociological). Its aim to correct the misrepresentations of the culture of Boasian anthropologists in Derek Freeman's shoddy, surmise-heavy "history" of American anthropology is obvious. Chapter 7 looks at a major department, the University of California at Berkeley's, which was somewhat becalmed during the 1950s with the retirements of its internationally known anthropologist superstars. This is the same department from which the psychological anthropology work discussed in the sixth chapter emerged (during its heyday) and one that reappears in chapter 13 as leading resistance to establishing a sociology department.

Chapter 8 turns to another periphery: doing fieldwork on Taiwan while American social scientists were banned from China and pretending to be studying "traditional Chinese culture," a more prestigious line of work than researching a hybrid culture under autocratic rule (that justified itself as restoring "traditional Chinese culture" to what had been a Japanese colony). We (the chapter was coauthored with Keelung Hong) show that there was variation by topical domain in how invisible in anthropologists' representations it was that the research was done on Taiwan. (The past tense is justified since American anthropologists fled democratizing Taiwan to work under the auspices of the autocrats in China once they could.)

Chapter 5 does not have a geographical base in terms of a particular anthropology department but looks at the field more generally in regard to field site locations. Although some American anthropologists looked beyond aboriginal America(s), looking at publication data shows that American anthropologist remained "Americanist" in the usual sense of American cultures and field sites.[2]

The ninth chapter shows that the pioneering empirical sociologist W. I. Thomas began as a Boasian ethnologist and ended as a behaviorist, although he has been read primarily as a voluntarist sociologist, especially by symbolic interactionist sociologists. (I do not think that he is read at all by twenty-first-century anthropologists, though some may nod at his pioneering collection of life histories from Polish emigrants to the United States.)

The tenth chapter focuses even more than the second one did on Edward Sapir, again in his Chicago years (1925–31), and the failure of ethnography of speaking or any other kind of sociolinguists developing there and then. Though Sapir was brought in to bridge disciplinary boundaries, he was involved in the fission of the sociology department at Chicago into separate sociology and anthropology ones, and his strongest personal bond to a Chicago sociologist was to the least ethnographic of them, William F. Ogburn (who had been friends with Boasian anthropologists at Columbia and was data-oriented but was not interested in language).

The eleventh chapter—looking at the reception of anthropological books in the three core American sociology journals—shows that cultural anthropology was highly valued by American sociologists until pronouncements by Margaret Mead, Hortense Powdermaker, and Clyde Kluckhohn made sociologists wonder whether what anthropologists understood of distant/alien societies was as off-base (invalid) as the facile claims they made about "American culture" (and the inner workings of Hollywood).

The thirteenth chapter, like the tenth, examines a case of postmaturity. Although anthropologists were not the sole opposition to the University of California (Berkeley) establishing a sociology department, Kroeber in particular was involved in delaying establishment of one. Keeping Dorothy Swaine Thomas—wife of W. I., student of and collaborator with William F. Ogburn, and later the first female president of the American Sociological Association—marginalized in the Department of Agricultural Economics seems to have been a major motivation, not only for senior male scholars in other disciplines but also for Margaret Hodgen, pioneer of history of anthropology, who was the woman heading the Department of Social Institutions. That department was an ad hoc institutional home concocted for her mentor, Frederick J. Teggart, who retired in 1940 and died in 1946.

The twelfth chapter also shows Dorothy Thomas being kicked around, by both an ambitious former research assistant and by senior staff at the University of Chicago who she thought would understand her wanting to control research for hire done by a research assistant, Morton

Grodzins. The subject matter of the data (the forced removal of Japanese Americans from the U.S. West Coast) and some artful dodging of truth made it possible for Grodzins to publish project data . . . and to take the position of his primary Chicago advocate as head of the University of Chicago Press, despite having no other background in publishing than getting his PhD dissertation published over the vociferous opposition of his former supervisors—including his dissertation supervisor, Charles Aikin, and Thomas, who was on his PhD committee in addition to being the head of the Japanese-American Evacuation and Resettlement Study (JAERS).

As with many of the preceding chapters, the final substantive one aims to correct misapprehension, this one that editors of core anthropology and/or sociology journals profit by increased citation of their work in the journals they edit.

The concluding chapter reviews what I believe I have learned from doing history of social science: a set of maxims rather than a cookbook. I think that understanding past thinkers as they understood themselves is ultimately impossible but nonetheless is a worthy aspiration, which is to say I consider my work "historicist." I do not think that trying to figure out what people in the past thought they were doing disallows criticism of how they did—and failed to do—what they wanted to do. Moreover, I find deplorable some of the goals—notably herein those of the anthropologists who worked for concentration camp administrators (as the Berkeley Japanese-American Evacuation and Resettlement Study staff did not) and those eager for access to fields in Taiwan—and do not confine myself to observing the self-defeating conduct of social scientists. My research and analysis of the history of American social science(s) is primarily internalist,[3] but by no means would I proscribe externalist work, particularly of the World War II and Cold War work into which some anthropologists plunged enthusiastically (garnering much more financial support than British functionalists received from the British colonial establishment), which David Price (1998, 2002a, 2002b, 2008) has been exploring (see also Solovey 2001; D. Wax 2008). George Lucas (2009) extends such valuable inquiry into this century's combats.

AMERICAN ANTHROPOLOGY & COMPANY

1

Anthropology and Some of Its Companions

Introduction

Before the Boasians

Though the chapters in this book do not form a teleology or test any specific theory, some readers might find the particular topics addressed as beginning in medias res and/or readers may lack background in the prehistory of academic American anthropology—a process that began in the last years of the nineteenth century. In addition to recommending accounts in Bieder (1986), Bieder and Tax (1974), Darnell (1998a, 1999, 2001), Hinsley (1981), and Jacknis (2002), I provide a whirlwind overview below.

From the beginning of European settlement of the Americas, missionaries tried to learn about Native American cultures and languages. Proselytizing in native languages and translating the Bible into them was an early and persisting commitment, along with understanding Others the better to manipulate them ("applied anthropology" *après la lettre*). Many Christians were interested in scrutinizing the native people to see if they were some "lost tribe of Israel" (Hodgen 1964:303–25; Stocking 1968:42–68). Rationalists during the eighteenth century also sought information about the native inhabitants of the Western Hemisphere to build and assess models of "the state of nature."

Thomas Jefferson

Thomas Jefferson was an American rationalist with wide-ranging interests. Prior to his election as president of the United States of America, he worked on problems of Native American philology and speculated about where Native people(s) came from. As president, he promoted the collection of information on Native Peoples, especially through the (Meriwether) Lewis and (William) Clark expedition to the Pacific coast (1803–6). Jefferson himself prepared a research memorandum for them and stressed the need to record languages and cultural traits. In his *Notes on the State of Virginia* of 1787, Jefferson set forth his own speculations about the ancestry of the American Indian(s), tabulated historical, descriptive, and statistical data on tribal groups, and reported on his own excavation of burial mounds.

In frequent correspondence with leading European and American intellectuals of his time, he "and others of his circle set an example by accumulating new knowledge regarding *Homo Americanus.* This was anthropology without a portfolio, pursued in our own frontiers" (Hallowell 1960:16).

Since Jefferson extended those frontiers, he also had less disinterested motivation for learning about the indigenous peoples. In his view, their cultures deserved respect. In the view of others, Native people were savages who happened to be in the way of what was later claimed to be the "manifest destiny" to supplant them with God's chosen northern European people (Anglo-Saxons) across North America. Once the new American government committed itself to the principle of recognizing native title to western lands, "it was of great practical importance for the government to have reliable knowledge about the Western tribes" (Hallowell 1960:18). Jefferson's own curiosity certainly extended beyond the practical needs of presiding over territorial expansion, but his wider humanistic motivations for inquiry were not necessarily shared by his successors, nor did they determine his presidential policies (see Wallace 2001). Jefferson institutionalized a connection between anthropological/linguistic inquiry, territorial expansion, and a responsibility for managing Native people within that encroachment.

Gallatin, Schoolcraft, and the American Ethnological Society

Together with Thomas Jefferson, whose secretary of the treasury and advisor on Indian affairs he was, Albert Gallatin (1761–1849) was one of the leading American Enlightenment figures. However, Gallatin "did not undertake serious ethnological studies until the 1820s, a time when Enlightenment assumptions about man were under attack" and German romanticism was increasingly influential (Bieder 1986:17).

Gallatin participated in the cultural, intellectual, and social institutions of the New York elite in the first half of the nineteenth century. John Bartlett, a fellow officer in the New York Historical Society, proposed to him "a new society, the attention of which should be devoted to Geography, Archeology, Philology and inquiries generally connected with the human race" (quoted in Bieder and Tax 1976:12). Gallatin was elected president of the new American Ethnological Society (AES) in 1842. Its dinner meetings were held in his home until his death in 1849. "The active members tended to be gentlemen of some social standing in the New York community who knew each other well, and while they had some intellectual pretensions, they were not 'ethnological experts.' Nearly all were professional men. . . . Very few of the members, even in the early and more fruitful years of the AES had any ethnological experience" (Bieder and Tax 1974:16).

Through most of the nineteenth century, "descriptions [of native ways] were often interpreted by gentlemen and philosophers who themselves had not had contact with native peoples. . . . This period gave way to one of incipient professionalism in which individuals labeled their work as anthropology and submitted it to evaluation by their peers, but were not themselves trained as anthropologists" (Darnell 1976:70–71).

Rather than develop (evolve) toward professionalism, the AES foundered (degenerated). Its sponsor died, leaving only dilettantes behind. Also, "philosophical disagreements had an adverse effect on the Society's fortunes. Many members quarreled about what was pertinent and legitimate for discussion. The crux of the matter lay in the fundamental division between the atheistic polygenists . . . and the clerics. . . . As physical anthropology became a topic of common discussion in the Society, discord erupted. The polygenist approach to physical anthropology disturbed both the clergy and other monogenist members, many of whom were mainly interested in Near Eastern antiquities and insisted on a literal interpretation of the Bible" (Bieder and Tax 1976:17).

That is, the AES was split by "paradigm conflict" despite its "prescientific" status. The Bible served as a paradigm for the monogenists, who explained diversity as stemming from degeneration (due to the lapsing of God's law) from the original unity of descendants of Adam and Eve.[1] Those who believed in multiple origins of humanity, language, and cultures necessarily challenged the sufficiency of Genesis as a description and/or explanation (Hodgen 1964:225–94).

Gallatin argued that Indian languages were primitive against those who saw "polysynthetic" languages as residues of a higher ancestral civilization (usually assumed to be that of a "lost tribe of Israel"). Mayan, Aztec, and Inca civilizations, which Gallatin insisted were indigenous, demonstrated the racial capacity to advance to urban, agriculture- and state-based civilization.

Henry Schoolcraft, now better remembered as the white discoverer and namer of the source of the Mississippi River (Lake Itasca, compounded from *veritas caput*) than as an expert on North American Native Peoples, was a geologist on an 1820 government expedition to Lake Superior and the Mississippi River led by governor/general Lewis Cass. In 1822 Schoolcraft was appointed Indian agent at Sault Saint Marie, Michigan. There he married Jane Johnson, an Ojibwa woman of mixed descent. Though spending more time in the field than most early ethnographers, Schoolcraft was typical in underacknowledged reliance upon the "tacit knowledge" of a long-term local resident (see Ogden 2011). Schoolcraft was less optimistic about Native Americans' racial capacity than Gallatin had been, often considering them "Oriental," which to him meant impervious to change, though he nevertheless believed the young could be Christianized and educated. Cass, a patron of Schoolcraft and of others studying Native Americans,[2] thought that Gallatin and others romantically overestimated the capacities of American Indians (see Cass 1826). Schoolcraft found—to his chagrin—that a "primitive language" (specifically Ojibwa, then called "Chippewa") was not as simple to master as Cass's theory of limited mental capacity of Indians ordained.

Frustrated by the difficulty of linguistic analysis, specifically with demonstrating the connections between Ojibwa and Hebrew, and by personal circumstances, Schoolcraft sought another, easier "royal road" to Native American history than comparative philology in folkloristics (Bieder 1986:158–173; Hallowell 1960:43). Despite the increasing dominance of polygenism (Horsman 1975), which made inroads even in the AES, Schoolcraft maintained the "Genesis paradigm."

Both by being innatist in science and by articulately criticizing genocidal policies, Schoolcraft and, later, Lewis Henry Morgan continued the Gallatin tradition, both in monogenist theory and in the practice of defending Native Americans from rationalizations for genocide. Indeed, his major ethnographic and ethnohistorical study of the League of the Iroquois was originally a series of "Letters on the Iroquois Addressed to Albert Gallatin" published in the *American Whig Review* in 1844–45. Although Schoolcraft and Morgan did extensive (if not intensive) fieldwork with particular peoples (Chipewyans and Iroquois, respectively), and although all three collated published reports and questionnaires sent to those familiar with different North American peoples ("tribes"), they all treated American Indians as a single people at the stage of "barbarism" in the evolutionary rise from "savagism" to "barbarism" to "civilization" (see Hodgen 1964). All three defended the model of monogenesis against an increasingly dominant polygenism in which American Indians were considered a distinct species doomed to extinction in competition for territory with the "Anglo-Saxon race."

Brinton and Putnam at Pennsylvania and Harvard

A firm believer in the psychic unity of mankind, Daniel Garrison Brinton, a Philadelphia physician, was active in many local intellectual societies. I would include among the local organizations Philadelphia's American Philosophical Society, of which Brinton was president in 1869 and in the *Proceedings* of which he published many anthropological papers. Brinton was also president of the (more truly national) American Association for the Advancement of Science in 1882.

Brinton was "technically the first university professor of anthropology in North America," appointed at the University of Pennsylvania in 1884. However, the appointment was an honorary one without salary. Moreover, Brinton did not actually teach classes or have students at the university (Darnell 1970:82, 85). The grandiose structure of courses listed in university catalogs went mostly untaught for lack of students. At least, he trained no professional anthropologists (A. Kroeber 1939:178, 1960:4–5). He was "committed to the development of an academic framework for anthropology" (Darnell 1970:83) but was at odds with the local patrons of the university and museum, who were primarily interested in classical and Near Eastern antiquities. Reacting against "lost tribes of Israel" and other interpretations of superficial resemblances, especially in myths and especially across vast spaces, Brinton maintained the probability of independent invention. Brinton's work had little posthumous influence (A. Kroeber 1960:4), except as the unnamed object of some of Boas's polemics between 1896 and 1911—though Boas was certainly not seeking to renew grand schemes of diffusion such as those Brinton had combated.

Frederic Ward Putnam came closer to being an organizational leader than Brinton did. Putnam was trained between 1857 and 1864 as a zoologist by Louis Agassiz, the preeminent natural historian in the Western Hemisphere. Putnam joined the Peabody Museum of American Archaeology in 1870 and held an honorific chair at Harvard similar to Brinton's at Pennsylvania between 1886 and his death in 1908. Putnam was not a Darwinian nor a Spencerian in any strict sense, albeit he was considerably more of one than was his patron Agassiz or his protégé Franz Boas. He "shared the prejudices and views of his contemporaries, although his commitment to a long historical perspective was tied to an advocacy of contact and borrowing more than in the case of his evolutionist contemporaries" (Timothy Thoresen:author, June 13, 1977).

As permanent secretary of the American Association for the Advancement of Science, Putnam had national ties in the world of science. His old New England family connections provided him access to the world of private philanthropy (Stocking 1968:279). Unlike Brinton, Putnam organized several enduring anthropological institutions, including the anthropological work for the World's Columbian Exposition in Chicago in 1893, which became the Field Museum, and for the American Museum of Natural History in New York (1894). He was also the nominal head of anthropological enterprises at the University of California beginning in 1900, although ill health kept him on the East Coast (A. Kroeber 1905). The Peabody Museum apparently did not pay him enough to live on, and he refused to give up his position there, but he could not realistically superintend day-to-day functioning of three institutions in three different cities. This overextension provided an opportunity for his protégés—Franz Boas in New York and Alfred Kroeber in California (see Thoresen 1975; Dexter 1989). Under their guidance, Columbia University and the University of California at Berkeley became two of the three preeminent institutions for training anthropologists in the twentieth century.

During the 1890s anthropology at Harvard produced fifteen PhDs—more than any other institution in the country. Following in the tradition established by Putnam, they were as a group predominantly interested in archaeology, without strong commitment to any major viewpoint in anthropological theory (Stocking 1968:279).

Putnam had no particular theory to push. Even in archaeology, where his own focus was, he did not found anything identifiable as a "theory group," nor did he provide distinctive intellectual leadership of the sort to found one. Even his importance as an organizational leader probably looms greater in retrospect because Boas and Kroeber, themselves important intellectual and organizational leaders, were among those Putnam sponsored and because archaeology continued at Harvard. He worked a number of years to place Boas and backed Boas's first (1901) Columbia PhD (Kroeber) more than Boas himself did (Thoresen 1975).

Major Powell and the Bureau of American Ethnology

The "gentleman amateur," engaged in fieldwork for a season or a shorter time, already encountered in the AES, was "most prominent in descriptive zoology and botany and in exploratory work in geography and geology," according to Randall Collins (1975:487). Although John Wesley Powell began his explorations of the Grand Canyon of the Colorado River as a professor of geology on a scientific expedition funded in part by his university, his early work fits that nonprofessional pattern, and the fruit of that first expedition was more journalistic adventure story than contribution to scientific knowledge (Stegner 1954:123). Powell was not primarily an anthropologist (and still less a linguist). He was a western explorer, "Washington scientific lion" (Scott 1976:27), and head of the Geological Survey of the Smithsonian Institution and, within it, of the Bureau of Ethnology, which he organized in 1879 (the name was specified to Bureau of American Ethnology in 1897). He was also president for the first nine terms of its existence of the Anthropological Society of Washington, which was later to become the American Anthropological Association.

As one of his successors recalled, of the collaborators he recruited to the BAE, "there's not one of them had training in anthropology, because there was no place they could train. . . . When I first went into the field, there wasn't a trained anthropologist in the whole lot. . . . Personal knowledge and interest gained them information" (Hodge 1955:80, 197). Although Powell lacked professional scientific training, built a staff of likewise self-taught scientists even in fields in which people with professional training were available, and was a major figure in amateur scientific circles in Washington DC, he was very oriented toward Theory. In his view, necessary observation could be made by almost anyone. Scientists such as himself then synthesized what amateurs reported (Hinsley 1981).

The self-made ethnologists whom Powell gathered together shared an evolutionary perspective. Morgan's (1877) *Ancient Society* and his view of unilinear evolution especially influenced Powell. While Social Darwinism was immensely popular in late nineteenth-century America (Hofstader 1944), Powell did not become a Social Darwinist. He preferred the progressivist-guided evolutionary doctrine of his protégé Lester Frank Ward.[3] While many of their contemporaries regarded the era of the robber barons as the inevitable pinnacle of human achievement, Powell and Ward stressed the role of intelligence and planning in human evolution—and were, therefore, implacable critics of Spencer and his view of mindless social forces (see Commager 1967:193–224; Hinkle 1980:184–213). Bureau ethnologists did not follow intellectual developments in Europe closely: "The subjects at home were so vast that it took all the time and research, the American Indians," as Hodge (1955:201) later rationalized.

The central problematic for BAE ethnologists was the observed "analogies and homologies" between human groups, particularly in North America. Since mankind was "distributed throughout the habitable earth in some *geological period* anterior to the present" one—and also "anterior to the development of organized speech"—what was common had to be accounted for by identical evolution (polygenesis) through fixed stages: "The individuals of one species, though inhabiting diverse communities, have progressed in a broad way by *the same stages*, have had the same arts, customs, institutions, and traditions *in the same order*" (Powell 1881:80). As a methodological principle, Powell asserted, "all sound anthropological investigation in the lower states of culture exhibited by tribes of men, as distinguished from nations, must have a firm foundation in language. Non-literate languages, representing a lower level of development, could profitably be studied with data from Native American tribes" (Powell 1881:xii–xv).

Powell and his subordinates were preoccupied with ordering the cosmos—and cannot be accused of gathering unconnected facts. Orderly classification of phenomena from the American "Wild West," such as Powell pressed for in geology, geography, hydrography, and ethnology, was useful to the government in Washington. Powell pioneered government science and tied it to a valiant attempt to plan development of the West based on understanding of its aridity.[4] Delineating Native Peoples was an administrative need of the federal government, responsible for their custody after the final expropriation of their lands (Holder 1966). Language was the obvious basis for groupings, so administrative needs and theoretical interests dovetailed.

The BAE classification of North American native languages bears Powell's name, and Powell (1891:218) claimed "full responsibility" (if not actual authorship) for it. The work of ordering the data on the premise that grammar relates to the stage of evolutionary development of the speakers of a language and that "the grammatic structure or plan of a language is forever changing" (Powell 1891:88) was done by Henry Henshaw, an ornithologist: "It was Henshaw who proposed and followed the biological method of linguistic stock precedence and nomenclature. ... Powell was the moving spirit, and the final result, expedited by the approaching appearance of Brinton's *The American Race*, was published in 1891, under Powell's authorship but with credit to Henshaw in the Seventh Annual Report of the Bureau" (Darnell 1971:83–84).

Powell created the BAE and organized the research to be done by others whom he recruited. He also arranged for the dissemination of findings. With Otis T. Mason, he founded the Anthropological Society of Washington. "The Society met twice a month, except in the summer, to hear from two to four scholarly papers. The papers read at these meetings seldom languished unprinted, but usually appeared in the publications of the Smithsonian. ... However, the need for a regular, official medium of publication was felt, and on Dec. 13, 1887, the Society became incorporated 'for the term of one thousand years' with the express purpose of bringing out a magazine, and the first number of the *American Anthropologist* appeared in January 1888" (Hallowell 1960:94).

If ever there was an organizational leader, it was Major Powell: "a genius at organization, [who] not only conceived a constructive program of research . . . but assembled the able men to carry it out" (Hallowell 1960:93), found positions for them, published and/or synthesized the resulting research, and "established a tradition which gave high priority to linguistic studies" (33). Powell designated what research was valuable and tied together the theoretical implications of the work done by subordinates into theoretically driven classifications.

The group that developed was not large. The number of full-time ethnologists in Powell's scientific empire was few, arguably none. Those involved were recruited in their maturity rather than trained by Powell. A nonstudent group with access to publication did not produce "revolutionary rhetoric." While rejecting then-influential Spencerism, Powell and his colleagues embraced the theoretical schema of Morgan. Celebrating their own lack of professional training as a virtue, Powell and his followers made no provisions to train successors. Despite successful

institutionalization—in government and in a "professional" society—
the failure to train a new generation of workers resulted in the eventual
eclipse of the Powell group and its paradigm by a university-based group.

Franz Boas

Though Boas and some of his students seem to have pushed the view
that all was darkness until Franz Boas came to Clark University and said,
"Let there be light," the material above shows this to be myth. Moreover, some anthropologists, Leslie White in particular, consider that Boas
brought darkness (theoretical nihilism) and obfuscation of evolutionary
patterns where there had been light (from Morgan in particular).

There is a vast literature on Boas, to which I have no interest in adding.[5] Not altogether advertently, he was central to relocating anthropological research from museums to universities. Quite advertently, he
taught cohorts of cultural and linguistic anthropologists at Columbia
University (where he was appointed in 1895) and established a paradigm
of ethnographic particularism often focused on cultural traits (the infa-
mous "shreds and patches"). The research in this volume begins with
the first generation of Boasians in fairly secure positions—inside the BAE
as well as in new academic departments (the Berkeley one not initially
a teaching department but turned into an important one by Alfred Kroeber) and at least represented in the old one at Harvard.

There was resistance to Boas's domination of American anthropology,
particularly from Harvard archeologists, and Boas was censured by the
American Anthropological Association in 1919 for decrying U.S. spies
posing as archeologists during the First World War, but his students ran
the association's journal, the *American Anthropologist*, and were embedded in decisions by funders of anthropological research.

Racial pseudoscience did not vanish but little of it emanated from
American university anthropology departments (Harvard again providing an exception with sometimes spy for the U.S. government Carleton
Coon). Theoretical discussions were between Boasians, as in the instance
examined in the first chapter, though in classifying languages there was
ongoing conflict between the splitter Boas and the lumper Edward Sapir. The latter, Boas's most prominent linguistic student, was also dubious about Boas's exclusion of those without academic training in
linguistics—and inclusion of some trained by Boas, matters I discuss in
Theory Groups (Murray 1994b).

The "normal science" of trait distribution studies of memory cultures (salvage anthropology) was, in Boas's own opinion, largely done, and I believe that he had no interest either in comparing the culture particulars amassed (generally by "white room ethnography" elicitations, also called "debriefing elders") or in attempting to try to make sense of North American prehistoric movements of peoples, cultural complexes, or culture traits. Boas claimed, "When I thought that these historical methods were firmly established I began to stress, about 1910[!], the problems of cultural dynamics, of integration of culture and of the interaction between individuals and society" (1940:311).

Whether influenced by psychoanalysis or not (his students definitely were), a shift to the integration of culture in personalities was a paradigm shift not brought on by rebels or revolutionaries but encouraged by Boas himself (see chapter 3; Darnell 1977). Similarly, established anthropologists (Alfred Kroeber, Robert Redfield, Lloyd Warner) rather than rebels or revolutionaries also encouraged expanding from studying "primitives" to studying peasants (see chapter 3).

Eventually there was an evolutionist counterrevolution in the decade leading up to the 1959 celebration of the centenary of the original publication of *The Origin of Species*. Some leading Boasians (Kroeber and Margaret Mead in particular) made this transition (led by Kroeber's former student Julian Steward, who became chair of the Columbia anthropology department in 1946 and trained many of the GI Bill generation of graduate students at Columbia). Later still, dissatisfaction with the failure to provide satisfactory explanations of change in term of "cultural contact," which was also the basis for history/"dynamics" within British social anthropology, led to comparative history, in the work of Steward's student Eric Wolf (1969, 1982, 1999) and others, in terms of trade (including the slave trade) and conquests.

1

Historical Inferences from Ethnohistorical Data

Boasian Views

Particularly under the stimulus of Jan Vansina (1965, 1986), the possibility of using oral traditions to draw historical inferences regained legitimacy within anthropology (see, for instance, K. Brown and Roberts 1980). The earlier debate in which consideration of any historical value in such data shows a lack of agreement with the Boasian "band of sons," a phenomenon also evident in the shock to the older sons about what intellectual daughters of "Papa Franz" did, is discussed in chapter 3.

The Cultural Elements Paradigm

Franz Boas, the prime mover both in the institutionalization of American anthropology and in overthrowing the paradigm of nineteenth-century unilinear evolution theory, purported to view the distribution of cultural elements as not only a basis for reconstructing the history of societies without writing but as the **only** objective basis. During the first decade of the twentieth century, he directed his students to chart the geographical distribution of institutions, beliefs, and material objects from which to infer the migration of peoples and the diffusion of objects. He and they believed that the center of these scattergrams was the point of origin, that the peripheries where diffusion most recently had extended, and that the wider the distribution, the older the trait was. Sapir (1916) provided the most systematic account of the method for inferring age from area (l distribution).

Gathering data and refuting theories were more congenial to Boas than using data for the purposes for which they ostensibly were gathered. When his students began to draw inferences about prehistory, Boas did not support their efforts and shifted to another kind of particularistic study of single cultures, their psychic integration and reproduction. Nevertheless, those already pursuing the first Boasian "normal science," the one in which they had been trained at the turn of the century, continued to try to solve the kinds of historical problems that were never seriously addressed by Boas or by his later students. Particularly in the project of salvaging memory cultures in California, Alfred Kroeber continued mapping cultural traits as reported by his students through the 1930s.

John Reed Swanton and Roland Burrage Dixon were the first Boasians to affirm some historical kernel of truth within folk traditions. Both received PhDs from Harvard, where Frederic Ward Putnam, a patron of both Boas and Kroeber, had established a center for anthropological research. Both had taken courses at Columbia from Boas. Swanton would later aver: "Whatever I have done is due to the inspiration of our teacher, Boas" (Swanton:Robert Lowie, July 30, 1957). Dixon, like Boas a veteran of the Jesup North Pacific Coast expeditions (see Freed and Freed 1983), was interested in language family reconstruction. As Kroeber noted in his obituary of Dixon, "Almost alone among their major contemporaries, he and Swanton maintained a sane and constructive interest in tribal and ethnic migration" (1923a:295).

This was the enduring interest that motivated Swanton and Dixon at least to consider whether folk traditions might contain grains of history. In their 1914 survey of the continent's prehistory they did not recommend uncritical acceptance of such traditions as offering transparent history; indeed, they cautiously suggested, "In investigating still existing people like the American Indian we can appeal in the first place to their traditions, which, although sometimes noncommittal and frequently misleading, gain weight when recorded with other data" (Swanton and Dixon 1914:402).

The far-from-wholesale endorsement was too much for the Machian positivist Robert Lowie, who was to succeed Swanton as editor of the *American Anthropologist* in 1923 and was, during the late teens, its book review editor. After claiming that "we are not concerned with the abstract possibility of tradition preserving a knowledge of events, we want to know what historical conclusions may safely be drawn from given oral traditions in ethnological practice" (Lowie 1915:597), Lowie appealed to the exemplification of sound practice provided by attorney-folklorist E. Sidney Hartland (1914). Lowie then proceeded to do nothing other than lay down his absolutistic ban of any even "abstract possibility" of such use of oral tradition: "I cannot attach to oral tradition any historical value whatsoever under any condition whatsoever. We cannot know them to be true except on the basis of extraneous evidence, and in that case they are superfluous, since linguistic, ethnological, or archeological data suffice to establish the conclusion in question. . . . From the traditions themselves, nothing can be deduced" (1915:598).

Dixon warned that "absolutely unqualified statements like that of Dr. Lowie's are usually dangerous" (1915:599), while Swanton defended folk traditions about movements as revealing at least of the direction of migrations. For Swanton (1915:601), an indicator that corroborated it in nine cases out of ten, when other evidence was available, could therefore be relied upon with some confidence in cases for which no other evidence was available. In Swanton's pragmatic view, some data were better than no data, but for Lowie, "it is our duty to doubt till the facts compel us to affirm" (Lowie:Paul Radin, October 2, 1920), which for Lowie, as for Boas, was never.

Boas's Columbia-Barnard colleague Alexander Goldenweiser, irritated by Lowie's attempted *reductio ad absurdum* in shifting from accepting reports of the direction of migration to crediting everything in creation myths, joined the fray, noting, "Dr. Lowie does not strengthen his case by citing creation myths as proof of deficient historical sense of the Indians. Commonly enough, the Indians themselves distinguish between a myth and a historical tradition. But even were that not so, who would doubt the word of a woman who tells of having witnessed a child being run over by a street car solely on the ground of his knowledge that the woman believes in ghosts?" (1915:764).

Goldenweiser also provided some less-colorful analogies:

Poor evidence is poor evidence, and the extent to which such evidence can be trusted is determined by the probability of it being true evidence, which again may be estimated from the frequency of agreement between such evidence of an intrinsically higher merit. Just as the physician is guided to his diagnosis of a disease by vague and doubtful symptoms until a positive one is forthcoming, just as the detective follows illusive and contradictory clues before establishing convincing proof of the crime, so the ethnologist in the absence of better evidence follows the lead of tradition until data of higher evidential value serve to confirm or refute his preliminary conjecture or hypothesis. (1915:763–64)

Lowie returned to his battle against native legends having any value as history with more straw men in his December 1916 address as outgoing president of the American Folk-Lore Society (a publication he saw fit to reprint in his collection of his most important ethnological papers), such as "How can the historian beguile himself into the belief that he need only question the natives of a tribe to get at its history?" (Lowie 1960:204) and issued another blanket rejection: "Indian tradition is historically worthless, because the occurrences, possibly real, which it retains are of no historical significance; and because it fails to record accurately, the most momentous happenings" (207).

In 1916 Edward Sapir—who was, with Goldenweiser, a member of what Lowie considered the Boasian "super-intelligentsia" (1959:133)[1]—in laying out the age and area "hypothesis," rebelled against the methodological asceticism of Boas and Lowie.[2] As in his own work on language classifications and phonemics (Sapir 1921a, 1925), Sapir preferred using imperfect data to throwing up his hands and not making historical inferences. In regard to trait distribution, Sapir went beyond Dixon and Swanton to infer the sources (that is, which tribe originated the trait), not just direction of migration, from folklore.

Lowie did not want to review Sapir's book but, having failed to get either Boas or Kroeber to do it, undertook the task. When his evaluation reached Sapir's discussion of "native testimony," Lowie produced an odd introduction: "Dr. Sapir's position with reference to certain moot questions is of interest" (1919:76). Considering that Lowie's own position had recently been attacked in the profession's core journal by four of his elders, including the journal's editor, "moot questions" is quite bold a definition of the situation! Besides which, I wonder how any answer to a "moot question" can be of interest. (Perhaps the word was understood differently a century ago?)

Just as he used creation myths to dismiss limited inferences about population movement in attacking Swanton and Dixon, Lowie set up a Sapirian straw man. Rather than multiple tribes agreeing that some other tribe invented something, Lowie switched to a hypothetical case in which each tribe claimed to have originated the trait and sententiously concluded that "the fact that one of them must be correct does not establish the methodological validity of accepting native traditions as history" (1919:76).

This account, internal to American anthropology (and, indeed, to the

American Anthropologist), does not consider the extent to which both Boas and Lowie had been doing battle against German diffusionism theories, as most completely crystallized in Graebner (1911). Boas rarely cited anyone, but he not only reviewed Graebner's magnum opus very negatively but also reprinted his 1911 review from *Science* in his collection of his major publications, *Race, Language, and Culture* (Boas 1940:295–304). Lowie devoted a presentation at the 1911 annual meeting of the American Folk-Lore Society (published in its journal: Lowie 1913) to attacking the assumptions (and "premature classification" of similarities in culture traits) in Graebner's magnum opus of a conception of mechanical cultural transmission in positing historical transmission of cultural traits (also noted by Boas, whom Lowie did not mention in this connection).

Aftermath

Although Lowie's critique came down (at least in the lore of the field, at least as far as the 1970s) as refutation (in the full Popperian sense) of pseudohistorical methods, closer examination of the whole exchange (or two exchanges) shows that Lowie's dogmatic condemnation of ethnohistorical data fit with the antihistorical wave of the future (ca. 1920) of American anthropology (functionalism, structuralism, culture and personality). It is not that Lowie refuted Swanton and Dixon, only that interests turned away from history of any sort in general and trait distributions in particular (as Lowie 1955:120 recognized). The lack of attention to such evidence in the following decades has less to do with the cogency of Lowie's criticisms than with a shift from historical reconstruction to ahistorical work on modal personalities in intact cultures and synchronic fieldwork focused on social organization.

After completing his combination of linguistic stocks into protofamilies (see Sapir 1921a; Darnell 1971, 1990a), Sapir was at the forefront of "culture and/in personality" theorizing (see Darnell 1990a, 1998b; LaBarre 1958:280–81) and arranged for the main carrier to North America of ahistorical functionalism, A. R. Radcliffe Brown, to come to the University of Chicago (see chapter 10; Sapir:Louis Wirth, November 25, 1931). Lowie would eventually write a national character study (Lowie 1954) and a social organization textbook (Lowie 1948). Yet, at the end of his career, he would recollect, "It was the reconstruction of the ancient primitive life that interested me" (Lowie 1959:169), despite his part in making such work seem neither possible nor worth doing (especially in Lowie 1937).

As already mentioned, staggering under the responsibility of salvaging knowledge about numerous California tribes (of considerable language family diversity), Kroeber persisted in collecting checklists of culture elements into the 1930s. By statistical analyses of data gathered by sometimes unenthusiastic students, Kroeber and Harold Driver sought to draw inferences about diffusion and to correlate cultural and environmental areas long after Boas had decreed the study of diffusion ended, and after even Clark Wissler had given it up.

Competing with his Berkeley colleague Frederick Teggart (see chapter 13), Kroeber continued historical correlations on a grand scale (A. Kroeber 1944 was his magnum opus); after World War II Kroeber (1955, 1961) championed Maurice Swadesh's development of a new mechanical discovery procedure for genetic reconstruction of languages, lexicostatisics (see Murray 1994b:207–11).

Above I quoted Kroeber writing that only Swanton and Dixon maintained an interest in tribal migration. Dixon's interests shifted from Native America to Polynesia (see Dixon 1916, 1928). Swanton continued careful sifting of whatever could be recovered from explorers' accounts (notably, Swanton 1932) and Native American traditions (Swanton 1930, 1942, 1952). Lowie recurrently used Swanton's work on the lack of clans in some American Indian tribes to refute evolutionary schema and presented it as the prime exemplar of Boasian ethnology in *The History of Ethnological Theory* (Lowie 1937:145).

And for my generation (and later ones), interest in the possibility of lore containing some valid knowledge (of history, or herbal remedies, and so forth) revived, along with scrutiny of accounts of vanished or greatly modified cultures made by nonprofessional (and still suspect) observers (the whole field of ethnohistory).

For the history of American anthropology, who won in either the short or the long run is less important than is revealing the quite heated disagreement within the fraternity (which it still was in 1915–20) of Boasian anthropologists. Boas's discomfort with Sapir's lumping of language families (from the profusion of the "Powell classification") and the discomfort of the first generation of Boasians with the methods of the later generation—most especially Margaret Mead, with her "vigorous omniscience" and lack of command of the languages of the people about whom she pronounced—are better known (the latter is discussed in chapter 3). And almost immediately following the dustup over migration accounts, there was a better-remembered conflict between Kroeber (1917, 1918) advocating considering only "superorganic" phenomena and Sapir (1917) defending psychology (no particular psychology, but the individual as the locus of cultural analysis).

I think that "Boasian paradigm" is a meaningful locution, though those trained after the First World War were pointed at other problematics than those that their elders had been aimed at. Boas remained a nihilist about drawing conclusions and even making generalizations. He may have taught (old-fashioned for the day) statistical methods, but he strikes me as having been incapable of thinking statistically, continuing to search for a single counterinstance to "invalidate" any purported pattern across space or time.

2

The Manufacture of Linguistic Structure

The human intellect, from its peculiar nature, easily supposes a greater order and equality in things than it actually finds, and while there are many things in Nature unique, and quite irregular, still it feigns parallels, correspondences, and relations that have no existence.

—FRANCIS BACON, *Novum Organum* (1620: L:xlv)

The observer who sets out to study a strange language or a local dialect often gets data from his informants only to find them using entirely different forms when they speak among themselves. . . . An observer may thus record a language entirely unrelated to the one he is looking for.

—LEONARD BLOOMFIELD, *Language* (1933:497)

Classic sociolinguistic work on variation and the permeability of speech community boundaries (Gumperz 1962, Labov 1972) made comprehensible what earlier generations of linguists regarded as "error" deviating from clearly delineated structures of a language. To properly use texts elicited and recorded by hand—in many cases the only records of languages no longer spoken—requires hermeneutic attempts to recover the intent of the recorders (linguists) and informants (not all of whom were native speakers) in the original elicitation context, as well as the problematic(s) motivating the work and the theories through which data were filtered and dictations were heard. The kinds of caution needed to use work based on classical elicitation procedures can be clarified by considering what was typical in the best elicitation-based (white room) fieldwork, such as that of Li Fang-Kuei (1902–87).

The fundamental lessons from the first generation of sociolinguistics (see Murray 1994b, 1998)—that context matters to the patterns of language use and that the world is not split into hermetically sealed units—calls into question the empirical status of linguistic structures derived from classic elicitation from a single informant when those analyzing unwritten languages believed that "text reveals structure" and that any fluent speaker would do, because there was a single structure to each language (and structural descriptions approximated "God's truth" rather than the "hocus pocus" of alternative structures, to use a famous distinction made by Fred Householder [1951]).

First, before the advent of portable sound-recording equipment, linguists necessarily slowed down their informants' speech to a pace at which they could write in phonetic script what informants said. This unnaturally slow pace and the focus on the transcriber hearing distinctly led to careful pronunciation. The unnaturally slow pace also provided informants opportunities to reflect on how they **should** speak—in contrast to how they usually spoke unselfconsciously. At a pace somewhere between a morpheme at a time and truncated clauses, distinctions not usually made may be made (Samarin 1967:54; Blom and Gumperz 1972:415) and syntax and phonology may be "cleaned up," because extraordinary attention is being paid to how the informant is speaking (see the systematic differences found by Labov 1972).

Second, as the codifier of American structuralist linguistics noted, "The difficulty or impossibility of determining in each case exactly what people belong to the same community is not accidental, but arises from the very nature of speech communities" (Bloomfield 1933:54–55; also see Gumperz 1962; Blom and Gumperz 1972); although he, and still more his followers, set out to chart idealized structures of particular, clearly bounded languages. When Chomsky (1965:3) asserted that the task of linguistics was to consider the language of an ideal speaker-hearer of/on a perfectly homogenous, monolingual speech island, he was not suggesting anything new but making explicit what was common practice in Geneva, Prague, Copenhagen, or New Haven structuralisms. Many of his predecessors and followers dealt in similar idealizations, while writing as if they were describing observable realities ("God's truth" analyses).

The Descriptivist Paradigm

Franz Boas attempted to reconstitute linguistic work on Native American languages with inductivist fieldwork done by those under his supervision and mostly trained by him. Boas was a "splitter" rather than a "lumper." He was especially eager to leave behind any talk of "primitive language" in general, stressing diversity between languages. Boas paid lip service to description being preliminary to comparison. Although the languages described in the first volume of the *Handbook of American Indian Languages* (Boas 1911) were chosen "to facilitate comparison of different psychological types in a single broad geographical region," the time for comparison had not arrived in 1911 (or by 1943, when Boas died), and "the *Handbook* on the whole is notably lacking in any sort of systematic comparison of one language to another" (Stocking 1974a:475).

Alfred Kroeber, the first of Boas's student to establish an independent institutional base (see Thoresen 1975; Jacknis 2002), was also the first to attempt to combine what John Wesley Powell (or at least the classification issued by the Bureau of American Ethnology under his name) presented as distinct languages (see Darnell 1971). During the early 1910s, while trying to organize the *Handbook of the Indians of California* (which was not published until 1925), Kroeber, working with Roland Dixon, attempted to reduce the number of stocks of California Indian languages from the twenty-two in the Powell classification.

Edward Sapir, who did graduate work in Germanic philology at Columbia before being turned into an Americanist by Franz Boas, was thoroughly familiar with the comparativist method and the uses to which it had been put in extracting reconstructions of proto-Indo-European languages from two millennia's accumulation of texts. In a letter to Kroeber dated February 11, 1913, Sapir cautioned him about the kind of evidence required, endorsed the neogrammarian principle of regular sound change (see Sapir 1921b), and urged Kroeber to proceed despite Boas's animus against historical reconstruction and the absence of historical texts: "I hope you do not have the idea that I am personally opposed to such syntheses. In fact, I feel strongly that there will be more of them made as our knowledge progresses." Inferring prehistoric links between languages—on the basis of texts then being dictated (i.e., synchronic data)—and combining languages into families on the basis of hypothesized links became an absorbing interest for Sapir, once he acquired an institutional base (Darnell 1971, 1990a). Sapir maintained an active correspondence with Kroeber, and Kroeber deferred to Sapir's superior training and talent, eventually reporting himself relieved to be "passing out of the game" (Kroeber:Sapir, November 25, 1919) as Sapir reduced Powell's fifty-eight stocks to six "super stocks."

Although he was a pioneer of synchronic structural description of language, the kind of linguistics that became the dominant concern of professionalizing North American linguistics, Sapir's interests through the 1920s were primarily historical. The synchronic fieldwork—much of it on Athabaskan languages—of Sapir, and—after 1925, when he took up a teaching position at the University of Chicago—of his students was motivated by historical comparative problematics.

Pliny Goddard's Athabaskan Fiefdom

In an era when one scholar could maintain a monopoly over not just a language or a culture but a whole family of languages, the one Sapir chose to focus on, Athabaskan, was the academic turf of Pliny Goddard.

Goddard went to the Hupas (in northern California) as a lay missionary for the Women's Indian Aid Association in March 1897. In 1900 he went to the University of California (in Berkeley) to study with its new president, Benjamin Ide Wheeler. Goddard received a doctorate in 1904. Wheeler arranged to provide for Goddard, first with a university scholarship and later with some of the money donated to the university by Phoebe Hearst that also brought Alfred Kroeber to the University of California. Together, Goddard and Kroeber began instruction in an anthropology department, although Goddard's primary interest was in being left alone to do fieldwork:

> I was wishing I could stay right in the field and record as long as there is anything left. (Goddard:Kroeber, August 16, 1901)
> I am getting deeper and deeper each in year in unpublished notes but am willing to go still further, hoping to work out in my old age when field work will be impossible. (Goddard:Kroeber, December 6, 1911)

Kroeber explained, "For Goddard it was not a duty but an intense satisfaction to secure his data and so far as possible present them in the native speech. . . . Analysis per se interested Goddard only slightly, and synthesis less. It was the data themselves, in their aura of experience by personalities that drew him and that he reproduced with felicitous fidelity" (1929:4–5).

Krauss (1980:12) suggested that the comparative material in Goddard's (1912) paper on Chipewyan was the impetus for Sapir's interest in Athabaskan, although Sapir must have been familiar with Morice (1907) and did fieldwork on Chasta Costa in 1906 (published in 1914).

Sapir's Incursion

In the late 1910s Sapir was combining superstocks and became increasingly interested in Athabaskan "dialects." He recognized Goddard's prior claim, reporting to Kroeber his frustrations at all he had to do "for the sake of peace and goodwill" and concluded, "I am willing to make some sacrifices but not to consider I have no moral right to do Athabaskan. The real fact is, Kroeber, Goddard's work is not very good—decidedly not . . . least of all in phonology. He is not really competent to write a thoroughly satisfactory comparative study of Athabaskan" (November 30, 1920).

Typical of his frustrations vented in correspondence is the following: "Athabaskan is not his scientific interest, but a kind of private mistress. . . . Why is he so damned personal about it? After all, nobody wants to have sexual relations with the Hupa language!" (Sapir:Kroeber, October 1, 1922)

Sapir's contempt for Goddard's ability to get Athabaskan phonology was based partly on the inconsistency of consonants (sometimes even in the same word) that Goddard reported, partly on Goddard's contention that tone was not used in all Athabaskan languages, and partly on Goddard's evidence for Algonkian influences. Sapir (see 1921b:196) was certain that Athabaskan languages were very conservative and resistant to any borrowing and viewed the variability Goddard reported as evidence of Goddard's incompetence. The clinching evidence, in Sapir's view, was Goddard's failure to hear tone: "As for tone not being important, that's a joke. It is twice as important as anything that Goddard has yet had to say about Athabaskan phonology. He admitted later he couldn't hear tone at all—it would have been hopeless for him to attempt to note it. What I dislike is his constant attempt to rationalize away his own disabilities" (Sapir:Kroeber, October 1, 1922).

Goddard recognized Sapir's brilliance and joined Sapir in doubting his own abilities: "Looking especially for tone, Sapir made his important field trip to Sarcee in 1922, and found what he was looking for" (Krauss 1980:15; see also Krauss 1978). Kroeber reported, "Goddard in his characteristic ambivalent mood about your Sarcee invasion. He says he did not get everything in Athabaskan and that you are doing better, but is somewhat hurt and just a bit bellicose at being superseded. In the main, however, his attitude is more one of sadness" (Kroeber:Sapir, September 22, 1922).

Once Sapir took up a teaching post (in 1925 at the University of Chicago), he began to train Athabaskanists. When the American Council of Learned Societies inaugurated a committee on American Indian linguists, administered by Franz Boas with advice from Sapir and Leonard Bloomfield, Sapir emphasized, "We must have first class quality in our work at the outset, as we must guard ourselves with the linguistic world. ... We must take our research people where we find talent and interest" (specifically, including missionaries, whom Boas and Bloomfield wanted to exclude from the means of linguistic production; see Leeds-Hurwitz 1985). He also noted, "I have one thoroughly excellent student, a Chinese Boxer indemnity man named Li, who has a good ear, tremendous enthusiasm and assimilative capacity, and a good sense of form. He should certainly be given a chance in the Athabaskan field" (Sapir:Kroeber, February 11, 1927).

The ACLS committee funded Sapir's California fieldwork in 1927 and Sapir took Li Fang-Kuei along for apprentice fieldwork under his supervision, ignoring Goddard's prediction "No Chinaman allowed in Humboldt County: ejected on sight" (reported in Sapir:Kroeber, June 28, 1927; on the widely forgotten virulence of Chinese exclusion in California, see Heizer and Almquist 1971:154–76).

Sapir and Li began by working together on the language Goddard knew first and best, Hupa. To his surprise and dismay, Sapir could not find tone in Hupa either: "It's disappointing to find that Hupas has no tone!" (Sapir:Kroeber, June 28, 1927). In his quest for pure, archaic (monolingual) Athabaskan he also lamented, "English is spoken with depressing frequency here by all Indians" (Sapir:Kroeber, June 28, 1927).

George Herzog worked with Sapir on Hupa, while Li worked on Wailaki and did "the best he could with such survivors who speak Mattole as he could find. I gather that he has some really valuable linguistic material, but it seems impossible to get texts" (Sapir:Kroeber, August 18, 1927).

Back at Chicago, Li worked up his Mattole materials and also took a course on dialects of Middle English from Leonard Bloomfield, who had just arrived after years at Ohio State University. Bloomfield suggested that Li recast his course paper into a dissertation (R. Scollon:author, January 15, 1979), but Li already had an MA dissertation, based on Sapir's Sarcee verb data (Li 1930a) and the material for a doctoral dissertation from the Mattole expedition of the previous summer. By May 21, 1928, Sapir reported to Kroeber that Li had completed the Mattole phonology, vouched for the great value of Li's work, and sought publication of it in the University of California series (it was instead published by the University of Chicago Press: Li 1930b).

Having passed his fieldwork "test" with flying colors (despite the absence of tone in Mattole and Wailaki), Li was ready to undertake a field expedition of his own, in Sapir's judgment. It was to Fort Chipewyan (in Alberta), where Goddard (and earlier, Lowie, according to Murphy 1972:23–26) had had many problems finding informants and extracting the kind of data he (as well as Sapir) wanted, that Li was sent—in effect to redo Goddard (1912).

Li found what was for his purposes a perfect local informant, which is to say someone not all typical of Fort Chipewyans. François Mandeville considered himself to be French rather than a member of any Athabaskan people. He had "not arrived at Fort Chipewyan until about 1925, when he was some 47 years old. . . . He was certainly not a native of that community. . . . [Moreover, he had] considerable experience with other dialects of Chipewyan and with other Mackenzie Drainage Athabaskan languages. It is said he could speak Chipewyan, Dogrib, Slavey, Hare Loucheux, and some Beaver. . . . For Li, Mandeville 'reconstructed' a maximally differentiated variety of Chipewyan out of his experiences in different speech communities" (Scollon and Scollon 1979:255, 154)

Fieldworkers of that era sought what they took to be the most "traditional" speakers they could find in whatever community in which they elicited data. Generally, choice fell on the oldest, least-traveled, and most ethnocentric speakers who could be found in order to minimize "interference" from other languages and, it was presumed, to best approximate the language used by the generation before that of the informants.

At Fort Chipewyan, where English had penetrated by 1776, at which time (Algonkian) Cree and (Athabaskan) Chipewyan had probably already converged (see Scollon 1979), and where previous fieldworkers had found both cooperation of informants and the production of Chipewyan "uncorrupted" by Cree to be impossible to secure, the Chipewyan Li recorded came from a much-traveled, not-at-all-ethnocentric, short-time resident. Mandeville was not only "modernized" (maximally differentiated form what the Scollons [1979] called "bush consciousness") but also had a long-standing interest in finding an orthographic system with which to represent the languages he spoke. Before Li's arrival, Mandeville already "could write in the syllable system which had been developed by the Wesleyan missionary, James Evans, as well as alphabetically" (Scollon and Scollon 1979:41), but he was dissatisfied with those systems. "When Li began recording his dictations in phonetic script, Mandeville realized that this was the writing system he was seeking" (255).

Linguist and informant together formed an academy in perfect accord in endeavoring to standardize a "pure" (archaic) Chipewyan, free— as the speaking of no one there and then—of any traces of Cree, just as the French Academy attempts to ban borrowings from English.

In the first dictations, Li heard and wrote down some of the same phonological variation heard and reported by Goddard (and others). Soon, however, Mandeville seized on their work as "an opportunity to produce his 'highest liturgical style' (cf. Newman 1955). . . . Mandeville's long-term interest in developing a 'high,' or if you prefer, a literary language was matched by Li's interest in recording a conservative, maximally differentiated Chipewyan" (Scollon and Scollon 1979:25). In very sloweddown and careful dictation, Mandeville in effect was producing something akin to "spelling pronunciations."

After "cleaning up" the variability and before standardizing the representations of sounds in the products refined from working with Mandeville, Li (1933a, 1933b, 1946) noted features that appeared to support Sapir's contention that Athabaskan languages were particularly impervious to borrowings. Unlike in Mattole, Li found tone in Chipewyan, though it went in the opposite direction from what Sapir (on the basis of Navajo) expected. Michael Krauss (1978, 1980) suggested that the absence of discussion of Chipewyan tone and Li's subsequent withdrawal from Athabaskan work are attributable to his mentors' inability to assimilate the never explicitly stated challenge of Li's findings.

Scollon and Scollon were quite right that earlier fieldworkers shared the goal of historical reconstruction and were abashed at the "noise" (variability) in the data they collected: "Lowie, Goddard, Mason, and Osgood all would have done an analysis much like Li's had they been able to. Their own comments on the futility of their research efforts indicate that they essentially agreed with Sapir in considering Li to have succeeded where they had not" (1979:258). (Goddard died in 1928, before Li had published anything on Chipewyan.)

While they failed to achieve their own goals motivated by then-current theories and interests, our contemporary research interests and theories make the variation Li suppressed from his publications of interest. That is, what was anomalous for older structuralist theories or contemptuously dismissed as incompetence on the part of the linguists when it was reported by Goddard is explicable in poststructuralist conceptions of convergences in genetically distinct language (Gumperz and Wilson 1971 provided an exemplar).

Similar idealization of linguistic and cultural distinctiveness probably typifies reports from early fieldwork about which we know less than (after Scollon and Scollon 1979) we know about Li's. Languages and cultures were sealed off from other languages and cultures by fieldworkers' reports rather than by "nature" or history (Samarin 1980). As Robert Murphy suggested, "Information idealized and rationalized past custom and they also standardized it. What was often elicited was not how a certain practice was done, but how it should have been done. The varieties of situation and expression were reduced to neat normative systems, a process of reduction that was aided and abetted by the investigator's own search for regularity and order" (1981:183–84).

Murphy's (1967) work on Tuareg kinship terms provided an extreme case in which a system (Iroquois) was elicited that is antithetical to the (Sudanese) one in use. Similarly, Jesse Sawyer told me that while there are no Spanish loanwords in the Wappo texts collected by Paul Radin, there was no lack of them in everyday language (though we do not know whether Radin or cooperative informants purified the language in the texts).

In drawing conclusions from the evidence of texts, it is necessary to remember that producing texts is an unusual speech event in which very deliberate speech occurs (Samarin 1967:79). While different languages were not invented for such occasions, the deliberateness of speech, facilitated by the slowing way down required in the pre–tape recorder era, invited purging of "impurities" and articulation of phonetic contrasts not usually made in normally paced speech. Problems of interinformant variability did not arise when the data came from a single informant.

3

Margaret Mead and the Professional Unpopularity of Popularizers

> Approval of those outside the specialist group is a negative value or none at all. . . . Scientists who attempt to find a wider audience for professional work are condemned by their peers.
>
> —THOMAS S. KUHN, *The Essential Tension* (1977:290, 347)

No other ethnographer has ever been so widely read and publicly visible as Margaret Mead (1902–78) was. Untold throngs of those dismayed with how life is lived in these United States and/or intrigued with how life is lived elsewhere followed her vivid accounts of her voyages of discovery to Pacific islands to learn about the range of human possibility— knowledge to be applied to solving social problems in her homeland and for planning social change here and elsewhere. At least until an alien (Australian Derek Freeman) attacked American cultural anthropology as represented by Mead in her first fieldwork (1928, 1930), students who undertook professional education found that her prestige within her chosen discipline was not as high as nonanthropologists supposed.

Because nonscientific audiences evidence a low tolerance for ambiguity and a total unconcern for statistical logic, seeking definitive answers that science does not provide, producers of science generally fail to consider that the members of the public might have a serious—if naive—interest in science. Scientists fail to apprehend how unintelligible research reports can be to those not trained to read them. Unaware of how much they routinely take for granted, scientists genuinely believe that anyone of reasonable intelligence who wants to learn about a line of work will be able to do so—and then reach the same evaluations of work they themselves have reached. This mistaken belief is enhanced by the tendency to forget that part of membership in a scientific community is knowing whose evaluations to credit. The internal hierarchies of status and professionally conceived boundaries of competence recognized (i.e., constructed and maintained) within a field of scientific endeavor are invisible to those outside of it. Authorities highly regarded within a research area are not distinguished from those judged merely competent nor even from those regarded as outright incompetent.

Experienced with incomprehension when they try, most scientists do not usually try to tell anyone but colleagues what they do not already know. Trying to inform nonspecialists burns through time that might otherwise be devoted to research and building the store of knowledge (and prestige) in a field. Frustration is increased by the widespread failure of interested members of the public (and, often enough, of those writing sensational headlines and stories about new discoveries) to distinguish between a hypothesis and well-established, replicated findings.

Moreover, "of the work [s/]he utilizes, no scientist personally checks more than a small fraction, even of that [s/]he is fully competent to evaluate," as Barnes (1972:287) noted. The norm of science that Robert Merton called "organized skepticism" operates at the superindividual level of science, not as an obligation incumbent on each and every individual scientist in regard to every scientific assertion she or he encounters. And what I call "scientific scorn" tends to be invisible: "Scientific communities rarely undertake public exposés of those they regard as incompetent; informal communication usually ensures that their work is treated as suspect, or, in some cases, written off" (287).

Informal evaluation is efficient **within** science. Laypersons (even scientists from other disciplines or specialties) are left to their own devices. Unsurprisingly, they often confuse what some credentialed scientist asserts with a scientific Truth that has been established. Dismayed by the way expert consensus is routinely cast aside and ideas ludicrous to specialists are propounded by those whom they consider cranks, scientists conclude that the public listens to what it wants to hear, so that there is no point in trying to devote time and energy to enlightening general publics.

From very early on, Margaret Mead sought a prophetic mantle and aimed to enlighten an audience that she saw as seeking a message that "things"—in her first work, the tribulations of adolescence and gender expectations—did not have to be the way they were in (WASP) American society. If arrangements in other societies were different, American arrangements could not be accepted as the inevitable product of "human nature."

The Boasian Paradigm(s)

Attacking any and all proposed conceptions of a singular "human nature" was the lifework of the man who recruited Mead to the calling of anthropology (away from sociology with a social work impetus). Franz Boas, who established cultural anthropology in American universities, trained the first generation of professional fieldworkers to find counterexamples that in his view refuted theories proposed by others. Although Boas taught statistics, considering statistical relations seems to have been alien to his iconoclastic and all-or-nothing temperament. In his view armchair ethnologists proposed theories and ethnographers in the field disposed of them. Boas relished "refutation" (by a single counterexample) of any theory, but his particular bête noire was unilinear social evolution.

The dominant (Bureau of American Ethnology, Lewis Henry Morgan, Harvard) paradigm—in opposition to which Boas institutionalized "empirical" anthropology done by credentialed (Columbia PhD) anthropologists—viewed "primitive" sociocultural arrangements as stages of evolution that Euro-American societies had passed through in their (pre) history. Boas and his students argued that those in "primitive" (in technology) societies are contemporaries, not ancestors, and that all cultures change over time. Substituting histories—often enough, histories inferred from the distribution of cultural traits and not native "myths" (the utility of the latter was a matter about which Boasians differed; see chapter 1)—of diverse peoples for a single History in which different societies of the time were at different stages was the major goal of Boasian anthropology from 1890 to the mid-1920s. Inventorying the distribution of ideas, institutions, and material artifacts over geographical areas was the method for documenting diffusion produced by historical contact between peoples (cultures). Boas's students were expected to document the areal distribution of cultural traits, and they did, one after another after another after another.

During the decade following the First World War, students of Boas and of his first Columbia PhD, Alfred Louis Kroeber, continued to collect and map particular culture traits and complexes of traits. In the absence of historical records, mapping distributions provided a seemingly objective basis for inferences about historical diffusion of specific traits and for postulating the point of origin in the center of the distribution. This Boasian methodology was codified by Edward Sapir

(1916) and expanded in terms of applications based in his own special-ization in comparative philology as a method for getting at historical sequences. Ruth Benedict, Boas's lieutenant during the 1920s and Mead's mentor, wrote a dissertation on beliefs in guardian spirits among ab-original North American "tribes." Mead's own (1925) doctoral disserta-tion, "An Inquiry into Questions of Cultural Stability in Polynesia," compared tattooing, house building, and canoe building in five Polyne-sian societies. The culmination and *reductio ad absurdum* of such trait distributionalism was *The Building of Cultures* by Roland Dixon. Dixon had studied with Boas but received his doctorate from Harvard, the oth-er major American anthropology program in the first quarter of the twen-tieth century. (Harvard's primary foci were in archaeology and physical anthropology rather than in ethnology and linguistic anthropology, the two primary foci at Columbia; thus a de facto division of labor rather than direct competition existed between the two leading North Ameri-can anthropology training programs.)

Coming of Age in Samoa (CAS) and *The Building of Cultures* were both published in 1928. Like Mead's dissertation, Dixon's book is an exem-plar of what the Boasian paradigm was and had been: comparison of various culture "traits" organized to show historical patterns of diffu-sion. CAS differs from both, prefiguring increasing influences of psycho-analytic ideas on American anthropology.

Mead's generation of anthropologists was tired of mapping trait dis-tributions. Mead, in particular, rebelled at salvaging memories of Native Americans (M. Mead 1965:xvi–xvii, 1972:128).[1] She instead longed to study a still-functioning "primitive" people. She sought out a relatively isolated and small-scale part of Samoa and then obscured the influenc-es of colonialism and Christianization there. This led her to write in the change-obscuring ethnographic present, even though she criticized her compatriots' writing about Native North America for the same practice. This attitude, along with her dismissing the necessity to understand the languages of the people she studied and the attention popularizers draw (see Murray 1980b, 1980d), explain some of the resentments toward and dismissals of Mead by her anthropologist contemporaries.

Other Paradigmatic Currents: Functionalism and Psychoanalysis

In wanting to observe a pure "primitive" society rather than recover memories of earlier times and in vigorously effacing evidence of western influences, Mead's practice fit with that of the social anthropologists of the British Empire, including her second and third husbands, Reo Fortune and Gregory Bateson.[2]

The major rival paradigm to the Boasian paradigm in the Anglophone world between the world wars, British social-functionalist anthropology, in which Derek Freeman was trained, ignored not only biology but behavior in order to posit functionally integrated social structures of colonized peoples treated as though they were aboriginal (see Strathern 1983:78).

Mead's Samoan publications—especially *Social Organization of Manu'a* (M. Mead 1930)—foreshadowed the ahistoric functionalism that would soon be taught by A. R. Radcliffe-Brown at the University of Chicago. While teaching social anthropology in Sydney, Australia, Brown (as the Boasians insisted on referring to him) was the official supervisor of Mead's second fieldwork (in New Guinea, in collaboration with Fortune). Mead's early books were more uncritically reviewed by Imperial British anthropologists than by American anthropologists (see Murray 1991).

Although they were not the foundation of culturalism, as Freeman imagined, Mead's Samoan research and writing were parts, even indices, of changes that some might want to call "paradigm shifts" in American anthropology. There are serious senses in which Mead abandoned American historicism for colonial British social anthropology, but CAS also constitutes a shift from Boasian particularism to neo-Freudian concern with individual "adjustment" and with childrearing practices, a shift that other Boasians rejected or ignored. Although presenting an essential(izing) ethos (of or for adolescent female Samoans), Mead carefully reported individual differences. In this she was doing some of what Sapir (1917) advocated in his polemic against Kroeber's advocacy of studying of the "superorganic," and providing some concrete evidence for adaptations of psychoanalytic conceptions by Sapir and by the sociologists who had influenced her before she encountered Benedict and Boas, that is, William Ogburn and W. I. Thomas. Ogburn (for whom Mead worked in 1923) was already discussing Freud with Sapir in 1917 correspondence, visited Freud in 1926, and later served as president of the Chicago Psychoanalytical Society. Thomas, the champion of gathering life history material to study the meanings of immigration and rapid social change, had published a massive study of "delinquent" American girls in 1923. Significantly, the psychological integration work done by Benedict and Mead began only as Boas neared retirement and despite his lack of enthusiasm for Freudian theory (mentioned by Benedict in a March 5, 1926, letter to Mead included in Mead 1959a:305). Beyond a willingness to write a preface for his student's first book, this shift to interest in childhood and adolescent socialization appears to have received little direct input from him and none from Kroeber, Lowie, Radin, Goldenweiser, Parsons, Spier, or other Boasian elders, except for Benedict (Murray 1991:404–5).

A "Boasian paradigm," as Freeman would have it, had crystallized prior to Mead's research (see Darnell 1977, 1998a, 2001), so neither Kroeber nor any other member of the first generation of Boas's students was waiting for Mead to demonstrate the existence of cross-cultural difference. The distinctions of race from culture, biological from cultural "heredity," and so on did not begin with Kroeber (1915a), as Freeman should have realized in quoting from Stocking (1968:264), since Stocking was referring to work collected in W. I. Thomas's (1909) *Source Book*. Stocking himself (1974b) chose 1911 as the cutoff point for the formulation of Boas's paradigm. Boas's key paradigm statements distinguishing race, language, and culture both appeared in that year.

The principles of Boas's anthropology were also well established by that year and were already being conveyed to a cohort of Columbia doctoral students. These principles included ethnographic and linguistic texts as the data base for ethnology and linguistics (as a way of getting at "the native point of view"); the definition of culture as a symbolic construct; the inseparability of language, thought, and reality; salvage fieldwork to record rapidly changing aboriginal cultures; and reconstruction of cultural history based largely on diffusion and present distribution of culture traits. Later Boasians moved toward recognizing their ethnographic subjects as consultants and collaborators rather than merely "informants," and long-term, often collaborative, fieldwork became a norm.

For Boas in the mid-1920s, normal science was gathering and mapping trait lists. He sent students off to fill in some of the parameters (see Darnell 1977, 2001). Mead's own PhD topic was comparative in precisely this diffusionist sense. There was no "crisis" (in the Kuhnian sense) of Boas and his followers desperately seeking some evidence of cultural differences, and the *Sturm und Drang* of adolescence was not a topic that any other Boasian took up.

For anyone seeking to establish the literally formative power of environment during the 1920s, Boas's (1912) measurement of the head forms of eighteen thousand immigrant parents and children in New York City would have provided far better evidence than any in Mead's first book. Although Boas's inferences were not entirely justified by the data (see Allen 1989), the point is what Boas and his followers believed at the time. (On Boas's biological anthropology generally and Freeman's misrepresentations of it, see McDowell 1984; Weiner 1983; Murray 1991.) Freeman's writings systematically ignored Boas's work in "physical" (biological) anthropology, in particular that Boas's empirical demonstration of environmental effects predated Kroeber's (1915, 1917) attempts to lay out a rationale for study of culture. Boas viewed his anthropometric work as providing direct evidence of environmental effects on human development; there is no reason to suppose that he was haunted by any need to find evidence of cultural effects. He was therefore not desperate to send Mead to the South Seas to find some. Indeed, far from choosing a field site and sending Mead to it, Boas was reluctant to approve her going to Polynesia at all.

If Boas foresaw her Samoan research as the crucial experiment to establish the Boasian paradigm, as Freeman claims, and/or if Mead was formless, will-less putty in his hands, would he not have taken some pains to lay out how she should measure the parameters? It is remarkable that Boas devoted so little time (a half-hour meeting) to giving her marching orders and gave no specific directions for what she should do in the field (see Boas's letters of July 24, 1925, in the appendix to *Journal of Youth and Adolescence* 29 [2005]).

As Weiner (1983:917) noted, anyone needing an example of relatively unstressful adolescence (and premarital intercourse) in the South Seas could have drawn on Bronislaw Malinowski's publications on Trobriand Islanders, especially the 1924 article Boas mentioned in his July 24 letter to Mead on the eve of her departure. Mead was well aware that what she was doing in questioning universals posited by western psychologists on the basis of observations of "primitives" in the South Seas was akin to Malinowski's work, more than to anything Boas ever did. On August 9, 1928, after her publisher sent Malinowski a copy of CAS, she wrote him that "no student who attempts to do psychological field work should fail to acknowledge the debt that is owing to you in the field which your[s] originated, plo[u]ghed, sowed and made fruitful for those who should try to do the same kind of work." Both in its locale and in its quasi-psychoanalytical focus, CAS is closer to Malinowski's work than to anything Boas wrote.

Boas's research program focused primarily on aboriginal inhabitants of North America, secondarily on Mesoamericans and Africans—not at all on Polynesians and not at all on the experience of adolescence anywhere. Before going to Samoa, Mead's knowledge about "traits" and "complexes" in and understanding of Polynesian cultures derived from Handy and other non-Boasians. Similarly, specific advice about how to do her first fieldwork also derived from Handy and others connected to the Bishop Museum in Honolulu, who had no stake in any "crucial experiment" about heredity and environment as explaining patterns of Samoan adolescence.

In contrast to the half hour Boas devoted to preparing Mead for a task that Freeman claims was vitally important to him and necessary to establishing his paradigm, the (non-Boasian) ethnologists at the Bishop Museum in Honolulu spent considerably more time preparing her to do the research that they thought should be done in Samoa (Mead 1972:138; also see Cressman 1988:131). E. Craighill Handy—whom Freeman (1991a:n13) conceded had produced the best account of a Polynesian culture available at the time (Handy 1923) and "who possessed a first-hand knowledge of Polynesia... that could not be matched by any other ethnologist then alive" (Freeman 1999:71) —"gave up a week of his vacation to prepare her" (M. Mead 1972:146). The only American anthropologists Mead (1930) cited had Harvard degrees (Dixon and Handy) or no degrees at all (E. W. Gifford). There are no citations of Boas or of any Columbia PhDs in Mead 1930, and no bibliography nor citational notes in CAS. In comparison, the foil in Mead's research proposal (see below), Miriam Van Waters's 1913 dissertation (of ninety-five pages) on adolescence in "primitive" cultures, included five citations to Boas and at least fifteen to his former students.

Freeman spilled rivers of crocodile tears that Mead spent more time gathering data on Samoan nonsexual culture than on her funded project on adolescence, contravening what he (mis)interpreted as commands to avoid inquiry and observation of other phenomena than adolescence (see Côté 2000). Oddly, his calculation of her allocation of time in the field did not make him wonder if Mead in Samoa was more a Handyian than a Boasian. Nor did his shock that Mead largely ignored what Freeman (mis)characterizes as Boas's "strict instructions" "to give all of her time" to researching the determinants of adolescent phenomena lead Freeman to reconsider that she was a fully committed tool of the cosmic mission of "proving cultural determinism" (1991b:108, 1999:57, 185).

Freeman (1991a:322) dismissed the criticism that Boas's suggestions to Mead in a July 14, 1925, letter of three interesting problems to investigate undercuts his interpretation that Boas wanted her to work exclusively on proving cultural determination of Samoan adolescence. It is, therefore, especially interesting that the only point Mead (1972:121) reported Boas making when he read the draft of CAS related to one of those problems (the contrast of passionate to romantic love), a matter also taken up by Lowie in his review of CAS in the *American Anthropologist* (1929:534).

Mead's Samoan Research Plans

Both the desperate need for some demonstration of the importance of culture Freeman imagined and the martinet ordering Mead to do nothing but gather data on heredity and environment in Samoa were absent in Boas's gently reassuring 1925–26 letters to Mead (see Côté 2000). Moreover, any plan to seek data about heredity is missing from her 1925 fellowship proposal. Surely it was obvious to those evaluating her proposal that Samoans differed in both heredity and environment from WASP Americans. Mead set out to contrast putative universals from "civilized" (i.e., WASP) experiences to "the individual experience of the primitive adolescent" she believed she would find in Samoa. It is hard to imagine that those approving her proposal supposed she was going to measure heredity. For Boas himself, I would suggest that any ardor he felt for Mead's project had more to do with the resentment he harbored against G. Stanley Hall (based on what Boas perceived as his early mistreatment at Clark University) than on any felt need for someone to provide some evidence for the importance of culture. It bears noting that the work that Mead's research proposal sets out to supplant was that of Miriam Van Waters's 1913 Clark University doctoral dissertation, "The Adolescent Girl among Primitive Peoples," which (like Mead's own dissertation) was based on library gleanings rather than on any direct fieldwork.

Although Boas counseled her not to try to do everything, it is obvious that he knew that Mead was going to gather data on diverse topics. Indeed, Boas himself suggested some possibly interesting topics in the very July 14, 1925 letter that Freeman calls an "interdiction" (1999:56) of ethnological research. That letter instead provides what could easily be interpreted as carte blanche to follow up on "anything that pertains to . . . the psychological attitude of the individual under the pressure of the general pattern of culture" that was extended by a November 7, 1925, letter. Mead did not try to hide from Boas or from the funders of her research that she was doing "general ethnological" work in cooperation with the Bishop Museum. This was explicit in her January 6, 1926, interim report to the National Research Council (NRC). Even her initial fellowship proposal of only 452 words explicitly stated that her research should "add appreciably to our ethnological information" (specifically about "the culture of primitive women"). Mead's plot to conceal from Boas and the NRC board that she was doing ethnography rather than measuring heredity and environment is a figment of Freeman's imagination. Freeman (1999) fantasized both Boas's interdiction and Mead's evasion of it.

Mead found it politic at various times to represent herself as an orthodox "Boasian," especially in her later career pronouncements about the history of anthropology and her own participation in the paradigm transition to more psychological questions. Nonetheless, she began her career already a strong-minded and resourceful young woman. She was no man's Trilby! Rather than being Boas's puppet (Freeman 1983:75), she selected what seemed useful to her from a large number of prominent male elders (such as Ogburn, Wissler, Handy, Sapir) and one female one (Benedict). Boas was certainly one, second in prominence in her own retrospective self-legitimations only to Benedict, who was in professional terms only slightly more senior than Mead and who was eager to be treated by her as a peer rather than as an authority figure. By her own report in various memoirs, Mead was never personally close to Boas. Ruth Benedict usually mediated their relationship and to Benedict Mead wrote that she thought she had never mattered seriously to Boas except as a student (May 16, 1937).

Mead is not the only anthropologist who, to get where she wanted to do fieldwork, wrote a grant proposal in the terms that she thought those controlling funds would approve. In the years it took to attain the rank of professor emeritus, Derek Freeman must have known of other instances. If the outrage Freeman (1991b, 1999) vented was sincere, he was very naive about how fieldwork support is often obtained.

Unlike many others, Mead wrote up findings about what she was fund-ed to study. However hastily researched and erroneous they may have been, a board that did not include Boas, but did include T. H. Morgan (who knew a great deal about heredity in the modern sense) and others with no cultural determinist allegiances accepted her final report. Frank R. Lillie chaired the Board of Fellowships in the Biological Sciences (of which the non-Boasian anthropologist A. V. Kidder was the ex officio member as chairman of the Division of Anthropology and Psychology). According to Freeman, "It can only be surmised that they [the board] did not seriously examine Mead's report but relied on the judgment of Professor Franz Boas" (1999:179). There was certainly time for at least Lillie to have read the manuscript before his initial acknowledgment of its receipt. In that Lillie did more than acknowledge receipt—express-ing his "gratification that your fellowship has resulted in such a very fine contribution" and adjudging it "an unusually full report for so relative-ly short a period of appointment"—and mentioned Honolulu reports about Mead while not mentioning any from Boas, the surmise that Lil-lie reached an independent opinion is more likely than Freeman's infer-ence. The other members had nearly three years to consider what Mead wrote about her problematic (and even to read reviews in both popular and professional periodicals). Perhaps all the members did not read it, but we should not assume that **none** read any of the twelve copies of CAS received by the board.

Moreover, far from attempting to hide from the research funders that she had done more in Samoa than work on her "particular problem," in transmitting her report, "The Adolescent Girl in Samoa," Mead explic-itly stated that she had "a mass of descriptive ethnographic materials [which] is now being written up as a monograph of the B. P. Bishop Mu-seum in Honolulu" (Mead:Lillie, April 24, 1927; earlier mentioned by Mead in a letter to the secretary to the board of the National Research Fellowships in the Biological Sciences, Edith Elliott, January 13, 15, 1926, January 9, 1928, August 10, 1928, and October 20, 1929). It is doubtful that this was unknown to the chairman, who wrote Mead that "during my recent visit to Honolulu I was delighted to find what a good impres-sion you had made in your approach to the subject" (Lillie:Mead, April 27, 1927). Moreover, the manuscript of the Bishop monograph was a part of the final report accepted by the board in February 1930 (Elliott:Mead, February 15, 1930).

Freeman's attacks on American anthropology—and on Margaret Mead's Samoan fieldwork that he mistook as Sacred Writ of culturalism—demonstrated a remarkably anachronistic sense of what "biology" and "heredity" meant in the United States in the 1920s, a reckless wrenching of words and phrases out of context, an obdurate refusal to consider alternative interpretations of phenomena (including anthropological texts and correspondence), and an unwillingness to acknowledge the extent of criticisms of Mead's work by Boasians and other anthropologists in the decades before publication of his 1983 book. Consequently, Freeman's account of the content and history of American anthropology is neither valid history nor an exemplification of how he read Karl Popper as saying scientists should behave. To the best of my knowledge, he did not accept a single corrective (from the many that were offered) to his long string of misrepresentations of American anthropologists' practices and products.

In particular, by selective quotation and the failure to refer to earlier critics of her work, Freeman (1983, 1999) consistently misrepresented the homogeneity of Boasian culture and the uncritical acceptance of Mead's revelations by American anthropologists. His "method" when it came to writing about anthropologists was to rip a word or phrase out of context and to repeat this word or phrase as an unambiguous endorsement of everything Mead wrote about Samoa—for example, see Murray 1991 on Freeman's lifting "convincing" to characterize Robert Lowie's (1929) very mixed and openly skeptical review of the methods and conclusions of CAS, or what Freeman claims was "the central dogma of Boasian culturalism, the supposition that 'the nature of man had to be derived from cultural materials'" (1999:175). When one looks at the source for this quotation (M Mead 1959a:16), it is at the end of a paragraph explaining that in 1923 in America, "there was no body of psychological theory by which smaller [than exhaustive collection of data] could be interpreted. The use of psychoanalytical theory, learning theory, Gestalt psychology, or ethology was all in the future. . . . Without any psychological theory which could both include and supplement cultural theory, the nature of man had to be derived from cultural materials." Rather than a timeless prescription, this last phrase was a specifically historicized explanation for collecting native-language texts and other "objective data" open to later analysis (see Darnell 1990b, 1999, 2000). In particular, psychological test data were not available.

Another egregious instance is his (mis)interpretation of the reprinting of Mead's "The Rôle of the Individual in Samoan Culture" (originally published in the [non-Boasian] *Journal of the Royal Anthropological Institute* in 1928) in Kroeber and Waterman's (1931) *Source Book in Anthropology* as an endorsement of Mead's claims about Samoan adolescence. According to Freeman, this is supposed to constitute evidence of Kroeber's "confidence in Mead's 'diagnoses' about Samoa" (1991:a325, 1999). "Diagnoses" alludes to an October 11, 1929, letter from Kroeber to Mead, of which there is not a copy in Kroeber's outgoing correspondence deposited in the Bancroft Library at the University of California, Berkeley. In the letter (in the Library of Congress) Kroeber wrote, "I think you have been able more successfully than anyone else to sketch the place of the individual in his particular culture. While some people complain that you do not give enough data to allow them to check up, this leaves me cold. Somehow I have confidence that your diagnoses are right even when your facts are few or not printed in full." Leaving aside genre considerations (i.e., the politesse of private correspondence from prominent elders to promising professionals at the start of their careers), the overt antecedent for Kroeber's acceptance is the relationship of individual and culture (the topic of the Mead article that would be included in Kroeber and Waterman 1931), not the relative weight of heredity and environment or the extent of adolescent *Sturm und Drang*. Even if "diagnoses" was as blank a check as Freeman interprets it as having been, it was not issued (or cashed!) in public. That is, there is nothing remotely repeating it in anything Kroeber or Mead published.

One would think that in half a century's participation in an academic field Freeman might have noticed that editors sometimes include work with which they disagree in books and journals that they edit. In the instance of Kroeber and Waterman 1931, there are selections from racialist eugenicists E. A. Hooton, Francis Galton, and R. S. Woodworth that are not merely un-Boasian but are antithetical to Boasian ideas. Moreover, Kroeber and Waterman explicitly stated, "The passages in this volume have been selected for their utility in stimulating discussion. They are included not because they present ultimate scientific truth, but because they embody facts and interpretations which are useful for the exercise of thought on some of the larger problems of anthropology.

... Passages have been included with whose conclusions the editors do not agree: Galton's on race worth, for instance. ... It is for the reader to analyze his[/her] interpretation and accept or reject it" (1931:vii).

In general, publication of a text does not establish that an editor accepts every point in the text or even that s/he admires the text as a whole. In this instance, there is a specific disavowal of any inference of agreement from inclusion. Reprinting Mead's article does not evidence Kroeber's acceptance of Mead's conclusions. Rather, it provides another example of Freeman's reckless disregard of data contrary to his theses (whether about Samoa or about American anthropology). The "Heredity and Race" section of Kroeber and Waterman (which is not the section in which Mead's article was included) has a selection from Boas, "Bodily Form of Descendants of Immigrants" (A. Kroeber and Waterman 1931:141–53), but Freeman fails to mention this, as he fails to mention Kroeber's own chapter on primates (472–88) that fits so badly with Freeman's view of fanatic rejection of biology by Kroeber and other Boasians.

The skepticism Kroeber expressed (in markedly Jungian terms) about Mead's New Guinea research applies directly to her Samoan work: "A gift of intellectualized but strong sensationalism underlies this capacity; also, obviously, a high order of intuitiveness in the sense of an ability to complete a convincing picture from clues, for clues are all that some of her data can be with only six months to learn a language and enter the inwards of a whole culture, besides specializing on child behavior" (1931:250). It is improbable that the applicability of this to her Samoan publications was lost on readers of the *American Anthropologist*.

Freeman (1983, 1987, 1991a, 1991b, 1999) vastly overrated the importance of Mead's "findings" about Samoan adolescence to Boasian anthropology. It is curious that, if Mead's book solved so important a problem for "the Boasian paradigm," Freeman could adduce acceptance for it from the first generation of Boasians only by misrepresentation of what Kroeber, Lowie, and Sapir wrote (and did, in the case of reprinting a paper of Mead's). Where was Roland Dixon, Kroeber's sometime collaborator and the first-generation Boasian who knew the most about Polynesia? Freeman (1991a, 1999) acknowledged that Paul Radin was critical of Mead, but where is the evidence that Boasians prominent by the time that Mead began her research—such as Fay-Cooper Cole, William Ogburn, Elsie Clews Parson, Frank Speck, Leslie Spier, John Swanton, W. I. Thomas, Wilson Wallis, and those already mentioned in this paragraph—accepted or built upon her claims about Samoan adolescence, a topic and a culture area about which they had little interest or expertise? If Mead's report appeared "decisive" to them, why did they not build on it in their subsequent scientific work or even mention it in their work aimed at wider audiences (including textbooks)?

Freeman asserted that CAS "continued to be accepted by the vast majority of anthropologists as presenting an accurate picture of the Samoan ethos as it had been in the 1920s" and that "its conclusions continue to be regarded by anthropologists and others as though they were eternal verities" (1983:107–8). Freeman retreated to "a sufficient number" (1991a:327), although, even with a list of examples light in Boasians (and very heavy on the 1930s anti-Boasian Yale tradition), it would be hard to apply "eternal verities" to the treatment of CAS by those on his list.

Mead's early (1928, 1935) books helped to disseminate a culturalism opposed to biologism to a mass audience but induced few (if any!) anthropologists (Boasian or other) to change their views of culture or of biology. Mead's claims about Samoan adolescent sexual behavior and stress had very little influence on anthropological research in professional/scientific publications (i.e., journals and monographs) and were far from being repeated "in an unbroken succession of anthropological textbooks" (Freeman 1987:392).

Presence in Textbooks

Introductory textbooks are not written for colleagues and are aimed at a mass audience more than at future professionals. Social science textbooks, in marked contrast to those in physical and biological sciences, typically describe divergent perspectives rather than laying out exemplary experimental solutions of scientific problems (Kuhn 1977:228–32; Latour 1987), so mention of Mead's views in textbooks does little to establish how influential those views were within professional anthropology. As Murray (1991:450) noted, Mead's claims about Samoan adolescent sexuality were ignored by as many pre-1983 introductory anthropology textbooks (eleven of twenty-six) as reported them without significant criticism or hedging. Freeman (1991a, 1991b, 1999) neglected to mention that more textbooks ignored or questioned CAS's findings than reported them without criticism and failed to acknowledge the distribution reported (either what Murray had provided him with in 1986 or the similar findings from a larger sample analyzed by T. Hays [1997:92] reported that only three of thirteen 1928–57 anthropology textbooks cited Mead on Samoan sexuality and/or adolescence, nineteen of forty-six from the years 1958–74, and eighteen of forty-three from 1975–83. In contrast, Malinowski's *Argonauts* [1922] was cited in 97.3 percent of the textbooks [T. Hays 1997:97; see Shankman and Boyer 2009]). Nor did Freeman report deployment of Mead's claims about adolescence in any of the textbooks written by her Boasian elders after 1928, the most notable of which (A. Kroeber 1948) was a widely assigned, encyclopedic textbook uniquely attended to by professional peers as well as by introductory students. Freeman (1999:200) cited the widely and long-used textbook by Ralph Beals and Harry Hoijer (who had been students of Kroeber and Sapir, respectively) as "uncritical acceptance." Although they did not attack her conclusions, Beals and Hoijer wrote that "emotional crises in adolescence are apparently culturally produced" and "adolescence in Samoa is apparently relatively free of emotional difficulty" (1953:586–87). Rather than "uncritical acceptance" or endorsement, "apparently" is an explicit hedge. Robert Lowie also wrote several textbooks that did not mention CAS. If CAS was as momentous as Freeman claims, why did Lowie not mention it in his 1937 *History of Ethnological Theory*? Such notable deficiencies in evidence did not lead Freeman to reconsider his characterizations of professional anthropologists' acceptance of CAS.

Citations in Social Science Journal Literature

In the social science journal literature of the 1970s, the decade before Freeman's onslaught on it, CAS was cited less often than three other books by Margaret Mead. *Male and Female* (1949), her most biology-exalting book, was cited nearly twice as often as CAS in journals covered by the *Social Sciences Citation Index* (217 citations to *Male and Female*, 176 to *Culture and Commitment*, 167 to *Sex and Temperament*, and 118 to CAS; in contrast, Freeman's most cited books received 11 and 13 citations during the 1970s).

For all its alleged momentousness for anthropology, before Derek Freeman's assault(s), only 7.6 percent of the 1970s citations to CAS were in anthropology journals. In comparison, 16 percent of the 1970s citations to *Sex and Temperament* and more than a quarter of the 1970s citations to Bronislaw Malinowski's popularized "sex among the savages" work from the 1920s were in anthropology journals. Just as it was not

Mead's most cited book, *CAS* was not even the 1920s sensationalization of "savages'" sexuality most cited in anthropology journals of the 1970s (Malinowski's 138 to Mead's 118).

Freeman asserted that "Mead's Samoan researches were not seriously questioned prior to the publication of [his] refutation by Harvard University Press in March, 1983" (1991b:55). Freeman continued to claim there was "no major questioning of Mead's conclusions" (1999:197). No doubt Freeman had some personal sense of what "serious" and "major" mean, excluding anyone who did not make all of the challenges he did. Most scholars would not expect serious critical analysis in a biographical blurb. Even if he was so naive as to look there for it, Freeman (1999:191) might have indicated that Spindler (1978:87) did not write that *CAS* was regarded "as the epitome of anthropology" by anthropologists but that Mead "has written books that are for many Americans the epitome of anthropology." Mead's work was never mentioned in the anthropology courses I attended across the span of the eight years immediately preceding publication of Freeman (1983).

The failure to acknowledge predecessors is the antithesis of scholarship, fully as culpable as the misrepresentations of earlier work of which Freeman (1983, 1987, 1991a, 1991b, 1999) is guilty. That most anthropologists ignored *CAS* rather than gathering data to refute it and that it is not unusual for scientists to proceed with their own work rather than denouncing what they consider suspect, or even view as erroneous, are points that Freeman, confusing Popperian prescriptions with descriptions of science, seemed unable to grasp. Silence is often dismissal rather than assent.

The Marginal Boasian Mistaken for the Epitome of American Anthropology

Mead recognized her marginality within academic anthropology, famous as she was outside it. In professing surprise at Lowie's invitation to write what became "Apprenticeship under Boas" (M. Mead 1959b), she wrote that she had "got accustomed to being treated as anthropologically non-existent" (Mead:Lowie, April 8, 1956). (Lowie did not list Mead [or himself] among those who were especially close to Boas [Lowie:Radcliffe-Brown, May 24, 1938]. Benedict was one of the eight he did list.)

Rather than being admired as single-handedly vanquishing biology and establishing cultural anthropology, Mead was widely regarded with contempt as an overheated romancer and popularizer by American anthropologists during the 1950s. Although some embraced her as a female role model in her last few years, most anthropologists did not take her seriously as a theorist.

Whatever Freeman (1983, 1999) may have done to "refute" her claims about Samoa (very little, in the view of other Samoaists), his ostensible history of Mead and the "Boasian paradigm" exemplifies far more than CAS does the misrepresentation of a culture (that of Boasian anthropologists) in order to prove a preordained point. Freeman's publications about Boas and Mead provide strikingly uncompelling exemplification of attempting to refute one's own pet theories—which is what Freeman interpreted the philosopher to whom he dedicated his 1983 book, Karl Popper, as having prescribed. Just as Mead's sometimes sensationalistic first book appealed to hopes for ameliorating repression in the 1920s, Freeman's sensationalistic and also heavily promoted book fit with the zeitgeist of the Thatcher-Reagan(-Fraser, for Australia) era of dismantling social engineering, rationalized in part by very Hobbesian notions of "human nature." Utopian aspirations and dystopian politics, respectively, fueled popular embraces of these books, while the obvious exaggerations and overgeneralization of both books have largely kept professional anthropologists from embracing either as adequate or valid models of Samoa or of "human nature." Although Freeman was silent about the welcome by antireformists and sexual counterrevolutionaries of his work and sarcastic about the welcome by more reformist and utopian readers of CAS, this statement is an observation of consequences that does not claim insight into Freeman's motivations.

Reasons for the Low Regard within Anthropology for Mead's Work Before Freeman's Attacks

Setting aside the disputed value of her research in Samoa and elsewhere and the differences in professional culture between British functionalists, sociologists, and Boasians mentioned above, I would suggest four social reasons for professional dismissal of Mead's work during her professional lifetime (before the disinterment and trampling on her bones by Derek Freeman).

The first of these is the simple fact of being a woman. While there were a number of prominent women in anthropology—more so than in other natural or social science fields—this does not mean sexism was absent in anthropology. Besides being a woman, Mead **studied** women (and children and sex). Focusing on low-prestige activities (rather than masculine pursuits like warfare and politics) exacerbated her peripherality. From my reading of criticisms, I have little doubt that a contempt for the "innately" intuitive "female mind" and a refusal to believe that women can be objective observers (especially of gender, sexuality, and childrearing practices and beliefs) rather than advocates quick to jump to undersubstantiated conclusions played some part. Whatever struck male anthropologists as silly in Mead's pontifications was seen as instantiating female fallibility, while equally silly pronouncements of male anthropologists were not attributed to limitations of the male sex.

A second factor that also reflects badly more on her detractors than on Mead is the feeling that she was a "rate buster," that is, too productive. She was exceptionally productive, both in the field and on her typewriter. Careful fieldwork, thoughtful analysis, and carefully hedged presentation took others longer, so that it was comforting to believe that Mead was failing in professional caution. Although "sour grapes" may account for some of the concerns about how much she wrote about how many different topics, it seems to me that there was some basis for distrusting her facility, along with envy at the amount she produced and the extent to which she was able to publicize her ideas, often in regard to U.S. culture(s) not based on any systematic research.

A third factor was annoyance at her personality, especially what Lowie called her "attitude of vigorous omniscience": smugness exacerbating glibness.

The fourth, which most interests me, is the suspicion directed at popularizers in all fields of science. Professional and popular enthusiasm rarely coincide. Although advertising a book as a "best seller" seemingly further increases its sales, "best seller" is a term of abuse to many scholars, and writing one is not a way to endear oneself to one's scientific peers. This phenomenon is not at all new. Writing in 1908, Frances Cornford sardonically described an academic norm: "The Principle of Sound Learning is that the noise of vulgar fame should never trouble the cloistered claim of academic existence. Hence, learning is called sound when no one has ever heard of it; and 'sound scholar' is a term of praise applied to one another by learned men who have no reputation outside the university, and a rather queer one inside it" (7).

Fueled in part by "sour grapes" discounting, seeking popular regard seems to many to be treason to the ascetic vocation of science. In professional socialization, scholars are taught that the only judgment of their work that is worth anything is that of their professional peers. To seek popular accolade is an implicit rejection of the sufficiency of the proper reward. To receive popular accolade—even without any apparent attempt to gain it—is grounds for suspicion; openly to write for an audience other than fellow specialists, as Mead already was doing in the 1920s, guarantees hostility.

Sometimes, superficial trappings of scholarship—dense syntax, arcane technical lexicons (jargon), polyglot documentation, and so on—are confused with the essentials. And, as already suggested, there may be some unexpressed jealousy for and resentment toward those who are reaping rewards that should be spurned as forbidden fruit—but that are not altogether unattractive.

Nevertheless, essentials of good scholarship are often jettisoned in works written for popular audiences. A single explanation is often pressed, and there are very few problems of any interest that can be solved with only one explanatory variable (often presented as "the gene" for this or that). Alternative explanations and evidence about limits of scope tend not to be considered. The evidence offered tends to be selective and one-sided, with self-confidence substituting for analysis and sensational examples as substitutes for systematic considerations of the evidence that is available and of other possible explanations.

Precisely these charges were leveled at Mead's work in the late 1930s and continued in professionals' expressions of reservation for her subsequent proclamations. Some of the same charges were made of such other anthropologist popularizers as Oscar Lewis and Ashley Montagu (and Loren Eiseley, who did not present himself as an anthropologist to his audience) as well as the art history of Kenneth Clark, economics of John Kenneth Galbraith, cosmology of Carl Sagan, political philosophy of Hannah Arendt (especially in regard to *Eichmann in Jerusalem*), and so on. Cases and quotations can easily be found by glancing through the reviews in professional journals of work widely disseminated beyond the audience of the author's discipline.

The popular writers of whom I am thinking are not quacks but are suspected of some quackery in their simplifications of topics their colleagues treat with greater caution (and more variables). Everett Hughes often observed that a quack is someone who is loved by his patients and loathed by his colleagues, and this extends to the portentous simplifications of popularizers of science.

Serious scholars who take the risks of drawing firmer conclusions for wider-than-professional publics than their colleagues do are likely to be held in lower esteem by their colleagues than by the public. Even those trained in seemly restraint may lose track of what they have demonstrated, confusing that with what data suggest.

Can scientists never write for nonspecialists without forfeiting peer esteem? There are at least two possible ways. The first is to alternate technical and nontechnical writing. To some extent, Margaret Mead attempted such alternation, even in reporting on Samoan culture (publishing her more restrained and technical report second, however). After winning a Nobel Prize, addressing nonspecialists will be treated with more tolerance. Mead made the mistake (i.e., a mistake if she was pursuing the approval of other anthropologists) of writing for general publics from the very beginning of her career. Worse still, she generalized from her research before she presented sufficient data from which to draw conclusions. In the report of her first fieldwork, she was taking a role appropriate for elders retired from active data-gathering and speaking with the wisdom of their long years of experience and technical contributions approved by those competent to judge them.

Although I have suggested ways to minimize the conflict between professional and popular evaluation, I must admit that—in the physical sciences at least—it is impossible to maintain even an extremely distinguished reputation for very long without new contributions. Recognition of most contributions by active researchers is gone after a year or two or three. In physical sciences, only the makers of a few exceptional contributions can rest on their laurels for very long without being bypassed—not even Albert Einstein. Punditry distracts one from doing new work within the discipline, so that status in the discipline suffers— quickly in physical sciences, more slowly in social sciences. Even in a relatively slow-moving discipline such as anthropology, it is difficult for a scholar to be taken seriously by his or her professional colleagues while simultaneously educating wider audiences. Some other American anthropologist examples are Loren Eiseley, Jules Henry, and Ashley Montagu, each esteemed by general readers while not being seen by anthropologists as contributing new anthropological knowledge.

4

American Anthropologists Discover Peasants

> The peasant is an immemorial figure on the world social landscape, but anthropology noticed him only recently.
>
> —CLIFFORD GEERTZ, "Studies of Peasant Life: Community and Society" (1962:1)

After the First World War, American anthropologists' focus on the distribution of aboriginal cultural traits faded and they gradually withdrew from salvaging memories of prereservation life from aging Native Americans (see Darnell 1977, 2001; S. Cole 2003). Anthropologists, particularly in the Midwest, began to pay attention to functioning contemporary cultures, albeit often continuing to look at atomistic traits ("survivals" of aboriginal culture) within a framework of "acculturation" (Redfield et al. 1936)—the third of these authors was the one preoccupied with "survivals," especially in *The Myth of the Negro Past* (Herskovits 1941)— and along geographic distributions that were taken as surrogates for historical changes—and while mostly continuing Franz Boas's rejection a priori of anything that had been written about a culture by anyone other than a professionally trained anthropologist.

The research by some University of Chicago anthropology graduate students who were fledged before an anthropology department split off from the preeminent sociology department was rooted in the "Chicago school" focus on urban "disorganization" (anomie, vice, crime) of immigrants to Chicago from rural backgrounds and the uneven assimilation of émigrés from peasant societies outside the United States. The exemplar of research on immigrant peasants in their society of origin and while struggling in the United States was *The Polish Peasant in America and Europe* (W. Thomas and Znaniecki 1927). Thomas was forced out of the University of Chicago, and his own, more general book *Old World Traits Transplanted* appeared bylined Robert E. Park and Herbert

A. Miller in 1921. Park, whose (1904) PhD was from the University of Heidelberg, played an important role in introducing German sociological ideas to America, including the *Gemeinschaft/Gesellschaft* (community/society) ideal types of Ferdinand Tönnies that were the prototype for Park's son-in-law Robert Redfield's romantic notions of homogeneous, harmonious peasant communities in contrast to conflict-filled, vice-ridden cities filled with "marginal" immigrants (see Park 1924, 1928; Wirth 1938; Bulmer 1984).

Everett Hughes, who was fledged with a PhD from the same department in the same year as Redfield was, and who told me that he and Redfield took all the same classes, recalled that although Redfield "was an exceedingly urban[e] man, yet he could not stand life in Chicago except around the University. He did not like cities" (1974:141). There is some merit in Charles Leslie's claim that "the symmetry of [Redfield's] analyses, which are the work of a restrained, ironic sensibility" (1974:158) are akin to classicism rather than to romanticism (and that Oscar Lewis's view was akin to operatic *verismo* [Lewis's own label for his approach was "ethnographic realism"; see Rigdon 1988:5]). However, *verismo* was related to postromanticist naturalism rather than to Herderian romanticism, and the "balanced reporting" Leslie asserted is difficult to sustain for Redfield's *Tepoztlán*, which is so focused on fiestas and ballads (*corridos*).

Such a Jeffersonian view of noble (genuine) yeoman (and suspect "city slickers" with a spurious culture) was not part of peasant studies by those who had been trained at the University of California, Berkeley (where there was no sociology department, an anomaly taken up in chapter 13 below), by Alfred Kroeber and Robert Lowie. In reporting a restudy of the community, Columbia-trained anthropologist Oscar Lewis (1944, 1947, 1951, 1953) vigorously challenged Redfield's representation of Tepoztlán. The controversy was explained away at the time by some (including Redfield 1955a:136) as reflecting differences in temperament between the observers (Redfield looking for harmony and looking at what people enjoyed in contrast to Lewis looking for and at their troubles).

Oscar Lewis "wondered why [Redfield] did not give more attention to the contrast between his own idealized version of peasantry and the sordid descriptions of the novelists" (1960:179), mentioning Balzac, Zola, Reymont, Turgenev, and Sholokov (but not Gogol!). Villa Rojas

(1979:49) attested to Redfield's familiarity with and keen interest in writers of the day, including, specifically, Sinclair Lewis. Along with Sherwood Anderson's *Winesburg, Ohio*, Lewis's work represented the intolerance of nonconformity in rural America (e.g., in *Main Street* and the early part of *Arrowsmith*) and the fervor of small-town American Christian zealots and those who stirred them up (especially in *Elmer Gantry* and *It Can't Happen Here*). In the years around the Scopes "monkey trial" and Mencken's recurrent assaults on the "boobocracy," the idealization of rural virtue stands out as particularly unusual.

By the time Redfield's glorification of "little communities" came under critical fire from some other anthropologists, a peasant-based revolution in China had interfered with Redfield's own research agenda. Moreover, the roots of Chicago anthropology's study of peasant communities in the immigrant assimilation "Chicago school" work had been forgotten, even though the German sociology to Robert Park to Robert Redfield lineage was remembered as the root of the folk/urban and little community/urban civilization typologies. Although Kroeber and Lowie were, in some senses, heirs of German romanticism of the *Völk* (not least as former students of Franz Boas), neither German sociology nor the Jeffersonian mythos of the yeomanry seemed to affect the work of Berkeley anthropology alumni. The German romantic traditions also had less discernible influence on Redfield's students than on Redfield. Indeed, "Redfield's students" presented themselves more as students of A. R. Radcliffe-Brown and participated in the cross-disciplinary paradigm of functionalism that was mixed with European social theory in the Harvard and Columbia sociology paradigm that eclipsed the "Chicago school" within sociology after World War II.

The Berkeley alumni had not worked directly with Radcliffe-Brown and, insofar as their work was functionalist, they seemed more interested in the cultural dynamics of Malinowski than in equilibrium-maintenance-assuming Radcliffe-Brown functionalism. At least one of the Berkeley alumni, Walter Goldschmidt—like Oscar Lewis, John W. Bennett, and Herbert Passin—did research on agriculturists in the United States and showed some awareness of what rural sociologists were doing (mostly in isolation from theorists and researchers in sociology departments).

The exception is Pitirim Sorokin at the University of Minnesota (before going to Harvard). Sorokin and his Minnesota associates introduced

A. V. Chayanov's conceptions of peasant family economies to Anglophone readers in the 1931 *Source Book in Rural Sociology*, but this eventually influential conception did not diffuse to American anthropologists working on peasantries until much later.

The First Generation of University of Chicago–Trained Anthropologists

The Early Research of Robert Redfield

Like Margaret Mead, in the mid-1920s Robert Redfield did not want to piece together fragments of memories of what aboriginal Native American life had been like forty or more years before. Even before the arrival in Chicago of A. R. Radcliffe-Brown, Redfield worried about records of cultures "no longer represented by the activities of living persons" (1930:149)—referring, specifically, to Ralph Beals's salvage of memory in northwestern Mexico. Redfield had no interest in the distribution of discrete traits and especially not in the distribution of remembered ones.

It is well known that Redfield was a student of the Boasians Fay-Cooper Cole and Edward Sapir as well as of his father-in-law, Robert Park, and of Ernest Burgess at the University of Chicago Department of Sociology and Anthropology. Less well known is that his impetus to study anthropology in general and México in particular came from another earlier student of Franz Boas, Manuel Gamio. Gamio went to Columbia in 1909, although his doctorate was not awarded until the publication of *La población del Valle de Teotihuacán* in 1922. On a trip to Mexico in 1923, the dissatisfied lawyer Redfield met and admired Gamio and decided to emulate him. After he returned to Chicago, Redfield began graduate studies during the fall of 1924. Under the supervision of Ernest W. Burgess's practicum in sociology, Redfield received a $500 stipend from the executive committee of Local Community Research (which was, in turn, funded by the Laura Spelman Rockefeller Memorial) to work half-time observing Mexicans in Chicago. He made over forty visits to the Mexican neighborhoods of Chicago as part of his practicum in sociology from October 5, 1924, until April 24, 1925 (Godoy 1978:51–52).

The rationale to the Committee on the Scientific Aspects of Human Migration of the Social Science Research Council (SSRC) for fieldwork in Mexico was very much in the W. I. Thomas–Robert Park tradition of Chicago sociology exemplified by *The Polish Peasant in America* (W.

Thomas and Znaniecki 1927) and *Old World Traits Transplanted* (Park and Miller 1921), in which immigrants constituted a social problem. Thomas pioneered research on the traditional organization of peasants at home and their personal and collective disorganization in U.S. cities. Having completed the massive report on Polish immigrants in 1918, Thomas was during the 1920s seeking support for comparative work on Jewish, Sicilian, and Swedish immigrants (see chapter 9). Similarly, Redfield claimed that "a description of the life of such Mexicans [from "semi-primitive village communities"] in their home communities would facilitate an intensive study of the problems arising out of the growing Mexican immigration into the United States" (1926 fellowship application, quoted in Godoy 1978:55). In 1926–27 the same committee was supporting Gamio's study of Mexican movement back and forth to the United States (Gamio 1930, 1931; Redfield 1929a, 1931; also see Massey et al. 1987)—what Redfield characterized as "the immigration problem" (1929a:434). In summarizing Gamio's "study of Mexican immigration with the emphasis on the immigrant and on Mexico rather than on the effect of the Mexican immigrant upon the economic and social organization of the United States," Redfield observed that "Dr. Gamio looks at the matter from the south side of the Rio Grande, although his experience with North America makes it also possible for him to consider some problems raised by the Mexican in our environment" (1929a:434).

In a summary of his PhD thesis, Redfield stressed that he was interested "not in the rescue of the disappearing vestiges of pre-Columbia culture, but in the culture as it exists today" and in "contemporary change in the present-day community under the slowly growing influence of the city and modern industrial civilization" (Burgess Collection, Regenstein Library, 189:1). He ignored the historical close connection of Tepoztlán to the Aztec capital of Tenochitlán (Beals [1961:10] noted that in Aztec times Tepoztlán had been the paper manufacturing center, with intimate ties to urban intellectuals rather than small-scale farmers. Redfield continued to insist that "in many respects Tepoztlán does conform with that imagine construct [the folk community]: it is or was isolated and homogeneous, with a traditional way of life. . . . I suppose Tepoztlán to represent the middle range, of peasant or peasant-like societies" [Redfield:Oscar Lewis, June 22, 1948].) and made no attempt to establish the representativeness of the field site, insouciantly stating that "this community is assumed to be more or less typical of the folk culture which characterizes the vast middle ground of Mexican civilization" and asserting that the social changes from the "slowly growing influence of the city" presented "a case of diffusion, occurring in an easily observed situation, so slowly as not to accomplish the disorganization of the community." It bears stressing that these are not "findings" of Redfield's fieldwork in Tepoztlán but were the rationale in a plan for studying it.

Paralleling the justification for Gamio's study, in his dissertation—"A Plan for a Study of Tepoztlán, Morelos"—Redfield wrote that "impetus to the project was given by the current practical interest in Mexican immigrants in the United States. A description of culture traits characterizing such immigrants would constitute, it was supposed, a description of the mental content and form which they would bring with them, and so indicate the amount of adjustment they would have to undergo in accommodating themselves in the new milieu" (1928b:8).

In an account of his stay in Mexico for a nonprofessional audience, Redfield similarly wrote of "collaborat[ing] with the sociologists in scientific study of foreign populations who do now and who promise even more to present practical problems to the people of the United States" (1928a:243)—this last a category that was narrowly conceived despite the annexation of considerable portions of what had been Mexico to the United States, for "the Mexicans, perhaps above all other peoples, present to us plenty of problems." In what is hard not to see as blaming the victims, Redfield explained that permanent immigrants "cause problems of status and race prejudice" (1929a:437). (He also reassured readers that "Dr. Gamio would not encourage permanent residence of Mexicans in the United States, but would encourage their temporary residence" [433].)

Although Redfield proposed nomothetic study of culture borrowing in his SSRC proposal and alluded to "traits" in his dissertation, he did not aim to inventory traits in the Boas-Kroeber manner but rather to explore "attitudes" in the Thomas-Park manner and ecological variation in culture/mentality in the Park-Burgess manner (Redfield 1928b:73, 231). Following the spatial logic of Chicago sociology research in the "laboratory" of Chicago and foreshadowing the synchronic treatment of "modernization" across the Yucatán (Redfield 1941), Redfield charted change across space (from the zocalo into different barrios) rather than changes through time.[1] Nonetheless, he argued (specifically, against Clark Wissler) that "culture change takes place by way of communication; not by way of geographic distribution" (Redfield 1930:148) and called for (more than exemplified) "noting the actual contacts and communications which are bringing about change" (151). Oscar Lewis would later emphasize that he (and his team of researchers gathering systematic data on fifteen times as many Tepoztlán residents as Redfield had) examined behavior, while Redfield wrote about "culture" primarily as "conventional understandings" (O. Lewis 1951:421; Cline 1952:224; cf. Redfield 1941:132).

With a $2,500 grant, accompanied by his wife, Margaret, mother-in-law (Clara Cahill Park), and two children under the age of three, on December 4, 1926, Redfield set up housekeeping in Tepoztlán, Morelos, the village suggested by Gamio.[2] Following a raid by the insurgent counterrevolutionary Catholic Cristeros on February 18, 1927, that Redfield would later breezily dismiss as a "minor disturbance" (1928a:247), he evacuated his family to Tacubaya, a suburb of Mexico City. "From February 28 until the end of June when his fieldwork ended, Redfield commuted from Tacubaya to Tepoztlán. From his correspondence there is no way of ascertaining with any degree of certainty how much time he spent in Tepoztlán and how much in Tacubaya" (Godoy 1978:69). Although four to five months was a relatively long period of fieldwork for American anthropologists of the mid-1920s, Redfield's was funded much better than most and, quite specifically, for a full year in the field. Cole wanted him to stay at least through the summer, but Redfield insisted he had worked hard enough, particularly given the four-hour round-trip commutes to and from Tepoztlán.

Cole was satisfied with the resulting dissertation, and Sapir was sufficiently enthusiastic about both the community study and the folklore materials (*corridos* mostly collected by Margaret Park Redfield) to advocate immediate publication in two volumes (Sapir:Redfield, July 8, 1928). In an undated reply to Sapir, Redfield claimed that he wanted to return to Tepoztlán before committing his preliminary study to print. In an apologetic preface to the book *Tepoztlán* two years later, Redfield explained, "The materials are now published only because it seems impossible that he will soon be able to return to Tepoztlán to continue the study here only introduced. . . . They are no more than a small sample of materials which might be obtained. They are far from constituting an ethnographic monograph on the people of Tepoztlán. Eight months is too short a time within which to secure the data for such a monograph.

.... Eight months is not even time enough to correct one's initial blunders" (1930:v). Eight months is also probably twice as long as Redfield was actually in Tepoztlán.

In the opening pages of the book, Redfield laid out his conception of "folk society" in contrast to urban literate society, romanticizing the "folk" and justifying not looking at written records (of, for instance, church parishes):

> The ways of the folk, largely unwritten and unremarked, constitute the real Mexico. . . . To learn and to set down the ways of the folk, one must encounter them directly and intimately; they are not otherwise to be found.
>
> What characteristics distinguish ["folk" peoples]? Such peoples enjoy a common stock of tradition; they are the carriers of a culture. This culture preserves its continuity from generation to generation without depending upon the printed page. Moreover, such a culture is local; the folk has a habitat. . . . Within the folk group there is relatively small diversity of intellectual interest; attitudes and interests are much the same from individual to individual. . . . And, finally, folk peoples are country peoples. (1930:1–2)

Tepoztlán appeared to Redfield to "represent a type intermediate between the primitive tribe and the modern city . . . analogous to the peasant communities of the more backward parts of Europe, of the Near East, and of the Orient" (216). In the final chapter of his book, Redfield presented Tepoztlán not as an approximation of the abstract type but as "a folk community [that] is slowly becoming more like the city. This change is a case of diffusion, occurring in an easily observed situation, so slowly as not to accomplish the disorganization of the community" (218)—"slow" still lacking any measurement.

Despite the admitted sketchiness of Redfield's ethnography and documentation of slow change (even through the recent revolution and the counterrevolution that led to his moving his family away), the book was well received by one of American anthropology's most critical evaluators (A. Kroeber 1931b:133 lauded it as a "landmark" and a "model" to be emulated), by the great Mayanist Alfred Tozzer, and by Robert S. Lynd (1931), the male coauthor of the most influential and thoroughgoing community study, *Middletown*. Lynd (1931) regretted the lack of categories for direct comparison of recent community studies. An unlikely advocate of participant observation, Ruth Benedict (1930) demurred from her own (then both past and future) practice of relying on informants ("white room ethnography" supplemented by library research), invidiously lauding the sociologist Lynds' participant observation of "Middletown" (Muncie, Indiana) to Redfield's fieldwork.

Although far from being a best seller—selling 786 copies in the first year after publication, 1,751 between 1930 and 1943 (undated report in the Redfield papers)—*Tepoztlán* established Redfield as the premier American anthropological authority on peasants and their acculturation. He moved on to consolidate this status by directing Carnegie work on Yucatán peasants along a folk-urban continuum.

An Atypical, New Yucatán Village

Chan Kom, the community Redfield himself studied the longest as a part of that research, was, at the time of his first visit (1930–31), not at all a traditional village. Chan Kom was not the most remote (from Merida) point of those chosen to illustrate (or test?) the rural-urban continuum. That was Tuzik, a place in which Redfield was particularly uncomfortable and one of the series in which "he failed to grasp that they [the inhabitants] were, and had long been a part of the modern world. They were not the small, homogeneous, meaning-filled, untroubled, family-oriented, self-sufficient social isolates of a more pleasant human past that Redfield imagined," as Paul Sullivan put it. "Drawing upon [Alfonso] Villa's work [published separately in 1945] as he did, most of Redfield's facts about the Maya of central Quintana Roo were accurate. But his selection, assemblage, and interpretations of them to constitute a portrait of folk society required prodigious feats of imagination and denial, particularly concerning the Maya's relations with foreigners like himself" (1989:158; "foreigners" refers to Americans but also the British of what was then British Honduras, now Belize, whom the Yucatán Maya tried to play off against Ladino/Mexican domination). Beals (1961:10) earlier noted that the supposedly rural peasants were refugees from hacienda peonage and had had long-standing contacts with British Honduras. The government of the Yucatán recognized Chan Kom as a pueblo (by granting it *ejido* land) only in 1926. Before the revolution of 1910–17, there was no village. Redfield and Villa Rojas noted that "few, if any of the villages of the southeastern part of the state of Yucatán have histories of undisturbed occupation." The vicinity was not cultivated during the War of the Castes, "which began in 1847 and cannot be said to have come to a definite and conclusive end, although real military operations ceased in the seventies." The predecessors of Chan Kom colonists "remained near or with the Whites during the war" and were pushed back by the Quintana Roo Indians (1934:23).

Agricultural techniques there were traditional and individualistic, but Chan Kom agriculture was not for subsistence only: in the early 1930s Chan Komians marketed half the maize they produced (Redfield and Villa Rojas 1934:51).

Redfield and Villa Rojas (1934:57, 100–101) noted "marked variation" between families' standards of living, and "considerable" differences in status, partly based on relative wealth. Yet they insisted that "there are no social classes. . . . Differences in status are not conferred by birth. . . . Superiority is not conferred by one surname rather than another" (101). Redfield (1950b:43, 76–78, 164) repeated the assertion that there were no class differences in Chan Kom, adding that occupational or status groups also were not recognized—despite the greater independence from growing maize of "leading families, who are all engaged in commerce" (55).

The factions involved in the religious schism of the 1930s described by Redfield (1950b:88–112) were family based. Political dominance and economic interests were clearly involved. As Redfield and Villa Rojas had earlier noted, "About one-third of the present families of Chan Kom have come from Ebtun, but these are the largest and the most influential families; leadership in Chan Kom has always resided with the Ebtun colonists" (1934:27; also see 212). This is one of many Chicago social scientist denials of the importance (or even existence) of class differences. (Also see the work of Lloyd Warner, Edward Shils, and Erving Goffman substituting status/prestige for class.) Reporting on a later study of Chan Kom, Victor Goldkind argued that "differences among relatively wealthy peasants, those who cultivate barely enough for subsistence, and the completely landless can be quite comparable, and just as important to the people involved as those occurring among the distinct classes or occupational groupings of the urban center" [1966:343]. Goldkind [1965, 1966] questioned the interdependence and homogeneity of Chan Kom in earlier decades [to those of Redfield's two studies], not just of the time of Goldkind's fieldwork. Also see the still-later study by de la Cruz [1996].)

The presence of American archeological expeditions to excavate Chichén Itzá had an influence on Chan Kom individual and collection aspirations. Rather than having a greater integration with mestizo Mexican culture, Chan Kom indigenes were influenced to an unusual extent by North American culture carriers. As Redfield wrote, "'The road to light' starts out toward Chicago rather than toward Mexico City. The changes in Chan Kom are in the direction of North American or cosmopolitan urbanized life rather than in the direction of Latin culture. . . . The two zestful sports, business and baseball, are surely not Latin. . . . Apparently the spirit of this people is not favorable to the adoption of Latin manners or mores" (1950b:153).[3] Moreover, construction of a road from Chan Kom to Chichén Itzá threw off the geographical calculation of distance from Merida as the folk-urban metric for cultural isolation. Both the relationships with Americans and the newness of the settlement made Chan Kom quite an untypical remote village (Beals 1961:10–11).

Similarly, Eustaquio Ceme was quite untypical a villager to provide the one life history published from Chan Kom (Redfield and Villa Rojas 1934:212–30). In addition to being unusually analytical (a native intellectualizer) and a leader, Eustaquio Ceme was raised in Ebtun, not in Chan Kom, and not by his parents. Unusually, even among Chan Kom residents he had been schooled in Spanish and was an aggressive advocate of modernization, opposing village shamans with a New Testament at the time of Redfield's initial fieldwork. At least in the view of Redfield (1950b:99), his prime informant led the village—two allied leading families descended from Ebtun in particular—into and then out of an evangelical Protestant sect.

Having championed "progress" (the spirit of capitalism and a Protestant ethic) in his youth, Don Eus later supported a gerontocratic revival of traditional religious ways, after the unseemly asceticism and youth-led Protestant adventure. Indeed, his general disappointment with the "modernization" he had had promoted undercuts the optimistic title of Redfield's second book on Chan Kom: *The Village That Chose Progress* (sometimes referred to as "The Little Village That Could," a play on the title of the children's book *The Little Engine That Could*). Redfield's use of "progress" may have been intended more ironically than it was read during the ascendancy of modernization theory. Clifford Wilcox (via e-mail) reminded me that the boosterist sense of "progress" is inconsistent with the romanticism of the folk and their expressive culture that I attribute to Redfield. Fred Gleach (also via e-mail) suggested that rather than "choosing" modernity ("progress"), Redfield may have changed his focus between the two books about Chan Kom (so that the "choice" had been made before Redfield first visited the village).

Don Eus was disillusioned by demoralization and the intrusion of hedonistic and individualistic values to the detriment of the frugality and hard work characteristic of the primitive capital accumulation and concomitant pueblo infrastructure building of his youth. By 1948 Don Eus appeared to have forgotten his own youthful independence from elders and the extent of his role in advocating new ways (see Redfield 1950b:118). To an extent that would alarm anyone looking for a representative sample, when Redfield wrote "Chan Kom," he often meant Eustaquio Ceme, a Yucatecan Maya Ogontêmmeli articulating an elaborate worldview, not the stoic, not-intellectualizing "common peasant."

The revolutionary political institutions (a federated Liga Local and agrarian committee), according to Redfield and Villa Rojas (1934:104–6), were not, in Redfield's view, especially salient, and were not mentioned at all in Redfield 1950b, but the amount of communal labor (*fagina*) in Chan Kom was exceptionally high. Also, the population was unusually young, made up of those seeking to better their lot by building a new community and willing to pay the price of devoting between a sixth and a quarter of each man's time to civic projects and/or to the overhead of local (independent pueblo) governance (Redfield 1950b:181). The age distribution in the pioneer settlement of 1931 and the established pueblo of 1948 remained the same, though the population tripled (contrasting Redfield and Villa Rojas 1934:14 with Redfield 1950b:68). Only one in fourteen Chan Kom residents was age forty-five or older at either point.

The village, in particular its leader, had already "chosen progress" in the early 1930s. Redfield and Villa Rojas emphasize that Chan Komians were peasants producing for markets with a well-developed "tendency toward the pecuniary valuation of all goods, even land" (1934:67). Indeed, the evidence for the atypicality of Chan Kom as an exemplar of a long-established local tradition is explicitly presented in the course of the first Chan Kom monograph, although later Redfield denied that "the relative progressiveness of Chan Kom" was a reason for its selection.

Rather, "the associations established with the Americans at Chichén and the presence of a teacher [Alfonso Villa Rojas] who was soon to become an ethnological collaborator determined the choice" (1950b:16).

Redfield spent ten weeks in intermittent periods in Chan Kom during the early 1930s. According to Villa Rojas (1979: 47–48), Redfield "had a facility for making friends with people; on the other hand, he did not really establish close ties with his informants. . . . He had a way of asking complex questions that informants found difficult to answer. . . . His interviews with the few informants who knew Spanish were well planned, although they were carried out in a deceptively casual manner. . . . He was enormously inquisitive, anxious to pursue to the smallest detail those topics that interested him."

"Despite his linguistic handicap," he also "liked nothing better than to be present, simply as an observer, at all kinds of gatherings and social occasions," according to Villa Rojas, who also recalled that Redfield "was able to go without sleep all night, so as to observe some special ceremony being carried out by a shaman; later he would interview individually all of the [few Spanish-speaking?] principal participants in the ceremony. In this way, he obtained a comprehensive and integrated understanding of everything he had seen" (1979:48).

Although Villa Rojas emphasized the meticulous recording of detail Redfield exemplified in the field and sought from Villa Rojas, Redfield's publications are more integrated than specifically detailed—overly integrated, in the view of some later anthropologists. For instance, Leaf (1979:267) wrote, "Redfield's work never did present, in an orderly way, most of the 'ethnographic' detail that one finds even in contemporary works of the same general tradition—like Evans-Pritchard's. The descriptions always retain a thin, abstract, and distant quality. . . . Without the support of closely analyzed data, Redfield's framework remained only programmatic, although it was the program most widely followed by anthropologists who were less interested in the reconstruction of 'tribal isolates' than in modern complex societies, in both the old and new worlds."

At the time of initial publication of *The Folk Culture of the Yucatán* (1941), even so sociologistic a critic as Durkheim-translator-and-explicator Harry Alpert (1941: 896), after noting the "assumption that the communities represent four successive stages of an ongoing historical process" and questioning the assumption of "one-to-one correspondence between isolation and homogeneity" (897), complained, "The analysis is much too abstract, too unpsychological. The author fails to make the established relationships meaningful in terms of the concrete behavior of specific individuals undergoing the process in question. We do not meet anyone in the throes of becoming secularized or individualized. We get no insight into the changing mentality of individuals. Our acquaintance is with cultural processes and social situations, not with people" (897; also see the January 19, 1962, letter from Oscar Lewis to Eric Wolf reproduced in Rigdon 1988:231).

Sicilian Peasants Studied by a Less-Famous Classmate of Redfield's

Redfield's classmate, Charlotte Gower, also began studying peasants by working with immigrants to Chicago. Her (also 1928) doctoral dissertation was based on fieldwork in Chicago's "Little Sicily."[4] Like work contemporary to it on Native American cultures, it was based on memory of nonmaterial culture from another time and place: "The material [on supernatural patrons] was gathered in connection with a preliminary study of the cultural background of Sicilian immigrants to America. It represents a reconstruction of a portion of Sicilian culture from the accounts of people already in this country, and literary resources" (Gower 1928:2). Her immediately postdoctoral fieldwork in "Milocca" (Milena) Sicily during 1928–29 was supported by an ssrc fellowship "because it was hoped that a knowledge of the background of the Sicilian immigrants to the United States might prove useful in understanding their problems in reactions to their new environment" (Chapman 1971:vii). Note the focus on the immigrants' problems rather than the immigrants being a problem, as in Redfield's formulations. Gower's book is, as King and Patterson (1991:106) noted, oddly silent on emigration, the original research problematic, as well as the justification for its funding.

Although her description is very normative with minimal discussion of intracultural variation, the book written in 1930 (finally published as Chapman 1971) stressed factionalism, stratification, lack of cooperation beyond the ranks of family and godparent ties, and the lack of a sense of solidarity even within age groups:

There is no sentiment of solidarity which binds a woman to her sex as a whole, or a youth to the aggregate of his coevals. . . . The sense of unity goes little beyond consciousness of kind. . . . Within these sex and age groups there is no cooperation. . . . This lack of a sense of solidarity in no way signifies that the sex and age groupings are without importance in the organization of Sicilian society. Everyone has the clearest idea of his place in respect to these groupings, and the majority of his actions and relationships are determined by his position in the structure. One is never merely a person, but a man or a woman, and, although here the precise limits are less strictly defined, a member of an age class. Of this he is perfectly aware. . . . In any particular set of circumstances he knows how it is expected that he will behave, and also knows in general what to expect from the members of the other groupings. (Chapman 1971:49, 48)

Even with the Mafiosi in jail, her picture of a western Sicilian village under Fascist rule is markedly less harmonious/pastoral than Redfield's romantic portraits of Tepoztlán and Chan Kom. Among other topics, she collected material on witchcraft beliefs. Although she collected proverbs, stories, and love songs, "insofar as possible, information was acquired by direct observation of the life of the community and by as full participation in that life as the circumstances and convenience would allow" (Chapman 1971:viii).

Unlike other ethnographers (and not just of that era!), she was very aware that she "could not escape affiliation with one of the two factions that divided the town, an affiliation that considerably limited my range of contacts among the leaders of the community" (viii). In being explicit about this, as in all regards, she was very conscientious about not overgeneralizing.

Gower was in the province of Caltanissetta more than four times as long as Redfield was in the state of Morelos. Still, like Redfield, she found that those she was studying were oriented more to America than to the national capitals (Rome in her case, Mexico City in Redfield's).

Redfield wrote to Livia Appel of the University of Wisconsin Press on July 27, 1937, that Gower's study "constitutes a contribution to scholarship of unusual merit and that both the simplicity and quality of exposition and the subject matter makes me feel that the book would have general appeal." Radcliffe-Brown wrote to Cole on January 28, 1941, that "in normal times, Oxford University Press would have published it." Despite the advocacy of Redfield, Cole, and Radcliffe-Brown for publication, both the University of Chicago Press and the University of Wisconsin Press failed to publish *Milocca* during the 1930s (Gower:Redfield, July 25, 1935, July 23, 1937), although 1938 correspondence between Redfield and Donald Bean of the University of Chicago Press evidences a plan to publish it simultaneously with *Pascua*, *St. Denis*, and *Suye Mura* (studies discussed below). William Foote Whyte (letter to Redfield, November 9, 1941) opined that *Milocca* was diffuse and lacking in a clear problematic, as good as *St. Denis* if not as tightly organized and well-written as *Pascua*; and earlier that year, Redfield had asked, "Can we do it this year? The series is going well" (Redfield:Cole, April 1, 1941). No answer has been preserved, and the Gower folder in the Redfield papers ends with his reply to Whyte, so it is unclear why the University of Chicago press did not publish *Milocca*.

Gower had left the University of Wisconsin for Lingam University in China in 1938 (recommended by Redfield, April 7). If she did a community study during her four years there or her later years in the employ of the U.S. Marine Corps and the Central Intelligence Agency (King and Patterson 1991:106; Lepowsky 2000), none has been published (yet?).

When it was finally published, *Milocca* was reviewed positively. Cronin celebrated "that the analysis is not encumbered by Redfieldian peasant theory, which denies, for example, the existence of such things as social class, or by an emphasis on value system without accompanying behavioral data" (1973:515; also see Cappanari 1973; Scarpaci 1973). And Migliore et al. (2009) found that Gower is remembered fondly in Milocca by descendants of those who knew her.

Redfield's Students

> The nature of a man's method is often clarified by seeing how it found expression in his students. Sometimes the nature of a method appears most clearly in some of its least cautious exemplifications.
>
> —ROBERT REDFIELD, Methods in Cultural Anthropology (Anthropology 340 syllabus) (1954b:8)

Having been raised to the rank of full professor and dean of the Social Sciences Division by 1934, Redfield was able to sponsor some of his students' work on other peasantries.

The Spicers' Study of Yaqui Villagers

Edward Spicer, who had been Dean Byron Cummings's student and assistant in archaeological projects at the University of Arizona, shifted to social anthropology as a doctoral student at the University of Chicago under Redfield and Radcliffe-Brown. Rosamond Brown, a fellow graduate student, took notes for him while he was hospitalized for tuberculosis. They were married in June 1936 and began a year's fieldwork at the Yaqui (Yoeme) village of Pascua on the outskirts of Tucson, Arizona. His PhD dissertation, a functionalist community study focusing on cultural persistence (of uprooted Yaquis at the edges of an American city) and "fictive kinship," and her MA thesis on the Pascua Easter ceremony emerged from this fieldwork.

Both of them were somewhat discouraged by Redfield's demands for generalization after reading what he considered overly detailed observations of particular events. In a June 8, 1938, letter to Redfield, Rosamond Spicer balked at providing account of a "typical festival," maintaining that she must describe "a specific event which took place March 1937 in Pascua. I cannot pretend to be studying other than a specific event." (Redfield replied soothingly, "You are right that you will have to report the specific ceremony that you witnessed. However, I think that your description can be so presented that the reader will understand what elements are more important than others, so that a sort of anatomy can become apparent" [June 14, 1938].)

Redfield wrote to Edmund Spicer (June 27, 1938) that his manuscript met the highest expectations and, for purposes of social anthropology, was one of the most useful written on a North American people. To Edward Sapir, in support of an SSRC application to extend Yaqui ethnography to the Mexican homeland, Redfield wrote that Spicer was "one of the very best students through Chicago. He has a clear sense of problem and of responsibility to the facts."

The study of Pascua was published by the University of Chicago Press as part of a quasi-series of community studies, with Redfield's own books, John Embree's Japanese village study, and the Quebec studies of Horace Miner and Everett Hughes (Hughes was Redfield's classmate in the then-joint sociology and anthropology department at Chicago; the others were students of Redfield and Radcliffe-Brown). Spicer was eager to have Redfield write an introduction to *Pascua*, writing to Redfield, "I still feel that an introduction, however short, by you would add a great deal to the book. I know of no one who could in a few words set it better in its proper theoretical context" (January 22, 1940).

Pascua was like Chan Kom (and unlike Tepoztlán) in being a new settlement with considerable influences by American culture and in being composed of indigenes (i.e., not mestizo Mexican). As a study of semi-integration of immigrants within the borders of the United States, Spicer's initial fieldwork was within the same Thomas-Park immigrant disorganization paradigm as Redfield's and Gower's fieldwork in Chicago.

Although ignoring relations of Pascua and Pascolas with the Tucson, Arizona, and U.S. governments, Spicer explicitly addressed factionalism. "We Yaquis [in Pascua] are not all from one pueblo; how, then, can we form one pueblo here?" Spicer (1940:149) quoted as a common saying. Diverse points of origin (and the "wild" versus "tame" histories of those places of origin in relation to the Mexican government) are what Spicer stressed. He argued that there was "little correlation between property possessed and village participation," that there was an "absence of class groupings based on income or property possessed," and that Pascolas did not consider "economic values" important (as did the "surrounding community" of Anglo- and Mexican Americans) (55). "Prestige in the village depends much more on ceremonial activity than it does on income or possessions of property," Spicer (55) wrote of Pascua, matching Redfield's representation of Chan Kom.

Whereas Pascua was an ethnic enclave of ex-peasants on the margins of a then-small American city, the Spicers went on to do fieldwork in the Mexican Yaqui village of Potam, Sonora (ca. 1941–42), also characterized by a lack of differentiation:

> The economic system which obtains in Potam is one characterized by very little specialization in production activities. All Yaquis produce approximately the same crops in about the same ways. All the men know and use similar agricultural techniques and all of them know, or are learning, similar techniques in house-building and in implement- and furniture-making. . . . To a considerable extent the variations in income through crops and money are equalized. Families whose crops are poor in a given year may have relatives, godparents, or *compadres* who have better crops and through these social relations obtain aid in the form of food and cash. They in turn in another year may have to use what surplus they have to help their relatives or *compadres*. (Spicer 1954:53, 52)

Spicer's primary focus was on "exotic" religious beliefs and practices, with an explicit functionalist (in the Radcliffe-Brown style) argument for "the consistency and interdependence of the behaviors and beliefs which characterize Yaquis" (2), the "close linkages of most aspects of Yaqui culture" (196). Considering both Spicer's interest in "acculturation" and the considerable disruption of Yaqui life by the Mexican Civil War and continued martial law, Potam is a remarkably pastoral account of a tightly integrated "traditional" village with practically no attention to state power. Spicer noted that "most Yaquis of Potam have fairly frequent relations of some sort with Mexican residents in Potam territory," going beyond selling produce and buying manufactured goods from Mexican storekeepers. For maintenance of order, the "governors [the leaders of the indigenous social structure] and other Poteños take the position that their own organization is perfectly adequate to serve all Yaqui interests, and that therefore the only function which the [Mexican state's appointed] municipality officials can serve is to preserve order and adjust the affairs of Mexicans or other non-Yaquis in the territories. ... The municipality officials do not interfere in the trials or other proceedings of the Potam governors" (110).

Although never focusing on class (or incipient class) differences between twentieth-century Yaquis, Spicer's magisterial "cultural history" of the Yaquis included three pages discussing (albeit minimizing) differentiation among nineteenth-century Yaquis and pointing out that the Yaquis (in Mexico) were not peasants then (Spicer 1980:219–21).

John Embree's Studies of Acculturation of
Japanese Peasants in Japan and Hawaii

Unlike those who studied the quite new and quite small villages of Chan Kom and Pascua, John Embree and his Japanese-speaking wife, Ella, undertook fieldwork in a long-established (more than seven centuries) village in the southern prefecture of Kumamoto on Kyushu in the fall of 1935. Suye Mura was also considerably larger. As John Embree wrote to Redfield on January 15, 1936, "We do not intend to produce any such complete report [as *Chan Kom*]. First alibi—Suye Mura 1600, Chan Kom 250; 2nd alibi—no time; and 3rd alibi—utter inability."

Although Redfield was interested in "survivals of traditional village ways," he urged Embree to study the role of literacy and generational differences (February 20, 1936). To a much greater extent than in Redfield's and Spicer's ethnographies, Embree considered incursions of state—a state explicitly trying to foment local organizations for identification and solidarity with national polity and policies. Whereas the neighborhood group (*buraku*/hamlet) had been the most important unit in the social structure of rural Japan, Embree showed that "the hamlet is part of a much larger and highly complex structure which is and has for some time been undergoing rapid change. . . . In abstract structural terms the hamlet is steadily losing its relative independence, and it as a group and its members as individuals are becoming more and more involved in and dependent upon relations with the wider social environment" (Embree 1937:xii), in part through increased communication that was supplanting the local dialect with standard Japanese.

Embree also explicitly recognized that "many unintended changes have come into Suye Mura, in addition to, and sometimes as the indirect result of, the carefully introduced changes directed by the government" (301). At the time of his observations, a cash economy was supplanting some traditional cooperation, and (along with improved roads) facilitating dependence on manufactured goods and producing internal stratification (158–61). Changes in traditional cultivation practices were being introduced by opinion leaders—a returned college graduate and a retired schoolteacher—rather than through unmediated influences of mass media (304–5, 311).

Embree was especially interested in forms of cooperation, including credit clubs and labor exchange. He included a chapter on the typical life history and looked closely at the mixture of Buddhism and Shinto in the beliefs and actions of villagers. Like Gower, unlike Redfield and Spicer, Embree discussed differences in class, both "new class groupings based on wealth" and old-time landed gentry (whose children were sent to high schools outside the village and were the only ones who went to college). He also found marriage to be endogamous by class: "upper groups taking brides from upper families, middle groups from middle families, etc.," with females occasionally "marrying up" but males not (161).

Suye Mura, the monograph resulting from the Embree's fieldwork, was a "durable classic" (R. Smith and Wiswell 1982:ix), of special interest as the only community study of the Word War II enemy "traditional Japan." Although remembered by Passin (1982), Shibutani (1990 interview), and other wartime students of Japan as the major resource, the book did not see a burst of sales following Pearl Harbor. Through 1941, 437 copies of the book had sold, with only 45 more copies selling in the first eighteen months of U.S.-Japan warfare. Restudy of the village (Yoshino 1954) did not result in the kind of challenges later studies of Tepoztlán and Chan Kom produced. Indeed, I cannot find any criticism of any of Embree's assertions. Moreover, the restudy noted that "at the outset the mayor was of the opinion that no further study was needed and that one could find out anything he might want to know from Embree's work. This attitude proved to be a handicap at various times during the course of the field study. However, the deputy, the assembly chairman and other 26 leaders of the village were very helpful and cooperative" (Yoshino 1954:26–27).

U.S. occupation and land reform brought about marked changes:

– the participation and interest of villagers in their local government and in public affairs has increased
– governing officials are more responsive to popular sentiment
– legal restrictions relative to women are gradually disappearing; for example, women can now vote, hold public office, and own property
– the current educational aim is to teach children to become socially responsible citizens rather than unquestioning followers
– the land reform program has improved the standard of living of the former tenant farmer

Least changed were

– the pattern of conformity to traditional rules of behavior
– the rigid hierarchical stratification system within the family and in most social relationships
– veneration of family ancestors and of the Emperor
– the system of exchange of labor and cooperative living (Yoshino 1954:155).

Unlike Thomas, Redfield, Gower, and Spicer, who did research on ethnic minority enclaves in the United States before doing fieldwork in the "source culture" (i.e., the homeland of the immigrants to the United States), Embree began with study of the source culture and then did fieldwork among émigrés from it. After taking up a position at the University of Hawaii, Embree undertook what he saw as a study of the acculturation of Japanese farmers in Hawaii (what became Embree 1941). In an October 31, 1939, letter to Redfield, Embree reported that (University of Chicago) sociologist Herbert Blumer had read and liked his study, which was too controversial for the University of Hawaii Press to risk publishing. Redfield wrote, "I wish I saw it as fitting into the Anthropology Series of our Press here, but the truth is I do not" (Redfield:Embree, January 11, 1940). It was not focused on the southwestern United State or Mesoamerica, but neither were *Suye Mura* or *St. Denis*.

The primary reason for exclusion appears to be that Redfield regarded Japanese Hawaiian farmers as not constituting a "traditional" peasant society. The Japanese farmers in Kona raised coffee for export and also tended to be small shopkeepers. In describing them, Embree discussed selective retention and adaptation of traditional rural Japanese institutions. Increased use of money and machinery did not have as much of a disintegrating effect on Hawaii as he had seen in Japan, although the Kona farmers engaged in less cooperative labor than did Suye Mura peasants. (About the same time, young Japanese American sociology students focused on structural barriers to assimilation on the West Coast of the United States. Miyamoto [1939] and Shibutani [1941] outlined potential sources of Nisei [American-born children of immigrants] disorganization.)

Embree also looked at residence and opportunity, ecology, and institutions rather than values or any national character based on primary socialization practices, the dominant focus of American anthropology throughout the 1940s. Embree (1950a) specifically criticized the culture and personality work that attempted to explain the conduct of World War II on the basis of childrearing practices.

Something else that troubled Redfield about Embree's Kona manuscript was that it had too much "case material and incident which I can't easily assimilate to any well-defined problem, and I miss the guidance of general ideas." Like Rosamond Spicer in being reluctant to operate on Redfield's level of abstraction, Embree replied that "as a benighted empiricist, I am against having a theme song drown out the words" (Embree:Redfield, June 4, 1940).

After conducting applied anthropology work during World War II and in Southeast Asia after it and before being killed in an automobile accident at the age of forty-two in 1950, Embree (1950b) wrote an article on the "loose" structure of Thai culture (in contrast to the tight interconnections of Japanese culture) that showed him quite able to produce thematic general ideas of the sort Redfield and others pursued through the 1950s in seminars on Asian civilizations ("great traditions") and local variations ("small traditions") (see Redfield 1954a, 1955b, 1956a) and that provided a framework for social anthropology of Southeast Asian peasantries (see Evers 1969).

Horace Miner's Study of Rapidly Changing Rural French Canada

Like Embree and Spicer, Horace Miner was a protégé of Robert Redfield (see Redfield:Donald Bean, January 8, 1938; Redfield:Lunt Upson, 1937; Redfield evaluation for the Julius Rosenwald Fund, March 28, 1939; Redfield:Miner August 6, 1947). Miner was also much influenced by Radcliffe-Brown-style functionalism as a University of Chicago anthropology student. Like Spicer, Miner focused on religion, the "deeply ingrained" Catholicism: "Lack of contact with persons of other convictions and the relative lack of functional problems in the mode of living mean that the particular native belief is rarely questioned. Life in St. Denis is a flow of traditional behavior. . . . Religious behavior and thought dominate all life" (1939:91, 100). Like Redfield, Miner aimed to provide an ethnographic description of a "folk culture in its least-altered existent form" (the most rural point of the folk-urban continuum) and to consider factors responsible for cultural change in the direction of urbanization and anglicization" (ix). Although Miner was interested in social and cultural change and urban influences on the countryside, St. Denis de Karmouraska at first seemed to him "so old French [that] I was worried there would be no outside influence. I lose no sleep over that now" (Miner:Redfield, August 3, 1936).

Redfield's introduction to *Saint Denis* framed it as a study of peasants: "The *habitants* live in terms of common understandings which are rooted in tradition and which have come to form an organization. The fundamental views of life are shared by almost everyone; and these views find consistent expression in the beliefs, the institutions, the rituals, and the manner of the people. . . . The sanctions which support conduct are strongly sacred. . . . There is little disorganization and little crime" (1939:xiii–xiv).

Redfield characterized "the French Canadians herein described . . . [as] almost the only North American peasants" (xv). Miner does not seem to have used the term "peasant" in the text, but when Redfield urged Miner to be frank about anything in the draft introduction that made him uncomfortable and specifically wondered, "Perhaps there will be objection to calling rural French Canadians peasants; they seem peasants to me" (Redfield:Miner September 9, 1938), Miner replied that "'peasant' does not disturb me at all; it is a common term of reference in Canada" (September 14, 1938). Miner's title had been *Quebec Folk* (with "St. Denis" in the subtitle; Miner:Redfield September 14, 1938), but in a 1963 foreword to a reprinting of *St. Denis*, he denied having "undertaken to illustrate or to 'test' any social typology," noting that the "context of peasant culture" was supplied in Redfield's introduction (vii).

Miner stressed that his "analysis of St. Denis was made along ethnological and structural-functional lines, strongly influenced by the teaching of A. R. Radcliffe-Brown." (It certainly has a Radcliffe-Brownian focus on kinship—and folk Catholicism was as exotic to Miner as to Redfield and to Radcliffe-Brown). Miner approached culture change as resulting from social "structural forces and from diffusion, not as a shift away from a folk type of culture" (vi). Redfield himself noted the increased money income and the export of labor to factories rather than the agricultural pursuits that had been de facto exclusive in the traditional/folk society.

While doing fieldwork, Miner disclaimed any "intention to be solely a reporter of the 'society' of St. Denis, but rather [sought to be] a commentator on how the present culture reflects the change which is going on at present, the directions of this change, the means of its introduction, and the forces responsible for it" and to provide a basis for comparison of social changes elsewhere (Miner:Redfield, November 30, 1936).

George Peter Murdock lauded *St. Denis* in an *American Anthropologist* review as the most genuinely cultural study of recent community studies and praised it for making "explicit the traditionally patterned norms according to which people behave and organize their interpersonal relations" and for providing an outstanding analysis of social and political organization. "Religion and its intimate interpenetration with all other aspects of the culture are admirably portrayed, albeit with a certain Durkheimian rigidity," Murdock (1940:324) wrote.

Miner later undertook an anthropological study of a corn-belt county in the United States (1949) and one of preindustrial cities in Africa, including a community study of Timbuctoo that was not published by the University of Chicago Press despite recommendations to do so from Redfield, Sol Tax, Joseph Greenberg, and William Bascom in 1948–49 and Miner's willingness to subvent publication. Eventually, it was published as a memoir of the American Philosophical Society in 1953 and criticized by Beals (1954) and Hansen (1954) as applying rather than testing the folk-urban model, confounding multiethnicity and urbanism, and failing to distinguish normative from descriptive assertions. Miner went on to psychological anthropology research on purportedly rural ("oasis") and "urban" samples of Algerians born in a small town at the edge of the Sahara Desert (Rorschach tests administered in 1950, analyzed in Miner and De Vos 1960). Miner seems to have done little research after the midpoint of the twentieth century, although he wrote some general pieces about African urbanism/urbanization and defending the value of the folk-urban continuum (Miner 1952, 1968).

Later Work

The folk-urban difference is not a classification. It is a mental construction of imagined societies that are only approximated in particular "real" societies.

—ROBERT REDFIELD memorandum about Oscar Lewis's criticisms, June 22, 1948

The Guatemalan fieldwork of Redfield (in the Ladino town of Agua Escondida and, briefly, in San Antonio Palopo) and Sol Tax (in Chichicastenango and Panajachel) challenged notions about the ubiquity of strong familial organization and lack of individualism in folk societies—even across Mayan peasant communities. From Agua Escondida, Redfield wrote to Alexander Leighton, "It is often said that the Highlands of Guatemala contain a great variety of cultures in a relatively small area. This is true in that each community has its own traditions, costumes, and forms of institutions . . . [but] now that I have been here several times the cultures of the Western Highlands seem to me very much alike in what one might call their fundamental character or in what [William Graham] Sumner would have called their ethos (December 12, 1938; see Tax 1937, 1941; Rubinstein 1991).

To Melville Herskovits, Redfield wrote of a surprisingly "thin culture":

"We are living here for a few weeks with a very agreeable, peaceful, orderly and happy people, who have less culture and less social organization than I had supposed compatible with stability and order" (April 1937; cf. the comparison Embree 1950b would later make between tight and loose structuring).

Comparing Chichicastenango to the Chan Kom described by Redfield and Villa Rojas, Tax wrote Redfield that "Chan Kom might as well be in Siberia for the feeling of differences that one gets. I'm afraid that if we ever write about Maya Culture, all we shall be able to talk about will be tortillas" (March 1, 1935). Four days later Tax dispelled any visions of harmony (and simplicity): "There seem to be as many conflicts as in Chicago; the culture is not that simple one we like to think a Folk has—in fact, I should be willing to gamble right now that it has all the complexities of a rural community of ten thousand in Illinois. . . . The only thing that holds the culture together—makes it as homogeneous as it is—is the political organization and the limitations imposed by little outside contact as well as strong conservatism" (Tax:Redfield, March 19, 1935).

Publication of Tax's systematic and detailed examination of small-scale capitalism, the manuscript of which he had drafted in early 1939 (see Rubinstein 1991:267–71), was delayed by wartime paper shortages and priorities until 1952. Redfield did not publish any Guatemalan community study—nor much else about Guatemala (two articles, 1939b and 1956b, are the exceptions), although he did refer to differences between the Yucatán and Guatemalan Mayas in his 1941 exposition of a folk-urban continuum—with Merida being the urban center then. The emergent international resort of Cancun has since become the antipode of Chan Kom for traditionalists, with "the homogenous community world envisaged by the ideological propaganda of los Antiguos elite" who abhor the worship of money among those influenced by or who have migrated to Cancun (de la Cruz 1996:156).

Along with arguing that an "ideal type" model cannot be falsified, Redfield insisted that "the comparison I attempted in the Yucatan was directed not toward a full understanding of Yucatecan society, but toward understanding a method of comparison" (Redfield:Helen Hughes, March 16, 1953, in regard to the manuscript of what became Mintz 1953). Redfield also insisted that "the Yucatecan hacienda, like Mexican plantations in general, was for generations not an industrial enterprise for profit but a way of life for people" whom he did not think should be considered rural proletarians. Mintz (1953:142) characterized as "impersonal" the relations between managers and workers in the henequen plantations of the Yucatan. Mintz proposed the plantation as another type of Latin American socioeconomic organization and very politely suggested that this "distinctive type [is] not amenable to the folk-urban construction," though noting that adding the plantation to the typology of communities in Latin America or the Yucatán in particular "might have upset, or at least modified the sequence from the 'folk society' of Tusik to the 'metropolis of Merida' and back again. To a very large degree, it would seem that Merida's very existence hinges on the continued success of the henequen plantations. The forces of change seem to originate not in the metropolis but in the world outside, and Merida is important in its intermediary relationship with the key economic area where henequen is produced" (142), not as an independent urban center from which culture change emanates (or a great tradition was maintained and elaborated).

In 1953 Sidney Mintz sought to elaborate Redfield's typology. A decade earlier George Peter Murdock (1943:136), who had been schooled in the Yale social evolutionary doctrines of the Sumner-Keller tradition, expressed concern about hyper-abstract models of form and process, noting that Redfield "is fond of playing with paired polar concepts such as cultural organization and disorganization, the sacred and the secular, collectivism and individualization. Like the evolutionists, he tends to conceive of cultural change, not in terms of a dynamics of process, but as an apparently inevitable transition from one conceptual pole to its opposite. The reader is irresistibly reminded of Herbert Spencer's all-embracing theory of evolution from undifferentiated homogeneity to differentiated heterogeneity. In theories of this order the present reviewer sees little nourishment."

Some other Redfield students, such as John Bennett and Herbert Passin, did anthropological fieldwork in the rural United States (as recalled by John Bennett 1988; on the folk-urban shift applied to the rural southern Illinois, see especially John Bennett 1943, 1948; see also Passin and Bennett 1943 on diversification of beliefs following increasing social heterogeneity).

Although interrupted by the purported applications of anthropology during World War II, and having even a project of surveying rural communities in China in 1948–49 thwarted by the civil war there, Redfield returned to "armchair ethnology" or comparative analysis of "the folk society" (in the singular) after the war with a special emphasis on Asia (see Redfield 1954a, 1955a, 1955b, 1956a; Mariott 1955). The focus of the work on examining the relationships of great tradition (civilization) to little (folk) traditions that Redfield directed during the early 1950s largely ignored the "economic and social development processes which had become a major concern of public policy [not least the Ford Foundation, which financed the Chicago comparative program] and international social life at the time. However, Redfield, [Milton] Singer, and others participating in the approach were concerned with scholarly matters like the meaning of religion in peasant societies, the symbols and values of Oriental religions, and the like," not with the relations between centralized states and localities, or with technological transformations, or with "traditional" means of production (John Bennett 1998:76–77), although they purported to provide holistic analysis "guided by a direct acquaintance with the culture and its expressive utterances and representations, and by collections of factual information about it" (M. Singer 1991:179).

The Berkeley Lineage

Although Kroeber (1948:284) would definitively lay out the anthropological conception of "peasants" as forming a "part society" ("definitely rural—yet liv[ing] in relation to market towns. . . . They lack the isolation, the political autonomy, and the self-sufficiency of tribal populations.") and some of his interwar graduate students at Berkeley would do pioneering work on peasants, Kroeber and Lowie taught about "primitive" peoples and civilizations without ever mentioning peasants (George M. Foster interview, April 13, 2000).

Ralph L. Beals

The first Berkeley-trained anthropologist focused on Mexico was Ralph Beals. He did summer fieldwork with the Nisenans (southern Maidus) and wrote an ethnological dissertation based on material on northern Mexico now in the Bancroft Library collection. After completing his PhD in 1930, Beals received a two-year National Research Council fellowship (in biological sciences) to study the Cahita peoples (Yaquis, Mayos, Opatas) of Sonora, a Mexican state that was under martial law with still-active Yaqui rebels inland. Elsie Clews Parsons visited Beals in the field and arranged for him to work with her among the Mixes in southern Mexico in 1932–33. "Essentially Boasian in outlook, Beals studied 'tribes' rather than communities" during the 1930s (Goldschmidt 1986:949).

Simultaneous with founding an anthropology department at UCLA, Beals returned to Mexican fieldwork for fifteen months in 1940–41 with four students from the Instituto Nacional de Antropologia y Historia. His community study of Cherán, a Tarascan town on a recently paved highway, was published in 1946. It marks a turn to applied interests and to the phenomenon of urbanization (see Beals 1951) and increased sensitivity to issues of sampling and ad hoc proclamation of "community" (see Beals 1954, 1961). Although a community study of a town that was being rapidly incorporated into mestizo Mexican culture, it was still organized as an inventory of culture traits on the model of the elicitation of traits of Native California peoples supervised by Kroeber and extended south into Mexico by Beals's survey of Cahita peoples. That is, while being a community study from rural Mexico, Beals's ethnographic work through the end of World War II did not theorize peasantry/ies.

In 1964–67, however, Beals returned to Oaxaca in a training program that, along with fieldwork on his own in 1972–73, resulted in his pioneering 1975 book on the peasant marketing system there, a study not of villages but of the selling in an urban center of what they produce (weavings being prominent, along with agricultural produce).

George Foster

George Foster also did a trait inventory of an indigenous California group (Yukis) based on elicitation of memories from elders. Foster did his Berkeley dissertation fieldwork in 1940–41 among the Sierra Popolucas in the Mexican state of Vera Cruz, inspired primarily by Herskovits's interest in economic anthropology (see Herskovits 1940; Foster had been an undergraduate student of Herskovits's at Northwestern University). Although traditionally *milpa* digging-stick subsistence farmers, following the Mexican Civil War the Popolucas raised coffee as a cash crop and used money in trade for manufactured goods. Although his dissertation and it publication labeled the Popolucas "primitive," they were indigenous peasants linked to the emerging Mexican national economy. (Foster noted that "similarities between certain so-called primitive economies and our own Western economy are frequently greater than between to primitive societies" [1942:2], hence the qualifier "Mexican" on "primitive.")

In 1943 Berkeley alumnus Julian Steward, under the auspices of the Smithsonian Institution Institute of Social Anthropology, hired Foster to teach (in Spanish) one semester a year at the National School of Anthropology in Mexico City and to take students to Michoacán (the home state of Mexico's president, Lázaro Cardenás) for collaborative fieldwork on Ihuatzio, a Lake Pátzcuaro Tarascan village, to compare to Beals's study of (inland) Cherán. The large party was not accepted (the local priest was particularly opposed, suspecting the anthropologists were Protestant missionaries in disguise: see Riess 1999:133). Foster instead undertook fieldwork in the mestizoized village of Tzintzuntzan in 1944.

His very comprehensive 1948 monograph *Empire's Children* described myriad aspects of the culture and economy of what, in the mid-1940s, still approximated a closed corporate community. "There's no theory in *Empire's Children*, but there are data on many things," Foster said in an April 13, 2000, interview. In his overview of Tzintzuntzan research he recalled that "as a student of Kroeber and Lowie, I was taught that all forms of behavior, all data, have meaning and that they are relevant to interpretation and explanation, even if this relevance is not apparent at the time they are noted or recorded" (1979:171) and added that, "in hindsight, I feel fortunate that I emphasized data rather than theory in the initial study" (176). In marked contrast to the seeming preference for taking geographical distances as a substitute for examining historical records (most notably in Robert Redfield's folk-urban continuum but also recurrently in the rejection by many Boasians of what had been recorded by nonprofessionals and substitution of inferences about the distribution of traits), Foster carefully worked through extant records from earlier times about Tzintzuntzan.

After returning, as a professor, to Berkeley in 1953 and doing fieldwork in Spain, Foster was able to return to Tzintzuntzan 1958. His intended restudy metamorphosed into longitudinal research as he made annual revisits into the 1990s (see Foster 1979). Long-running observation of behavior and attitudes of Tzintzuntzeños was the basis for Foster's theorizing about peasant worldviews and social organization. His 1967 book *Tzintzuntzan* focused on the image of a limited good and dyadic contracts as organizing principles that explained much about the Tzintzuntzan peasants of the 1940s (the ethnographic present of the book, although supplemented by data from later times), particularly the lack of communal cooperation. In regard to his model of "the limited good," Foster wrote that it "is accurate, I believe, for traditional Tzintzuntzans, perhaps to about 1965, although with a decreasingly good fit during the years immediately preceding that date" (2002:267; 1965 was also the date of publication of it as a model of peasant worldview).

In addition to research on changes in how Tzintzuntzeños lived and understood their lives, Foster organized comparisons of peasants around the world in a reader, *Peasant Society* (Potter et al. 1967), which he co-edited and for which he wrote an analytical introduction.

The view of noncooperation of Tzintzuntzeños deeply suspicious of each other and of any gains being possible except at the expense of others (the zero-sum of the "limited good") contrasted with Redfield's optimism about Chan Kom as a village that "chose progress" (Redfield 1950b) and was characterized by extensive communal labor (Redfield and Villa Rojas 1934) and with Redfield's (1954c) representation of the peasant view of the good life. Foster's writings about "folk society" linked to Oscar Lewis's (1951) very critical presentation of a restudy of Tepoztlán. Although in my 2000 interview Foster said that he had not intended to criticize Redfield, Foster and Oscar Lewis cited each other in support of their representation of chronic suspiciousness and noncooperation in Mexican peasant communities (though Lewis [1970:253] questioned whether Tzintzuntzan was a peasant community, since less than a third of its residents engaged in farming). Each also enlisted Sol Tax's (1952) study of Panajachel, Guatemala, *Penny Capitalism*, as an illustration of individual(istic) "calculatingness."

Lewis—whose restudy of Tepoztlán involved a team of half a dozen Mexican fieldworkers (plus his wife and local residents trained as assistants) and at least twice as long a residence in Tepoztlán as Redfield's and ten times as long as many interviewees'—followed villagers to the metropolis (Mexico City) and also challenged Redfield's characterization of the "disorganized" urban end of the folk-urban continuum (O. Lewis 1952, 1970). Over time, the émigrés from Tepoztlán fade away in Lewis's publications of research on Mexico City slums. Rather ironically, Lewis increasingly focused on a culturalist (cultural determinist) essence as abstract as any of Redfield's, albeit one linking to the pessimistic view of Tepoztlán. Paddock (1961) recognized this early on. Although continuing to coordinate research by teams of researchers, over time Lewis wrote more and more about fewer and fewer individuals.

Foster's student Robert Kemper similarly extended the research on Tzintzuntzeños to the capital (Kemper 1977, 1979; see Foster 1979).[5]

Walter Goldschmidt, Julian Steward, and Eric Wolf

Another future American Anthropological Association president who worked extensively on rural society, Walter Goldschmidt also began graduate work at Berkeley in 1935. In the interwar turn in American anthropology from "primitive"/"tribal" peoples to community studies, Goldschmidt's 1997 recollection singled out Redfield's *Tepoztlán* (1930) as "a penetrating, if idealized view of peasant life", the Lynds' (1929) *Middletown* as the pioneer U.S. community study, and Warner and Lunt's (1941) first "Yankee City" book. "These studies," he noted, "tended to treat the community as if it were a tribe; that is, as being largely self-contained rather than dependent on the nation-state of which it was a part. They also treated them as if they were representative of the nation, or, at least, the region" (Goldschmidt 1997:viii). He suggested that the undertheorized body of material in such community studies aimed to provide "detailed empirical documentation of the rural side of the rural-urban dichotomy, a counterpart to the empirical work on cities inspired by Chicago [sociologists]" (ix)—ignoring the considerable body of research by rural sociologists, although his own early work on (nonpeasant) agriculture in California's Central Valley (1942, 1946, 1947) showed great awareness of what rural sociologists had been doing (i.e., was not so professionally ethnocentric as the writings of Ralph Beals during the 1940s)—and did not cite any of the community studies Goldschmidt (1947) singled out as pioneers in *As You Sow*. Goldschmidt recalled that his work in the early 1970s on "the general character of peasant society" (1997:x) was stimulated by Martin Yang's (1945) *A Chinese Village: Taitou, Shantung Province* and Arensberg's (1937) *The Irish Countryman*, the latter of which had been published before Goldschmidt's work on California Central Valley agriculture, as had the landmark *Peasant Life in China* (Fei Hsiao-Tung 1939).

Goldschmidt had found that "from industrialized agriculture one reaps urban life" even in the countryside, with impersonal pecuniary-driven social relationships, rampant materialism, and class conflict between a rural proletariat and capitalist owner/growers: "Industrial agriculture blurs the border between town and country and renders the urban-rural dichotomy meaningless" (Goldschmidt 1997:xii; see also Goldschmidt 1947:222–38).

When Kroeber's earlier student, Julian Steward (PhD 1929), turned from "primitive" North and South American societies to coordinating a study of Puerto Rico during the late 1940s (work reported in Steward 1956), he also compared villages, although these were chosen for their differing economic pursuits rather than along a rural/urban continuum as in Redfield's Yucatán work. Although citing the earlier Chicago studies of peasant societies, Steward's only reference to Puerto Rican peasants was to some small landowners in the coffee-growing San José region (studied by Eric Wolf). Although materialist and focused on economic "base" rather than ideological "superstructure," Steward's approach was as typological as Redfield's comparisons of civilizations ("great traditions") during the 1950s, and "the fact that the separate communities were really parts of a larger whole—the functionally interdependent political economy of the island-nation—somehow escaped the Steward research program and vitiated many of its conclusions. There was no theory of larger systems" (John Bennett 1998:87). Near the end of Steward's life, he coordinated a set of case studies of modernization of peasant societies across four continents (and three volumes: Steward 1967) that still treated the localities in isolation even while pursuing an evolution that looks rather unilinear (see R. Murphy 1981:199–200).

During the 1950s one of Steward's students-turned-colleagues, Eric Wolf, continued typologizing peasantries (with the goal of formulating "cultural laws") and distinguishing semiautonomous closed corporate communities from peasant communities with less control over their lands (1955, 1957), then increasingly focused on the relationships of peasantries and states, stressing that cities are "a likely, but not an inevitable product of the increasing complexity of society. . . . The city is but one—though common—form in the orchestration of power and influence, but not its exclusive or decisive form" (1966:11; see Foster 1967b:6).[6] The smoothly functioning microcosm of Redfield, Radcliffe-Brown, and Chicago students of the two disappeared in Wolf's synthesis of historical materials about peasant revolutions (E. Wolf 1969). By the end of the 1960s closed corporate community peasant societies (insofar as they had ever existed) disappeared and functionalist studies of rural communities maintaining equilibrium ceased to seem plausible as American anthropologists increasingly examined state influences on even remote localities and documented histories, conflicts, and dysfunctional sociocultural arrangements.

Conclusion

As the supply of "primitives" ran out (along with the dwindling of the supply of Native Americans who remembered prereservation life) and as the fate of peasants first in the Soviet Union and then in China became of increasing concern to U.S. policy makers, some anthropologists discovered peasants as peoples to study. The "discovery" and initial fieldwork was not as "recent" as Clifford Geertz supposed in 1961, however. Following the sentence used as this chapter's epigraph, Geertz wrote, "Only since World War II with the entrance of the major peasant-based nations of Asia, the Middle East, and Latin America onto the stage of international politics has any notable shift of interest toward the study of peasant life occurred" (Geertz 1962:1). This is quite a startling statement to have issued from an anthropologist at the University of Chicago, where many of Redfield's associates were still active. Geertz's survey of the literature mentioned Redfield's great/little tradition conception from the 1950s and George Foster's research in Spain but not Redfield 1930 or Redfield 1941 or Redfield and Villa Rojas 1934 or Embree 1937 or Fei Hsiao-Tung 1939 or Spicer 1940 or O. Lewis 1951 or any of the publications of Ralph Beals or Sol Tax or Nathan Whitten. (I also wonder how, in Geertz's view, the oil-rich Middle East nations in particular had not been of international political interest before 1945!)

Geertz did not comment on the romanticizing of rural life and the negative view of urban life in the German tradition of celebrating the *Völk*. Although Oscar Lewis, the primary later critic of romanticizing peasants/peasantries, termed the idealization of "simple" peoples and societies "Rousseauian" "cultural primitivism," it seems to me more in the Jeffersonian tradition of regarding the yeoman as a bulwark of a healthy, egalitarian society (see Benet 1963) than in the proto-romantic valuation of "noble savages" of Rousseau. Many functionalist assumptions about stability and tradition were extended to rural agriculturists, as was a focus on religion and cognitive phenomena rather than on class differences, conflict, political relations of locality to national governments in synchronic "community studies" that mostly ignored documented history,[7] and even outbreaks of violence while the field researcher was present, as in the case of the Cristero raid on Tepoztlán that led to Robert Redfield evacuating his family and leaving Mexico altogether far ahead of schedule.

The ethnographic work by Berkeley alumni (along with Columbia alumni Oscar Lewis, Sydney Mintz, and Eric Wolf and the Harvard alumnus working under the aegis of Lloyd Warner, Conrad Arensberg) provided a less rosy picture of peasant life than Robert Redfield's generalizations about "folk" society. Their work paid more attention to those who owned no land and to differences in income within communities represented as less homogeneous and less harmonious than in Redfield's typology, in which "folk" was an "ideal type" in more than one sense (normative ideal as well as abstract type). Many of the critiques by anthropologists of the folk-urban continuum were published in sociology journals (e.g., Mintz 1953, O. Lewis 1953; along with the considerable concessions to critics of the continuum in Miner 1950, 1952; also see Tumin 1952 on stratification within a peasant community: San Luis Jilotepeque, Guatemala), while sociologists criticized urbanism as a dubious entity within a dubiously unilinear evolution and challenged both the valuations and the simplifications of the rural-urban dichotomy (e.g., Caplow 1949; Duncan and Reiss 1956) and the genuine/spurious contrast underlying it in Redfield's deployment (Tumin 1945). Movement along the folk-urban continuum was also challenged as an adequate model of social change both for peasants in the countryside and for emigrants from the countryside to cities.

Although the Mexican revolution, which was a "peasant revolution," especially in the *part* of the country (Morelos) in which Robert Redfield undertook fieldwork, and although Redfield's later work was in a part (the Yucatan) that experienced long-running insurrection during the nineteenth century, the initial American anthropological theorizing of peasants and their "folk society" glossed over local conflicts and conflicts with state authority. As functionalism became the dominant discourse in anthropology after the retirement of Franz Boas, history and ("dysfunctional") conflict were not considered interesting topics, and Radcliffe-Brown influenced Redfield and University of Chicago students of both of them to focus on (local) equilibration. Whether influenced by the specter of Maoist peasant revolution in China (a society from which some functionalist ethnographies by "natives" had been encouraged by Redfield, Malinowski, and Radcliffe-Brown) or simultaneous with it, an assault on the image of rural harmony and comity in Mexico was launched by Oscar Lewis and augmented by George Foster, both students of prominent Boasians. By the time of U.S. engagement in an Asian land war, different aspects of peasant life were theorized by Eric Wolf and others.

5

The Non-eclipse of Americanist Anthropology
during the 1930s and 1940s

Before undertaking the research for this chapter, I accepted too easily the conventional view ("folklore" in the pejorative sense) that American anthropologists' turn away from studying Native North American peoples began with Margaret Mead in Samoa and Robert Redfield in Mexico during the late 1920s, became more general with the importation (partly by Mead and Redfield and directly by the American sojourns of A. R. Radcliffe-Brown and Bronislaw Malinowski at, respectively, the University of Chicago and Yale University) of British functionalisms during the 1930s, and was established decisively with the mobilization of anthropologists into the U.S. war effort during the 1940s. When I looked more closely, I saw that the eclipse of Americanist work was lesser and later than many Americanists suppose.

Clearly, Mead and Redfield and the visiting functionalists articulated an already widespread impatience with listing and mapping traits salvaged from the memories of those no longer living in aboriginal societies (see chapter 1). They and many students of the 1930s sought to study the functional integration of intact, distinct "primitive" cultures and scorned examination of how Native Americans lived on the reservations to which they had been confined. These anthropologists' own fieldwork was mostly far from intensive and often did not even involve prolonged residence with the people studied.[1] About the Omahas, with whom she reluctantly—and, I might add, clandestinely[2]—worked in the summer of 1930, Mead wrote that "there was very little out of the past that was recognizable and still less in the present that was aesthetically satisfying. . . . I had the unrewarding task of discussing a long history of mistakes in American policy toward the Indians and prophesying a still more disastrous fate for them in the future" (1972:190–91).[3] As Hymes noted,

"Some anthropologists stopped studying Indians in the 1930s, because they had become like any other minority group" (1974:31). For instance, Elizabeth Colson (1985:178), whose first fieldwork was in California, recalled, "Many of us thought by the 1930s that what could be recorded here at home about the Native Americans' pre-conquest past had been recorded, and we wanted a chance to write about living people. Today we no longer share a regional focus and probably have not done so since about 1950."

In addition to stressing that last date—coincidentally the year of my birth and the high tide of British functionalist social anthropology of Africa—I would note that interbellum Americanists had practically no systematic knowledge of reservation life to apply. Kelly (1985:129) discussed the critique Scudder Mekeel and Julian Steward made in 1936 and Steward (1977:336) reiterated that "in 1934 anthropologists were ill-equipped with basic understanding of culture change in the modern world" because "ethnologists were not interested in the factors, processes, and dynamics of change that had occurred during the many years following European contact" (also see Villa Rojas 1979:50).

The acculturation studies of the 1930s continued to focus on (shared/normative) cultural traits, not on communities, let alone communities in the context of states. Indian reservations could have been, but were not, the site of community studies. I don't think that anyone thought to treat the Native Americans living in the 1930s as outside of history or as examples of endogenously maintained social equilibrium, as social anthropologists treated groupings in colonized Africa as being.

[Radcliffe-]Brown did not undertake fieldwork during his Chicago tenure (1931–37) and greatly antagonized many Americanists, including Edward Sapir, who had been partly responsible for bringing him to Chicago.[4] Although she put in some time on a reservation, Mead was very emphatic that she did not want to make a career as an Americanist and famously insisted on going to Polynesia for her first fieldwork in defiance of Boas's wish for her to work with some American tribe (M. Mead 1972:128–30; see chapter 3). In that Derek Freeman (1983) has cast her as the Boasian archetype (see chapter 3), there is a special irony in her refusal to study Native Americans. The irony is increased by the markedly nationalistic American defense of Mead in that she was heavily influenced by British functionalists before almost any other American was and in that no one since Radcliffe-Brown had occasioned so uniform and nationalistic a rejection as an uppity alien disrespectful of what American anthropologists do as had Derek Freeman, even though what Mead did was much closer to the work of the detested Radcliffe-Brown than to that of her Boasian elder brothers. She was even "under the direction of Radcliffe-Brown" in her first Admiralty Islands fieldwork (M. Mead 1959a:553n34). In contrast, as discussed in chapter 3, her Boasian "elder brothers" were uncomfortable with her methods and epistemology. Robert Lowie (1929, 1940) was particularly troubled (specifically by M. Mead 1928, 1939; also see the dismay in A. Kroeber 1931a). However, neither in published reviews nor in unpublished correspondence do I see any of the locus of their discomfort (bordering on anxiety even) being her abandonment of Native America as a research site.

Mead and Redfield were certainly harbingers of functionalism, of disregarding material culture and history (whether written or derived from archeological or linguistic evidence), and of globalizing the scope of American anthropology, but when I looked more closely at who was doing what when, the marginalization of Americanist work within American anthropology appears both more gradual and less complete than many Americanists suppose. Anthropology PhDs from the 1930s, especially from Berkeley and Yale, and to a lesser extent from Harvard, mostly worked on Americanist dissertation topics (Ebihara 1985: table 1).

It is indisputable that professionalizing Canadian and U.S. anthropology began with attempts to identify general/normative traits of what the oldest then-living members of pacified North American aboriginal tribes remembered (Darnell 1969, 1971; D. Cole 1973; cf. Preston 1983). However, it is useful to recall that especially Roland Dixon, Edward Gifford, Alfred Kroeber, Berthold Laufer, and Robert Lowie had broader interests than aboriginal North America and considerable erudition. Boas-trained anthropologists such as Fay-Cooper Cole, Laura Watson Benedict, and William Jones studied indigenous groups in the colony of the Philippines that the United States seized in 1898. Zora Neale Hurston and her enemy Melville Herskovits, both of whom were Boas students, did fieldwork in U.S.-occupied Haiti. Herskovits and Ruth Landes worked among Afro-Brazilians during the 1930s, while Lowie and Benedict fostered fieldwork in the South American jungles. Lowie also conveyed and amplified Baron Nordenskiold's pressure on the National Research Council's Division of Anthropology and Psychology to survey South American Indians in 1932, which led to the Bureau of American

Ethnology's *Handbook of South American Indians*, edited by Julian Steward (1946–50) during the 1940s (Frantz 1985:89–90).[5]

It is apposite to remember that, depending on whether one counts Anglo-America, Benedict's (1934) ever-popular restatement of cultural description as personality was either two-thirds or three-fourths Americanist and that before World War II her fieldwork was Americanist. So was most American anthropologists' work on acculturation and much of the work on culture and personality.[6] Practically all of George Devereux's ethnographic publications are on Native Americans, as is most of Weston La Barre's ethnographic and historical work. Even much of the culture and personality work done in the decade and a half after World War II—notably that of Irving Hallowell, Anthony F. C. Wallace, John Honigmann, Victor Barnouw, and George and Louise Spindler—was Americanist. Ralph Linton, probably the most influential non-Boasian, non-Chicago anthropologist of the 1930s and 1940s and the author of the most widely used textbook of the late 1930s, obviously got around. Before going to Madagascar, he was Field Museum curator of North American ethnology and worked up Pawnee material from notes of George Dorsey's work with James Murie (A. Linton and Wagley 1971:25). During his Wisconsin tenure Linton worked on Comanche, and once he got to Columbia, he pulled together Columbia Americanist students' fieldwork in *Acculturation in Seven American Indian Tribes* (1940). His own chapters in that book, along with what he wrote in *The Study of Man* (1936) seem to me relatively continuous with Boasian study of the movement of culture "items" and "traits" and their adaptation into "complexes"—Roland Dixon's study in particular, as A. Linton and Wagley (1971:14) noted. Although not exclusively an Americanist, Linton clearly did Americanist work.

I also consider Melville Herskovits's African research as seeking antecedents for African American culture and thus in a serious sense "Americanist," as is that of the third member of the Social Science Research Council acculturation subcommittee, Robert Redfield, in the Yucatán and Guatemala (and, arguably, also in Morelos). Redfield notably continued the substitution of space for time in analyzing processes ("acculturation" in the Yucatan). Linton sponsored Charles Wagley's fieldwork in Brazil and Carl Withers's in "Plainsville" (A. Linton and Wagley 1971:52–53), also "Americanist" in the wider-than-First-Nations sense.

With the exception of John Embree, Brown's Chicago students also worked on Native American topics.[7] Indeed, it seems fairly obvious that Brown came to America believing that he would sort out Native America as he had aboriginal Australia (DeMallie 1994:6–7)—and that some Chicago students thought that they accomplished this under his tutelage. Brown's Chicago students became and remained Americanists. Indeed, there is a sense in which Brown's Chicago tenure and the reaction of Boasians stimulated a renewal of theoretical interest in Native America rather than an abandonment of work on Native American peoples. At the very least, his stay produced some Americanists who might otherwise have worked elsewhere.[8]

Although they produced a florescence studying kinship "system" studies, neither Radcliffe-Brown nor his Chicago students produced holistic ethnographies of Native American "social systems." And they did not "progress" toward modeling how local groups are affected by nation-states and world economies. As late as 1950, even ethnography done as part of early "area studies" continued to fail to relate parts to any whole, moving Julian Steward to note, "Most studies have treated the community . . . as if it were a self-contained structural and functional whole which could be understood in terms of itself alone. . . . Individual communities are often studied as if the larger whole were simply a mosaic of such parts" or "as if the larger society did not exist" (1950:22). Steward (1956) set out to remedy this in the project on (the U.S. territory of) Puerto Rico he directed.

Redfield's introduction and Sol Tax's opening chapter in *Social Anthropology of North American Tribes* (Eggan 1937) pressed [Radcliffe-] Brown's claims to be developing a science of society with rigorous "scientific laws" against Boasian theoretical nihilism and historical inferences based on geographical distributions (Dixon, Kroeber, Wissler). While struggling diplomatically to give Boas his due—for doing what was needed at an earlier time[9]—Redfield proclaimed that "no one in America has offered a strictly nonhistorical scientific method, equipped with a self-consistent body of concepts and procedures for getting specific jobs done in relation to ultimate scientific objectives. Radcliffe-Brown has done just that. . . . Radcliffe-Brown has offered an explicit and systematic method for the scientific study of societies" (1955a:xii).

Redfield also attempted to anticipate the objections that Julian Steward was going to make (in his 1938 review of the book in the *American Anthropologist*) to the sterility and unimportance of the results.[10] Three-quarters of a century later, I do not think many anthropologists are impressed with the vapid so-called social laws promulgated by "Radcliffe-"Brown (e.g., 1952b:44–45) or are expecting any to emerge from his approach. Lowie invidiously noted, "Newton did not tell us that bodies either rise or fall" (1937:225) but managed to be more specific in promulgating laws of gravitation. Many of us would agree with Steward's 1938 criticism that "Radcliffe-"Brownian dogma "precluded serious attention to available history and that concern with standard behavior largely prevented inclusion of material on individual differences," not just in *Social Anthropology* but also in the oeuvre of his student Robert Redfield, among others.[11] Still, for all the arrogant dismissal of Americanist work Brown and his Chicago students made, despite the bad manners of their revolutionary rhetoric. And despite his own lack of acquaintance with "every day facts of life in particular [Native American] societies"—Steward (1938:720) quoted this desideratum from Tax (1937b:14), noting Tax's lack of intimate knowledge of California peoples (in implicit contrast to Steward's and Kroeber's considerable knowledge) and of Brown's lack of Americanist fieldwork, Brown did not divert Chicago students from working on Americanist topics.

He did not even entirely stifle historical research by them. One of the chapters in *Social Anthropology of North American Tribes* even dealt with a social process (nativist religious revivalism) in an intercultural community, using archival records, rather than with the kinship system of an aboriginal "tribe." Concerned with the rejection of historical data by Radcliffe-Brown et al., Steward extolled Nash's "well-documented" chapter as illustrating "the value of history in giving the fullest meaning to the function of an institution" (1938:722). Within the Radcliffe-Brown school in England, Daryll Forde's insistence on historical and ecological considerations perhaps owed something to his Berkeley sojourn in the late 1920s (as well as to his initial archaeological training).

The volume's editor, Fred Eggan, who had been a student of Cole, Sapir, and Leslie Spier before Radcliffe-Brown arrived, was more cautious in making claims than was Brown and continued to focus on circumscribed, historical comparisons and to avoid the rhetoric of a functionalist revolution against Boasian historicism. Although he did fieldwork in the U.S. colony of the Philippines before Japan conquered it, his major theoretical and ethnographic work remained Americanist (DeMallie 1994:12).

It bears stressing that the early twentieth-century shift of anthropology's primary institutional basis from museum to university (Eggan 1955:488; Darnell 1969; Hinsley 1981) did not lead to a de-emphasis on (Native North) America. Not that the shift in institutional base and fieldwork practice was without theoretical consequences. George Foster (1982) contrasted a period in which fieldwork involved a summer visit to a reservation or "white room ethnography" with key informants interrogated off a reservation to a community study period.[12] The length of study rather than the choice of a particular people to study yielded more data, which made it possible for some anthropologists to write synchronic, non-comparativist monographs. The earlier focus on "ethnological specimens"—that is, culture-wide "traits"—undoubtedly related to the museum base of research. Because they had to be generalists, Boasians at least implicitly considered cultures holistically (Foster 1982:146–47)—more so, I would argue, than British social anthropologists did, despite the rhetoric about integrated "systems" the latter mouthed. Excluding language and psychology and "material culture," Radcliffe-Brown and his students chose to ignore what Boasians saw as evidencing cultural configurations. In particular, functionalists' de-emphasis on "material culture" collection is inseparable from the lack of interest in technology and physical environment that is a hallmark of social anthropology of the Radcliffe-Brown school, in maximal contrast to Americans such as Julian Steward, Leslie White, and (to a lesser extent) Ralph Linton. Boas and most of his students wanted to know how people did things, including weaving (Gladys Reichard), making pots (Ruth Bunzel), hunting (Frank Speck), and even making blueberry pies (Boas). (Also see Edward Hall [1992:74–75] on "frozen motor habits" [specifically in making pots] and the Whitings' [1978:42] recollection that the most important lesson they learned from Leslie Spier was that if you describe something, you must know how it works [specifically a Paiute rabbit trap].)

Creative British work on the social implications of technology came not from social anthropologists but from the chemist turned historian Joseph Needham and archaeologist Gordon Childe, influenced, like Steward, by Marxist (albeit undialectical) materialism.

New Deal agencies funded ethnographic and historic research on American communities and made some attempts to apply scientific knowledge to rural America, including Indian reservations. If the Rockefeller Foundation had continued to expand support for anthropological work, as many expected, rather than curtailing it in 1933, globalization might have begun in earnest during the 1930s, but this did not happen.[13] Moreover, before the United States began to win the war and think about administering territories from which the Japanese would be driven—and Japan itself—the U.S. government employed anthropologists in administering the concentration camps of West Coast Japanese Americans (P. Suzuki 1981; Starn 1986; see Gregg and Williams 1948:607; research on the involuntarily relocated not paid for by the incarcerators is discussed in chapter 12).

In common with other anthropologists, Americanists have at least indirectly maintained colonial and neocolonial administration and domination.[14] Some anthropologists have been eager to serve power—few more explicitly than Malinowski and Radcliffe-Brown—but customers have been few and strikingly successful "application" of "knowledge" nonexistent. Admittedly, some anthropologists have sometimes challenged particular policies, but few have exerted real influence in long-term policy. One Chicago-trained anthropologist, Philleo Nash, was Indian commissioner from 1961 to 1966 (see P. Nash 1979). Gordon Macgregor was for a short time agency superintendent of the Oglala Pine Ridge Reservation, before moving on to the Indian Health Service.

To the best of my knowledge none has produced an ethnography of, say, the U.S. Department of the Interior, although anthropologists have given (mostly informal) advice to Indian organizations on how to manage such bureaucracies and have written—decades later—of mistaken attempts to employ anthropologists and to apply anthropology (e.g., Steward 1977:33–36; P. Nash 1979; E. Hall 1994).

Although foreshadowed by earlier research in the Philippines, service by American anthropologists to colonial domination seems to me to have begun in earnest only with the Roosevelt administration, which reorganized the Indian reservations[15] and later established the Japanese American concentration camps. John Collier, Roosevelt's commissioner of Indian affairs, sold anthropologists to Milton Eisenhower, warden of the Japanese American concentration camps, as a means "to perfect the science of human management" that would be useful in "our post-war job in the Far East" (quoted in Kelly 1985:135). At the very least anthropologists were complicit in attempts at ethnocide (see P. Suzuki 1981; Starn 1986; and R. Wax 1971:69–174).

How many copies of Alexander Leighton's (1945) *The Governing of*

Men reached the Allied armies of occupation and whether this new knowledge on "human management" or the "culture at a distance" discourse including Ruth Benedict's (1946) *The Chrysanthemum and the Sword* was applied are historical topics that have yet to be researched.

Americanist work remained predominant not just through the 1930s but into the 1950s, despite the mobilization and dispersion to many places of American anthropologists in World War II. In a major and quasi-official historical retrospect, Robert Murphy wrote that, until World War II, "The bulk of our research had previously been in the study of the American Indian, which served more than any other influence to produce the rather flat, descriptive tone of our writings. It was the reservation situation, the culling of memory culture unvitalized by extant patterns of activity, that led to American nominalism, and not the anti-evolutionism of Boas" (1976:6). Murphy also considered Native American "deculturation" as an explanation for the resistance to the shiny new toys of functionalism: "However handy [a model of society in which norms guide actions, which then feed back to reinforce the system of norms] may be as a starting point for the analysis of functioning social systems, it was less than useful when studying the shattered remnants of American Indian societ[ies]" (1976:12). "Financed by an influx of new funds that were clearly responsive to the country's expanded overseas interests, [American anthropologists] broke out of their traditional insularity and embarked on research on global scale" (1976:6; also see Geertz 1995:103).

He further asserted that "the change in scale of the research subject wrenched anthropology out of its age of innocence and ended forever ethnographies written from the head of one old informant sitting in the anthropologist's hotel room" (R. Murphy 1976:7), adding "until ethnoscience" resurrected the omniscient prime informant.

Looking at the immediately postwar volumes of the official journal of the American Anthropological Association does not substantiate this, as table 1 shows. More than half the articles dealing with specific locales that were published in the *American Anthropologist* between 1946 and 1951 (the first column) were Americanist, and almost all of these were North Americanist. Into the 1990s, a plurality of articles with specific locales still were North American, as the second column shows. The decline from a majority to a slight plurality is considerable, but the immediate post–Second World War period shows that the internationalization

TABLE 1. Areal Distribution of Articles in *American Anthropologist (AA)*, *American Ethnologist (AE)*, and *Man/Journal of the Royal Anthropological Institute (Man/JRAI)*

Geographical area	AA		AE	Man/JRAI
	1946–51	1989–93	1984–93	1981, 84, 87, 90, 93
North America	49	24	26	7
South America	3	14	12	7
Africa	11	22	18	22
Asia	16	4	16	21
Oceania	13	15	17	23
Europe	2	11	11	14
Australia		1		6
Urban North America		9		

of American anthropology was still beginning, that the wartime mobilization had not reduced the status of Native North America to just one place among many. It still held the privileged place for research that was accepted for publication in the flagship journal of U.S. anthropology.

Similarly, contrasting the third and fourth columns shows that during the 1980s (the end of the Cold War) and beyond the *American Ethnologist* published substantially more Americanist work than the official *Journal of the Royal Anthropological Society* (previously known as *Man*). There were fluctuations but no trends in percentage of articles that were Americanist within these time spans.

In Canada around 1980, Burridge (1983:309) classified the regional expertise of 57.8 percent of 270 Canadian ethnologists as New World, along with 79 percent of the dissertation field sites for 142 ethnology PhD degrees from Canadian universities.

Linguistic Anthropology

In 1925, when the Linguistic Society of America was founded, there were more than nine philologists and more than ten teachers of written languages for every two anthropological linguists (Murray 1994b:162; nearly all of the latter were Americanists). In the first fifteen volumes (1925–39) of its official journal, *Language*, 8.5 percent of the articles about a language group dealt with Native American ones. In the next decade this dropped to 6.6 percent (while the percentage of articles on languages that were not Indo-European, not Semitic, and not Native American rose from 5.0 to 13.5).[16]

If not within American linguistics, at least within linguistic anthropology, Native American languages remained central. The major focus in linguistic anthropology during the 1950s, the so-called Whorf hypothesis, was rooted in assertions about Hopi language and culture, while Dorothy Lee's writings on values and worldview were rooted in research on Wintu and Lakota; the Navajos and their neighbors were the central site for Harvard Social Relations contrast of diverse value patterns within in a particular habitat (Vogt and Albert 1966), as well as for trying to test what was interpreted as Whorf's claim.[17] The neo-Bloomfieldians who attempted to extend linguistic methods to cultural classifications and social interaction during the 1950s and 1960s, notably C. F. Hockett, Kenneth Pike, and George Trager (with Edward Hall) were all Americanists first and foremost. Although some of the important exemplars (by Harold Conklin and Charles Frake) of ethnoscience derived from the Philippines, those of Floyd Lounsbury, Brent Berlin, Duane Metzger, and Gerald Williams were based on Native American data, and other major exemplars were Americanist in the broader sense, that is, Anglo-American (see Murray 1994b:403, 410). Certainly the analysis of ethnopoetics in recent years has been mostly Americanist (e.g., Hymes 1981; Tedlock 1993), along with outstanding analyses of creolization (Scollon and Scollon 1979), linguistic play, and intercultural stereotyping (K. Basso 1979).

Structuralist and Postmodernist Anthropological Work

As for reflexive accounts of fieldwork, I would recall Diamond Jenness, whose participant observation was as early as Malinowski's—while being more intensive, more extensive, and more sympathetic to the people being studied. Gladys Reichard's (1934) *Spider Woman* provides another early example of reporting on participation. And in the more recent self-conscious literature, Jean Briggs's (1970) *Never in Anger* continues the genre of writing about living with Inuits inaugurated by Jenness. It also continues to strike me as being the best exemplar of reflexive writing that conveys something about another culture, not just about the anthropologist's sensibilities. Also, two of the three sites discussed in the more instrumental pioneering discussion of fieldwork in R. Wax 1971 were Native North American ones.

Lévi-Strauss's structuralist mill ground up North and South American native materials. George Peter Murdock's fieldwork was Northwest Coast and Leslie White's was Pueblo, although I am among those who do not see how the theorizing of either relates to his ethnographic work. Julian Steward's development of ecological analysis more clearly derived from his Americanist work (this is especially clear in Steward 1937), as did the influential theorizing about nativist revitalization movements by Linton, Wallace, and others; Wallace's explorations of intracultural variability; and Wallace's and Steward's exemplary use of documented history. Lowie remained a force through much of the 1950s and Kroeber through the entire decade.

Certainly Mesoamericanists (e.g., Ralph Beals, George Foster, John Gillin, Edward Spicer, Eric Wolf) and some South Americanists (Jules Henry, Charles Wagley) were prominent by the 1950s, while Lloyd Warner and his students (including Erving Goffman) mostly studied American groups other than First Nations/Native Americans.

I have already noted that Radcliffe-Brown's Chicago students did not turn away from Native America. Insofar as the dominance of functionalism was accompanied by such a turn, it was postwar Harvard Social Relations students such as Clifford Geertz, David Schneider, and Robert Bellah and Yale students such as Ward Goodenough, Harold Conklin, and Charles Frake who looked west of the American West Coast, not the Chicago students of Radcliffe-Brown. Looking at 1946–60 in the *American Anthropologist* greatest hits collection (R. Murphy 1976), one notes that the authors who were not trained as Americanists were mostly not from North America (Fredrik Barth, Meyer Fortes, Siegfried Nadel), along with Goodenough and Geertz and linguist Zellig Harris, who was trained as a Semiticist philologist but at the time was working on Cherokee. Those I classify as "Americanists" from that collection are John Adair, John Atkins, Fred Eggan, Goffman, Steward, C. F. Voegelin, Evon Vogt, Leslie White, and Eric Wolf.

Although there are more Americanists in academia now than there were in the decade after World War II, the number of specialists on other areas increased more rapidly during the 1950s and 1960s. Still, I think that it would be difficult to construct a plausible claim that Africanists or Oceanists or Europeanists or Asianists have succeeded Americanists in dominating American anthropology at any time.[18] There are "theorists" who have worked outside the Americas, but it seems to me that they are not concentrated in the study of any one other particular place or area. I certainly have heard anthropologists whose work is outside the Americas complaining of being marginal, marginal to "theory" in particular.[19] I do not mean to underestimate the extent to which area studies were underwritten by Cold War interests, the extent to which the illusion of cultures outside history continued, or the extent to which functionalists' derision of detailed Americanist data collection as theoryless has outlasted the dominance of functionalist theory and the recognition that cultures are neither as discrete, as unchanging, nor as integrated as functionalists supposed.[20]

There was wartime mobilization of anthropologists and a quest for systematic information about how to avoid unnecessarily roiling local sensibilities in places that U.S. forces would occupy. The interdisciplinary Institute of Human Relations at Yale, funded by the Rockefeller Foundation, and the U.S. Navy–commissioned (lieutenant commander) George Peter Murdock were the readiest to serve up standardized cultural data in what became the Human Relations Area Files (see Morawski 1986, Price 2002b), and Murdock and company were supported to advise and collect cultural data on Micronesian islands that became U.S. territory, Truk and Yap in particular (see Bashkow 1991).

In addition, I would suggest at least one more general component in the postwar diversification of American anthropology. The GI Bill spurred expansion of university enrollment in general—as well as rapid growth of the number of anthropologists in particular—on the magnitude of 71 percent between 1947 and 1951 (Goldschmidt 1985:179). Demographic pressure pushed U.S. anthropologists' fieldwork beyond Native American reservations.[21] Areal studies were well funded, but simultaneous with the pull of money was the push of diversifying to avoid competition. As Durkheim (1893) recognized in *The Division of Labor in Society* and Hagstrom (1965) applied to scientific specializations, an expanding labor force usually leads to specialization. In the case of anthropology, this has meant that an anthropologist has his or her own village or own cultural domain within a culture with several fieldworkers, instead of having a monopoly over a culture or (still earlier) over a culture area. Replication, though nominally regarded as desirable, has not been common. Flight from American research sites seems to me, historically, in part, to have been a means to avoid competition and the concomitant scrutiny of the validity of ethnographers' claims about particular cultures.

I think, as Regna Darnell (1999) also contended, that Americanists in recent years have been more cautious than other kinds of anthropologists about rejecting native interpretations and trampling native sensibilities.[22] In that more and more tribal governments restricted who could study and publish what and set priorities for those employed or allowed to do fieldwork, Americanists in recent decades have had to take native concerns seriously or not have access to new data. While I think that increased sensitivity to native concerns is a positive value, I think that it was forced on anthropologists more than spontaneously developed by them. Whatever its sources, I would suggest that important examples of native analysis, of genuine dialogue between natives and alien analysts, of encouragement of native texts (particularly individual narratives[23]), along with careful, comparative use of historical materials[24] have the potential to overcome such stigmatization of Americanist anthropology as lingers on after totalizing functionalist and structuralist paradigms have themselves been discredited, and as stories people tell about their experiences have become not merely respectable but the preferred object of anthropological attention.[25]

6

The Pre-Freudian Georges Devereux, the Post-Freudian Alfred Kroeber, and Mohave Sexuality

University of California (Berkeley) dissertation defenses during the 1930s had programs that provided very visible genealogies. Georges Devereux (né Gyorgy Dobo in Lugos, Transylvania, 1906–85), who defended his dissertation on December 9, 1935, had a particularly stellar one. After completing his baccalaureate at Turnu-Severin in Rumania in 1926, he went to Paris. There he earned diplomas at both the Institute d'Ethnologie and the École Nationale des Languages Orientales Vivantes (National School for Living Oriental Languages) in 1928 and a license ès lettres from the Sorbonne in 1932. He had taken courses in theoretical physics and radiation from Marie Curie and in anthropology and primitive religion from Marcel Mauss and became a Rockefeller fellow in 1932–34. The curriculum vitae of his dissertation defense did not list any anthropological classes in Paris other than the two from Mauss. In Devereux's 1978 retrospect he wrote that he "learned anthropology primarily from Marcel Mauss, but also from Paul Rivet and L[ucien] Lévy-Bruhl (whose work seems to me to merit infinitely more attention than it receives today). The craft of anthropology I learned from Kroeber and Lowie" (365–66). The program listed Hopi and Mohave fieldwork in 1932, fieldwork in Papua, New Guinea, in 1933 (with the Karuamas and Rotos), and in French Indochina (with the highland Sedang Mois) in 1933–34, along with graduate work at Berkeley in the fall of 1932 and in the spring and fall of 1935.

At Berkeley Devereux had taken courses on mythology and on field techniques from Robert H. Lowie, courses on California ethnography and of individual study with Alfred L. Kroeber, and a course on animal domestication taught by Kroeber and cultural geographer Carl Sauer (see Sauer 1936). Devereux's dissertation was a relatively orthodox descriptive work on an indigenous California culture, except for its focus on sexuality. Sixty of the 115 endnotes were to publications by Alfred L. Kroeber. There were 10 to Darryl Forde, who had been a Commonwealth fellow at Berkeley in 1928–30, and 6 each to Berkeley Anthropology Museum curator and faculty lecturer Edward Gifford and to a Boasian contemporary of Kroeber and Lowie, Leslie Spier. Nothing by Lowie (or Boas or Freud) was cited or included in the bibliography. Devereux acknowledged with gratitude unpublished fieldwork materials by Thomas Waterman (who had been Kroeber's first doctoral student, then junior colleague) and Abraham Halpern, a linguistic anthropologist specializing in Yuman languages. Kroeber was also the author of more cited works (six) than anyone else (followed by Spier with three) and of the most frequently cited (the 1925 *Handbook of the Indians of California*).

Though there was by that time substantial interest in Freudian doctrines and dicta in American culture in general and American anthropology (as a subfield, "culture and personality") by the mid-1930s (see P. Bock 1999 and the memoirs in Spindler 1978), Devereux clearly had not had his conversion to Freudian theory by the end of 1935. The only references to Freudians in the dissertation are one to Wilhelm Stekel (1933) and four to Géza Róheim (1932)—both authors' works incompletely listed in the dissertation's bibliography. What strikes me as the most contemptuous dismissal in the dissertation is: "Róheim is obsessed by Freudian ideas and is obviously so ignorant of data from other Yuman tribes that he mistakes type—'dreams' made up largely of legends from true dreams" (Devereux 1935:96). Some would contend that Devereux's later work applying Freudian notions to Greek myths and tragedies (e.g., Devereux 1953, 1976) is open to the same criticism.

That Devereux's dissertation was completed before he turned Freudian is significant, because both recent analyses of Mohave and anthropologists' ontological conceptions of sexual categories retroject the later Freudianism back on what Devereux wrote in the mid-1930s. One of the few scholars who evidences actually having examined Devereux's 1935 dissertation, Will Roscoe (1998:139, 149), casts Devereux as already Freud-blinded ("orthodox" is his characterization). More seriously—and repeatedly—Gilbert Herdt (1991:490–501) reads Devereux's (1937) best-known and most often cited article through Devereux's later Freudian orthodoxy (and a functionalism that had not yet affected Devereux in 1935–36), particularly Devereux's "Normal and Abnormal" (1956), which was written while Devereux was working with psychiatric entrepreneur Karl Menninger, founder of the Menninger Clinic in Topeka, Kansas.

Devereux himself unequivocally stated that "having (to my misfortune) read in Indochina one of Róheim's books. which my ignorance of psychoanalysis did not enable me understand, I remained an anti-Freudian until 1938. . . . Until 1938, I read practically only non-Freudian psychological and psychiatric works" (1978:366).

Devereux's 1937 article expanded upon the four-page section describing homosexual transvestites (heterogender homosexuality, in current terms). *Alyhâ* (transgendered natal males) and *hwamê* (transgendered natal females) are Mohave terms (indeed, unless I missed another, the only ones). Devereux reported that both were "intended to exist" (i.e., from the creation of the world). The *alyhâ* and their (masculine male) spouses were lucky at gambling and *alyhâ* shamans could cure venereal disease, according to Devereux's report of Mohave beliefs. Those men who married *alyhâ* were teased, but the *alyhâs* never were, Devereux wrote repeatedly.

For the increasingly prominent, kinship-focused functionalism of the day, probably the most interesting assertion in Devereux's discussion of homosexuality in his dissertation was that the incest prohibition extended to same-sex couplings; that is, that persons of the same clan did not couple and that "only prominent persons are able to obtain *alyhâ* wives" (1935:72).

I find particularly interesting the conventional assumptions about the weakness of women (belied by the literature on "women warriors" among Native North American groups—see Roscoe 1998:67–92) and the "natural promiscuity" of masculine men in the following: "*Alyhâs* were happier, I believe, than *hwamê*, because men were always willing to get married for a while, for fun with an *alyhâ*, while women who threw in their lot with a *hwamê*, had more trouble in "going straight" and remain[ing] free of jesting reference. Being female, *hwamê* could not protect their spouses with physical force from insults and seducers, as did *alyhâs* and their male husbands. A *hwamê* woman's wife was fair game, because no one feared her female husband . . . [and] their wives were teased mercilessly" (Devereux 1935:75).

In the discussion of cosmology later in his doctoral dissertation, Devereux noted with approval that the Freudians "Róheim and Stekel as well as others have made out a pretty good case for inversion being made possible through the fact that hermaphroditism preceded sexual differentiation regardless of what the psychologic mechanism might as an efficient cause ultimately be responsible for actual cases of inversion" (1935:156). The sentence following this particularly infelicitous one makes certain that he meant that "hermaphroditism preceded sexual differentiation" phylogenically ("the curious phylogenic coincidence with the culture pattern"). In Devereux's view (169), Mohave belief that the original beings were sexually undifferentiated and had zoomorphic ancestry paralleled the evolution of the human species in scientific biology and deserved reporting.[1]

By 1935 the "ontogeny recapitulates phylogeny" model had been generally discredited (see Gould 1977). Individual development repeating species development appealed to Freud (most vividly exemplified in the highly speculative prehistory of *Totem und Tabu* [Freud 1913]) and his followers but had no currency in American anthropology, even among those sympathetic to psychoanalytic ideas. After dabbling in psychoanalytic practice himself, Kroeber (1920) had dismissed such "just-so" stories and the pseudohistory of *Totem und Tabu*.

Influences of his Durkheimian elders on Devereux's dissertation are remarkably slight. There is a lone reference to anything by Marcel Mauss, a 1904 analysis of Australian data gathered by others, and passing reference to the foundational sociological analyses of suicide rates by Émile Durkheim (1897) and Maurice Halbwachs (1930) that suggest their inapplicability to "primitive" societies" (with "mechanical solidarity," in Durkheim's terms). Devereux contended that "true suicide" did not occur among the Mohaves.

He also contended (1935:50) that only shamans masturbated. Later in life Devereux wrote much of what he called "pseudohomosexuality." Even his 1937 article on "institutionalized homosexuality" (by which he meant gender inversion, not all males having sex with other males and not even all who were sexually receptive to other males) began with the assertions that "although [1] there is little or no objection to homosexuality among the Mohave at present, [2] there is no avowed homosexual living on the reservation." He went on to mention three men who "are at present accused of active and passive homosexuality." All three lived together (two were half brothers) and "are usually referred to as each other's wives and are said to engage in rectal intercourse" (499). The three men did not cross-dress and were not called *alyhâ*. Devereux wrote that none had "officially [?] submitted to the transvestite initiation ceremony" (499), as if such ceremonies still occurred or had occurred in living memory (and conflating "transvestite" and "homosexual"—a pair of terms corresponding to "gender" and "sexuality" in now-current distinctions but that Devereux used interchangeably in the 1937 article). There is an implication, which I think came from Devereux rather than from the surmises of Mohaves alive during the 1930s, that the *alyhâ* desired to "pass" as a woman (cross genders).

Devereux's 1937 expansion of his dissertation section on homosexuality makes it clear that all the data on *alyhâs* who had husbands came, via translation into English, from one shaman, Hivsû Tupôma, who had never seen an *alyhâ* and who was telling what he himself had been told by Kuwal, who had married two *alyhâs* (not at the same time). Even if Devereux had sought to try to determine whether the Mohaves of a century or more earlier conceived of *alyhâs* as crossing over from male to female gender or constituting a third or intermediate (1.5) gender, the institution was too long gone to answer the question. Hivsû Tupôma's rendition of what Kuwal told him many years before refers both to "the *alyhâ*" and "my woman" and quotes a woman (who wanted to fellate Kuwal) referring to Kuwal's *alyhâ* wife as "another woman." Mohave (Hivsû Tupôma recalling Kuwal's stories, at least) used the feminine pronouns in English, but that is not at all conclusive, given that the only pronouns in English for individual human beings are "he" and "she."

Field Methods

In contrast to such 1930s Berkeley anthropology graduate students as Ralph Beals and George Foster, who recalled receiving no preparation for fieldwork, the list of Devereux's courses on his dissertation defense program included a course in field techniques taught by Robert Lowie. From the same source, however, it seems that any such course must have been after Devereux's (then Dobo's) fieldwork, since it also lists him as being a graduate student in the fall of 1932. For 1932, the program lists both Hopi and Mohave fieldwork, with fieldwork in New Guinea and Indochina filling 1933–34 and more graduate coursework at Berkeley in the spring and fall of 1935.

Devereux cannot have spent much time with the Mohaves in 1932, because he was thrust upon Leslie White's field school (under the auspices of the Laboratory of Anthropology in Santa Fe, New Mexico) that was working Orayvi Hopi. According to William Peace, who here as else-where accepts Leslie White's views as factually accurate and sufficient,

> Devereux was added to the field session at the request of Stacy May, director of the Social Science Research Council and the Rockefell-er Foundation (May to White, 9 Aug. 1932). . . . When Devereux ar-rived it became apparent that he was woefully unprepared to conduct fieldwork. Both his fellow graduate students and the locals realized Devereux was hopelessly naive, and he quickly became the brunt of many practical jokes. Placed in an impossible situation, White had to help Devereux, which caused him to neglect his own work, and Devereux, to make matters worse, resisted White's offers of assistance. White sent blistering reports concerning Devereux's be-havior and disruptive influence to Jesse Nusbaum, director of the laboratory (White to Nusbaum, 18 and 20 July 1932). In White's es-timation, Devereux was a lazy and incompetent fieldworker. Nus-baum responded that it was a "situation that requires handling with kid gloves." Nusbaum stressed that "we cannot afford to have trou-ble develop in the field party, and more particularly when we have accepted a student from abroad under a fellowship from the Rock-efeller foundation at the request of the Social Science Research Council" (Nusbaum to White, 22 July 1932). (Peace 2004:62–63)

According to Peace, White eventually arranged to have Hopi informants speak to Devereux.

Not least for the already-mentioned lack of native terms in his dis-sertation and a dearth of material based on observations, it seemed to me that Devereux worked in English, questioning Mohaves through in-terpreters. This is not mentioned in the dissertation, but interpreters are mentioned in the 1937 article.

From the 1935 curriculum vitae and from Devereux's 1978 retrospec-tive, it seems that the only time of any duration that he could have spent with Mohave informants was during the summer of 1935 and that he wrote up what he had been told during the fall semester back at Berke-ley. In regard to the transgendered roles, the "ethnographic present" was forty or more years earlier. As Roscoe put it, "The last known *alyhâ* and *hwamê* lived in the generation of the parents of Devereux's infor-mants. Devereux himself made no direct observations of either male or female berdaches, relying instead on the memories of informants re-calling individuals and events of the late nineteenth century and often relying themselves on second-hand reports" (1998:163, 149).

Like other anthropologists writing about the Mohaves in the first half of the twentieth century, Devereux evidenced not even a passing thought to any reverberations in "traditional Mohave culture" of Spanish incursions (which resulted in horses spreading beyond any direct Spanish-aboriginal contact, among other things) and treated the second- or thirdhand memory culture he elicited as "Mohave culture": "Kroeber, Spier, Stewart, Fathauer, Devereux, Wallace, and a few more—seem to have assumed that the life they observed was much as it had been in aboriginal time, changed mainly after the beginning of Anglo-American domination in 1859" (C. Kroeber 1973:1). Moreover,

> With all the old people gone, and with very few written sources dating from before the 1850s, we still have no ethnohistorical study of how the tribal culture changed during its last independent generation. . . . That last generation of freedom must have been turbulent, with new stimuli and challenges, a time of swift cultural change encountering strong resistance from attitudes and customs that were deeply rooted. For many years the Mohave had been safe in their valley. Their remaining enemies, the Cocopa and Maricopa, never came there to raid. Now the Mohave discovered what accurate gunfire could do against their hand-to-hand, club-wielding style of fighting. Now they could be surprised at any moment by small parties of enemies who had no nearby homeland and who came heavily armed on horseback. They saw camels and steamboats in Mohave Valley. They witnessed the gradual humiliation and subjection of their friends the Quechan. They heard that everywhere to the eastward the white man was subjecting the Indian. They had seen such a thing, even earlier, in coastal California. (C. Kroeber 1973:1, 6)

It is the memories of the children and *grandchildren* of those Mohaves who had passed puberty before 1859 that Devereux elicited, three decades after Alfred Kroeber spoke to the last of those with preconquest memories.

Devereux's dissertation includes a "Note on Methods." Its three pages have nothing at all to do with field method (from anxiety to method of anything more specific about from whom he elicited data, in what language, etc.). Rather, it is a highly abstract reflection, with allusions to theoretical physics, about the possibility of turning cultural materials that are not consistent or rational and contain several patterns into rational (structural) models. He asserted that "social science will need to evolve a symbolic logic of their own, little related to mathematical logic," and mentioned Edward Sapir and Paul Radin (1935:173–74).

Although the material Devereux discussed in his dissertation seemed to Kroeber likely to excite reproof from state legislators if published by the university press, the preface that he drafted for publication elsewhere (where is uncertain) provides what was intended to be a public stamp of approval (with assurance that what Devereux reported fit with what Kroeber and other researchers had found among Yuman cultures). He also expressed hope that other research would be done on Native American sexuality:

> This monograph is the first systematic study of the sexual life of any American Indian tribe. From Oceania, we have Malinowski's *Sexual Life of Savages*, dealing with the Trobriand group, Margaret Mead's studies in Samoa, the Admiralties, and New Guinea, Róheim's work on Australia. For the primitive people of Africa and Asia, there are a number of monographs which give at least fairly adequate consideration to the place of sexuality in the culture. Why, with the enormous amount of field study of the American Indians in the past generation, the sexual aspects of their society have been so consistently neglected, is not altogether clear. Perhaps the prime factor is the temperament of our Indian, which is covered by deep layers of reserve. But again the puritanism may have been not wholly on the part of native informants: American ethnologists in the main have shown no great interest in penetrating the Indian's reserve on this side of his life. The first field studies were undertaken in a period of Victorian attitudes, and to some extent the techniques then established appear to have been adhered to without reformulation.
>
> The Mohave, together with a group of related tribes of the Yuman family, centering about the Lower Colorado River where Arizona and California adjoin, are exceptional among American Indians in being relatively tolerant and outspoken in their behavior

and attitudes about sex. This fact rendered the present study more easily successful. But it also makes it necessary to guard against considering the Mohave as a typical American Indian tribe. They are conspicuously uninhibited, where almost all other tribes show varying degrees of inhibition and restraint. The historical cause of this difference remains as obscure as the fact is evident, and sets a most interesting problem for future interpretation.

Before this problem can be seriously approached, reasonably comparable knowledge will have to be secured on several tribes of other types. Also, comparison will then have to be made not only in terms of the respective sex attitudes and behaviors, but in terms of the several cultures as wholes. A special type of sex life can hardly be anticipated to exist without corresponding modification in other parts of the culture, if indeed it is not largely conditioned by the remainder of the culture. The pertinent facts in each culture will be both objective, such as established, specific customs, and subjective, in the nature of psychological trends.

For instance, among the Mohave and allied Yumans, it is evident that there has taken place considerable shift from the American Indian norm in the areas of life respectively covered by the introverted and extroverted components. Introversion is unusually heavy in their religion. Ritualistic elements, usually so conspicuous in primitive life, have been reduced to the vanishing point. Individual dreaming takes their place. This must occur according to certain patterns, else it does not count as religious inspiration in the Mohave view, as Dr. Devereux has shown. Also, it is only in part actual dreaming; the rest is imagined, or waking day-dream. Nevertheless, all religious sanction in these tribes depends on essentially introverted functions. Side by side with this, however, the Mohave and other Yuman tribes prosecuted warfare actively for distraction or pleasure as well as honor; and much of their sex life is also strongly extroverted.

As compared with them, the Pueblo Indians, immediately to the east in Arizona and New Mexico, and the southern California Indians on their west, gave the dream a much less important place in their religion and ritual expression a much more elaborate one. On the contrary, these neighboring tribes fought unwillingly, chiefly under pressure of self-defense or some irremediable humiliation;

and withdrew their sex life as much as possible from public cognizance and participation instead of exposing it.

It is differences such as these, differences in underlying psychological trend or configuration, that characterized the several types of native cultures occurring among our numerous Indian tribes. It is to be hoped that with the ice once broken by Dr. Devereux's monograph, other studies will follow which will make possible the more exact definition and comparison on which, in turn, must rest both functional and historical interpretations.

The general culture of the Mohave and associated tribes of the Lower Colorado River is now rather well known from a series of studies on the Mohave, Yuma, Cocopa, and Maricopa, which Dr. Devereux has cited. The results of his investigation, therefore, integrate into what is known of the total life habits of the same people. This integration reciprocally affords a solid control for his findings. I began to study the general aspect of Mohave culture over thirty years ago, and find that all of Dr. Devereux's special determinations fit into the broader but less intensive results which I then secured. (Undated typescript, Alfred Kroeber collection, Bancroft Library, University of California–Berkeley)

After 1935

The conversion from "anti-Freudian" to "orthodox" Freudian Oedipal (etc.) theory occurred in 1938, as already noted, probably after the undated Kroeber preface intended for publication of the dissertation. Thereafter, Devereux displayed the zeal of a convert. When his 1937 "institutionalized homosexuality" article was reprinted in Hendrik Ruitenbeek's *The Problem of Homosexuality in Modern Society* (the "modern society" of nineteenth-century Mohaves?!), Devereux substituted a Freudian case study of the *alyhâ* Sahaykwisa (as recalled and told by Hivsû Tupôma) published in *Mohave Ethnopsychiatry and Suicide* (Devereux 1961) for the briefer and un- or pre-Freudian one in the 1937 article.

Devereux served in the U.S. Navy during the Second World War; he began his own psychoanalysis with Marc Schlumberger in Paris. He returned to the United States and worked as a psychoanalyst with Karl Menninger at the Menninger Clinic at the University of Kansas at Topeka (from 1946 to 1953), mostly with Native American veterans suffering traumatic neuroses. In 1952 he finished training as a psychoanalyst and became a member of the International Psychoanalytic Association and the Philadelphia and New York Psychoanalytic Societies. He taught at the medical school of Temple University in Philadelphia.

In 1961 he published *Mohave Ethnopsychiatry and Suicide*, "a study of the Mohave's knowledge of psychological and psychosomatic disorders" that in his view "could actually serve as a textbook from which budding Mohave shamans, preparing to specialize in psychiatry, could learn their craft" Devereux 1978:371), a statement that confuses me about the book's "ethnographic present" and makes me wonder if he supposed Mohave cultural categories were timelessly fixed (though he proudly proclaimed his view that personality and culture alike are constructs, "a view incompatible both with culturalism and neo-Freudianism" [385]).

The series of papers Devereux published about Mohave sexuality were, Devereux averred, "written from the start to constitute chapters of a book for which I have not found a publisher. It should be borne in mind that they were written in the 1930s and 1940s" (1978:394). It was this statement that led to my unsuccessful attempt to bring that plan for "Sexual Life of the Mohave Indian" to belated fruition in 1981 (his proposed table of contents is included in Murray 2009).

Devereux expressed his frustration at the unsubstantiated concern for contemporary Mohave prudery about their ancestors' sexual beliefs. "In 1935," he wrote, "Kroeber said U. C. could not publish it for Sacramento politicians would object" (Devereux to author, February 8, 1983). This establishes the reason for Devereux's dissertation not being included in the usual publication outlet for Berkeley dissertations, the University of California Publications in Anthropology series. In a letter to me dated May 12, 1982, Devereux wrote that Kroeber insisted on a short thesis. In a June 1, 1982, letter (twenty-two years after Kroeber's death) he wrote me that "relations between us (K[roeber] and me) have been quite bad for many years" (in response to my writing that I had found the preface Kroeber had written for publication of Devereux's dissertation, reproduced above).

Herdt recalled that Devereux told him "that his doctoral thesis on Mohave sexuality remained on restricted access to readers even in the late 1970s; he insinuated that Kroeber was responsible for this" (1991:491n39). Aside from Kroeber having died in 1960, access to **all** dissertations on any subject at Berkeley is restricted, and during the late 1970s most of the books in the Berkeley anthropology library (and all the dissertations) were in the "locked cage" (the dissertations still are—all of them, not just Devereux's).

Devereux's best-known title (and, perhaps, best-known book), *From Anxiety to Method in the Behavioral Sciences* was published in 1967, though Devereux went out of his way to note that "some of the questions it asks go back to my adolescence; at least one of its key theories (chapter 22) was formulated in 1931, [and] most of the book was drafted in Indochina (1933–35)" (1978:373), that is, purportedly, before his summer of Mohave fieldwork.

He recalled that he "decided I had no future in anthropology in the United States" (Devereux 1978:366) and moved back to Paris in 1963, where he became a member of the Société Psychoanalytique de Paris in 1964 and taught ethnopsychiatry and psychoanalysis at the École des Hautes Études en Sciences Sociales until 1981. He suffered from worsening emphysema until his death in 1985 and continued to be frustrated that his collected (and highly redundant) articles relating to Mojave sexuality were not published. (For an overview of his career from a pro-psychoanalytical perspective, see Kilborne 1987.)

7

University of California, Berkeley, Anthropology during the 1950s

The origins of anthropology at Berkeley—Franz Boas's patron, Harvard's Frederic Ward Putnam, being in nominal charge of the collection of antiquities Phoebe Apperson Hearst gave to the University of California —and how Boas's first Columbia PhD, Alfred Louis Kroeber, went to California and began teaching anthropology at Berkeley—have been thoroughly explored by Timothy Thoresen (1975) and Ira Jacknis (1993a, 1993b, 2000, 2002). As the Ethnological and Archaeological Survey of California (established in 1903) led to the *Handbook of the Indians of California* (A. Kroeber 1925) and beyond, Kroeber presided over salvage elicitation of information about California Native Peoples whose cultures seemed irremediably shattered and whose languages seemed on the verge of extinction. Although more of native cultures and languages has persisted than seemed likely early in the twentieth century, material was elicited from the last speakers of a number of languages and memories of prereservation life were gathered, even though the data collection through the 1930s tended toward checking off lists of cultural traits, an endeavor that seemed frustratingly old-fashioned to 1930s graduate students sent out on salvage missions (see Beals 1978; Foster 1976)—and even to Kroeber's teacher, regarded by many as the arch-particularist, Franz Boas (see Jacknis 2002:525–26).

George Foster and Ralph Beals wrote (and were recorded by interviewers) about the seemingly detached and very busy figures with national reputations who taught them ethnology and sent them to sink or swim in the field, following Boas's example. The more approachable University of California Museum director Edward W. Gifford began offering some courses in 1920 (although he did not officially become a professor until 1938) and Robert H. Lowie was hired from the American Museum of Natural History to teach at Berkeley in 1921.

When Kroeber was able to add another faculty member he had many choices, but he chose the undistinguished but loyal alumnus Ronald L. Olson as a junior staff member to take on teaching introductory anthropology and other drudgeries. Not without reason, many have inferred that Kroeber did not want charismatic competition or competition in running what had de facto been his department from before its official founding.

Robert Lowie was content to let Kroeber run the department. Moreover, an undistinguished scholar could not have been brought in when Lowie was hired, so this earlier hiring of a major anthropologist does not constitute convincing evidence against the surmise that Kroeber wanted, if not a flunky, at least someone providing no competition. (Perhaps he saw in Olson something others did not see and a promise that did not materialize.)

After Kroeber, After World War II

I have chosen to focus on the 1950s in part because the early decades of Berkeley anthropology have been well described in print and Berkeley of the 1960s has been much written about. Berkeley anthropology of the 1950s has not. In addition to recapitulating the example of avoiding competition that characterized not only Kroeber's hiring of Olson but his allocation of "tribes" to one anthropologist who could then with perceived legitimacy object to "poaching" by others, my choice of the 1950s is motivated by interest in what Weber called the routinization of charisma.

The charismatic founder of the institution, Alfred Kroeber, retired in 1946 and went back to his alma mater, Columbia, where he drew a number of productive students. He spent his summers in northern California and continued to be consulted by his successors in the Berkeley department until his death in 1960. Indeed, when the department finally added a linguistic anthropologist, as he had been advocating—after retirement—it was one of whom he more than approved (Dell Hymes). Kroeber took an interest in the Berkeley students of the 1950s and was regularly informed about them and other matters of departmental importance. Lowie retired in 1950 and also had successes in teaching in various places, including Berkeley, after retirement.

Cultural anthropologist David Mandelbaum, who had been a student of Edward Sapir at Yale and was well established on the University of Minnesota faculty, and archaeologist Robert Heizer, a departmental alumnus, were hired in 1946 at the time of Kroeber's retirement and the start of the surge of university enrollment propelled by the GI Bill and by the postwar growth of the California population. Kroeber had been more interested in Peruvian than in Californian archaeology and the Peruvianist archaeologist/ethnohistorian John Rowe was hired in 1948. Rowe became the faculty member supervising the most graduate students during the 1950s. Through the end of the 1950s, Rowe also taught a course on language in culture that was taken by students (e.g., William Bright, William Samarin) in the new linguistics department that was the home of the Survey of California Indian Languages.

After a rapid rise in enrollments in 1946–48, enrollments in anthropology declined somewhat in the years 1948–55 and then increased steadily during the rest of the 1950s (Chairman David Mandelbaum:Dean A. R. Davis, June 10, 1955; also see Kerr 2001:74). The department had hired psychological anthropologist Cora DuBois, one of its alumni, to start in 1950, but she refused to sign the loyalty oath that was not ruled unconstitutional until 1952, by which time the University of California was under censure from the AAUP and others. The department remained entirely white male through the entire decade of the 1950s.

Clark Kerr, who had been a professor of labor economics before being appointed Berkeley's first chancellor (in 1952) and then president of the University of California system (1958–67), successfully advocated for a system of faculty tenure and took an active interest in promoting Berkeley social science florescence. "Political science and sociology were given special encouragement" (after sociology was blocked for decades by a coalition including but not led by Kroeber; see chapter 13), and restoring history to its earlier eminence was a particular interest of Kerr (2001:85), who was well aware that through the 1940s that "science was king at Berkeley and the humanities and social sciences were resentful" (349). Moreover, Dean of Letters and Science "Lincoln Constance and [Kerr] tried to move [the language departments] toward a more general concern with 'culture' in addition to language and literature" (Kerr 2001:86). There was a conscious effort to bring in people representing "modern developments" in the field of anthropology, such as Claude Lévi-Strauss, Siegfried Nadel, Anthony F. C. Wallace, Daryll Forde, Julian Pitt-Rivers, Clyde Kluckhohn, and David Schneider, only the last of whom was eventually (if briefly) hired (Mandelbaum:Davis, June 10, 1955; Mandelbaum:Kerr, April 5, 1956; Wallace:McCown, June 26, 1952;

McCown:Schneider, April 20, 1953), plus Forde for a summer. Each annual report to the chancellor reiterated a wish to hire someone to supervise rural California community studies. No candidate was specified, though the early work of department alumnus Walter Goldschmidt fits the description.

Latin America was the predominant geographical area for Berkeley graduate students during the 1950s, but the department staff of cultural anthropologists diversified, both in terms of areal specialties and theoretical perspectives (see table 2). David Mandelbaum's doctoral work had been on Native Americans (Crees), although he began focusing on South Asia during the late 1930s. Gerald Berreman, hired at the end of the decade, repeated the pattern (having worked on Aleuts, then specializing in India) and John Hitchcock also worked in South Asia. David Schneider had worked in Micronesia, then with Mescalero Apaches (see Schneider 1995:135–66), and Clifford Geertz worked briefly on Clyde Kluckhohn's Rimrock Five Cultures project, though he was (and is) primarily an Indonesianist (who later also worked in Morocco). Robert Murphy's doctoral research was in Amazonia, and he also conducted Shoshoni fieldwork before going to Berkeley (and worked on North Africa while a Berkeley professor). Edward Norbeck's geographical area was Japan, William Bascom and Lloyd Fallers were Africanist, René Millon a Mesoamericanist, Richard Salisbury a Melanesianist, and Raymond Smith worked in Guyana and the Caribbean. George Foster had worked steadily in Mexico but on and in Spain as well.

The distribution of doctoral dissertations by area supports the argument I have made elsewhere (chapter 5) that work on Native Americans was not so eclipsed and not so early as Robert Murphy (1976:6) and variously wistful and/or aggrieved Americanists have claimed (see table 3). There were nine doctoral dissertations on Native North American phenomena, five on South American, three on Mesoamerican, four on Asian, two on Middle Eastern, and one on Australian, plus two comparative ones that considered Native North America. The chronological listing of dissertations does not show any shift over the course of the decade, despite the addition of staff in the latter half of it.

Despite the loyalty oath debacle making recruiting more difficult, by discerning hires, Theodore McCown, David Mandelbaum, and Robert Heizer built a new department as prestigious and more diversified than the department over which Kroeber presided during the 1930s and 1940s.

George Foster was brought back and retained. William Bascom was hired as museum director in 1957, and the eminent physical anthropologist Sherwood Washburn was hired in 1958. But during Foster's chairmanship, a mass exodus of junior faculty occurred.

Robert F. Murphy elaborated on his characterization of "the Berkeley department of the late 50s [as] riven with conflicts of personality and ideology, each masquerading as the other" (1990:69), writing, "But in the final analysis, we all left because our theoretical directions were best expressed in the more intense intellectual climate of the east, where the basic problems posed by Marx and Freud were still relevant" (November 25, 1986, memorandum, seemingly to Grace Buzaljko, in the department archives in the Bancroft Library). Murphy also recalled the irony that the shockingly "revolutionary doctrine being imported by the eastern breed [specifically, Harvard's Social Relations Department] was structure-functionalism."[1]

Murphy wrote that when he "went to Africa in 1959, we had the most exciting department in the country; when I returned in 1960 it had moved east. Schneider, Geertz, and Fallers had gone to Chicago, Salisbury to McGill, René Millon, though still there, was being dropped. Although I was given tenure in 1960, I knew I would soon follow." Despite assurances from Foster and Washburn of their support for his own further promotion, Murphy opined that "the chief problem was difficulty in integrating the new, feisty World War II generation into the department." In a further elaboration, he wrote that "although Berkeley was to recoup these losses with the appointments of many able people, it would never regain the community of theoretical interests they [the departed junior faculty] represented . . . [and the] dialogue among the younger people that would later reach fruition in other universities, which was theoretical by a concern for the classic sociologists, for the embodiment of symbols in social activities" (March 5, 1987 memorandum; also see R. Murphy 1976:11–12, 15).

Murphy (1990:68–69) acknowledged that during the late 1950s and early 1960s he had been making a career of drinking. An undated communiqué from Gerald Berreman characterized Murphy as an acerbic department member, Schneider as abrasive, hostile to the "old guard," whom he suspected of anti-Semitism, and the most eager to leave.[2] Schneider recalled finding it "impossible to live with these people" (1995:172), that is, in a split department engaged in incessant infight-

TABLE 2. Berkeley Anthropology Department Faculty of 1950

Alfred Kroeber (1906 [instructor, 1901–5], emeritus 1946–60)

Robert H. Lowie (1921; emeritus 1950–57)

Ronald L. Olson (1931; emeritus 1956–79)

Edward W. Gifford (1938 [instructor and museum director, 1920–37], emeritus 1954–59)

Theodore D. McCown (1938–69)

Robert F. Heizer (1946–79)

David Mandelbaum (1946–87)

John H. Rowe (1948–2004)

Robert F. Murphy (1955–61)

Lloyd Fallers (1955–60)

William Bascom (1957–81)

David M. Schneider (1957–60)

Richard F. Salisbury (1957–61)

(John T. Hitchcock and Raymond T. Smith were listed in 1957–58 catalogs)

Sherwood L. Washburn (1958–2000)

René F. Millon (1958–61)

Gerald Berreman (1959–)

Clifford Geertz (1959–60)

Additions during the 1950s

George M. Foster (1956– [1954–55 visiting professor, then acting museum director, 1955–57])

Edward Norbeck (1954–58)

Chairmen

McCown, 1950–55

Mandelbaum, 1955–57

Heizer, acting chair, 1956–58

Foster, 1958–61

ing, and reported being stunned by one anthropology department professor's animus to tenuring an Irish Catholic. (Schneider had arrived with tenure).

Both Dean Lincoln Constance and éminence grise Alfred Kroeber tried to persuade Schneider to stay, and Schneider recalled telling them bluntly how "fucked up" the department was (1995:32–33). There were new hires from Harvard Social Relations during the early 1960s, Dell Hymes and Laura Nader, who also seemed to have bridled at the perceived paternalism of the senior faculty. An attempt to bring in Clyde Kluckhohn as a visiting professor fell through earlier (Kluckhon:Clark Kerr, September 14, 1956).

Schneider gives himself and Fred Eggan credit for taking Fallers and Geertz along with him to Chicago, though both went to the University of Chicago Committee for Comparative Studies of New Nations, under the auspices of Edward Shils and David Apter, and Fallers and Geertz had cross-appointments in the anthropology department.[3]

Jeffrey Dickemann (e-mail to author, October 24, 2002), who was a Berkeley graduate student through most of the 1950s and remained in

TABLE 3. Berkeley Anthropology Doctoral Dissertations, 1950–1962

1950   Hohenthal, William D., "An Investigation of the Evidence Relating to South American Tribes Reported as Non-Agricultural"

1951   Lowrimore, Burton S., "The Concept of Dualism in American Indian Folklore"

1951   Osborne, Homer D., "Excavations near Umatilla, Oregon: The Archaeology of the Columbia Intermontane Province"

1952   Libby, Dorothy R., "Girls' Puberty Observances among Northern Athabascans"

1953   Chard, Chester S., "Kamchadal Culture and Its Relationships in the Old and New Worlds"

1953   Nelson, Harold, "The Armenian Family: Changing Patterns of Family Life in a California Community"

1954   Beals, Alan R., "Culture Change and Social Conflict in a South Indian Village"

1954   Goins, John Francis, "Huayculi: The Quichua of Cochabamba Valley, Bolivia"

1954   McCorkle, Homer Thomas, "Community Persistence and Cultural Change on Margarita Island, Venezuela"

1954   Riddell, Dorothy, "The Late Ica Pottery of Ancient Peru"

1955   Bushnell, John Hempstead, "San Juan Atzingo: An Interpretation of Folk Culture in Central Mexico"

1955   Hoffman, Bernard G., "The Historical Ethnography of the Micmac of the Sixteenth and Seventeenth Centuries"

1955   Kennedy, Mary Jean, "Culture Contact and Acculturation of the Southwestern Pomo"

1955   Madsen, William. "Christo-Paganism: A Study of Mexican Religious Syncretism"

1955   McKern, Thomas W., "An Anthropometric and Morphological Analysis of a Pre-Historic Skeletal Population from Santa Cruz Island, California"

1955   Roney, James Givens, "A Study of Skeletal Maturation in Central Iran"

1957   Clark, Margaret, "Sickness and Health in Sal Si Puedes: Mexican-Americans in a California Community"

1957   Orenstein, Henry, "Caste, Leadership, and Social Change in a Bombay Village"

1957   Wallace, Dwight T., "The Tiahuanaco Horizon Styles in the Peruvian and Bolivian Highlands"

1958   Dickemann, Mildred, "The Reaction of Nonliterate Peoples to the Introduction of Western Education: A Comparative Study"

1958   Freed, Ruth S., "Culture Change, Acculturation, and Types of Communities"

1958   Pilling, Arnold R., "Law and Feud in an Aboriginal Society of North Australia"

1959   Hammel, Eugene A., "Wealth, Authority, and Prestige in the Ica Valley, Peru"

1960   Broadbent, Sylvia. "A Grammar of Southern Sierra Miwok"

1960   Lanning, Edward P., "Chronological and Cultural Relationships of Early Pottery Styles in Ancient Peru"

1961   Coult, Allan D., "Conflict and Stability in a Hualapai Community"

1962   Kennedy, Kenneth A. R. (MA 1954), "The Balangodese of Ceylon"

northern California, stressed that McCown was never part of the "dictatorial old crowd" and was much liked by students of his generation and shunned by the moralistic senior faculty for leaving his wife for a younger woman. What used to be called "moral turpitude" was also used to force Edward Norbeck to resign after he had been arrested for indecency in a public restroom (Dickemann 1997:14).[4]

From the early 1960s the mid-1980 Berkeley was a major training center in linguistic anthropology (see Murray 1998), though by the early 1990s there were no linguistic anthropologists in the department and the departmental guide introduced the discipline as comprising three subfields.[5] A very generous early retirement package offer led to an exodus of senior faculty during the mid-1990s, 20 percent of the campus's full professors in two years.

The department now, like the American Anthropological Association more than a hundred years old, continues and a later owl than I can evaluate whether the luster has been or will be recovered.

8

American Anthropologists Looking through
Taiwan to See "Traditional" China, 1950–1990

with KEELUNG HONG

Taiwan is a small, densely populated, and now highly industrialized island on which American social science research on "Chinese" culture
and society was concentrated from the late 1950s through the late 1970s,
at the same time as Taiwan was rapidly industrializing. Japanese and
Chinese anthropologists working on Taiwan prior to the 1950s studied
the aboriginal enclaves in the mountains of Taiwan or on smaller, neighboring islands. Bernard and Rita Gallin (1974b) recalled that they found
sociologists at National Taiwan University, not anthropologists, interested in their work during their first trips (during the late 1950s and early 1960s) to do fieldwork in rural Taiwan. Arthur Wolf similarly recalled
that, into the 1960s, "Chinese and foreign anthropologists studying Taiwan practiced a strict division of labor. The Chinese studied the aborigines, and the foreigners studied the Chinese [from the context, it is clear
that this meant Taiwanese, not refugees from the Kuomintang (KMT)
defeat in China]. The two groups exchanged reprints and dinner invitations, but when they went to the field they went in different directions
to study different problems" (1985:3).

   American anthropological work has focused almost exclusively on
rural Hokkien- (Holo-) and Hakka-speakers whose ancestors left behind
the elaborate lineages of southern China, mostly between the seventeenth and nineteenth centuries—prior to Japanese occupation in 1895.
"Taiwanese" includes those of Austronesian descent (which, to some
degree, most Taiwanese are) and the children of those born in China
who arrived on Taiwan during the late 1940s (referred to as "Mainlanders"), between the defeat of Japan in World War II and the final defeat
and evacuation of surviving remnants of the KMT bureaucracy and army

from China in 1949. There is a great deal of anthropological literature, if hardly any in English, on aboriginal tribespeople;[1] scarcely any on Mainlanders' children and grandchildren who identify themselves as Taiwanese. Our review of representations by American social scientists recapitulates the concentration on Holo- and Hakka-speakers but is not intended as endorsing the narrowing of the category "Taiwanese" to exclude anyone born on Taiwan who identifies as Taiwanese.

Arthur Wolf and the Unthinkability of "Taiwanese"

Arthur Wolf was one of the first American social scientists to do fieldwork in rural Taiwan. His publications and those of his wife during his early fieldwork on Taiwan, Margery Wolf, are the most frequently cited anthropological work dealing with Taiwan and have considerable recognition outside East Asian/West Pacific studies. Having found what he was not originally looking for—a predominance of "minor marriages" in the southwestern portion of the Daiba ("Taipei") basin—he related his research on the implications of this phenomenon to a wider audience of social scientists than those interested in East Asia or in Pacific islands such as Taiwan. The high levels of daughters-in-law adopted at early ages (*simbû'a*) and of uxorilocal residence, which Wolf and others found to have been very common in northern Taiwan (41 and 15 percent, respectively), do not fit with the norms for the "traditional patriarchal Chinese family" at all (as A. Wolf and Huang, 1980:125, 318 acknowledged; also see Pasternak 1989). The high rate of uxorilocal marriage, however, should not have come as a surprise to anyone familiar with the scant literature about Taiwan that was then available in English, since George Barclay (1954:228–29) had reported that 15 to 20 percent of Taiwanese marriages between 1906 and 1930 were uxorilocal.

Division of household assets (*pun ke-hoe*) during the lifetime of the father would seem to constitute another anomaly to "traditional China."[2] Such patterns, though later attenuated, would seem to evidence important cultural differences between "traditional Taiwan" of the first four and a half decades of the twentieth century and mainland "traditional China."[3] That these patterns anomalous to patriarchal Chinese family structure have been the central focus of Wolf's work makes his practice of promoting a view of a single Chinese essence all the more startling to those unacquainted with the investment of the (KMT) regime that welcomed Wolf had in being the preserved "Chinese tradition."

Wolf, who continues to find the archival records of the Japanese Empire the best place to study traditional (imperial) China, asserted that only historians "still insist on treating China as though it had the internal consistency of rice pudding" (1985:15). Although, in this passage and elsewhere, Wolf seems to acknowledge diversity, it is always within a singular "Chinese society" or a singular "Chinese culture." Also, since he and his students deploy a single one of the Chinese languages, Beijinghua ("Mandarin"), his statement that "most anthropologists are now convinced that Chinese society is as varied in expression as the Chinese language" may concede very little. For that matter, rice pudding is often not homogeneous and does not merely blend together its diverse ingredients but frequently includes (unassimilated alien) elements like raisins that remain distinct from the rice. Despite Wolf's nominal recognition of diversity, his practice is one of relentless analysis of *Chinese society* in the singular.

Data from Taiwan are at least the major ingredient, when not the only source, of Wolf's data. Yet invariably, singular nouns modified by "Chinese" and not "Taiwanese" appear in Wolf's titles, even though he recurrently acknowledges that the data from Taiwan may not be representative of Chinese sociocultural patterns. For instance, "Considering the source of most of the original data we are presenting, this book might appropriately have been entitled *Marriage and Adoption in Rural Haishan*. We chose *Marriage and Adoption in China* because we believe our argument has implications for the study of Chinese domestic organization generally, not because we view Haishan as representative of China" (A. Wolf and Huang 1980:ix–x). In that Wolf and Huang marshal data from various areas of Taiwan, not just from Haishan, "Marriage and Adoption in Taiwan" or "Marriage and Adoption in Japanese-Ruled Taiwan" would have been more precise. Modesty in claiming generalizability somehow just never makes it into Wolf's titles, although his students sometime skip to the local level in theirs (e.g., "Religion and Ritual in Lukang" [De Glopper 1974]). "Taiwanese society," "Taiwanese culture," and "Taiwanese family" are literally unthinkable to Wolf and to some of his students.

In his contribution to *The Anthropology of Taiwanese Society* (Ahern and Gates 1981) Wolf covered "domestic organization." He brought himself to use "Taiwanese" six times—in contrast to twenty-five "Chinese" and "Hakka" or "Hokkien" seven times. Even in a volume manifestly about Taiwan, he used the phrase "Chinese family" exclusively. Wolf and other anthropologists writing about religion based on field materials from Taiwan end up with gods, ghosts, and ancestors and/or Buddhism, Confucianism, Daoism, animism, and perhaps Christianity as "Chinese religion," which remains in the singular, as in *Religion and Ritual in Chinese Society* (A. Wolf 1974).

A contrasting treatment by anthropologists of multiple religious realities is provided by Thailand. Even though, unlike Taiwan, Thailand has a state religion (Theravada Buddhism) that the king has special obligations to protect, as Herbert Phillips noted, there are "four internally consistent and clear, but different belief systems—Buddhism, Brahmanism,[4] a Thai version of traditional Southeast Asian Animism, and simple naturalistic explanations—each of which has certain explanatory functions, but which villagers (often the same individual) also use interchangeably and inconsistently" (1973:71). Even A. T. Kirsch (1977:241–66), who sees a functional division of labor between religious traditions in Thailand and some systematicness to alternation and syncretism there, distinguishes historical strata and divergent types of religion. No one speaks of an entity, "the Thai religion," in the singular. A similar unconcern for theological distinctions typifies syncretic Japanese religious beliefs and practices[5]—and even American "popular religion." As Donald De Glopper, wrote, "There is no more reason to expect various Taiwanese customs or beliefs to form a coherent, logically consistent, and uniform system than there is to expect the doctrine of the Trinity, the tooth fairy, and Easter eggs to fit together into a consistent 'American popular religion'" (1974:44).

If four "world religions" and a widespread "folk religion" do not suffice to trigger the plural "Chinese religions," it is unlikely that "Chinese societies" can be conceived, especially by those whose research has been sponsored, facilitated, or merely permitted by the "Republic of China" (ROC) government. It had its own reasons for maintaining a view that there is only China and pretending that the government that happens to be located on Taiwan should be recognized as the legitimate singular *China*, since it clearly did not give proportional representation to those whom it actually ruled. A separate entity called Taiwan was not at all "good to think" for them. Indeed, "Taiwan" remains a dangerous thought for the KMT (and various parties led by former KMT members), even now.

That a concept "Taiwan" is so unthinkable to the most-cited anthropologist who has done fieldwork on Taiwan makes one wonder what danger it constitutes for him, why it was not "good to think" for him. Fear of losing access to data seems a likely possibility for someone relying heavily on government archives. In recent decades, loss of access to the means of production of data has been a salient concern for anthropologists, not just in Taiwan. Fieldworkers unpalatable to the regime were denied entry to Taiwan by the KMT ROC government, just as were native Taiwanese (including coauthor Hong) who criticized the government while studying outside Taiwan. American anthropologists familiar with Taiwan cannot be unaware of the KMT's restriction of access. As Hill Gates (1987:240) put it, "Where we can do fieldwork, our researches are constrained by tight governmental limits on the pursuit of topics that might undermine national policy. Where we cannot do fieldwork, we can do anthropology only on the safely dead. Intellectual issues thus come to be defined conservatively, and research topics become studies in the art of the possible."

Arthur Wolf has done both: not only has he avoided thinking or writing about "Taiwanese culture," but he has concentrated on the safely dead, writing about "traditional China" on the basis of Japanese colonial records.[6] Japanese population records, covering two generations, have been widely used by American social scientists to examine demographic changes. The massiveness of these archives has been taken as prima facie proof of the validity of the records, as if, because there is so much, it must be accurate. With Wolf's confidence in the homogeneity of "Chinese culture," he did not even consider the possibility that there might be variability among Taiwanese by class or by locale in their understandings of *ge* (family) in writing, "The Japanese settled on the *chia* [*ge*] as the basic unit and wisely left it up to the natives to define the term. All that was required of people was that they register as members of one and only one *chia*. Thus we may be confident that the family preserved in these records is a product of Chinese customs and not an arbitrary creation of the Japanese colonial bureaucracy" (A. Wolf 1985:31–32; also see A. Wolf and Huang 1980:chapter 2).

Although he does not consider that Taiwanese may have manipulated definitions and registrations for their own purposes, he at least acknowledged a bias in the records against joint families: "They followed Japanese custom in designating the head of the household. When a head died or retired the headship passed to his eldest sons regardless of whether or not the family included the former head's brothers. Since the Japanese must have known that Chinese custom favors brothers over sons, my guess is that primogeniture was introduced as a clerical convenience" (A. Wolf 1985:33). Other biases or invalidities Wolf did not discuss. Yet in the major mid-1950s survey of community studies in Japan itself, Richard Beardsley (1954:44–45) cautioned against accepting abundant official records as transparent: "This method, though particularly enticing in Japan where any government office has a wealth of statistics on many different subjects, has very serious limitations, since many statistics touch on matters of taxation and government control, on which the government statistics collector finds it almost impossible to learn the true state of affairs. Careful check of the records against independent surveys of land ownership, occupation, and population in the small communities studied in the Inland Sea has invariably shown discrepancies; sometimes, indeed, the figures bear very slight resemblance to reality."

If the detailed statistics for Japan itself are unreliable, there is little reason to suppose that similar statistics collected in other languages by Japanese officials in a colony are obviously valid or reliable. Huang Chiehshan (1989 interview), who spent a decade working for Wolf on data from the registries, contended that they were more reliable than records from Japan because of the tighter police control on Taiwan than in the homeland or in Korea—or in China under any dynasty. The lack of usable registration data from China is strong evidence that the institution was imperial Japanese, not imperial Chinese. There has been little (if any) concern about the procedures and motivations of those recording in or reporting to population registries, although Melissa Brown (2001, 2004) has shown systematic bias in the household registries' recording of ethnic classification and intermarriage rates. Studies on the ethnography of official record collection (e.g., the locus classicus; Kitsuse and Cicourel 1963) are apparently unknown to those working on the demography of Japanese colonial Taiwan. Wolf once wrote that, "given that the Japanese household registers are the best source of evidence we will ever have for studying family composition in late traditional China, one of our research priorities must be to discover how people interpreted the term 'family' when registering with the Japanese police" (A. Wolf 1985:12). He has not, however, published work bearing on this research priority.[7] It will soon be too late to ask any Taiwanese who reported on their households to Japanese officials about their understandings of requirements and categories for registering household members.

In his preface to Huang's and his magnum opus, Wolf claimed that the Japanese "household registers allowed me to determine the precise composition of every family from 1905 through the end of the Japanese occupation in 1945" (A. Wolf and Huang 1980:viii). Who it was in the family that decided whom to include as being part of it, by what criteria, and for what purposes are not problematics addressed within Wolf's work on the colonial Japanese archives.

Asking about responses made to Japanese police is "salvage anthropology" that is not being done and soon will be undoable, but researchers could ask similar questions about registering with the KMT police now. We know from the Gallins' research on emigrants from the Jianghua village that they call "Xin Xing" that some longtime resident in Daiba continue to be registered back in the village (1974a:344–46; the disparity between actual residence and registration was already noted during Bernard Gallin's 1958 fieldwork and reported in B. Gallin (1966:34–35). On the basis of censuses of two Daidiong (Taichung) villages conducted by students from Dunghai University, Mark Thelin (1977) found that the ROC household registries overcounted households, undercounted the number of persons within the households, and suggested motivations relating to taxation for household members to misreport to the official records. (One cannot extrapolate directly from these discrepancies to the Japanese period. Although the KMT took over the institution of household registration and increased police surveillance, short-term and long-term migration to Daiba and to other cities was clearly higher than in the Japanese era, providing an increased opportunity for registering family members who were living in other places than where they were officially counted.) Similarly, Tang Mei-Chun (1978:179–83) reported that, in comparing official registrations with a 1969 census of a town that has been engulfed by Daiba, the existence of households and the kinship relationships of those within households were consciously misrepresented. As in the village studied by Thelin, even in the aggregate, Yellow Rock households were overcounted, although there were under-registrations as well as over-registrations. Less socially prestigious kinship relations (including the one that was Arthur Wolf's long-term focus, *simbû'a* and matrilocally resident couples, plus illegitimate children) and occupations were systematically misrepresented. Other systematic biases in the registers remain to be explored. Given that these registers bear such a weight in the study of "late imperial China" (and, coincidentally, for the study of colonial Taiwan), we can only hope that someone pays attention to the research priority suggested but ignored in practice by Arthur Wolf.

Within the Japanese colonial data set, if Wolf and Huang's data are disaggregated (by year as well as by place), we may be able to see that, even within the half century of Japanese rule on Taiwan, in addition to considerable regional differences within Taiwan, there may have been temporal differences, so that the social structure (marriage patterns) in even Wolf's microcosm (Haishan) of the timeless essence "China" was changing, as had been reported (by Barclay 1954:228–29) before the Wolfs first went to Taiwan (also see Pasternak 1989:105–6). Arthur Wolf acknowledged that "changes initiated by the Japanese occupation began to have significant effects" about 1930 (A. Wolf and Huang 1980:viii). Wolf's coauthor (Huang, 1989 interview) stressed that increased literacy undercut paternal authority, making it possible for sons to refuse to marry girls who had been adopted for future marriage. Bernard Gallin also mentioned "increasingly open opposition of young people" but stressed that an increasing ratio of females to males and improved financial conditions made brides "both easier to find and easier to afford" (1966:165). In arguing for the essential unity of a singular China (despite linguistic differences between southeastern province, and the nonacceptance of foot-binding among the Hakka whom he studied in Taiwan), Cohen (1990:123) adduced the use of Qing dynastic dates in account books in southern Taiwan for five years after the transfer of Taiwan to Japan as evidence of the hegemony of the (dubiously Chinese) Celestial emperors. Five years to change something so fundamental to business practice and everyday thinking as dating seems rapid to us and a better argument for Japanese imperial hegemony as early as 1900. (Besides having a different standard for communist hegemony in China and Chinese hegemony in Taiwan, Cohen appears not to understand *hegemony*, since he can write that "hegemony in modern China received no commonly accepted legitimization through culture" [130].)

Folk Religion

Over time, as American anthropologists came to view "kinship" as a less-than-transparent or intersubjective category (see Wallace and Atkins

1960; Schneider 1968), the initial focus of anthropological research on Taiwan shifted from kinship and lineage organization to religion, usually with an implicit or explicit assumption that "traditional Chinese religion" had been preserved on Taiwan (and had been successfully extirpated by the communist rulers of China). Researchers on "world religions" found on Taiwan often have been oblivious to folk religion being a marker of ethnicity in Taiwan. Participation in Taiwanese festivals has long been scorned by those born in China as "backward superstition." The ethnic minority governments (Manchu, Japanese, and Chinese) recurrently attempted to suppress, or at least limit the frequency, duration, and expenditure on, festivals derogated by Mainlanders as only one step removed from the extravagant goings-on of barbarian headhunters.

In the view of the Qing official who gladly arranged to give the island to the Japanese, Li Hongzhang (Li Hung Chang 1913), the nonaboriginal Taiwanese were even more degraded than the aboriginal "wild beasts" headhunting in the hills. In reporting the Mainlander derogation of Taiwanese, we do not intend to denigrate the aboriginal population and (obviously!) do not accept the equation of *Chinese* with *superior*.

The pantheon of a "Chinese religion" held in contempt by the ruling Chinese minority on Taiwan and by their Beijinghua-speaking offspring is supposed by some specialist researchers (prominent among them, Arthur Wolf) as mirroring a real political structure. In the Durkheimian tradition, cognitive structures in general, and religion in particular, are reflections of society. Indeed, it is society that is worshipped, in Durkheim's view. As Wolf put it, "It is clear that the peasant's conception of the supernatural world was molded by his vision of society" (1974:8). In the anthropology of religion on Taiwan, however, it is an earthly power that never exercised effective control on Taiwan and that surrendered responsibility for Taiwan more than a century ago—that is, a political order that is beyond the recall of anyone living on Taiwan. As Arthur Wolf's then-future wife, Hill Gates Rohsenow, wrote, not just Taiwan but the areas of southeastern China from which settlers derived "were largely on their own for a significant part of the later Qing dynasty. . . . It is paradoxical that the [current] iconography derives from an otiose and powerless dynasty several generations past, while the authoritarian and all-pervading present governments are rarely alluded to in its symbolism" (1975:488).

To say, as Wolf did, that "the supernatural world is never a simple projection of the contemporary world" (1974:8) is to put it very mildly.[8] It is no doubt salutary to "begin the study of Chinese [or of Taiwanese, a level of analysis between the village and China that never seems to occur to Wolf as a possible one] religion with the social and economic history of particular communities" (1974:8), but will careful local history explain the relevance of an extinct social order never particularly salient in the region (northwestern Taiwan) about which Wolf and others write? "To understand the beliefs held at any point in time, one must examine the history of the community as well as the contemporary situation" (9), Wolf continued, but, just as his demographic work is focused on the Japanese period, what he and his associates have written about religion tends to ignore contemporary situations in general, and ethnic domination in Taiwan in particular. As Rohsenow wrote, "The struggles of the present are brushed over very lightly. . . . What events of contemporary life keep century-old animosities alive? . . . An analysis which attempts to show the relationship between religious symbols and social organization should make clear the nature of the social relations the ritual sphere is purported to express" (1973a:479).

Some other anthropologists have seen religion as a potential expression of rural ethnic protest, although they too put *Chinese* rather than *Taiwanese* in the titles of works dealing with data from Taiwanese history and contemporary culture (e.g., Weller 1987). As Bernard Gallin suggested, "The proliferation of religious activity in Taiwan and increased importance of the supernatural might be viewed as a nativistic movement to mark and enhance Taiwanese identity—as opposed to the Mainlanders . . . [who] are openly disdainful of what they refer to as Taiwanese superstition" (1985: 55–56). A resurgence of long-suppressed popular religion (along with a renaissance of elaborate funerals) also emerged as part of southern resistance to the northern and iconoclastic communist regime in China (see Luo 1991; Friedman 1993).

Even Myron Cohen eventually wrote that what he called "traditional Chinese culture on Taiwan became very much transformed into a modern assertion of national identity, but in this case the identity was Taiwanese and the nationalism was linked to the movement for Taiwan's independence" (1990:132). The primordial/ethnic basis of self-identifying as "Taiwanese" has declined as children and grandchildren of the post–World War II influx from China have lived their entire lives on Taiwan and increasingly intermarried and become bilingual or multilingual. That is, self-identification as "Taiwanese" is increasingly oriented to the hoped-for future of democracy and prosperity rather than to the rampant injustices of the KMT arrival, slaughter, and persecution of the majority population by a privileged and newly arrived Chinese minority (see Corcuff 2002; Chu 2000; Ho and Liu 2002). Nonetheless, credence in and support of temples predating the imposition of Chinese (mis)rule continues to distinguish Taiwanese from Chinese.

Historical Sources of Taiwanese Invisibility in American Anthropological Discourse

Some American academics (e.g., Mendel 1970; Lo 1994) have studied movements for Taiwanese independence, but anthropologists have not (even when venturing to research social movements on Taiwan, e.g., Weller 2000). Despite the well-known exemplary studies of nativist resurgence by Anthony F. C. Wallace (1956, 1970, 2003),[9] American anthropologists have largely avoided investigation of the resurgence of Taiwanese religion and its connection to Taiwanese struggles for self-determination. Given that American social scientists are generally liberal and that anthropologists dote on cultural differences, one would expect most of them to be sympathetic to self-determination and cultural maintenance anywhere—in Taiwan as much as in Slovakia, in Tibet as much as in Zuni. American social scientists marching in lockstep with a right-wing dictatorship legitimating—rather than treating skeptically—an ideological construct so shaky as "Taiwan is the most traditional part of China" is a puzzle. Although such a representation is overdetermined, we can suggest several partial explanations of how this status quo came about.

First, the triumph of the "People's Army of Liberation" on mainland China was traumatic for American China experts—not as traumatic as for the KMT, but still traumatic. First General Patrick Hurley and then right-wing congressmen blamed the "loss of China" to communism on the China experts who had warned of the popular hatred of the KMT in China, as if observers were responsible for the reality they observed (Grayson 1979:34–47). Shooting the messenger carrying bad news is a venerable reaction to frustration about military and political outcomes.

A second component to the acquiescence of American social scientists with the representation of Taiwan as typically Chinese is that the Maoist state made research inside China impossible—just at the time when anthropologists were beginning serious study of peasants and post-peasants (see chapter 4), and just when there were some Americans with the linguistic means to do ethnography in Beijinghua, and just when some studies of communities on mainland China by Chinese natives were becoming available (Fei Hsiao-Tung 1939; Fei and Chang 1945; Yang 1945; Hsu 1948; Lin 1948).

Robert Redfield abandoned plans for fieldwork in China. A few Sinologist anthropologists who would later become prominent started fieldwork in China between 1945 and 1950. Morton Fried did fieldwork in China after the war in an area still controlled by the KMT, though not where the Beijinghua he had studied was spoken. Having had to leave Sichuan without his field notes in 1950, G. William Skinner did fieldwork among Chinese in Thailand for his (1954) PhD dissertation. During the 1950s, no one had yet noticed Taiwan was the place where Chinese culture was best preserved. Taiwan had not yet become the most traditional part of China. In the 1953 *American Anthropological Association Memoir* dealing with China (A. Wright 1953) there is no mention of Taiwan (or Formosa). Similarly, what would soon be represented as the most traditional part of China was unmentioned in Karl Wittfogel's *Oriental Despotism* (1957), although he included analysis of places such as Bali and southwestern U.S. pueblos that are farther from China and the usual senses of *Oriental*. Those who wanted to study Chinese culture where Mao hadn't blocked them during the early and mid-1950s went to Southeast Asia, not to long-colonized Taiwan or Hong Kong.

Along with the first generation of researchers who began fieldwork in Taiwan in the late 1950s and early 1960s (Myron Cohen, Norma Diamond, Bernard and Rita Gallin, Burton Pasternak, Arthur and Margery Wolf), Skinner and Fried taught many of those who later did fieldwork in Taiwan. When their students began their fieldwork, they were preoccupied with finding continuities with what their teachers thought of as *Chinese* and had studied in China (Gates 1987:237). A later series of conferences, which led to Stanford University Press collections during the 1960s and 1970s, viewed by James Watson as "provid[ing] the very substance upon which Sinological anthropology depends for its corporate identity" (1976:364), "foster[ed] a generally conservative tendency to assume Chinese continuities over time and space," as Gates (1987:238) charged.

Researchers who wanted to study China were welcomed by a government pretending to **be** China. Moreover, being open to foreigners—whether social scientists or businessmen—at the time that KMT state capitalism was changing to encourage foreign investors—helped demonstrate that there was a "free China," in contrast to the larger, but closed, Maoist China. Writing in English about a timeless, essentialized "Chinese" culture and society in Taiwan was the safest kind of free speech for a regime that until the end of the 1990s restricted other kinds of discourse—especially any discourse about ethnic differences and Taiwanese autonomy. In return, social scientists were grateful for a chance to study at least something they could label "Chinese" in their publications (thereby getting more attention for them).

The KMT was eager to facilitate research legitimating its view of reality, arranging access to archives, forcing cooperation from village officials, providing assistants, and even financing some research by Americans. Hill Gates noted that "the Nationalist [KMT] need for legitimacy caused them to emphasize cultural continuities with China. . . . Often writing in English, and clearly for an American audience, Nationalist supporters in Taiwan and the United States based many of their arguments on the premise that Taiwan was an integral part of China, and its people were wholly and essentially Chinese" (1987:232).

Wishful thinking on the part of those who wanted to study China dovetailed with the need of a government claiming to represent all China but not sufficiently secure about its legitimacy as a minority in the only territory it controlled to drop martial law for four decades. Social scientists who sought the legitimacy of being experts on "the world's oldest continuous civilization" or the world's most populous country shared the KMT interest in claiming that "traditional China" had been preserved by caretakers of the Japanese colonial régime for a half century on Taiwan to provide foreign observers a sort of Ming theme park. For instance, Taiwan is a particularly good setting for comparative work, according to Baity, because "the Chinese live there as an overwhelming majority of the population, govern themselves[!] according to more or less traditional Chinese principles, and are relatively free of the influences of a present or former colonial power" (1975:2). The fantasy that the Japanese were caretakers of "traditional Chinese society" is explicit in the introduction to *The Anthropology of Taiwanese Society*: "Taiwan is the only province of China that has not undergone the sweeping changes of a socialist revolution: Chinese life has greater continuity with the past there, it can be argued, than anywhere else. During fifty years of rule, the Japanese did not intentionally alter Chinese customs and social relations; subsequently, the Kuomintang [KMT] government actively promoted adherence to Confucian ideals of social order. Anthropologists have therefore gone to Taiwan to study what they could no longer study in other provinces. It was Taiwan's representativeness, not its special qualities, that first attracted their interest" (Ahern and Gates 1981:8).

Gates later acknowledged that the Japanese wished to "Japanize the Taiwanese" (1987:232), that the impact of Japanese control has been underestimated. She also stressed that "we must demonstrate continuities [with the Chinese past], not assume them" (232). She had earlier faulted Burton Pasternak's naivete in dismissing the importance of Japanese influences on Taiwanese social structure (Rohsenow 1973b:78). (On Japanese education on Taiwan and the effort to promote the Japanese language through education in Japanese, see Sugimoto 1971.)

Just to call Taiwan a "province of China" is to take a stand with the KMT and against the right of self-government of the people on Taiwan. Moreover, *province of China* has little historical warrant. Until 1886 Taiwan was a territory of the province of Fujian, although Qing forces controlled only one-third of the island's land mass (Chuang 1988). The Japanese did not classify Taiwan as a "province." While Chen Yi was looting the island after World War II and while the KMT still controlled some territory on the Asian continent, Taiwan was not considered a province. Within the fantasy "Republic of China," Taiwan contains three provinces. Thus, in the four-plus millennia of Chinese civilization(s), Taiwan was considered a province of China only for seven years before the Qing Dynasty unloaded what its chief negotiator with the Japanese (Li Hongzhang) regarded as a bleeding ulcer on the motherland. Before the Chinese government transferred its claim to sovereignty over Taiwan to Japan, the dangerous frontier outpost was certainly not considered typically "Chinese."[10]

In combing the literature on Taiwan, we have not encountered any nineteenth-century claims that Taiwan was the most representative part of China or the best place to understand Chinese culture and society. It is hard to imagine anyone seriously believing that Japanese imperialism made Taiwan more Chinese instead of more Japanese. If half a century of Japanese rule is "a bridge to the past," as Ahern and Gates (1981:9) characterized it,[11] the claim rests on the quite unusual assumptions that colonial rule that introduced universal education—conducted in Japanese, not in any Chinese language, and aiming to assimilate (*dôka*) Taiwanese as Japanese (see Ching 2001)—"pacified" the aboriginal population of Taiwan so that peasants could concentrate on agriculture and forget about defense, presided over the demographic transformation from an island with the death rate equivalent to the birth rate to one with the birth rate double the death rate (Taeuber 1974:362), and also built a network of roads and railroads that markedly increased the access of the countryside to production for export (see Grajdanzev 1942; Ho 1978; Barrett and Whyte 1982) somehow simply preserved "traditional culture."

Generally, production for export is considered an indication of "modernization." As a Japanese colony, Taiwan was integrated into the world economy more than any part of mainland China was. An early "green revolution" made it far more productive than any part of mainland China was (or is). Nowhere else in the world is integration into the world economy taken as an indication of wholesale "preserving tradition." Those who want to study "traditional Chinese culture" on Taiwan ignored that the "bridge to the past" was a Japanese bridge to the past—and, once on the other side, one had to ignore the influence of the Dutch East Indies Company recruiting, sponsoring, and supervising the Hakka- and Hokkien-speaking men leaving their lineages behind in southeastern China to clear land and grow crops for export. Of course, in the view of those who wish to find "traditional Chinese culture," neither the European supervisors nor the aboriginal Formosan tribes they fought and with whom the migrants intermarried were of any cultural importance. Having gladly transferred claims on Taiwan to Japan, Li Hung Chang (Li Hongzhang) wrote,

> Formosans are neither of us nor with us, and we praise all the ancestors that this is so! In all Asia, in all the world, I believe there are no tribes of animals called men more degraded and filthy than these people of Taiwan. And have we not enough of criminals and low creatures to deal with on the mainland? These people are not farmers, they are no hill-men, nor hunters of wild beasts whose skins bring in money and keep men's bodies warm in the cold winters. No, they are not even fit to be soldiers in trained armies, for they

have no discipline, nor could they be taught. Neither would they make good sailors on regular ships though many of the coastmen are good enough as wild pirates and buccaneers of the sea. They are cut-throats, all of them, along the coasts and back into the jungles. And so they have been from the days of Chia-Ch'ing to the present time. No, they are not all even of so good a class as that! For what are opium smokers, head-hunters, and filthy lepers.... A very large number of these people are opium users of the lowest kind, and those who do not use this hellish concoction only abstain from it because it is not within their power or means to obtain that dirtiest of evil drugs. (1913:268)

This late Qing official did not anticipate that anyone would claim that Ming culture was transported wholesale to Taiwan in the final years of the Ming Dynasty and there alone lived on through the Qing Dynasty and beyond. In 1895 the island was viewed as unimportant to China and as quite abhorrently un-Chinese.

If, rather than efforts of seventeenth-century European or twentieth-century Japanese curators of "Chinese culture," it was the retreat of the remnants of the KMT army to Taiwan that made Taiwan the most representative or traditional part of China, one might expect that anthropologists would have studied the Mainlanders, using their memories to reconstruct what Chinese life was like before 1931 (when Japan invaded Manchuria), much as Native Americans told the first two generations of professional American anthropologists about prereservation life. Although the KMT supporters who fled to Taiwan constitute a quite unrepresentative sample of the population of China, at least they grew up in China and had not been socialized within the Japanese Empire. Insofar as there has been "salvage anthropology" on Taiwan, however, it has concerned either the aboriginal Formosans or research in the Japanese archives. Studies of the "memory culture" of China, akin to the classic works of Yang and Lin, have not been encouraged or elicited from Mainlanders resident on Taiwan by American social scientists (or by their Chinese and Taiwanese students). As already noted, American social scientists beginning in the late 1920s preferred studying functioning cultures to eliciting recollections and sorting through them to compare "culture elements." The functioning culture of units small enough to be studied in a year or so of fieldwork was a Taiwanese village, not one of the urban enclaves of exiled Mainlanders, despite the urban focus of Fried's and Skinner's work.[12]

One particularly striking failure of anthropologists on Taiwan is that they did not look at what Mainlanders did about forming lineages when they were separated from their natal lineages during the late 1940s and were dwelling in a hostile frontier area, dominating but outnumbered by natives. A great deal of early work, especially by Columbia-trained anthropologists, dealt with the conditions of lineage formation in the eighteenth and nineteenth centuries on Taiwan, but this interest did not extend to seeking to observe this feature of Chinese culture among contemporary Mainlanders in protracted exile on Taiwan. It is also odd that the "sojourner" conceptualization—developed by "Chicago school" sociologists to account for Chinese in North America who planned to return to China (P. Siu 1952, 1987)—has not been applied to studying Mainlanders on Taiwan. (In both cases, most "sojourns" lasted the rest of the sojourners' lives.)

Although there has been some painstakingly systematic work in Japanese archives and other government records, another characteristic of an early age of faith in cultural homogeneity and easy access to it continues. As Fried (1954:24) noted in his review of community studies done on mainland China, "since the subjects of anthropological research in the past were almost invariably [treated as/conceived to be?] of a simple homogeneous nature, there was little need for the field worker to concern himself with the source of his information, other than to be reasonably certain that he was not relying too heavily on the reports of people who were recognized within their own culture as being markedly deviant."[13]

Anyone, in any place—Indonesia, Malaysia, Singapore, Thailand—would do for eliciting "Chinese culture." Who needed sampling if communities and individuals were interchangeable and "Chinese culture" static and homogeneous? Sampling is not one of the strengths of American anthropology and was even less so in the 1950s, when only a few anthropologists grappled with intracultural variance.[14]

Gates suggested a third, related basis for studying Taiwan as a surrogate for rural China—not Ming or Qing China, but the China in which a communist peasant revolution had just triumphed—in order to try to understand conditions leading to that revolution and to look for possible ways to prevent other, similar revolutions:

By the late 1950s it was clear that American anthropological field-workers would not be welcome in the People's Republic of China for the foreseeable future. It was beginning to appear too that the Mc-Carthyist destruction of China scholarship in the United States was hampering the American ability to understand events in China proper. Support [from foundations] emerged for anthropological investigation of everyday Chinese life in Taiwan, where, it was assumed, traditional Chinese culture had been preserved from the changes set in motion by the Communist revolution. . . . The anthropological literature contains a marked bias toward seeing Taiwan as a sample of an essentially homogeneous Chinese whole. (1987:236, 232)

It would have to be admitted that Taiwan would have been an excellent place to study the KMT officials and army who "lost China" as well as being a place to monitor their tactics after retreating there to ensure that they were not pushed farther east—that is, into the sea. Following the massive wartime effort to develop expertise about the areas in which American troops were fighting or in which the government anticipated military action and/or postwar occupation, and preceding the counterinsurgency research such as Project Camelot, the decade of the 1950s was a boom time for area studies. The "Truman doctrine," and its enthusiastic extension by Eisenhower's secretary of state John Foster Dulles, made it the responsibility of the United States of America to save the world from communism, which seemed seductively attractive to peasants. Whether land reform and rural reconstruction might halt the "Red Tide" was an important policy question even before the escalation of American military presence in Southeast Asia led to grasping for the "hearts and minds" of peasants suffering through a guerrilla war there. Although land reform would seem patently "un-American," given the importance of land speculation and large landholdings in U.S. history and current agricultural production, it does seem to have been approved and even prescribed for other parts of the world, in particular during the military occupation of Japan.

A fourth factor in explaining why American social scientists looked through Taiwanese culture without seeing it is a general problem of "Orientalism." Edward Said, who is a member of another group that was politically invisible until very recently to Americans, wrote a comprehensive critique of western research on the Middle East. As he wrote, the "Orient" has "a kind of extrareal, phenomenologically reduced status that puts it out of reach of everyone except the Western expert. From the beginning of Western speculation about the Orient, the one thing the Orient could not do was to represent itself. Evidence of the Orient was credible only after it had passed through and been made firm by the Orientalist's refining fire. The Orient is eternal, uniform, and incapable of defining itself; therefore it is assumed that a highly generalized and systematic vocabulary for describing the Orient from a Western standpoint is inevitable and even scientifically 'objective'" (1978: 283, 301).

With the substitution of "China" and "Sinologist" for "Orient" and "Orientalist" these (and much else of his critique) apply directly to the fabrication of a singular "Chinese culture."

Said noted that in the study of Arabic, Indian, Chinese, and even Japanese culture, western scholars were preoccupied with a glorious, classical past as preserved in old texts rather than with making sense of the messy, living present. He noted a general flight from the disorientation of direct encounters with living carriers of a culture to the safety and manageability of documents. One does not expect to encounter this pattern among anthropologists, but it does seem to occur among some who work on civilizations with long written traditions. Reading American Sinologists, one feels that they want to skip over not only the Japanese occupation of Taiwan and of northeastern China but the whole Manchu period, to reach back to Ming China, or beyond—M. Suzuki (1976:259) related twentieth-century Taiwanese *dang-gi* directly back to the epoch of the Warring States in ancient China. Said shows that the positing of timeless entities such as "Chinese society" is a recurring habit. The most distinguished comparativist sociologists interested in China—Wolfram Eberhard, Max Weber, and Karl Wittfogel—often treated materials from different millennia as part of a single, static "Chinese society." For Taiwan, Japanese and KMT household registration records, rather than ancient literature and court records, provide the escape of preference from complicated contemporary realities to documents. H. Murphy provided two apt analogies to the standard operating procedures of Sinology: this literature is like what Asians might write about Europeans "if they felt obliged to avoid the confusion of referring to Germans, French, and Italians as different peoples . . . [and is] as if Asian scholars were explaining current European attitudes by reference to material from the early Roman Empire" (1982:39).

Into the 1960s, if "primitives" were not available for study (and after half a century of Japanese rule, the Formosan aboriginal cultures could not be so classified even by those eager to ignore any changes in Hakka and Holo cultures on Taiwan), then anthropologists studied peasants. In either case, the "classical manner in ethnography may be summarised thus: It is assumed that within a somewhat arbitrary geographical area a social system exists; the population involved in this social system is one culture; the social system is uniform. Hence the anthropologist can choose for himself [/herself] a locality of any convenient size and examine in detail what goes on in this particular locality. He then generalises from these conclusions and writes a book about the organisation of the society considered as a whole" (Leach 1954:60; see Barth 1993:171–73).

Although the "whole" for work on Taiwan is often "China," this was not the case for ethnography done in China prior to the victory of the "People's Liberation Army" in 1949. In the community studies done in China before any western community studies in Taiwan—with the telling exception of Francis Hsu's study of non-Han villagers in the Chinese periphery of Yunnan (Hsu 1948)[15]—there was "little tendency to overstate the significance of the results in terms of the area to which they applied. Indeed, most of the authors leaned the other way, inserting a prominent caveat that the community described is not China but an aspect of a huge and diversified society" (Fried 1954:22).

Moreover, there was also a thoroughgoing critique in American anthropology of *village* as a "natural unit" of analysis for peasant societies (see Geertz 1959; and, for China, Skinner 1964). Again, Bernard Gallin showed another, better way: *Hsin Hsing, Taiwan* was exemplary in stressing that "Hsin Hsing and the other villages of the immediate area are far from being small, isolated units" (1966:45). This pioneer study of a Taiwanese village aimed to describe change, not an incarnation of that timeless essence "the traditional Chinese village." Although change was not the problematic of her community study, Norma Diamond was also careful to point out that the Dailam (Tainan County) fishing village she studied in the early 1960s had been "subjected to modernizing influences for some 60 years [and so] it should not be mistaken for a picture of traditional China" (1969:2).

In trying to understand why some American anthropologists writing

TABLE 4. Country(ies) Listed in Titles of Books and Articles Reporting Research on Taiwan by American-Trained Anthropologists, by Institution of PhD Training

University where trained	Percentage of publications with			
	Only China[a]	China primary[b]	Taiwan primary[c]	(N)
Berkeley	78	0	22	(9)
Washington	67	0	33	(6)
Columbia	64	14	22	(36)
Stanford	55	4	41	(22)
Harvard	50	0	50	(8)
Cornell	41	9	50	(54)
Other[d]	19	9	72	(68)
Johns Hopkins and Michigan	18	9	73	(11)
Michigan State	0	20	80	(10)
Total	39	9	52	(223)

[a] *China* or *Chinese* in title without *Taiwan* or *Taiwanese* in title or subtitle.
[b] *China* or *Chinese* in title with *Taiwan* or *Taiwanese* in title or subtitle.
[c] *Taiwan* or *Taiwanese* in title, *China* or *Chinese* in subtitle or in neither title nor subtitle.
[d] Universities whose alumni published fewer than five publications based on research in Taiwan are combined as "other."
$X2 = 53.2, 1$ 8 d.f., $p < .0001$.

about Taiwan have followed Hsu rather than the other early writers of Chinese community studies in claiming "the typicality of his population" and equating it without major reservation to "a generalized traditional Chinese norm" (Hsu 1948:22; also see 19–20), perhaps the key is precisely that Taiwan and Yunnan are peripheral areas with strong historical, non-Chinese influences, as well as being under KMT martial law at the time Hsu and other ethnographers were working in these places. (Even the southeast China from which Taiwanese ancestors emigrated is dubiously "traditional China" or even Han: see H. Siu 1993.)

Nonetheless, there are also works closer to the Taiwanese ground. In effect, there is intracultural variation within American anthropology. The Taiwanese basis of research is more readily visible in the titles of books and articles by anthropologists not trained at Berkeley and Columbia, as can be seen in table 4.

There is no diminution over time of Taiwanese invisibility in American anthropological work done on Taiwan. Indeed, there is a slight (though statistically insignificant) increase in Taiwanese invisibility in the titles. Early book-length American ethnographies of Taiwan, such as Bernard Gallin's *Hsin Hsing, Taiwan* and Norma Diamond's *K'un Shen, a Taiwan Village*, included "Taiwan" in their titles—in English, at least.[16] Before producing the string of titles with "Chinese," even Arthur Wolf titled his (1964) dissertation "Marriage and Adoption in a Hokkien Village."

There are, however, also (statistically significant) differences by topic of research. As shown in table 5, research on kinship and religion especially evidences participation of American anthropologists in the imposition of "traditional China" on Taiwan. Research on ethnomedicine and research about working women is by no means unconcerned with the "great tradition" of Chinese civilization but has generally contained closer attention to Taiwanese distinctiveness. In addition to professional socialization in some places in keeping the Taiwanese location out of titles, significant variation can be accounted for by whether research was done in Daiba Guan (Taipei County) or further from the capital.

Using stepwise regression of a dichotomous dependent variable of whether *Taiwan* or *Taiwanese* occurred in the titles of 223 books and articles based on fieldwork in Taiwan by American-trained anthropologists published before Lee Tenghui's first election, we found that training at Columbia University, the University of Washington, or the University of California at Berkeley in contrast to training at institutions other than these three to be the best explanatory variable. Research topics involving kinship, medicine, or religion versus other topics and research in Daiba Guan versus elsewhere also had statistically significant effects. Betas were .37, .23, and .20, respectively. The same three variables were the only ones accounting for significant variance in *China/Chinese* receiving primacy in the title (whether or not *Taiwan* was also visible there), with betas of .37, .24, and .14, respectively. The multiple Rs were .46 and .43, respectively. In addition to interaction effects of the variables with statistically significant correlations to the two specifications of the dependent variable, year of publication, book versus article, and alternate combinations of topic were included in the analysis but did not have statistically significant effects. Still, the positive effect for year of publication (indicating increasing Taiwanese invisibility) makes dubious the claims that there was a widening sensitivity to essentializing a monolithic "Chinese culture" and greater re-

TABLE 5. Taiwanese Visibility by Topic in Publications of American-Trained Anthropologists

| Topic | Percentage of publications with | | | |
	Only China[a]	China primary	Taiwan primary	(N)
Medicine	62	0	38	(13)
Family/kinship	51	9	40	(23)
Religion	54	0	46	(85)
Other	28	8	64	(85)
Women	18	6	76	(17)
Total	39	9	52	(223)

Note: Includes publications without *Chinese*, *China*, *Taiwanese*, or *Taiwan* in the title.
[a] Includes four titles with *Taiwan* or *Taiwanese* and *China* or *Chinese* in the subtitle.
$X2 = 2$ 9.2 with 8 d.f. $p = .001$.

straint exercised before American ethnographers moved on to the People's Republic of China (PRC).

Ahern and Gates claimed that anthropologists "develop an instinct for telling if a book with 'China' in its title deals with Taiwan, Hong Kong, the PRC, or the T'ang dynasty" (1981:7). Other than by recognizing the authors on the basis of their earlier work, it is unlikely that this supposed "instinct" develops. For a previously unfamiliar American anthropologist's publications, it is necessary to look into the book or article to find out if it is based on research done in Taiwan. Even then, especially in Ahern's work, it is sometimes difficult to distinguish assertions that are generalized from Taiwan to China from those based on mainland Chinese sources. Moreover, it was not always necessary to depend upon developing such an "instinct" to know whether a publication described Taiwan.

Ethnomedicine

The study of folk medicine blossomed on Taiwan during the 1970s. Although more likely than research on other topics to have *Chinese* rather than *Taiwanese* in titles, the medical anthropology literature based on fieldwork from Taiwan was more likely to record native terms in whichever language was used by healers and their clients, rather than imposing Mandarin ones. Most of the illustrative material in Arthur Kleinman's very widely influential 1980 book *Patients and Healers in the Context of*

Culture was from Taiwan.[17] In addition to establishing explanatory models of illness rather than of disease as the proper focus of medical anthropology, that book made Taiwan the exemplary case of medical pluralism. The families of sick Taiwanese do not merely "doctor shop" but (often in succession) pragmatically try healers from different medical traditions. These include western medicine with its focus on microorganisms (viruses and bacteria) and its often high-tech remedies; Chinese medicine (*diong-i*), with its humoral etiological theory and herbal remedies; geomancy (*hong-sui*), providing insights into problems resulting from improper alignment of houses or tombs; and Taiwanese spirit mediums (*dang-gi*), exploring illnesses caused by ancestors and other spirits, who must be palliated in order for the ill person to recover. Each kind of practitioner offers explanations of what went wrong to bring about illness as well as attempting to provide remedies for the presented problem. Some of the remedies work in some cases, and some of the explanations are accepted. However, there is considerable variance in attribution of which treatment was efficacious (not even temporal contiguity, i.e., the remedy closest in time to recovery, is an adequate predictor of which medical belief system will be substantiated by the illness trajectory), and the standards in everyday use for confirming the validity of diagnosis are also quite elastic.

In contrast to analyses of "Chinese religion" in the singular on Taiwan, medical anthropological work done on Taiwan during the 1970s stressed the pragmatic diversity in medical behavior and intracultural variation in the salience and content of medical beliefs. Bernard Gallin cautioned against inferring commitment to a medical tradition (i.e., assuming that what is tried is salient to those—not necessarily the "patient"[18]—who decide to try some kind of healing): "Utilization of the traditional systems does not necessarily imply belief in these forms of medicine. Many people 'go through the motions'" (1975:277), just as they do in the realm of religious rituals. As he had described "Hsin Hsing" villagers earlier, "not even the most skeptical are entirely convinced that the rituals are ineffectual" (Gallin 1966:264). Gallin also cautioned, "We must be more careful not to attribute the same knowledge, perceptions, and behavior to all member[s] of Chinese society[/ies]. For too long, we took for granted the universality of the knowledge and even the behavioral manifestations of the tenets of the great Confucian tradition among the Chinese population[s]" (1975:278).

De Glopper (1977: 356) puts it even more bluntly:

> There is no single, pristine Great Tradition of Chinese medicine. There are several distinct schools, and when you look at what actual practitioners are doing, the variety is even greater. . . . People commonly utilize several therapies at the same time. . . . They do not place their entire confidence in any single practitioner, whether M.D., traditional doctor, diviner, or spirit medium. In my experience on Taiwan a tendency to keep one's options open and to prefer multi-causal explanations is common among ordinary people, as is an appreciation of the unique qualities of a very particular case or event. What cured one may not cure another, or what cured someone at a particular time may not work later, because the circumstances are different.

In contrast to the situation in other research specialties, Taiwanese culture is visible and recognized in medical anthropology work. This does not mean that the anthropologists had any particular interest in Taiwanese (medical) culture. As in other specialties, fieldwork shifted from Taiwan to China when researchers could go there at the end of the decade (with Kleinman again in the lead). Nevertheless, they did not posit a consistent, overarching entity, "Chinese medicine," for comparison with "western medicine."[19] The data on local and individual diversity in medical belief systems in retrospect might seem unmistakable, but anthropologists have demonstrated a considerable capacity for ignoring intracultural variation in presenting models of this or that culture. Moreover, during the same period, "Chinese religion" remained an authoritative construct despite data of similar pluralism in religious practices from Taiwan.

One partial explanation for the difference between these research specialties is that the typically Orientalist fascination with texts was markedly lower in the work on medicine on Taiwan than in the work on religion, despite the huge corpus of Chinese texts in various medical traditions.

Another reason for the difference in visibility of Taiwanese materials is that medical anthropologists were much more concerned with ethnosemantics than were anthropologists writing about "Chinese religion"[20] and were, therefore, more leery about translating native terms into Beijinghua.

As Judith Farquhar (personal communication, 1990) pointed out, the heavy repetition of some Taiwanese terms, notably *tang-ki* (*dang-gi*), gives the appearance that Kleinman used more native terms than he did in writing about the research he did on Taiwan. For instance, in Kleinman 1980:218 the six underlined "*tang-ki*" jump out at the reader, but he used (more discreetly italicized) Beijinghua terms for the symptoms of "depressed" and "anxious" rather than what the Taiwanese consulting the *dang-gi* used to label the problems for which they sought help from the possessing deity.

Furthermore, although medical specialists were certainly a focus of attention for medical anthropologists, religious specialists, particularly Daoist priests, were more central in the anthropological discourse about religion in research done in Taiwan. That is, the behavior and beliefs of those mixing or successively using divergent medical technologies received more attention than the structured behaviors and beliefs of the expert professional practitioners. Medical anthropology was and is more concerned with messy, varying practices; the anthropology of religion tends to construct clean-cut, neat cosmologies with little consideration of the variability of knowledge of the cosmology or in credence of particular beliefs. (A notable, albeit not American, exemplar is Marcel Griaule's (1965) *Conversations with Ogotemmêli.*)

One "messy" Taiwanese practice in particular, viewed with considerable distaste by Chinese Mainlanders on Taiwan, spirit possession, was a central concern of anthropology during the 1970s (see I. Lewis 1971; Samarin 1972; Bourguignon 1973; Fry 1976), although for research locales other than Taiwan it tended to be considered in the domain "religion" rather than the domain "medicine." The lack of possessed healers in central and northern China has led to other problematics emerging from fieldwork there and to a lack of comparison to what was studied on Taiwan during the 1970s. Nonetheless, due to the centrality of Kleinman's 1980 book to a paradigm shift within medical anthropology, the diversity and complexity of Taiwanese reality was unusually visible in that research specialty, and not just the specifically East Asian/West Pacific work within it.

The recognition of Taiwanese (culture and language) within medical anthropology of the late 1970s and early 1980s was more apparent than real. During that same period (the last burst of anthropological work on Taiwan before western anthropologists were welcome in the PRC), there was one subspecialty of American anthropology that clearly examined

Taiwanese patterns without subsuming them in "Chinese tradition" or "Chinese society."

Working Women: The Exception to the Pattern of Finding "Traditional China" on Taiwan

The wide distribution of industrial enterprises to the countryside of Taiwan attracted the interest of many social science observers. Elsewhere, industrialization was an urban phenomenon. Landless workers from the countryside migrated to urban centers. During the first Industrial Revolution in Europe, only mines and lumber mills—both processing raw materials where they were—blighted the countryside. Otherwise, the "dark, satanic mills" were located in cities. Noting the rising standard of living in Taiwan, many observers were euphoric, considering Taiwan as a model for rural industrialization without urban social problems. The widespread pollution of the environment went all but unrecorded in the enthusiasm for an example of "spatially equitable" economic development.[21]

The exception to this euphoria was some feminists (Linda Arrigo, Norma Diamond, Rita Gallin, Hill Gates, Lydia Kung) who studied women working in urban and rural factories and who saw and remarked that small family enterprises were practically unregulated in terms of worker safety and treatment. They also noted that Taiwanese women constituted a reserve labor army, by postponing marriage and childbirth, much as had the poor families who sold their labor in nineteenth-century British factories. Taiwanese women constituted

> a submissive, docile, and transient labor force, willing to accept low pay and unlikely to remain in one job long enough to agitate for wage increases or improved working conditions. With their minimal training, they are also prepared to accept the lackluster and poorly paid jobs available in labor-intensive industries. . . . To ensure sustained production at low cost during periods of economic growth and political stability during periods of economic recession, the Taiwanese [*sic*; The government of the Republic of China, about which she was writing, was anything but "Taiwanese"! Although we advocate clear distinction of *Taiwanese* from *Chinese*, the government on Taiwan circa 1984 was a Chinese oligarchy.] government encourages an ideological environment that relegates women

to menial labor and household tasks. The marriage of patriarchal ideology and contemporary capitalism allows the family, the nation, and the international market economy to take advantage of women's unpaid domestic and underpaid public labor without altering cultural definitions of male and female roles or transforming the structure of male status and authority within the family. (R. Gallin 1984:397–98)

Most of the unmarried young women's earnings were turned over to parents, who often invested this income in the education of sons. Diamond (1979) reported that women factory workers who lived with their natal families gave 70 to 80 percent of their earnings to their parents. Those moving farther away and living in factory dormitories also remitted nearly half of their earnings. Diamond and other anthropologists and sociologists who did fieldwork among women factory workers on Taiwan during its industrialization did not find substantial increases in the independence of these women from decisions made about their lives by men. For the most part, the young women maintained traditional views about the appropriateness of female subordination (see R. Gallin 1984:396; Diamond 1979), although attitudinal surveys reported Taiwanese men and women stating that women had increasing or equal say in decisions about expenditures (Yang 1970:449). The economic importance of daughters has increased with marriage postponement. Stafford (1992) showed reassessment of investment in daughters as they take increasing responsibility for ancestor worship and funding family investments of other sorts.

At least through the 1970s, factory work was a station at which many young women "repaid" parents the cost of raising them prior to marriage (and the benefit of the family into which they passed). The median age of females leaving employment (ca. 1972) was twenty-nine (Speare et al. 1988:103). With no prospects for advancement within the workplace and with widespread discrimination against the employment of married women, factory discipline was succeeded by subordination to a husband for women who worked for wages until marrying. The relatively short-term involvement in the labor force, in turn, has been used to justify not promoting women, who are viewed as "fickle" and/or who "will just get married and leave anyway"—a rationalization not unknown in the United States. The criticism of the exploitation of women factory workers as a reserve of labor to be used or let go with fluctuations in business cycles and to be routinely exposed to toxic materials in unsafe working conditions is the exception to widespread celebration by American social scientists of the "Taiwan miracle" (e.g., Kuo et al. 1981; Gold 1986; Clark 1989). This insulting-to-Taiwanese locution is embedded in discourse on political economy arguing against "dependency theory" (e.g., Winckler and Greenhalgh 1988; Gates 1987:50–67). It is also an important exception to subsuming "Taiwanese" under the rubric "Chinese."

With shortages of labor during the 1980s and early 1990s, the pattern changed, and according to official statistics, "In 1986 52% of Taiwan's female employees were 30 years of age and older; 42% were married" (R. Gallin 1989:374). These statistics raise questions about the continued application of analyses of working Taiwanese women during the early 1970s. The "reserve" may have been "called to active duty" and/or the demands for more skilled labor may have made workers less interchangeable, as also in South Korea (see Cho 1989:469).

Research on Taiwanese working women remains an exception to the conception of shared, traditional, Confucian Chinese worship of whomever has power that is advocated by the ROC government and is exemplified by researchers whom it supported and was supported by.

The Aftermath: Fleeing Democratization

To many Taiwanese, it seems that American anthropologists are afraid of democracy and believe that they must depend on authoritarian states to force people to be studied by ignorant aliens speaking (though usually awkwardly) the language imposed by that state. When no opposition to the KMT was permitted and the KMT ruled Taiwan under martial law, American anthropologists were abundantly present—writing about "Chinese culture," using Beijinghua as a lingua franca to villagers whose mother tongue was Holo or Hakka and who had been schooled in Japanese. Then, when those who had been schooled in Beijinghua started to grow up, the KMT began including Taiwanese at higher levels in the party, and democratization began to follow upon Taiwanization and increased prosperity, almost all of the American anthropologists fled. Seemingly, they were not interested in observing democratization and/or were not comfortable when the ROC government could not so easily impose foreign social scientists on Taiwanese and stopped pressing claims to Chineseness and to constituting the rightful government of China (thereby having less interest in anthropologists calling what they observed "Chinese culture").

Most of the anthropologists who were interested in doing fieldwork fled democratizing Taiwan for China, where the authoritarian government was still able—and now was more willing—to impose foreign social researchers on its people. I know that motivation is more complicated than fearing democracy and seeking the protection of authoritarian sponsorship, though these elements seem at least to be involved. Those who had been looking through Taiwanese people, culture, and society to write about "Chinese" this or that had not wanted to work on Taiwan or to pay attention to Taiwanese people except as surrogates for the unavailable "Chinese." China is what interested them, where they wanted to but could not go.

Coeditor of *The Anthropology of Taiwanese Society* Hill Gates wrote candidly, "In the 1960s, the United States forbade its citizens to visit China, and neither side was prepared to have social investigators living there. Instead, I did fieldwork in Taiwan" (1999:1). When it became possible to work in the PRC, "after two decades of depression, my energy was back, and I was ravenous to begin the China anthropology that had so long eluded me" (2). Her book about her "adventures in China" discussed how Chinese women in Sichuan were forced to cooperate with her research. Gates had the grace to be uncomfortable with the element of coercion that procured her "informants" and data. She was also candid that the academic rewards for research on China are higher than those for research on Taiwan (though she underestimates the importance of this by labeling it "academic snobbery"), writing in a 1988 journal entry, "No matter what superficialities I return with from Chengdu, they will count for something simply because they come from China, and not Taiwan. I am going to obtain data by what are primarily fetch-me-a-pygmy [i.e., coerced informants], yet I am already [at the start of her fieldwork in Sichuan] receiving invitations from real universities to lecture on this perhaps too-quick research. More fuss will doubtless be made about my four months here than has ever been over the four years of sweat, tears, and lowered serotonin levels that the Taiwan findings have cost me" (reproduced in Gates 1999:68–69).

The theorists little inclined to fieldwork continue to (over)generalize from written materials and bits of their earlier, thin ethnography to "Chinese culture." The anthropology of religion using Taiwanese data continues to be a domain in which data from Taiwan has been most insistently forced into the "Chinese" rubric. This has continued to be the case in the heavy theorizing books, such as Feuchtwang (1992) and Sangren (1987, 2001).

Arthur Wolf (1995), continuing to prefer poring over records extracted by plantation-like neocolonial laborers (see Chun 2000:589) rather than doing ethnography, produced his magnum opus on childhood association's de-eroticizing daughters-in-law adopted as children. As in his earlier work, its primary basis on Taiwanese evidence was occluded from the book's title (*Sexual Attraction and Childhood Association: A Chinese Brief for Edward Westermarck*).

Hill Gates (1997, 1999), Melissa Brown (1996), and Robert Weller (1987, 1994) explicitly compare material from Taiwan and material from China. Perhaps from having become accustomed to peripherality (and little competition from other anthropologists?), American anthropology professors who have shifted their fieldwork from Taiwan to China have mostly chosen to work not in the central plains, which are the heartland of "traditional Han Chinese culture" and the basis for the appellation "Middle Kingdom." Instead, they have gone to Han peripheries (e.g., Hill Gates, David Schack) or have focused on non-Han peoples within the PRC (e.g., Burton Pasternak and Stevan Harrell). Evidence of the continued heedlessness by anthropologists to complicity with domination is the pathetically circumscribed scope of "fieldworkers' responsibilities in China" posited by Pasternak (1983:61–62): he does not consider anything problematic about contributing to the legitimacy of ethnic (or any other kind of) domination and systematic state ethnocide but addresses the need to give lectures while in the field in China.

Social scientists, mostly Taiwanese sociologists, who have published on an increasingly democratic Taiwan in which even the KMT was Taiwanized have empirically examined the previously taboo topic of ethnic identity and cultural differences on the multiethnic island,[22] even if the source of the data as Taiwanese is sometimes still occluded by western anthropologists (e.g. Stafford 1995). A 2000 special issue of the *International Journal of the Sociology of Language* included scrutiny of language use and Taiwanese identity by Huang Shuanfan, Liao Chao-Chih, and John Kwock-Ping Tse (also see Sandel 2003). Identity politics and party (re)alignment has been analyzed by Kim (2000a, 2000b), H. Lu (2002), You (1994), and N. Wu (1992, 2002).

Gender, the dominant discourse within American anthropology during the most recent two decades (see Murray 1994a), has been a major focus of anthropological research done on Taiwan (see Moskowitz 2001; Wen 2000). The presence of women in the paid-labor force has remained the primary interest, but rather than the unmarried temporary factory workers living in dormitories described by Diamond (1979) and Kung (1984), the later research has focused on women doing piecework at home (Hsiung 1996; A. Lee 2000) or those who are capitalist entrepreneurs (Gates 1997, 1999; Y. Lu 2001; Simon 2000, 2003b; Wilen 1995). Diverse patterns of continued employment for women after marriage and giving birth were elucidated by sociologists Yi and Chien (2001) and Yu (2001), while Chang (2002) found systematic discrimination against female workers in state-owned enterprises as well as in private companies.

Conclusion

Social scientists have too often supported—in their words, in their presence, and in their deeds—the paternalistic claims of rulers suppressing the very cultures the anthropologists want to study. Social science work dealing with Taiwan routinely legitimated substitution of the language of Beijing for the language used by those observed and justified ignoring Taiwanese culture by subordinating consideration of its specific features to writing about Chinese civilization, just as Taiwanese were economically and politically subordinated to the fictitious "Republic of China." The "China" that Arthur Wolf and others serve in return for support of their research on what purports to be China is an egregious, but unfortunately not unique, example (see Asad 1973; Winks 1987:43–51) and has continued in publications of research done by anthropologists on Taiwan since 1990, including in the best-selling and widely diffused resurrection by Margery Wolf (1990, 1992) of a 1950s case of a woman whose claim to spirit possession was rejected by villagers.

Some Anglophone anthropologists writing about Taiwan, such as Charles Stafford, continue to seek the greater prestige of studying Chinese culture with titles (and discourses) that obscure the site of their fieldwork. Most of the American anthropologists who did fieldwork on Taiwan when China was closed to them moved on to their real interest when the post-Mao communist regime allowed foreigners greater access to China. Some (e.g., Steven Sangren, Arthur and Margery Wolf) have continued to draw on material gathered earlier on Taiwan while continuing to package what they write as being about "Chinese" phenomena. A few, such as Weller (1999) and Gates (1997), are interested in contrasting lifeways and associations in Taiwan to those in China, though mostly seeming to regard Taiwanese phenomena as possible harbingers of the future for China—rather than as remnants of Ming Dynasty China, as in much of the anthropological writing based on materials from Taiwan during the 1950s and 1960s.

We do not mean to suggest that the published descriptions of Taiwanese communities are without value, though their usefulness as history of the KMT era is reduced by a general reluctance to describe state terrorism by the regime that permitted anthropologists to do fieldwork in Taiwan and mystification of the identity and language of those studied. The price of admission to do fieldwork on Taiwan during the KMT era seems to have included obscuring power relations and paralleling the Chiang dictatorship's portrayal of Taiwan as a Chinese culture, though in most conventional senses Taiwan was more "modern" than China was when Chiang was driven out of China and took refuge on Taiwan. Despite a turn to reflexivity in recent American anthropology, there has been a notable lack of reflection on the ideological service anthropologists have provided either to the right-wing Leninist ROC regime or to the left-wing Leninist PRC one.

2

*Sociology's Increasingly Uneasy
Relations with Anthropology*

Introduction

Considering that the Rockefeller-endowed University of Chicago looms large in part 2 and that the focus herein remains on the initially porous boundary between sociology and anthropology, there is less need to elaborate on the intellectual and institutional bases of early American sociology than there was for the compressed tour of pre-Columbia history of American anthropology I undertook at the start of part 1.

Anthropologists sometimes claim Heródotos as "the father of anthropology." In that the comparative morphology of Aristotle's *Politics* is less prescriptive and more systematic than the *Republic* and *Laws* of his teacher, Plato, I'm surprised that American sociologists—at least from Albion Small (1926), longtime chair of the Chicago department and editor of the *American Journal of Sociology*, through functionalist-turned-Marxist Alvin Gouldner (1965)—root study of the *logos* of society in the very prescriptive and proscriptive Plato rather than in the more descriptivist Aristotle (though it should seem "natural" to me in that my own introduction to the history of sociopolitical theory began with *The Republic*).

Both the words *sociologie* and *positivisme* were coined by the French antimetaphysician Auguste Comte (1798–1857), who promoted a Newtonian, verifiable science of society and social change, especially the changes wrought violently by the French Revolution's totalizing central state's assault on "organic" social institutions and lifeways, in particular (see Nisbet 1943, 1966). Alexis de Tocqueville and Émile Durkheim brought a comparative perspective to bear on societies, social institutions, and social change (evolution for Comte and Durkheim, continuities even across *la revolution* for Tocqueville). The founders of sociology programs in U.S. institutions were more directly influenced by analogies from biological to social evolution than were Tocqueville and Comte, both of whom were dead before *The Origin of Species* was published in 1859.

The first president of the American Sociological Society (1895), the "American Aristotle" (Chugerman 1939), Lester Frank Ward, was the resident evolutionary theorist for Major John Wesley Powell and his Bureau of American Ethnology. As noted in the introduction to part 1, Ward offered an alternative to the "social Darwinism" of Herbert Spencer while pioneering notions of social control.

The founder of the sociology program at Yale—who also was the first person to teach a course called "sociology," one focusing on the program of Comte and the claims of Spencer—William Graham Sumner "married evolutionary theory to economic [classic] liberalism and arguments for a minimal state, and thus contributed to the popular stereotype of social Darwinism as a rationalization for the market competition of the Gilded Age" (Calhoun 2007:5). *Mores*, Sumner's most enduring notion, were for Sumner "beliefs and practices held to be not merely convenient but good and/or true" (5), which in German Romantic guise was the particular "genius" of a particular people (*Völk*). Sumner is also credited with coining *ethnocentrism*, which he saw as a "natural" rejection of the ways of other peoples by those enculturated in a worldview and particular lifeways.

The founder of the sociology program at Columbia, Franklin Giddings, "staking a position between Ward and Sumner, emphasized that mere gregariousness among animals was not the same as [purposive] human association because it was not mediated by speech and consciousness of kind" (9). Giddings was hired to provide a scientific background for education of social workers and for social reform(s).

Though hoping that knowledge about society would be applied to bettering social arrangements, Giddings and Small, like Franz Boas, were scientistic in clearing out competition in researching and theorizing culture and society. Giddings (and his prize student, William F. Ogburn) championed quantitative work on, among others, immigrants (on whom research was also done by Boas [1903, 1912]). As Sica (2007:718) wrote of Small, "Despite his own theological background and his passionate belief that sociology should ultimately serve some meliorative societal purpose, he was married to the idea of 'objectivity' as the distinguishing trait of 'true' sociological research." Small (1916:748) wrote of the American sociological "movement" in terms of the "*demand for objectivity* in social science which found voice in Adam Smith" (emphasis in original). (Giddings's "consciousness of kind" was rooted in Smith's *Theory of Moral Sentiments* [1759], conceptions from which also foreshadowed some of Sumner's ideas [not least the operations of the market's "invisible hand"]. As Calhoun (2007:2) noted, "Adam Ferguson and Adam Smith pioneered the notion of self-organizing civil society and developed a sociological approach to key issues in political economy."

Peasant immigrants' mores being followed back to their source societies already loomed large in chapter 4, and "Negro" lifeways in the Americas were explored by some prominent students of Franz Boas (Zora Neale Hurston, Melville Herskovits, Ruth Landes) and by sociologists including African Americans W. E. B. DuBois (whose early work in Atlanta and Philadelphia pioneered quantitative methods in the United States), Charles Johnson, and Franklin Frazier (see Blackwell 1975; McKee 1993:216–18). Chapter 9 focuses on the seminal researcher on immigrants (in both their place of origin and in America), W. I. Thomas, before and after that work, work that is also important background for the potential and actual developments analyzed in chapters 10, 12, and 13. The urban ethnography "Chicago School" of Robert Park (Robert Redfield's father-in-law) grew directly from the conceptions and monumental research of Thomas, and W.I. and Dorothy Thomas had been working with the Myrdals before Gunnar Myrdal was hired by the Carnegie Foundation to research *An American Dilemma* (results published in 1944) with help from many American sociologists and anthropologists.

For more detail on the nineteenth-century developments to/of American sociology see Small (1916, 1924, the latter heavy on the German historiographic tradition[1]); on the founders of American academic sociology see Bernard and Bernard (1943) and Hinkle and Hinkle (1954); on exemplars of sociological research (including a chapter on *The Polish Peasant*, one on Parkian social ecology, and one on *An American Dilemma*) see Madge (1962). Historicist publications on the history of American sociology are markedly scarcer than work on the history of American anthropology, economics, or psychology. A journal on the history of sociology (on the editorial board of which I served) collapsed in 1987, not for lack of material being submitted but for lack of financial support (Sica 2007:714). The American Sociological Association has a website with biographies of its presidents from its founding in 1906 through its 2005 centennial at www2.asanet.org/governance/pastpres.html (paralleling the volume of biographical sketches of presidents of the American Anthropological Association edited by Regna Darnell and Frederic Gleach [2002]).

9

W. I. Thomas, Behaviorist Ethnologist

W. I. Thomas's role in pioneering the kind of empirical research that is identified as "the Chicago school of sociology" is well recognized (see Bulmer 1984; R. Faris 1967; Kurtz 1984). That most of his writings were intended as contributions to ethnology has been forgotten by later generations of sociologists and anthropologists, and even by historians of social science. The fame of the monumental *Polish Peasant in Europe and America* overshadows both his earlier and later work collating ethnographic details gathered by others. The book was originally published in five volumes between 1918 and 1920, the first two by the University of Chicago Press, then all five by Richard Badger (Boston). Having consigned *The Polish Peasant* to sociology, anthropologists (and their historians) neglect its priority for work on acculturation by American anthropologists. Leslie White, who, typically for anthropologists, considered *The Polish Peasant* a work of sociology, not anthropology, believed that Thomas's anthropological books "have not been appreciated at their true worth by American anthropologists—probably, I believe, because Thomas was not a 'member of the union.'" (White:Fred Mathews, November 29, 1964; cf. Lowie 1945:416). In this chapter I attempt to reclaim Thomas for the history of American anthropology, especially the move within it toward "culture and personality" work after the Boasian "refutation" of nineteenth-century evolutionisms.

I also show that, although the personality and interests of Frederick Starr undoubtedly obstructed the "professionalization of scientific [which in the context is to say *Boasian*] anthropology" at the University of Chicago, as many scholars have noted (R. Faris 1967:16; also see Eggan 1974), Fay-Cooper Cole did not introduce Boasian doctrine to the University of Chicago Department of Sociology and Anthropology. There were two admirers of Franz Boas there two decades before the "takeoff" of anthropological research during the late 1920s led by Cole, Edward Sapir, and Robert Redfield. (On the later developments see Eggan [1974]; and chapter 10.) Thomas himself was something of an early Boasian convert, albeit "prematurely" interested in acculturation.

Original Interests and Training

William Isaac Thomas was born in Virginia in 1863 to a father who combined preaching with farming. In 1880 W. I. enrolled at the University of Tennessee, and in 1886 he received the first doctorate it ever granted. He began teaching (English, Greek, natural history) before completing his degree and continued until the all-but-obligatory year of study in Europe. During the 1888–89 academic year he went to Göttingen and Berlin, where he could learn firsthand about folk psychology and ethnology as practiced by Heymann Steinthal and Moritz Lazarus. On his return to the United States, he took a position at Oberlin College. He took a leave of absence in 1893–94 for graduate work in sociology at the University of Chicago with Albion Small and Charles Henderson. However, at Chicago he took more courses in brain anatomy from Adolf Meyer and physiology from Jacques Loeb than sociology courses. Having already taught natural history, his graduate work at Chicago was that of a physical anthropologist. That summer he was appointed an instructor in the Department of Sociology and Anthropology.

After earning a second doctorate in 1895 (with a thesis titled "On a Difference of the Metabolism of the Sexes"), Thomas became an assistant professor in the department (Janowitz 1966:xi–xiii). He was promoted to the rank of associate professor in 1900, to full professor in 1910. Although Thomas was a protégé of Small rather than of the senior, albeit prescientific anthropologist in the department, Frederick Starr (whose own PhD was in geology from Lafayette College in Easton, Pennsylvania; see Miller 1975; Bulmer 1984:39–40), Thomas taught courses on primitive races, women, folk psychology, primitive art, primitive education, racial development, occupations, and sex. He does not seem ever to have been much impressed by Starr. Nor was Thomas subordinated to Starr in a department run by Thomas's sometimes teacher Albion Small. Starr and Thomas managed to coexist physically removed from the sociologists in the Department of Sociology and Anthropology. (After noting that his courses were being given in the Walker Museum, Thomas wrote President Harper on January 17, 1896, "I desire to be located with the Department of Anthropology, as my books are to be combined with those of Mr. Starr.")

Starr was an exceedingly popular lecturer, and the anthropological part of the "science of society" at Chicago began auspiciously at the graduate level as well: two of the first seven PhD dissertations of the department dealt with "primitive" groups and were clearly supervised by Starr (even though each is far better grounded than any of Starr's work). These were David Barrows's "Ethnobotany of Coahuila Indians of Southern California" and Merton Miller's study of Taos. A student of Thomas's who wrote a 1904 MA thesis on the "hunting pattern of mind" and went on to pioneer intensive ethnography among the Bagobo of Davao, Laura Watson Benedict, went to Columbia to write up her results under Boas's direction (Bernstein 1985).

Thereafter, studies of peasant communities and urban ethnic enclaves increasingly predominated as Chicago thesis topics, and such topics were "not anthropology" in the view of anthropologists of that day. The work Thomas was reading and attempting to synthesize, however, was anthropology. Moreover, surviving correspondence with President William Rainey Harper from 1896 onward shows that Thomas wanted to expand graduate training in anthropology, while Starr preferred his status quo as a popular lecturer and resisted Boasian professionalization of anthropology (Darnell 1998a). Ironically, Starr, like Boas, nursed a grudge over how the Columbian Exposition anthropology collection was transformed into the permanent Field Museum without including a job for him: Starr blamed Boas's champion Frederic Putnam for his exclusion; Boas blamed the Washington/Smithsonian group for his (Miller 1975:56; Stocking 1968:281).

The Boasian Thomas

In a brief autobiographical sketch Thomas (1973:249) listed Franz Boas as having more influence on him than his teachers of sociology. He was also influenced by some of the same German "folk psychologists" who were Boas's formative influences (e.g., Wilhelm Wundt, Adolf Bastian, and Heymann Steinthal; see Kluckhohn and Prufer 1959; Stocking 1968:133–60). There is no evidence that Thomas encountered Boas between Thomas's arrival in Chicago as a graduate student in 1893 and Boas's departure from the Field Museum in 1894 or during Thomas's Berlin sojourn with Steinthal (1888–89). By 1907, however, George Dorsey and Thomas were scheming to bring Boas to Chicago to reorganize anthropological instruction (Thomas:Boas, March 26, 1907; Dorsey:Boas, March 26, 1907). (Boas only accepted an offer to teach at Chicago during the summer of 1908; see Darnell 1969:163.) Boas's influence on Thomas seems to have been mediated originally by Dorsey, a student of Putnam's who joined the Field Museum in 1896 and had a nebulous appointment at the University of Chicago to teach physical anthropology between 1905 and 1915 (Evan A. Thomas:author, October 23, 1978; also see Miller 1975). Thomas (1973:249) himself wrote the he was "more influenced by trends of thought and method than by particular persons," so perhaps it does not matter exactly how he was first exposed to the emerging Boasian paradigm. He was on terms of mutual regard with Boasians and drew heavily on their ethnography for his ethnology (W. Thomas 1909; Alfred L. Kroeber:Thomas, June 6, 1910; Theodora Kroeber, 1977 interview; Lowie 1945:416).

Thomas's *Source Book for Social Origins* (1909) included a chapter by Boas. At the time he was preparing that volume Thomas had not yet cast off the influences of Herbert Spencer and Friedrich Ratzel, but he wrote about race and sex in increasingly more Boasian (i.e., less Spencerian) terms during the first decade of the twentieth century.

From the distance of 1927 Thomas wrote, "I was influenced by Spencer, by his evolutionary and anthropological view of the development of institutions, but I was never a 'Spencerian.' . . . His suppression of inconvenient data and selection of convenient data were little less than dishonest. One of my early studies was a checkup of his generalizations in his *Principles of Sociology* and the data in his *Descriptive Sociology*, on the basis of which he prepared the former work. It turned out that he had ignored all the data which did not conform to his theories" (250). That there is a touch of retrospective illusion in this denunciation of Spencer is obvious from Thomas's earliest writings and also his own statement in the same memoir that "I was about 40 years old [1903] before I assumed a critical attitude toward books and opinions" (W. Thomas 1927:248). As all his books demonstrate, Thomas's wish for novelty was sufficiently dominant to take note of diverse phenomena and string disparate materials together without much synthesis. Fragments of life histories follow one another in Thomas's *The Unadjusted Girl* (1923), as do snippets from his extensive reading of ethnographies in *Primitive Behavior* (1937).

Moreover, Thomas's almost obsessive respect for particularistic facts and unwillingness to compare detailed materials ostensibly gathered for comparison resembled that of Boas, who also defined *science* as rejecting the selectivity of theorists such as Spencer.

Boas's work received more than passing note in the 1909 compendium, and work by "Boas school" and "Cambridge school" (see Langham 1981) anthropologists replaced such nineteenth-century theorists as Herbert Spencer in Thomas's coverage in *Primitive Behavior* (1937). Sociological theorists of Thomas's own generation were discussed at most in passing.

The materials for *Primitive Behavior* were furnished by publications of Boasian Americanists, Riversian Melanesianists, and German Africanists (especially Bruno Guttman [1926]—by the reckoning of Jürgen Winter [1979:11] Thomas quoted twenty thousand words from Guttman). Were they used for "anthropological" purposes? Presuming the debate between W. H. Rivers and Alfred L. Kroeber about kinship terms and behavior occurred within anthropology and that work on "primitive" law and government was not sociology, the answer to this question is affirmative. The topics of Thomas's long chapter on language are eccentric (against the standard of Kroeber's first *Anthropology*), but the discussion of obligatory grammatical classification is closer to Sapir's *Language* than the Tardean rejection of regular sound change in Robert E. Park and Ernest W. Burgess's (1921) classic codification of Chicago sociology; the different facets (aspect instead of modality here, animate instead of gender classification there) are in no developmental order, merely alternative patterns from the various possible means of ordering the universe parsimoniously: "In each language only a part of the concept or mental image is expressed" (W. Thomas 1937:60).

A rejection of instincts and any racial differences in mental endowment was common to Boasians and sociologists (notably Thomas's former students, Luther Bernard and Ellsworth Faris), and "pattern diffusion" was of interest to Boasian sociologists like William F. Ogburn as well as to Boasian anthropologists (W. Thomas 1937:23).

What seems to me clearly to distinguish *Primitive Behavior* from work by sociologists of the 1920s and 1930s is the extended discussion of kinship. This emphasis, even more than the focus on language, marks the book as "anthropology," rather than plundering examples from anthropologists to build sociological theory. Kinship classification was the language-and-culture problem par excellence of American anthropology through much of the twentieth century, and the meaning of kinship classifications was the major grounds for conflict between American and British anthropologists. To most sociologists, on the other hand, kinship terms are and were uninteresting data on which anthropologists are puzzlingly fixated. Like an anthropologist, and unlike a sociologist, Thomas considered kinship terminology before discussing sex or social rank. Moreover, his conception of "patterns of distinction" is closer to Robert Lowie's conceptions than to sociological work on stratification. The first three cultural domains Thomas compared in different cultures—couvade, personal names, and conceptions of twins—recur in anthropological discourse but not in sociological writing.

Like Dorsey's (1925) *Why We Behave Like Human Beings*, Thomas's book had considerable sales and went through many printings but had no discernible influence on social scientists (of any disciplinary allegiance). Although *Primitive Behavior* gathered up many pieces of cultural data from Thomas's vast reading and note taking, there is no theoretical innovation, and the empirical data are taken from clearly identified others. As Ellsworth Faris noted in his admiring review, "Even those concepts for which many of us are indebted to Thomas himself are largely neglected in the interpretation of this material. Scant mention is made of attitudes, or values, and the 'four wishes' seem to suffer from neglect. The 'definition of the situation' is . . . a 'definition' in only a metaphorical sense" (1937b:169–70).

Sociologists during the late 1930s were increasingly concerned about the validity of the kind of materials Thomas relied upon, and the epistemological critique that Herbert Blumer leveled against *The Polish Peasant* was extended to ethnographic inference by a number of sociologists (Blumer 1979).[1] There was no methodological discussion of how ethnographies were sampled for *Primitive Behavior*. Seemingly having abandoned the conceptual armaments of *The Polish Peasant* to collect Frazerian ethnographic trinkets, Thomas's book was of little use to sociologists. Anthropologists would seem to have been better prepared to follow the argument through the vast delta of lengthy quotations from ethnographies, but they ignored the book. It was not even reviewed in the *American Anthropologist*.

If Thomas's academic career had not been permanently disrupted by his scandalous firing in 1918, a revised version of his *Source Book* would probably have appeared during the early 1920s, along with other works of Boasian synthesis (see Darnell 1977).[2] By 1937, the time *Primitive Behavior* actually appeared, the Boasian message had been received and comparative work was more Durkheimian (influenced by Radcliffe-Brown), but less global.

Interdisciplinary Approaches to Personality

In addition to being concerned with topics mostly considered by anthropologists—such as kinship, language, "primitive" law, and sexuality, which were not generally discussed by sociologists contemporary to him—Thomas, from the teens of the century onward, was very interested in conceptions of personality and of social influences in personality development. There was little concerted attention given by anthropologists to personality before the mid-1920s, although the later popularity of "culture and personality" work obscures the earlier situation. In *The Polish Peasant* Thomas and Florian Znaniecki had discussed a typology of personalities and the sociocultural molding of impulses and temperaments. They wrote, "Social personality as a whole manifests itself only in the course of its total life and not at any particular moment of its life and is not a mere empirical manifestation of a timeless metaphysical essence, always the same, but is a continuous evolution in which nothing remains unchanged. . . . It is relatively easy to classify temperaments and characters, but this classification is entirely unproductive unless it is used as a mere preparation for the study of their evolution, where the aim is to determine human types as dynamic types, as types of development" (1927:1835–36).

As the leading figure in national research councils, Thomas dominated the symposia during the late 1920s from which "culture and personality" work derived. Together with Dummer, Thomas organized the Symposium on the Unconscious and presumably edited the resulting proceedings, but K. Koffka was credited on the title page (Koffka 1928; see Janowitz 1966:xvi–xvii). Platt (1992:29) quotes an undated letter in which Dummer declines to be listed as editor of the volume (on her rehabilitation of Thomas by contracting him to interpret case records of "unadjusted"/"delinquent" girls, see pp. 26–30). Platt also quotes a November 30, 1925 letter from Harriet Thomas to Dummer, crediting her "confidence in him and the backing you have given him [with] hav[ing] done more than anything to push back into their proper limbo the prejudices that interfered with his chance of being heard" and one from Miriam van Waters crediting her with "sav[ing] a splendid mind and to free it for the highest type of service" (28). Platt makes clear that Dummer's contributions to sociological research on delinquency and other social problems were not only financial. Thomas was also the dominant fomenter of interdisciplinary investigation of personality during the 1920s. Supported by Rockefeller Foundation funds, he planned to follow his earlier monumental work on Polish immigrants with a contrast between Swedish and Sicilian personality and culture, alongside his long-running analysis of Jewish immigrants. Plans for collaborative work between Gunnar and Alva Myrdal and Dorothy and W. I. Thomas, made just before the stock-market crash and subsequent international depression, were a victim of harder times. Only a brief discussion of Swedish pronoun avoidance in W. I. Thomas's *Primitive Behavior* (1937:84–85) along with D. Thomas's austere 1941 monograph on Swedish historical demography derived from the research in Sweden. Janowitz (1966:xxviii) and Bressler (1952) discuss the unpublished work W. I. Thomas did on Jewish American assimilation. As Faris said of the influence of Thomas on the quantitative work on attitudes done by Samuel Stouffer and Lewis Thurstone after Thomas had left Chicago: "Not that Thomas ever measured attitudes. He had no mathematics and came into contact with statistics through marriage. But only because of the work of Thomas did this development take place" (1951:877).

In the American Psychiatric Association colloquia on personality investigations, it was W. I. and Dorothy Thomas, rather than Sapir, who had plans for new research and the experience of working with life histories, including their recently completed *The Unadjusted Girl* (W. Thomas 1923). Edward Sapir, popularly conceived by anthropologists as the apostle of using life histories to analyze individual personality, had neither collected nor analyzed life history materials with which the Chicago sociologists' data could be compared at the start of the first colloquium (APA 1928:12; see chapter 10; Dollard 1935; Darnell 1986; Leeds-Hurwitz and Nyce 1986).

Thomas's opening statement to the first Colloquium on Personality Investigation sounded a call for a research program on rates of behavior that seems closer to John B. Watson and Ogburn than to the interpretation of life histories Thomas pioneered. He went out of his way to aver that "sociological journals suffer from a metaphysical-philosophical holdover and contain too much speculative essay writings" and that psychiatrists' publications "contain a considerable proportion of irresponsible, fantastic and incredible statements" (APA 1928:9–10). Given that "the incidence and character of mental disturbance among the races and nationalities" (8) was a Chicago preoccupation, it must have been the radical behaviorism that provoked from Robert Park, Thomas's ostensible disciple, the comment, "He called himself a sociologist, as he was talking here this morning, but he was certainly talking a language that was quite strange to me as a sociologist. I don't know what has happened to him" (22).[3]

Watson's influence is part of what had happened to Thomas in New York. Along with the influence of Ogburn directly and indirectly through Ogburn's student and collaborator, Dorothy Swaine Thomas, whom Thomas married, Leslie White recalled, "John B. Watson, the great 'behaviorist' of the 1920s, gave a course at the New School when I was there, and Thomas 'took' the course just as I did—for which I loved him" (White:Fred Mathews, November 29, 1964). He took Watson quiet seriously, as few psychologists at the time did (see Samelson 1981), and, surely, some of the reason for a shift from a source book on social origins to a compendium of primitive *behavior* can be attributed to a behaviorist conversion achieved personally by Watson.[4] In the second colloquium (in 1929) Dorothy Thomas reported, "My work has been concerned entirely with overt behavior in the field of social interaction. We are approaching the problem of personality as manifested by the individual differences in overt behavior reactions in social situations [specifically, nursery schools]" (APA 1930:20).

Unlike other participants who studied pathologies (e.g. Harry Stack Sullivan, Ernest Burgess, and Clifford Shaw) or were bystanders to research on personality (e.g. Sapir), she was studying "normal" children's early socialization in a resolutely behaviorist manner: "The problem is to select specific overt behavior acts and record their recurrence in all sorts of situations. . . . We are not concerned with the individual's own record of his inner life" (APA 1930:23). In his statement of his research, W. I. Thomas also stressed "behavior" and "habits" and recast *The Polish Peasant* as showing that "the more rapidly people change their habits in a new habitat, the more disorganization ensues" (42). He also revealed his plan "to make a study of behavior problems, especially [those related to] the child and crime," contrasting Sweden and Italy (42). He did not accept the early determination of personality proclaimed by Sigmund Freud (and his American disciples), and it seems likely that the research on childhood behavior by the Thomases during the late 1920s and early 1930s was undertaken at least in part to refute Freudian dogma. Morris Janowitz's characterization of Thomas as "fiercely anti-Freudian" (1966:xxii) strikes me as overstated, but Thomas's appreciation for the play of Freud's mind was akin to Ogburn's. (For a view of Thomas more sympathetic to Freud, see Znaniecki 1948:765–67.) Indeed, Thomas's comment on Freud's *Leonardo* as "artistic phantasizing" (in Janowitz 1966:152) repeats Ogburn telling Sapir about the book a decade earlier: "It is truly wonderful (not as science necessarily—but for the insight)" (Ogburn:Sapir, December 31, 1917, National Museum of Man Archives, Ottawa).

Thomas could not accept a view in which motivation or personality is determined in early childhood. During the second personality colloquium he expressed his "distrust [for] the finality of the assumption that behavior is structuralized exclusively on the infantile level. . . . While the infantile period is very properly very heavily weighted now, I think it is disproportionately weighted" (APA 1930:41). Later he reiterated, "The evolution of personality should be continuous and stabilization should approximate the point of death rather than the point of maturity" (99).

Thomas himself was far from being permanently set in his ideas and impermeable to later effects. Another of the new stimulations for Thomas in the late 1920s was the real organizer of the personality colloquia, Harry Stack Sullivan. Along with almost every other American social scientist interested in the possible contributions of psychiatry to understanding normal human behavior (e.g., Sapir, Harold Lasswell, Leonard Cottrell, Bingham Dai), Thomas was intrigued by Sullivan, who was, like himself, prominent in national forums without having any academic affiliation (see Perry 1982). Thomas's association with another major figure in the rapprochement between social science and psychiatry, Adolf Meyer, dated back to courses at Chicago from Meyer on brain physiology before the turn of the century.[5] Whether Meyer's evolving social psychiatry influenced Thomas's focus on personality forming over the entire course of life, or whether Meyer was influenced by Thomas's thought, cannot easily be unraveled. Similarly, parallels with Alfred Adler's conceptions are "very pronounced and not likely to be a case of wholly independent development," nor of some general zeitgeist (Coser 1977:545).[6]

During his visiting appointment at Harvard (1936–37), Thomas taught a sociology seminar on depth psychology, but as Leslie White observed of Thomas's classes at the New School, "He did not teach anthropology or sociology or psychology or any other ology. He taught what W. I. Thomas had done and thought and wondered about wherever human beings were involved. He exhibited things in a way which made you see things you had never seen before. He made you think about things in novel ways" (White:Fred Mathews, November 29, 1964).

Dorothy Thomas (1952a:664) similarly noted that her husband's interests were so catholic that their work *The Child in America* (1928) "might properly have been called 'The Child and Other Matters in America and Elsewhere.'" What systematicness there is in *The Polish Peasant* must owe much to Znaniecki.

During the second personality colloquium (in 1929), Thomas expressed his view of a need for experiments with young children to get some order out of the chaos of various psychoanalytical claims and reformulate hypotheses (APA 1930:120). Although Dorothy Thomas did not continue such research after taking an appointment at Berkeley, the Yale Institute for Human Relations, which they left, did (see Darnell 1990a; Samelson 1985).[7]

Thomas is tangled in the roots not only of "symbolic interactionism" in sociology, and in measuring attitudes (see E. Faris 1937b:577),[8] but also in the Yale behaviorist work of John Dollard, John and Beatrice Whiting, and others associated with the Institute for Human Relations. He may also have been involved with the pre-behaviorist George Peter Murdock project of sorting through ethnographic reports that later became the Human Relations Area Files at Yale, as well as with Boas and two generations of his students. He was a recurrent participant in the Edward Sapir/John Dollard seminar on the impact of culture on personality at Yale (which he may originally have proposed to Rockefeller funders; see Darnell 1986). Although it is difficult to determine where the center of Thomas's thought was, its peripheries were everywhere in interwar American social sciences.

10

The Postmaturity of Sociolinguistics

Edward Sapir and Personality Studies in the
Chicago Department of Sociology

> An academic discipline is at once a group of men in persisting social rela-
> tions and a method of investigation. . . . The two kinds of relations, social
> and methodological, are mutually influential, but neither determines the
> other.
>
> —ROBERT REDFIELD, "Relations of Anthropology to the Social Sciences
> and to the Humanities" (1953:728)

In launching the sociology of science from the rostrum of an American
Sociological Association (ASA) presidential address in 1957, Robert Merton focused the specialty on the timing of discoveries. Merton's earlier
discussions of the sociology of knowledge (e.g., 1941, 1945) had drawn
out implications of the notion of zeitgeist, and still earlier work with Sorokin (1937) had dealt with sociological aspects of time and the hospi-
tality of a zeitgeist for some theories and discoveries rather than others,
but these earlier works did not inaugurate a research tradition as the
1957 address did (see J. Cole and Zuckerman 1975). In the decade that
followed, Merton (1961, 1963, 1968) pursued specification of simulta-
neity of discoveries and began to discuss "premature" discoveries (also
see Westrum 1982), that is, theoretical formulations or empirical discoveries that were too far "ahead of time" to be understood or built upon
by sciences preoccupied with other problems and proposed solutions.
In 1974 Harriet Zuckerman presented the first, fascinating fruits of the
research of a multidisciplinary team of scholars (including Merton) attempting to define empirically the other logical category to accompany
on time and early: late. "Postmature contributions," according to Zuckerman, are "those which competent judges say could have been made

substantially sooner if only their cognitive ingredients were required for the outcome" (Zuckerman 1974). As an operational definition, this leads all too easily to "credentialism": Who is "competent" to judge? And what if other judges disagree? Rather than be caught up in such squabbles, I would suggest that "postmaturity" is an essentially contestable interpretation for which there is no final solution. The concept may, however, be valuable if the explanations for cases of postmaturity suggest that scientific progress is not linear and broaden the understanding of the role of noncognitive processes in the history of science. Responses merely to the provocation of asserting a specific "might have been" may yield interesting historical data. One generalization Zuckerman made from the case of recombinant bacteria—"The opportunity to work on high risk investigations is not distributed equally, but falls to the comparatively well established in science or those in deviant career paths" (1974)—makes the case of postmaturity to be discussed here all the more striking, because it involved central figures in interwar American social science, some of whose career paths were quite deviant (Robert Park, W. I. Thomas, Ellsworth Faris, Harry Stack Sullivan, and to a lesser extent, Edward Sapir), who clearly could "afford" to innovate, both because they frequently did and because social science disciplines were less ossified into distinct entities during the 1920s.

The postmaturity problem is that given the importance of language in the work of George Herbert Mead and the "symbolic interaction" that claimed intellectual paternity from him, the interest evidenced by Robert Park on retention of immigrant languages (namely, non-English presses in the United States), the earlier anthropological interest of W. I. Thomas in language (discussed in chapter 9), and the location in the Chicago sociology department of the scholar to whom the founders of sociolinguistics accord their intellectual paternity, some convergence would seem to have been possible at Chicago in the late 1920s, rather than involving Sapirian anthropologists and Everett Hughes during the mid-1960s (see Murray 1994b:310–14, on the Social Science Research Council Sociolinguistics Committee). The explanation proffered here is that although Chicago sociologists' work influenced later "culture and personality" work in anthropology by way of Sapir's exposure to their work, Sapir failed to show Chicago sociologists how to analyze language variety. To claim that there was a possibility of convergence requires showing that Chicago sociologists were interested in language, culture, and personality. This demonstration deconstructs "the Chicago School" into three groups: (1) social psychologists led by Ellsworth Faris and inspired by George Herbert Mead, (2) the followers of William Fielding Ogburn pursuing cultural explanations of social change and of mental illness, and (3) the urban ethnography tradition usually traced Thomas-Park-Burgess-Hughes. Faris and Ogburn were in some sense Boasian; Thomas was influenced by Boas and some of his students; Park and Hughes were at least interested in anthropological work and directly interested in social consequences and determinants of language usage. Moreover, Chicago sociologists were quite familiar with psychoanalytic work, Sapir's other major interest at the time he was in Chicago (1925–31) and beyond. Thus, the "intellectual environment" of the Chicago sociology department cannot be considered to have been hostile to Sapir's intellectual roots. The Rockefeller money that paid to transplant Sapir to Chicago was given to foster a synthesis of social sciences at Chicago and provided for the institutional basis of the desired synthesis. As will be shown, however, Sapir was personally close to the leader of the group least likely to develop sociolinguistics and pushed for the institutionalization of a fourth group in a separate department of anthropology.

The first obstacle to conceiving a real possibility for convergence is to overcome now-current conceptions about what is sociology and what anthropology. Later preoccupations of and differences between the professions of sociology and anthropology obscure the location and even the nature of earlier disciplinary channels. To many, it will come as a surprise to see in table 6 the extent to which works by anthropologists before midcentury were reviewed in sociology journals and the extent to which prominent anthropologists published in sociology journals, including the first and most prestigious one, edited by the Chicago sociology department, the *American Journal of Sociology* (AJS). It was in its pages that Sapir (1924) took a first stab at theorizing "culture," one at odds with the relativistic "shreds and patches" Boasian orthodoxy. Moreover, American sociologists, before American anthropologists, were interested in what would later be called acculturation and intergroup contact throughout the world (if especially in U.S. cities). Chicago sociologists pioneered ethnography at a time that Boasian anthropologists were still eliciting idealized memories of what indigenous cultures had been like a generation or more before the time of fieldwork and were mapping distributions of cultural traits to infer prehistoric tribal move-

TABLE 6. Number of Articles by Some Leading Anthropologists and of Reviews in the *American Anthropologist* and Core American Sociology Journals, 1913–1950

	Articles				Reviews			
	AA	*AJS*	*ASR*	*SF*	*AA*	*AJS*	*ASR*	*SF*
Benedict	7	1	2	3	1	3	2	
Devereux	2	1	2					
Dollard	2	1	3	2	1	6		
Goldenweiser	9	2	1	3	1			
Hallowell	12	1	1	1	1			
Herskovits	9	6	1	7	10	5	6	3
Kroeber	26	3	12	5	5			
Linton	20	1	1	7	3	5	2	
Lowie	20	5	12	1	5	2		
Mead	4	5	10	6	4	6		
Murdock	2	2	2	1	1			
Opler	16	2	2	2	1	1		
Powdermaker	1	1	1	3	1	2	3	
Provinse	1	1						
Redfield	5	5	2	2	3	4	4	2
Sapir	17	3	7	2				
Wissler	4	3	5	1	2			

Note: *AA = American Anthropologist*, 1913–48; *AJS = American Journal of Sociology*, 1913–48; *ASR = American Sociological Review*, 1936–51; *SF = Social Forces*, 1924–53

ments and contacts (see Sapir 1916). In particular, the ethnographic technique anthropologists view the post-Canadian Sapir as championing, the individual life history, was a well-established tool of Chicago sociologists (see W. Thomas and Znaniecki 1927; Krueger 1925; Cavan 1926; Shaw 1930, 1931). "By 1929 a total of 75 articles and books in sociology dealing with life histories had been published" (Hinkle and Hinkle 1954:24). The "intellectual leader" of the first generation of Chicago sociologists, W. I. Thomas asserted that "personal life-records, as complete as possible, constitute the perfect type of sociological materials. If social science has to use other materials at all it is . . . a defect, not an advantage of our present sociological methods" (W. Thomas and Znaniecki 1927:1831–32).

The "intellectual leader" of the second generation of Chicago sociologists, Robert Park, recalled (from retirement in a letter of October 12, 1938, to Louis Wirth), "My studies of personality are mainly based upon life histories of a generally psychoanalytic bias. These histories are designed to throw light on the nature of the intimate and relatively closed moral and personal order to which the individual person is most responsive, and they throw light also on the processes of acculturation which take place within the limits of such a minor [sub]cultural unit."

Given that Sapir had not evidenced any interest in the method of life history before joining the Chicago department, it is plausible that his later championing of the genre derived from exposure to sociologists' use, quite likely from his first summer in Chicago, during which the department's Summer Institute had as its theme "personality" (Bulmer 1984:116), while Sapir was teaching the psychology of culture.

Long before studies of either acculturation or contemporary communities were considered legitimate in American anthropology (see the famous 1936 tabled motion to permit the former to appear in the *American Anthropologist*; Lowie 1959:32), Chicago sociologists were producing both—and with a focus on individuals quite like that Sapir came to advocate. Indeed, the keen interest of Chicago sociologists in individuals (whether Park's marginal man or symbolic interactionists' concern with the genesis of the self) seems to have been grounds for the suspicions of sociologists elsewhere that Chicagoans were insufficiently sociologistic, indeed that they were camouflaged psychologists. Suspicions of such treason seem to have been involved in the organizational revolution within the American Sociological Society during the 1930s against the Chicago department's dominance (Lengermann 1979; Kuklick 1973). That such suspicions were not unmerited is evidenced by the Chicago journal's contents during the 1930s: when AJS ceased to be the official journal of the society, psychiatrists filled the pages heretofore filled with publications by non-Chicago sociologist (Kuklick 1973:5, 10), and "in the AJS from 1895 to 1930 the only topic attracting an ever greater percentage of articles was 'Personality—the Individual and the Person.' . . . As Louis Wirth said, the relationship of the individual to the group had become "the central problem of sociological theory" (Kuklick 1973: 11–12).

Moreover, the social psychology advanced by the third generation of Chicago sociologists followed Charles Horton Cooley rather than George Herbert Mead in rejecting the "superorganic" (paralleling Sapir's rejection of Kroeber's "superorganic" sociologism): "It was in the aftermath of this political defeat of the Chicago group that Blumer (1937) officially christened and launched his 'symbolic interactionism.' . . . [In common with Sapir] Blumer finds the locus of every social act in the individual. . . . Blumer's individual remains absolutely sacrosanct and detached from any degree of social determination" (J. Lewis and Smith 1980:252, 173).

The chairman of the department Sapir joined, Ellsworth Faris, had prolonged field experience in a functioning primitive society and had defended (against French "theory of primitive mind" (in the singular); Lucien Lévy-Bruhl) "the mental capacity of savages" with, among other cudgels, a morphological analysis of Bantu languages.[1] Though no one else provided so empirical an exemplar of Boasian "scientific antiracism" as did Faris (1918, 1925) in the pages of AJS, several Boasians had there explained the goals and achievements of Boasian anthropology prior to Sapir's Chicago arrival (A. Kroeber 1918; Lowie 1918; and, most extravagantly, Goldenweiser 1925; see the AJS columns of table 6). Faris repeatedly attacked presumptions of racial incapacity/stasis, drawing on Bantu responses to European contact, and prefigured Evans-Pritchard in noting that "to say that the culture is magical does not mean that all things are held to be animate or endowed with mystical power. . . . Most of their [Bantu peoples] life goes on with the aid of commonsense technique. . . . [Moreover,] among modern peoples it can be shown that fixed ideas exist and collective representations abound" (E. Faris 1937a:243–45).

With his withering critiques of Levy-Bruhl's "mentalité chez société inferieur" and McDougal's instinct explanations, Faris (1931) also took on the universality of the Oedipal complex, arguing it was inapplicable where fathers and uncles are permissive and diffuse authority figures and where the mother may have a succession of spouses and/or where there is a bevy of co-wives. "The psychological basis of the family is a more variable phenomenon than is usually assumed" (219) was a conclusion congenial to Boas and shared by his students. Indeed, Faris drew frequently on Lowie's writings to bolster his relativizing.

Moreover, it was Faris who pressed to build anthropology within the department. As Odum recalled, "The department was designated 'Sociology and Anthropology.' Frederick Starr was the lone anthropologist, [and although a popular lecturer] out of favor with the administration and embittered. When he did retire, the president was quite content to let anthropology fade out of the picture, but Faris busied himself, securing Ralph Linton [briefly], then F.C. Cole" (1951:182), a Boas student who, together with Faris, then successfully pushed to change the explicit policy of the Laura Spelman Rockefeller Memorial (the predominant source for social science funding prior to the Depression) against providing support for new positions. The sum of $13,500 was appropriated for Sapir to be appointed associate professor at Chicago (Bulmer and Bulmer 1981:389).

As discussed in chapter 9, W. I. Thomas, the real founder of "the Chicago school" (third PhD from the department, 1896), listed Franz Boas as having more influence on him than his teachers of sociology, was on terms of mutual regard with Boasians (Kroeber:Thomas, June 6, 1910; T. Kroeber 1977 interview; Lowie 1945:416), and drew heavily on them in his 1909 *Source Book*.

Even the arch-advocate of quantification in American sociology, William F. Ogburn, who arrived in Chicago two years after Sapir, was a Boasian intimate (see the "anthropology picnic" picture facing p. 82 in Goldfrank 1978) and particularly close to Lowie. As long ago as Becker and Barnes it was recognized that a "result of the training provided by the Columbia [sociology] department was the close relationship it established with anthropology. Although Giddings himself made little use of the great advances in ethnographic and ethnological knowledge achieved by Boas, the greater number of Giddings' students and associates assimilated enough to start cultural sociology on its way. Ogburn, Willey, Chapin, and many others arrived at the conviction that the products of man's hands and brain, i.e., material and non-material culture, are far more important than the climatic, topographic and biological factors once rated so highly" (1938:977–78).

Abel (1930:741) lumped Ogburn together with Wissler and Goldenweiser as engaged in what Abel considered intrinsically impossible, a cultural sociology synthesizing "school of Boas"–style descriptions into generalized explanations. Decades later, Huff similarly maintained that Ogburn was too influenced by Boasians' (namely, Lowie, Kroeber, Wissler) conception of culture, about which he "threatened" to write a book (Ogburn:Lowie, March 7, 1917), so that "only by breaking out of that scheme was he able to resolve the conceptual contradictions of his theory of social change" (Huff 1973:272). Ogburn arrived at Columbia about the time Sapir left, and they did not meet until 1915, when Sapir was working with Ishi in San Francisco. Sapir knew Giddings well enough for Giddings to approach Albion Small about publishing "The Social Organization of West Coast Tribes" in AJS (Small:Sapir, January 7, 1915).

Ogburn began writing Sapir about psychoanalysts with whom Sapir was unfamiliar (e.g., Jung in a September 8, 1915, letter; Adler, July 9, 1917). Ogburn closely followed anthropological literature (Sapir:Ogburn, June 30, 1917), taught extension courses on anthropology (Ogburn:Sapir, February 9, 1916), at least thought about doing fieldwork in Washington beyond a three-week foray to the Hopis, and contemplated writing the already mentioned book on culture. Thus he could be as skeptical as Sapir of psychoanalysts' forays into explaining mythology and the rituals of primitive peoples. Ogburn also seems to have been as able as Sapir to regard Freud as brilliant, insightful, and unsound all at the same time (in telling Sapir about Freud's [1916] analysis of Leonardo da Vinci in 1917 letters), quite out of keeping with the image now dominant of a positivist Ogburn. Moreover, his interest in psychoanalysis was sufficiently deep and sustained for him to serve as president of the Chicago Psychoanalytical Society (H. Hughes 1959:2). On a European sojourn earlier, Ogburn had seen much of figures as prominent and diverse as Marcel Mauss and Viennese psychoanalysts, including "the great Freud himself" (Ogburn:Lowie, March 28, 1926). Both Sapir and Ogburn wrote Lowie of their liking for each other (1929 letters in the Lowie collection), and two of the thirty-three works in Sapir's list of suggested readings for his course The Impact of Culture on Personality (undated list from David Mandelbaum, in author's possession) were by Ogburn. Insofar as there was a rift between ethnographers and quantifiers at Chicago, Sapir was on the side of Robert Park and Park's many students, opposed to the psychologists led by Thurstone. One of Ogburn's students, Philip Hauser (1977 interview), recalled Park emerging from a meeting in which Thurstone had described his strategy for keeping up on the literature—namely, to read tables and skip over everything else in journals. Park growled that this was like a child being toilet trained, looking through books upside down, or looking only for pictures. Ogburn's interests in psychoanalysis and ethnography, in contrast, were keen. Work by students of Ogburn on rates of psychoses was explicitly comparative. Ellen Winston (1934) argued that the Samoan rates reported by (Ogburn's former assistant) Margaret Mead were as high as those in the rural United States. Winston (1935) argued against a constant increase in rates of mental illness with increasing social complexity. Robert Faris (1934) marshaled what information about schizophrenia he could find (Mead again, his father's observations, and Seligman's) to try to assess the cross-cultural validity of a relationships between cultural isolation and schizmogenesis.[2] John Dollard also attempted to see "the psychotic person culturally" in 1934.

Ogburn was one of the first American social scientists to see relevance in psychoanalysis for both the concepts and the methods of would-be human sciences (see 1922, 1927). He not only preceded Sapir into this discourse but also had a much clearer idea that the implications of psychoanalysis included undercutting the omniscient observer. While Sapir was more than willing to apply Jungian labels to whomever he encountered, it seems to me that he was as unwilling as Margaret Mead to consider his countertransferences to native informants. Even after he realized that "psychology" was what Thurstone and Hull did and what he was interested in was some kinds of "psychiatry," it does not seem to me that Sapir subjected his own field methods to the kind of psychoanalytical scrutiny Ogburn applied to his own.

It might also be mentioned that Sapir (1930) carried Ogburn's discussion (published in 1928 but laid out as early as a March 21, 1915, letter to Robert Lowie) of the shift of American families from production units to "companionship" to a nonprofessional audience. The shift/decline of family functions was a major Chicago focus, central to John Dollard's MA and PhD theses and to such later Chicago syntheses of family theory as Burgess and Locke (1945) and Ogburn (1955). While we might consider "convergence" of interest on psychiatry, that Sapir was influenced by Ogburn (and probably by a student of both men, John Dollard, as well) seems to me indubitable, if not earthshaking. Sapir only occasionally adumbrated the Margaret Mead of *And Keep Your Powder Dry* (1942), pontificating about American culture, delaying the reaction by sociologists to that kind of impressionistic generalization that occurred after the Second World War (see chapter 11).

The discussion of changing functions of the family should suffice to demonstrate that Ogburn's interest in social change was not confined to easily measurable quantitative trends. The plea not to leave the rich materials of social history to historians in the last article he wrote (Ogburn 1959) should be recalled as well as his famous conception of "culture lag."

In addition to being the bastion of ethnography in American social science during the 1920s, Chicago was also the institution at which George Herbert Mead (1913, 1924) had been formulating a theory of the genesis of the self a decade before Freud even began to theorize about the ego and its genesis. Faris, himself a student of Mead and Dewey and with them as unflagging a critic as Franz Boas of the use of "instincts" or racial inferiority in explanations (see E. Faris 1922, 1937a; R. Faris 1967:92–94), directed his own sociology students to Mead (J. Lewis and Smith 1978). Two of them, Herbert Blumer and Leonard Cottrell, extended Mead's conception of socialization to general theories of interaction.

While at Chicago, Sapir, too, became increasingly interested in the genesis of personality. Indeed, he published the only one of his papers that comes close to suggesting a method for studying any aspect of personality in AJS (Sapir 1927c, discussed below). Furthermore, through his Chicago colleagues' connections, Sapir was able to become involved in national efforts to foster the study of personality in relation to culture that were pressed by W. I. Thomas. As was noted in chapter 9, in the American Psychiatric Association colloquia on personality investigations it was Thomas rather than Sapir who had plans for new research and the experience of working with life histories. Sapir had neither collected nor analyzed life history materials with which the Chicago sociologists (Shaw, Burgess, and Park, as well as Thomas) could be compared at the start of the first colloquium. Despite his vicarious exposure to work on life histories at Chicago and his programmatic exhortations to focus on individuals, Sapir never did publish an analysis of an individual (cf. Dai 1941, 1944; R. Faris 1944 with Sapir 1938a, his unanalytic foreword to Dyk, *Son of Old Man Hat*).

The "Chicago School" Conception of Language

Although quite ignorant of linguistics (which it must be remembered had the most tenuous development as a distinct science during the 1920s), Chicago sociologists were very interested in language—particularly in how language is involved in primary socialization (a concern of Mead and Faris and also of Charles Horton Cooley, with whom Sapir exchanged books in 1922 and whom he visited in Ann Arbor the next year). During the early 1920s Park was also much interested in immigrant groups' language retention (Park 1920, 1924). (The psycholinguistics and sociology of language that have developed during the past half century have been preoccupied, respectively, with language acquisition and language loyalty.)

The "Green Bible," as Chicago sociology students dubbed the 1921 Park-Burgess textbook, took the speech community as the primary collectivity larger than the family (50, 458) and foreshadowed what has been called the "Sapir-Whorf hypothesis" by noting, "There is a petrified philosophy in language" (169). There is also in Park and Burgess (169–74) a discussion of the evolution (namely, simplification in form) of lexicon and of writing quite similar to Sapir's ([1921] in Mandelbaum 1949:382–83). In addition, there is (what was even then) a wholly spurious rejection of the neogrammarian explanation of sound change. Although specifically building on methodological principles derived from Boas and Lowie,[3] Park and Burgess (1921:18–20) followed Oertel (1904) in accepting Gabriel "Tarde's theory of imitation as an alternative explanation to that offered by Wundt for 'the striking uniformity of sound changes' which students of language have discovered" (Park and Burgess 1921:22).[4]

In E. Faris 1937a:158 there is a rejection of elements smaller than the word that would have seemed even more wrongheaded to Sapir. The point, however, is that there was a clear interest in explaining how language makes social interaction possible. Sapir could convincingly defend phonemics and neogrammarian claims; indeed, his clearest demonstration of sound change was published in a casebook the impetus for which came from Ogburn (Sapir 1931). However, there is no record of Sapir trying to correct the views disseminated by the "Green Bible" earlier or more directly. Neither does the fascination with the Chinese language common to Park and Sapir seem to have led to discussion between the two scholars, or between Sapir and Park's Chinese students, who included one who wrote a thesis on the history of Chinese characters (Tan 1925) and another who wrote a thesis on glossolalia (Dai 1932) at Park's suggestion (Dai, quoted in Rauschenbush 1979:105). Dai, who was the only contributor to the basic culture and personality anthology (Kluckhohn and Murray 1948) to cite Sapir, after receiving a PhD in sociology at Chicago was analyzed by Sullivan and was a member of Sapir's culture and personality seminar at Yale. He went on to pioneer work on social psychiatry, strongly influenced by Sullivan (see Dai 1941, 1952). Dai reported that Park "unreservedly encouraged my interest in personality" (1970:xxii).

Speech and Personality

> The human personality always grows up in association and communication. . . . There is no such thing as language in general. . . . Society does not mold the individual, for molding is too passive a term. Individuals do not produce a culture, for collective life has its own laws and its own procedures. Society and the individual, culture and personality: both are useful and necessary abstractions.
>
> —ELLSWORTH FARIS, *The Nature of Human Nature* (1937a:158, 215, 238)

Sapir's famous paper "Speech as a Personality Trait," published in AJS in 1927, has as little to do with rigorous analysis of linguistic materials as the musings about vocalizations in the evolution of interaction in Park and Burgess. There is not even anecdotal illustration of how to distinguish what is individual from what is social in speech. Indeed, rather than exemplifying how to study a personality by his/her speech, Sapir devoted most of his second major paper in AJS to warning against using characteristics of speech to judge personality characteristics! For instance, Sapir argues that one should not conclude Japanese have less affect than Italians by comparing their intonations: any indication of personality afforded by an individual's usual range of intonation must come from contrast to the normal intonational habit of one's speech community (1927c:539). In other words, compare the Neapolitan to other Neapolitans, not to someone from Tokyo. The analyst must know what the social norms of production are in a community before distinguishing allowable departures from the anomalous utterances that mark personality. "You cannot draw up an absolute psychological scale for voice, intonation, rhythm, speed, or pronunciation of vowels and consonants without in every case ascertaining the social background of speech habit. It is always the variation that matters, never the objective behavior as such" (542). At each level of speech, Sapir stressed, one must understand the background social pattern before one can recognize what is significantly personal. Among all the (eminently Boasian) exhortations of caution, nowhere in the article did Sapir provide sociologists any guidance in determining what should be taken as the social group or the speech community for comparison. He could not point to "baseline" data from any speech community to which individual variation could be contrasted and did not concern himself with who was going to collect the data or with how it should be collected.

The article warns against facile personality typifications, especially intergroup stereotypes reinforced by group speech patterns. Though we know of Sapir's interest in the study of personality, this now-famous paper is—in common with much Boasian discourse—far more concerned with telling the analyst how not to proceed than with telling one how to proceed in distinguishing the social from the personal. Nor is there any promise of what successful methods would yield—what one might learn after avoiding all the traps of confusing personality with mere group habits. The paper is not an exemplar. No one's personality is illuminated. Moreover, the features or "levels" of speech—the voice, voice dynamics, pronunciation, vocabulary, and style—are discussed so vaguely that no linguist in 1927, not even one ready to extend the method of phonemic analysis to such phenomena, and still less any 1927 sociologist could have followed the program to study personal variation within a speech community. Although now we can easily read into the paper prescription of an emic analysis of differences within a speech community, Sapir did not explain to sociologists how sounds are patterned (Sapir 1925), nor did he explain how the very recent triumph of phonemics could be recapitulated in analyzing idiolects. He was able to explain the difference between phonemic analysis and purely acoustical measurements of differences in a nontechnical manner for a nonspecialist audience. Indeed, in the same year, in his paper for the symposium on the unconscious, he did exactly that. Any chance of sociologists taking up the research depended on Sapir introducing them to phonemics, because three (or four) of the five levels of speech he discusses are phonological, and then as now, sociologists are not notable for any ability or training in analyzing phonological differences. Although this paper has had enduring influence among linguistically trained scholars interested in personality, it has had no discernible influence in the discipline of the journal in which it was published. As an exemplar for sociologists of how to do the kind of research advocated, Sapir 1927c was a failure. The failure was not remedied by discussion of Radin's materials in AJS (Sapir 1927b) either.

Life Histories Purged of Linguistic Data

What might appear to be a source of data for distinguishing what is individual personality from what is culturally standard is the corpus of life histories of persons from thoroughly studied cultures. As stressed earlier, Chicago sociologists pioneered such elicitation and actually analyzed the material they gathered rather than merely passing it on as necessarily valid narrative. As Leeds-Hurwitz and Nyce (1986) noted, sociologists and psychologists routinely sought to assess the authenticity of reports in life histories by interviewing family members and other observers, that is, what the individual said was only part of a case history, while anthropologists presented personal narratives alone and uncritically. They exemplified Renato Rosaldo's (1976:147) apt characterization: "Most anthropologists have assumed that the life history is a natural and universal narrative form. If crudely unmasked it might not be too much of a parody to say that the prevailing anthropological view is as follows: place a tape-recorder in front of Mr. Non-literate Everyman and he will tell the 'real truth' about his life."

Dollard (1935) analyzed two life histories published by Chicago sociologists. This student of Ogburn and Sapir, who would have a major impact on American psychology and community studies, could find no Native American life history to analyze, nearly two decades after Sapir's rejection of a "superorganic."

The genre of life history that did develop without Sapir's leadership systematically edits out not only individual speech style but all traces of oral production. As Kluckhohn (1943:268) wrote in an acute analysis of the problem endemic to the genre that obstructed any fine-grained analysis, "The serious student wants to know at first-hand on what subjects the Hopi did tiresomely repeat himself. Every omission by the editor, every stylistic clarification takes us one more step away from what Don actually said. The specification of the role of the investigator also leaves something to be desired."

Kluckhohn (1943) also tackled the problem of assessing what was culturally typical, what was individually variant about a Hopi who would produce a life history. In contrast, on the two occasions Sapir wrote about Native American autobiographies—his 1927 AJS review of Radin's *Crashing Thunder* and his 1938 foreword to Dyk—he did not make any attempt to point out what was individual personality distinct from cultural replication in the documents. In all the years after his critique of the "superorganic" he not only failed to gather any data about any individual, but he also failed to analyze data gathered by others.

In practice Sapir was quite ready to reify "the language" (see chapter 2) and "the personality," while critical of reifying "the culture" (and "the society"). All of these would seem to be "metaphors," "convenient abstractions," patterns abstracted from (the flux of) behavior or analysts' "conventions" (1938b). It is difficult to believe that Sapir failed to notice that personality is also a hypostatization. Yet he could write, "There is **never** a serious difficulty in principle in imputing to the stream of his experiences that causative quality which we take for granted in the physical universe" (in Mandelbaum 1949:576, emphasis added). In contrast, Ellsworth Faris repeatedly stressed that not just culture and society but also language and personality are abstractions. Another prominent sociologist who extended the Sapirian kind of critique of "the superorganic" to "the personality" was the coauthor of *The Polish Peasant*, Florian Znaniecki (1938, 1942), whose critique of anthropologists reifying personality applies as well to Sapir's musings as to Sapir's student Morris Opler's Apache ethnography: "No individual can experience and exact more than a small part of the culture in which he shares; nor is any life history ever fully integrated—any more than a culture is. As an individual performs different social roles in successive periods of his life or during the same period in different social circles, in each role a different fragment and aspect of the culture enters the range of his active experience" (Znaniecki 1942:725). Similarly, Robert Park (1973 [1927]:255) took from William James the view that "the universe is not a closed system [society] and every individual, having his[/her] own peculiar experience, has some insight into the world that no other mind could have. The real world is the experience of actual men and women and not abbreviated and shorthand description that we call knowledge."

For Chicago sociologists (including Ogburn, Mead, and Faris, as well as Park, Burgess, Wirth, and Thomas) the social/cultural less-than-total determination of individuals was the precondition of innovation. Along with such catastrophic cultural contacts as conquests and large-scale population migration, individual innovation was the mechanism of social change (in contrast to the stasis glorified by functionalists as well as by the Sumner tradition and by nineteenth-century social evolutionisms).

In subsequent decades, not only within the Chicago tradition (Lloyd Warner, Everett Hughes, their student Erving Goffman, and Herbert

Blumer and his many followers) but within the rival Harvard-Columbia tradition (Robert Merton, Talcott Parsons, Robert Bales, and the many students of each), the multiplicity of roles rather than a static personality has been the heuristic for work on interaction, socialization, and even "collective behavior." Hallowell (1954:701; 1955:77) generalized that "personality" could not be regarded as a domain distinguished in all cultures, and in his Huxley lecture of 1938 Marcel Mauss suggested that, even in Western Europe, a psychological being was not conceived before Fichte. Thus, "far from being a primordial, innate idea clearly inscribed since Adam in the deepest part of our being, we find the category of the self still being slowly erected, clarified, specified, and identified with self-knowledge, with the psychological consciousness, almost into our own times" (Mauss 1979:87).

Departmental Fission

According to the folklore of anthropology, Cole and Sapir thought sociologists were unfairly harsh to Leslie White when he defended his (to the sociologists, atheoretical) dissertation. An inversion of the myth is propounded by Carneiro (1981:213), namely that Faris rejected White's thesis proposal as too theoretical. Both accounts attribute the fission of an anthropology department to reverberations from White's treatment. The available documentation is a letter from Fay-Cooper Cole to acting university president Frederic Woodward (November 26, 1928) proposing a separate department, that is, a year and a half after White's defense and longer still after his thesis proposal could have been considered, not exactly a fast and furious response. Moreover, the letter goes out of the way to aver "our relations with Sociology have been most cordial and we feel especially indebted to Prof. Faris for his lively interest and help. As a matter of fact, we have delayed several months in bringing this matter to your attention because of the feeling of indebtedness to Prof. Faris and our reluctance to do anything which might reflect on him. In this request for a separate department, nothing of a personal nature is involved."

I would not want to underestimate the amount of duplicity of which academics are capable nor the tenure of Sapir's grudges. However, I do not think Cole was particularly duplicitous nor prone to nurse grudges. Both Cole and Sapir were ambitious and therefore inclined to want a fiefdom of their own. Another possible motivation is Sapir's seeming distaste for competition. The attenuation of his claims to be a poet once he was somewhere where there were poets is one indication that he preferred to shine alone. Similarly, rather than working with colleagues who had advanced ethnography, the collection and analysis of life histories, or the application of psychoanalytic principles, he withdrew to a smaller pond. He could easily outshine Cole, not so easily the Chicago sociologists.

On the basis of what Cole, Redfield, and Ogburn told him, Fred Eggan (personal communication, 1984) suggested that the real reason had nothing in particular to do with Leslie White's treatment or with Sapir's intolerance for competition and was obscured by what is available in the official record quoted above. Rather, he maintained, the proposal to break off was a preemptive move to avert a plan to reorganize the sociology department into "cores," which would have distributed the three anthropologists into three different cores (Sapir to social psychology, Redfield to social organization, Cole to comparative sociology), shattering the growing anthropology molecule into atoms within sociology molecules and foreclosing development of archaeology (which Cole had undertaken) and physical anthropology (which Cole turned over relatively quickly to a student, Wilton Krogman). Prior to building the Chicago program, Cole had given little or no attention to archaeology and physical anthropology. Redfield had intellectual (as well as affinal) ties to sociology at least as strong as those to ethnography.[5] Whether subsuming Sapir within social psychology would have fostered the development of sociolinguistics is at least conceivable. However, like Chomsky, for all his talk about psychology, Sapir was not about to subordinate linguistics to psychology (cf. Homans's (1961) and Murdock's (1971) acceptance of the subordination of their original discipline, sociology, to one kind of psychology).

The opportunity for the integration of social sciences afforded by Sapir's appointment to the Chicago sociology department—and intended by the foundation that paid for it—was not taken. As can be seen in table 7, some of Ogburn's students took some of Sapir's courses, but Park's held back (or were held back). Overall, Sapir had less influence on sociology students being trained at Chicago than did some other nonsociologists. As table 8 shows, even Cole was more often cited in dissertations than was Sapir. Of course, Sapir established his own coterie in Chicago, and even more so at Yale, where Murdock nourished a grudge against

Boas. Murdock seems to have been viewed as "the enemy" by Sapir's disciples, who were outraged that Murdock rather than Leslie Spier was made chairman of anthropology when Sapir was incapacitated.[6] Although making little use of any of Sapir's work, Murdock appears to have been compunctiously correct to Sapir and always to have credited Sapir with urging him to undertake Haida fieldwork during the summer of 1932. But the injection of his judgment "that the permanent contributions of Sapir to cultural theory are relatively slight" in the preface to *Social Structure* (Murdock 1949:xv) is too gratuitous not to indicate that the antipathy was mutual. Citing Bloomfield rather than Sapir on linguistic drift in the same volume (198) is a marked slight. And in his late renunciation of cultural and social explanations of human behavior, Murdock (1971:23) seems to me to have gone out of his way to distinguish his critique of supraindividual theories from Sapir's. Indeed, Sapir's is the only name Murdock mentioned to exemplify the brilliant, complex theorizing irrelevant to "science" that Murdock dismissed rather than attacked.

Sumner's successors at Yale (among whom Murdock numbered himself) were intent on comparing social formations, considering anthropologists' descriptions grist for their own theoretical mills. The link between Sumner and Murdock, Albert Keller, felt Yale had no need for an anthropologist. In 1931, when he returned from a sabbatical year to find that a Sterling Professor had been appointed without his being consulted (or himself appointed!) and moreover had brought a platoon of his own followers along with him from Chicago to Yale, he was outraged. Keller insisted Murdock be appointed to the nascent anthropology department to safeguard "The Science of Society" from degenerating into particularistic barbarology (which is how he saw Boasian anthropology). Keller's animus likely contributed to Sapir's blackballing at Yale and the continuous pressure to absorb anthropology back into the Sumner-Keller science of society. Yale sociologists were neither ethnographers nor much interested in the development of personality. They were not sufficiently interested in what Sapir knew to care whether he felt slighted (as he usually did). Even at Chicago, where there was a tolerant community of scholars with similar interests, Sapir's hypersensitivity prevented his working together with his peers. Unable to see when he was well off, Sapir went off to the multiple, tragic personal and intellectual rejections of Yale.

That the importance of social relations might outweigh that of allegiance to theory or method should not come as a shock to many soci-

TABLE 7. Chicago Student Enrollment in Sapir and Ogburn Courses, 1925–1932

	Sapir courses	Ogburn courses	Dissertation year	title
Bowers, Alfred W.	3	1	1948	A History of Mandan and Hidatsa
Dollard, John	1	8	1931	Changing Functions American Family
Griffin, James B.	1	4	1936	Norris Basin Ceramics (Michigan)
Hoijer, Harry	16	1	1931	Tonkawa Grammar
Laves, G. K.	6	1		
Leh, L.	3	1		
Mekeel, Scudder	4	1	1932	History of Teton-Dakota (Yale)
Osgood, Cornelius B.	8	1	1930	Ethnology of Northern Dene
Provinse, John	4	1	1934	Underlying Sanction Plains Culture
Rappaport, D.	2	2		
Redfield, Margaret Park	1	1	1936	MA Folk Literature of a Yucatecan Town
Redfield, Robert	2	1	1928	Tepotzlan Study Plan
Sassaman, Wm. H.	7	1		
Stephan, F .F.	1	5	1926	MA, Social Uses of Telephone
Stouffer, Samuel	1	4	1930	Comparison of Statistical and Case Study Methods
Talbot, Nell	1	4	1928	MA Social Factors in the 1928 Presidential Election
Thompson, Edgar	1	1	1932	The Plantation
Watkins, Mark H.	10	1	1937	Grammar of Chichewa
Sapir courses only				
Bunzel, Ruth	7		1932	Zuni Ceremonialism
Dyk, Walter	6		1933	Wishram Grammar (Yale)
Eggan, Fred R.	4		1934	Western Pueblo Social Organization
Eggan, Olive	4			

	Sapir courses	Ogburn courses	Dissertation year	title
Gower, Charlotte	4		1928	Sicilian Supernatural Patron
Haas, Mary R.	1		1935	Tunica Grammar (Yale)
Hart, C. W. M.	4			
Krogman, Wilton H.	4		1929	A Study of Growth Changes in the Skull and Face of Anthropoids
Li, Fang-Kuei	11		1930	Mattole Grammar
Newman, Stanley	8		1931	Yokuts Grammar (Yale)
Riste, Victor E.	5			
Swadesh, Morris	7		1931	MA, Nootka Aspect
White, Leslie A.	3		1927	Southwestern Medicine Societies
Wirth, Louis	1		1926	The Ghetto

Ogburn courses only

	Sapir courses	Ogburn courses	Dissertation year	title
Blumenthal, Albert		5	1933	Small Town
Cottrell, Leonard		1	1933	Marriage Study Test
Faris, R. E. L.		5	1931	Insanity in the City
Hauser, Philip M.		2	1933	MA, Motion Pictures in Prison
McCormick, Thomas		5	1929	Rural Unrest
Stonequest, Everett		4	1930	The Marginal Man
Winston, Ellen Black		8	1930	Statistics of Mental Disease

Courses from neither Sapir Nor Ogburn

	Sapir courses	Ogburn courses	Dissertation year	title
Blumer, Herbert			1928	Method in Social Psychology
Dai, Bingham			1932	MA, Speaking in Tongues or Glossolalia
Hughes, Everett C.			1928	The Chicago Real Estate Board
Rosario, José			1931	MA, The Jibaro of Puerto Rico
Shapiro, Deba			1929	MA, Tribes of the Chicago Region

Source: University of Chicago instructors' grade reports

TABLE 8. Citations to Selected Faculty in University of Chicago Sociology
PhD Dissertations, 1920–1935

Faculty member	Percent citing			Total citations		
	1920–24	1925–29	1930–35	1920–24	1925–29	1930–35
Nonsociologists						
Sapir	11	15	8	3	5	2
Cole	0	27	4	0	21	5
Merriam	0	12	27	0	6	11
G. H. Mead	11	12	27	9	15	26
Thurstone	0	19	27	0	8	30
Sociologists						
Ogburn	11	8	23	3	4	29
Thomas	63	35	50	63	78	50
Faris	5	31	62	2	31	65
Burgess	5	54	81	32	96	120
Park	74	65	77	78	141	210
N	(19)	(26)	(26)			

Sources: R. Faris 1967: appendix A; Lewis and Smith 1980: table 9

ologists (nor to Robert Redfield, with whose wise observation—perhaps of the cleavages within Chicago?—I began). Lengermann (1979) shows some of the same characters aligning quite at odds with theoretical cleavages. Eggan (personal communication, 1984) remarked that in the sociology doctoral exams he attended, Faris and Park each protected their own students from the other. Within what has been subsequently perceived as a "school" and was at the time resented as a monolith (see Lengermann 1979), the elders seem to have been like Schopenhauer's porcupines: too sensitive to come very close together. J. Lewis and Smith (1980) blamed Park's prickliness for the backwardness of the social psychology in Park and Burgess (1921). That Faris was Mead's champion in sociology did not move Park toward Mead's ideas with any great alacrity (though they seeped in via students). Park's wife and Ogburn's wife loathed each other, according to Robert Faris (personal communication, April 2, 1984), which interfered with their husbands' rapport (see, however, Ogburn's generous tribute to Park at the Chicago memorial service for Park, and Helen Magill Hughes's 1959 tribute to Ogburn as a "free-ranging" and "great man"). And the polemical zeal of the younger generation (Stouffer vs. Blumer) found various outlets as well.

What appears now to have been an opportunity to work with American sociologists exploring interaction, personality development, and assimilation was not taken. The reason for this was far less any resistance to ethnographic methods and Boasian theorizing on the part of sociologists than the prickly personalities of Edward Sapir and Robert Park (along with the combative personality of Ellsworth Faris). Sociologists' preference of "role" rather than "personality" as an explanatory tool certainly must be considered a "cognitive" basis for resistance to the culture and personality work that issued during the 1940s. The sociolinguistics that finally emerged during the 1960s and proclaimed Sapir its father, however, has been resolutely interactive, so this factor is unlikely to have been the decisive obstacle to convergence during the 1920s. Exactly what the interactions of Chicago professors were like during the 1920s is not recoverable (and was not visible to those who were students then and there, as Robert Faris and Edward Shils stressed to me). The only sociologists with whom Sapir can be shown to have been intimate are Ogburn and Wirth, while his relations with Faris, Park, and Burgess seem to have been formal (and there is no indication Sapir and Mead knew each other). Certainly, no collaboration ensued. Given the various department colloquia and research organization Bulmer (1984) discusses, and given that Park is legendary for practically living in his office, there was no shortage of opportunities for interaction. If they did not occur, it is plausible (albeit unpalatable to many sociologists!) to attribute lack of interaction to personality (rather than to role or to structure). The nonconvergence of Sapirian and Chicago sociological work at Chicago shows something Sapir frequently argued, that the individual personality can make a difference, sometimes fueling innovation and forging theory groups, sometimes making it unlikely ideas will be integrated or followed up by others with similar interests. I believe it also shows that investigation of "postmaturities" can be revealing, even if no "postmaturity" can ever definitively be proven to have existed.

The Reception of Anthropological Work
in American Sociology, 1921–1951

During the 1940s American sociologists began to express in print their misgivings about the reliability and validity of observations by cultural anthropologists. This is later than one with a focus on boundary disputes (Kuklick 1980) might expect, but nearly four decades before Derek Freeman (1983) contended that he first "discovered" that there were weaknesses in the modus operandi of the second generation of Franz Boas students. The years surrounding the end of the Second World War might seem a strange time for interdisciplinary attacks, considering wartime cooperation on areal studies, work on propaganda and military morale, and the ubiquity of postwar interdisciplinary conferences and projects (see Heims 1977). Additionally, the GI Bill funded previously unparalleled academic growth, so competition for resources between disciplines was muted during the late 1940s. Moreover, the boundaries between social sciences were more permeable then than now. One indicator of this is that American anthropologists published significant work in the same sociology journals in which blistering attacks on anthropological field methods were later published.

By examining how sociologists reviewed anthropological work between the two world wars in the three leading American sociology journals—the *American Journal of Sociology* (*AJS*), the *American Sociological Review* (*ASR*), and *Social Forces* (*SF*)—I hope to show that sociologists' attacks during the 1940s were not bolts from the blue. Rather, they were rooted in an increasing recognition of the fallibility of generalizations with little basis on observation about national cultures made by anthropologists.

In order of foundation, *AJS*, *SF*, and *ASR* remain the core sociology journals. Traditionally, American anthropology has consisted of four subfields: cultural, linguistic, physical, and archeological. Applied and psychological anthropology have been subsumed under cultural anthropology, the largest subfield in number of practitioners. Although *SF* reviewers were attentive to conclusions from physical anthropology, there was not ongoing, systematic coverage of physical, linguistic, or archeological anthropology books in the journals considered here, so "anthropology" can be considered an abbreviation for "cultural anthropology."

The *American Journal of Sociology*

AJS, the oldest American sociology journal, founded in 1895, has always been edited within the Department of Sociology of the University of Chicago for the University of Chicago Press. From the founding of the American Sociological Society in 1905 until 1936, it was also the official journal of the society (Rhoades 1981:16–17, 31–32), although relatively little used as a publication outlet by East Coast sociologists.

In the first three decades of the twentieth century (as detailed in chapters 9 and 10) the intellectual environment within the sociology department at Chicago was open, even attuned, to anthropological work. All three groupings in what is commonly termed the "Chicago School of Sociology"—social psychologists trained by Ellsworth Faris and inspired by George Herbert Mead, those trained by William F. Ogburn to quantify cultural explanations of social change and of mental illness, and the urban ethnography tradition usually traced from W. I. Thomas through Robert Park and Ernest Burgess to Everett Hughes—were avid consumers of reports on cultures other than those of Anglo-America. Thomas, Faris, and Ogburn were in some sense Boasian, and Boas and some of his students influenced Thomas (as detailed in chapters 9 and 10). Park and Hughes, along with Herbert Blumer and Louis Wirth, were sophisticated readers of analyses of other cultures. Moreover, Chicago sociologists were quite familiar with the psychoanalytical ideas at the base of the developing "culture and personality" study within American cultural anthropology of the 1930s and 1940s.

Also, as discussed in chapter 10, long before American anthropologists, Chicago sociologists were interested in what would later be called acculturation. They pioneered ethnography in both urban and peasant settings at a time when Boasian anthropologists were still eliciting idealized memories of what (analytically insularized) "primitive" cultures had been like a generation or more before the time of fieldwork and were mapping distributions of cultural traits to infer prehistoric tribal movements and contacts (see chapter 3; Darnell 1977). In particular, the ethnographic technique that anthropologists view Edward Sapir as championing, the individual life history, was already a well-established tool of Chicago sociologists before his arrival in the Chicago department. Before studies of either acculturation or contemporary communities were considered legitimate in American anthropology, Chicago sociologists were producing both. And these works focused on individuals, not on "superorganic" entities (cultures, societies, etc.).

For Chicago sociologists (in all three traditions) the social/cultural less-than-total determination of individuals was the precondition of innovation. Innovation was fundamental to their view of social change. They believed that along with such catastrophic cultural contacts as conquests and large-scale population migration, individual innovation was a major mechanism of social change. This perspective sharply contrasted with the stasis glorified by functionalists such as A. Radcliffe-Brown (who became the dominant intellectual figure in a separate anthropology department after Sapir and many of his students went to Yale), as well as with the Yale tradition of William Graham Sumner, the smooth diffusions posted by Clark Wissler, and nineteenth-century social evolutionism's inexorable stages of development. Thus, demonstrations that individuals in "primitive" societies were not slavish followers of customs were eagerly sought in the anthropological literature by sociologists, supplementing those of Ellsworth Faris (1918, 1925).

Psychoanalytical ideas were also discussed in *AJS*, but much more critically than the work of Boasian or functionalist anthropologists. Although a special issue of *AJS* dedicated to Freud was put together by Burgess at the end of Freud's life (in 1939), one prominent motif in *AJS* discussion of anthropological work was rejection of Freud's determinism and Freudian anthropology. For example, in 1929 Blumer welcomed Bronislaw Malinowski's annihilation of the historical fantasies of *Totem and Taboo*. The next year he lauded Ruth Bunzel's *Pueblo Potter* for discrediting the psychoanalytical approach to culture. Even within the special issue dedicated to Freud, Salo Baron reviewed Freud's *Moses and Monotheism* as "a magnificent castle in the air" and Linton questioned the dogma that personality was completely formed in childhood. A remarkable facet of *AJS* critiques of Freudian work is that most were written by scholars interested in individual variation (Blumer; C. W. M. Hart) or by prominent proponents of wider application of psychoanalytic ideas (Linton, Morris Opler, Harold Lasswell, Bingham Dai) (Blumer, *AJS* 34 [1930]:393–94; 35 [1931]:663–64; Salo Baron, *AJS* 45 [1939]:471; Ralph Linton, *AJS* 45 [1939]:480).

Over the course of the 1930s critiques of data selectivity extended beyond discussion of psychoanalytical work and the theorizing of Lévy-Bruhl. Sociologists tired of Boasian anthropologists "breaking all cultures up into arbitrary fragments" while "talking endlessly about each culture's having a 'pattern.'" Even their old friend Ogburn expressed some "unease." Robert Redfield found Margaret Mead's first book disappointing and her thesis unconvincing; Ernest Mannheim considered her method to be "dangerous." Hart blasted "unsupported statements" by Boas himself as "personal opinions of the writer's masquerading as generally accepted propositions."[1] Although this blast prefigures later concerns about subjectivity and selectivity in anthropological work, Boas continued to collect encomia in *AJS*. Wilton Krogman, a fellow Chicago student of Hart's, saw in Boas's collected essays "the inception of many of our current concepts of human life, biological and cultural. The book is not Boas—it is American anthropology" (*AJS* 47 [1942]:224). Malcolm Willey (1929) was nearly as enthusiastic about Kroeber's *Anthropology* as Krogman was about Boas's essays, and despite some unease about ripping traits from their cultural context, Ogburn (*AJS* 40 [1936]:847–48) lauded Lowie's accomplishments. Despite growing concern about the validity even of American (Boasian) anthropology, rival (foreign) schools of anthropology were scorned as mercilessly in the pages of *AJS* as in Lowie's (1937) exceedingly partisan *History of Ethnological Theory,* a sort of compendium of what Boasians considered anthropological heresies. For instance, *AJS* book reviews included attacks by resident anthropologists Fay-Cooper Cole and Robert Redfield on the then-popular "children of the sun" thesis (see Langham 1981) and a remarkably Boasian critique of Émile Durkheim's (1893) *Division of Labor* by Ellsworth Faris: "The work accepts as accurate the crude misconceptions of the 1880's concerning the life of primitive man as set forth in the books of those who were no more competent to describe them than a botanist would be to write a treatise in his field without ever having seen a plant" (1935:376–77).

Anthropologists wrote most of the reviews of anthropological works in *AJS*: 76 percent of 136 reviews in volumes 30 through 50. Blumer and

TABLE 9. Reviewers of Three or More Anthropology Books in the Leading American Sociology Journals, 1921–1951

Reviewer	Training	SF	ASR	AJS	Total
Robert Redfield	Chicago, sociology and anthropology	2	26	28	
Franklin Hankins	Columbia, sociology	20	1	1	22
Luther Bernard	Chicago, sociology	20		1	21
Fred Eggan	Chicago, anthropology	2	2	12	16
John Embree	Chicago, anthropology		4	9	13
Fay-Cooper Cole	Columbia, anthropology		2	8	10
John P. Gillin	Harvard, anthropology		2	8	10
C. W. M. Hart	LSE and Chicago, anthropology		3	5	8
Irving Hallowell	Pennsylvania and Columbia, anthropology		7	1	8
John Honigman	Yale, anthropology	5	3		8
Morris Opler	Chicago, anthropology	7	1	8	
Bernhard Stern	Columbia, sociology	3	3	2	8
Melville Herskovits	Columbia, anthropology	1	4	2	7
Leslie White	Chicago, anthropology		1	6	7
Ellsworth Faris	Chicago, sociology		1	5	6
Guy Johnson	Chicago and North Carolina, sociology		6		6
Ralph Linton	Columbia and Harvard, anthropology		2	3	5
Margaret Mead	Columbia, anthropology			5	5
Robert Park	Harvard and Heidelberg, philosophy		1	4	5
Richard Thurnwald	Berlin, anthropology		3	1	4
Harry Barnes	Columbia, sociology	3			3
Ruth Benedict	Columbia, anthropology	1	2	3	
William Bennett	Chicago, anthropology			3	3
Herbert Blumer	Chicago, sociology			3	3
Everett Hughes	Chicago, sociology			3	3
Scudder Mekeel	Chicago, anthropology			3	3

Note: AJS = *American Journal of Sociology*; ASR = *American Sociological Review*; SF = *Social Forces*; LSE = London School of Economics

Faris wrote some reviews of "technical" works, but successive editors relied heavily on anthropologists trained at Chicago by Cole, Sapir, and Radcliffe-Brown (each of whom was also called on for reviews), especially Robert Redfield and Fred Eggan but also, if to a lesser extent, Leslie White and C. W. M. Hart (see table 9). Robert Park's daughter, Margaret Park Redfield, reviewed many folkloric works not included in the computation of anthropological works.

Trained by Boas's students and by sociologists who admired Boasian anthropologists, AJS reviewers of anthropology were well acquainted with the principles and trends of cultural anthropology—especially the work on the psychological integration of culture. For the most part they reviewed American and some British anthropological works sympathetically. Still, beginning in the late 1930s criticism of American anthropological work began to appear in AJS along with expressions of doubt about foreign schools of anthropology.

The *American Sociological Review*

As part of the organizational rebellion against Chicago domination of the American Sociological Society (see Lengermann 1979), AJS was replaced as the official journal in 1936 when the society inaugurated ASR. The new journal reviewed anthropological monographs with regularity, its early editors drawing upon a more heterogeneous group of anthropologists for reviewers than did AJS editors. The only two who made frequent appearances in the pages of ASR book reviews were anthropologists Irving Hallowell and John P. Gillin. The former was highly visible in national research councils, and the latter was a son of a prominent sociologist. Although no other single anthropologist reviewed more than three anthropological books in the first twelve volumes of ASR (see table 9), the proportion of anthropological works reviewed by anthropologists was the highest of any of the three core sociology journals: 81 percent ($N = 124$).

Perhaps because of the later starting date, proportionately more ASR reviews seem to have a cutting edge than reviews in the other two core sociology journals. Some impatience with the first generation of Boasians' listing of tribal "shreds and patches" must owe something to the influence of American sojourns by Malinowski and Radcliffe-Brown. The one specific criticism in ASR, however, came from a former student and avowed admirer of Boas, Bernhard Stern (ASR 3 [1938]:373), rather than from any of the advocates of functionalism. Boas's collected essays were greeted with something approaching rapture (Howard Becker, ASR 5 [1940]:684), and the reissue of his *Mind of Primitive Man* received pious praise (A. Irving Hallowell, ASR 3 [1939]:580–81). In 1941 Fred Eggan lauded Kroeber's use of culture areas (viewed as "old hat" by many anthropologists then—especially by those who, like Eggan, had been influenced by Radcliffe-Brown) as "the most important study of American ethnology in recent years" (ASR 6 [1941]:139). In contrast, the other prominent school of diffusionism (that of Father Schmidt) was denounced in ASR as "dangerously metaphysical." There were shots in ASR at "flights of Freudian fancy" (Raymond Kennedy, ASR 6 [1941]:412) and what seems to be quite a "late hit" of James Frazer by George Peter Murdock (ASR 2 [1937]:932).

ASR reviewers tended to be as skeptical of psychoanalysis as AJS reviewers. Also like AJS reviewers, ASR ones praised demonstrations that individuals in "primitive" societies were not slaves of custom. Concern was expressed by one psychological anthropologist (Hallowell, ASR 2 [1937]:559) about ignoring the variation of actual behavior from norms, whereas another (David Mandelbaum, ASR 7 [1942]:293) invidiously contrasted the normative rules in W. H. R. Rivers's classic Toda ethnography to Verrier Elwin's Baiga ethnography, in which there "are men and women, not bloodless repositories of curious customs." Surprisingly, a leader of the Durkheim revival in American sociology, Harry Alpert (ASR 6 [1941]:896–98), criticized Redfield's *Folk Culture of the Yucatan* for being not only too abstract but also too unpsychological. Almost equally incongruous was Murdock's (1943) review in the *American Anthropologist*.

Donald Collier expanded on Hallowell's criticism of ignoring intracultural variation from abstract norms: "Since it seems to be true that even the most conservative groups do not adhere completely to the ideals of their social pattern, knowledge of the extent of divergence is important." (ASR 6 [1941]:413). One of the authors of the pioneer work on acculturation and exemplars of using life history materials, Florian Znaniecki, really lowered the boom against reifying modal personality to characterize a culture in 1942 (quoted above, p. 186).

Although John Dollard and Neal Miller's fusion of Freud and Clark Hull attracted some potshots, the circular culture and personality formulations of Abraham Kardiner and Clyde Kluckhohn drew frontal attacks. (For sharp criticisms of Kardiner, see F. Hankins, ASR 10 [1946]:574;

Read Bain, *ASR* 5 [1940]:759–60. A searing attack on Kluckhohn's "confused, weird, unworkable" eclecticism was delivered by Herbert Blumer, *ASR* 14 [1950]:563–65.)

If anything, the view of anthropological work on alien cultures expressed in *ASR* indicated an acceptance of data about diverse social arrangements hedged somewhat by a concern that the reports were overly neat, thereby masking behavioral divergence from ideal norms. Throughout the period considered in this chapter, statistical approaches to describing and explaining intracultural variation were becoming increasingly dominant in sociology. Indeed, quantification is supposed to be the intellectual battle line in the revolt against Chicago dominance that led to the founding of *ASR*. Occasionally, comparative work would increase caution about ethnographers' impressions. As Ogburn's student, Ellen Black Winston (1934), had demonstrated in contrasting Samoan and rural American rates of mental illness, more statistical care could vitiate the pronouncements about patterns and exaggerated distinctions between "primitive" and "modern" societies made by overly omniscient ethnographers.

As we shall see, the critique of unsubstantiated impressions was taken up more earnestly against anthropologists' pronouncements about national character—especially American national character, a phenomenon about which American sociologists had impressions of their own, and even "hard data." Generally, however, between the world wars work on other cultures was welcomed in sociology journals, perhaps most so in *SF*, the one that least relied on anthropologists as reviewers and least covered technical anthropological work.

Social Forces

Founded in 1922, *SF* was the journal of the sociology department of the University of North Carolina. Howard Odum, a sociologist trained at Columbia who sought to give voice to a "New South," ran both the journal and the department. Odum was very interested in African American folklore and in the comparative study of folkways in various regions to which African slaves had been imported, particularly the Caribbean. Allied with Boas in antiracist endeavors, Odum's program dovetailed with the African and African American ethnology of Melville Herskovits, a polemical Boasian and a frequent contributor to Odum's journal.[2] Boasian works intended to synthesize more technical work on cultural diversity and to criticize claims of racial or geographical determination or evolutionary stages of cultural development were particularly well received in *Social Forces*.

Surveying work on folk from areas other than the southern United States for *Social Forces* was done predominantly by book review editors Frank H. Hankins and Harry Elmer Barnes. Both of them, like Odum, and other recurrent reviewers of anthropological work, such as Ernest Groves and Bernard J. Stern, were Columbia graduates. In the period between the wars Hankins (who had sent Odum to study with his own master, Giddings) wrote twenty reviews for *Social Forces*, most of them surveys reviewing between three and forty books about race and biological explanations of social phenomena. Although Hankins did not go so far as some Boasians in rejecting any kind of racial explanation,[3] in the zeitgeist of eugenics, Hankins's was a voice raised against the pretensions of "Nordic" superiority advanced by Madison Grant and the instinctivism of William MacDougall. Hankins was a critic of residual social Darwinism, stressing both that "one must rid himself of the notion that natural selection always favors the superior, as judged by certain human valuations" (1927:409) and that there are no absolute differences between races: "With reference to any particular trait, one so-called race differs from another more or less as to type but with a greater or lesser degree of overlapping in the statistical distribution of individual members. Since all races are human, differences must be those of degree or quantity rather than those of kind or quality" (408). Hankins wrote Lowie (in a letter dated November 22, 1927) that their difference was "one more of emphasis than anything else," reiterating, "I certainly would not wish to be construed as in any way implying that present cultural differences constitute reliable evidence of differences in racial endowment."

Another author of broad surveys of books about other regions (especially Latin America), Luther Bernard, was, along with Ellsworth Faris, the sociologist champion in jousts with MacDougall. Barnes, who had an encyclopedic command of seemingly everything ever written about society, completed the *SF* triumvirate, surveying the social science scene between the wars. Stern (*SF* 8 [1929]:271), Hankins (*SF* 6 [1928]:449–500, 8 [1930]:469–70) and Barnes (*SF* 8 [1929]:271) went out of their way to laud Boasian work even when praising work from other traditions. Indeed, their stance adumbrated in many details the catechism of Lowie's

1937 *History of Ethnological Theory*. For instance, the "good" (early) Rivers was detached from his heliocentric corruption; the inadequate basis for Freud's, Lévy-Bruhl's, and especially Róheim's equation of children and "primitives" was mercilessly attacked. Although Malinowski was better appreciated in *SF* than by Lowie (1937), even his demonstration that "primitives" are not slaves of customs was invidiously contrasted to Lowie's work. Work associated with Harvard (Alfred Tozzer and Arthur Kidd, not Roland Dixon or E. A. Hooton) was also welcomed as supplementing—not in any way challenging—Boasian work (Harry E. Barnes, *SF* 3 [1924]:196–202; Clark Wissler, *SF* 4 [1925]:244–46; Frank H. Hankins, *SF* 4 [1926]:425; Luther L. Bernard, *SF* 7 [1929]:609–10). Mostly, *SF* sociologists deemed themselves sufficiently expert to evaluate work from other disciplines. Anthropologists were summoned less often than by the other core sociology journals: between volumes 6 and 18 there were only two reviews by anthropologists, and one of them was by Murdock, who was trained as a sociologist. Boasian anthropologists still trampled rival doctrines when they got the chance: for example, Ruth Benedict's sarcasm about Lévy-Bruhl (*SF* 3 [1925]:557–58) and Wissler's rejection of Róheim (*SF* 4 [1925]:244–46).

Just before World War II, a new generation of anthropologists (Eggan, Gillin, Harry Hoijer, Kluckhohn, Loren Eiseley) began to be invited to review more technical works than the anthropological work usually reviewed in earlier volumes. In the first twenty volumes of *SF* the only anthropologists authoring more than one book review were Wissler and Eggan. Only 8 percent of the identifiable reviewers (of seventy-three books) were anthropologists. Odum's closest collaborator in the study of African American folklore, Guy B. Johnson (a former Chicago student of Park) reviewed such landmark anthropological works from the 1930s as *Naven* (Bateson 1936), *A Black Civilization* (Warner 1937), and *Mitla* (Parsons 1936) (*SF* 17 [1938]:131–35). In general, *SF* promoted a Boasian line on race and culture. The works of synthesis and generalization that appeared after the First World War were welcomed and held up as models against any competitors, foreign or domestic. Works by anthropologists directed less at explaining the gains of anthropology to wider audiences (popularizations) than at "getting on with the work" of anthropology (technical contributions not aimed at general audiences) received less attention than in the other two journals. Despite admiration for Malinowski's work, there were traces of unease about his generalizing to all "primitive" societies from a single case and with his over-statements of functional integration (Frank H. Hankins, *SF* 6 [1928]:500; Bernard J. Stern, *SF* 10 [1931]:294; also see Stern, *ASR* 1 [1935]:1018). From his Chicago base, which included access to *AJS*, Radcliffe-Brown does not seem to have exerted any influence on the *SF* watchers of the sociology-anthropology boundary(ies). Although the editor of Radcliffe-Brown's festschrift, Fred Eggan, began to review books in *SF* it was the "student of Sapir" rather than the "student of Radcliffe-Brown" who praised the vivid view inside Eskimo life in *Kabloona* (19 [1940]:116–18) and looked askance at the lack of psychological data for psychological claims in Linton's *Acculturation in Seven American Indian Tribes* (*SF* 20 [1942]:519–20). Similarly, it was not for analyzing social structure, but rather for opening a window into Apache lifeways that Loren Eiseley (*SF* 20 [1941]:520) praised the book by Opler criticized by Znaniecki. In volumes 19–29 (1941–51) 60 percent of the identifiable reviewers of (thirty-five) anthropological books were anthropologists, especially two North Carolina faculty members, John P. Gillin (four) and John Honigmann (five), Gillin continuing Bernard's Latin America focus.

In *Social Forces* during the 1920s and 1930s cultural sociologists interested in anthropological data and sympathetic to Boas's antiracism welcomed American work (which was predominantly Boasian) while criticizing work from other (national) anthropological schools (except for the British "school" of Rivers and Malinowski). As in *AJS* and *ASR*, when Boasian work on the distribution of cultural traits was succeeded by synchronic and psychological problematics such as those considered by Margaret Mead, relatively sympathetic attention to work on acculturation was accompanied by unsympathetic scrutiny of culture and personality work. The methods and conclusions of culture and personality work stimulated skepticism about the validity of ethnographic observations in general.

Poaching in Sociologists' Territory: The United States

Until the late 1930s, despite some expressions of concern about overgeneralizing from a single case and about overly schematic accounts of cultures that took insufficient account of variation from norms—especially when a trait was sundered from its ethnographic context for use in ethnological illustration—sociology journals generally shared American anthropologists' judgment about what was sound work on other cultures and what was untrustworthy. Most of the work regarded as sound was done by professionally trained/academic anthropologists. Though some of what was judged unsound came from Harvard (namely, E. A. Hooton), and from popularizers (including some with professional credentials, such as George Dorsey and Margaret Mead), most of it came from non-professionals lacking training in and/or commitment to Science.

In general, whatever anthropologists asserted about the lifeways of a distant island in the Pacific Ocean or indigenous tribes of North America was likely to be credited by sociologists, who could not easily compare their own impressions of these cultures. However, assertions about American culture or the social structure of American regions were not so safe from informed questioning by sociologists. When sociologists saw that anthropological methods yielded dubious results in the United States, they began to wonder if anthropologists' assertions about remote locales were similarly flawed. The "honeymoon" described thus far in this chapter ended when anthropologists "came home" to write about American culture(s) rather than exotic lifeways of remote islands. Insofar as there was a "gathering storm" of interdisciplinary acrimony within American social science before World War II, the border incidents occurred around W. Lloyd Warner and his associates as they studied American culture.

Warner worked with Lowie at Berkeley before becoming the one student there drawn into Radcliffe-Brown's orbit during his visit to Berkeley en route to Australia in the summer of 1925. Radcliffe-Brown used some of his Rockefeller Foundation funds to support Warner so he could join him in Australia. There Warner did fieldwork on the Murngin from 1926 to 1929, which was reported in his monumental *Black Civilization* (not published until 1937).

Warner never finished his doctorate. Nevertheless, he taught anthropology at Harvard between 1929 and 1935. During that time he began a massive collaborative study of a Yankee community (Newburyport, Massachusetts). This project included fieldwork in rural Ireland by Conrad Arensberg and Solon Kimball and in "Yankee City" by platoons of students. Warner also suggested some observational methods to the industrial psychologists who were concluding a series of studies (also funded by the Rockefeller Foundation) of the Hawthorne Western Electric plant with the Bank Wiring Observations. Despite the complexity of his far-from-finished Massachusetts projects, Warner chose to leave Harvard and rejoin Radcliffe-Brown at the University of Chicago in 1935. From Chicago Warner took an active part in work sponsored by the American Youth Commission on black youth in Mississippi—though most of it was done by sociologists who had left Chicago before he arrived (Charles S. Johnson, E. Franklin Frazier, John Dollard).[4] The first Mississippi reports were published simultaneously with *Black Civilization* in 1937, before the "Yankee City" volumes began to appear.

Although no sociologist knew anything about the Murngin of Australia, many of them knew a great deal about the American South. The first report from Mississippi, *Caste and Class in a Southern Town* (Dollard 1937), resting on short-term observation by a Yankee and life histories of three women and six men, may have had a larger sample than many early holistic ethnographies, but a sample of nine was not very impressive to sociologists. Lyn Smith wondered in *ASR*, "Is psychoanalysis a technique which sets a premium upon unrestrained flights of the imagination?" (2 [1936]:797) and balked at generalizing to the entire South or the whole nation. In reviewing the book Smith adumbrated much later criticism of facile analyses of sketchy data by Margaret Mead, Geoffrey Gorer, and others: "It is the usual experience of those engaged in social research to find that the problems to be solved become more numerous and complex as the project moves along. Apparently, Dr. Dollard was not confronted with this difficulty. In his book there appear few indications of perplexity or uncertainty; he has a ready answer for every situation; and he easily disposes of all questions of fact and theory. A single observation frequently calls forth a torrent of highly speculative premises, hypotheses, and conclusions, together with not a few corollaries, explanations, and applications" (797).

More than the authors of *Deep South* (Allison Davis, Burleigh Gardner, and Mary Gardner, 1941), it was Warner who was criticized (by Lewis Copeland and Robert Schmid) for their overemphasizing caste and class and for attempting to study white southerners as if black southerners did not exist. Sociologists were quick to point out that the southern United States did not consist of isolated coral atolls, where one culture could be studied in isolation. Schmid, in particular, zeroed in on the unnecessarily intuitive "method" of social anthropologists:

One is struck constantly in reading the book by the authors' propensity for the use of comparative terms which are unnecessarily vague and impressionistic. . . . One wonders if the writers are merely guessing or if they are embroidering their information with personal hunch. In general, it would seem that the authors have missed many opportunities for quantitative statement. . . . Can even the social anthropologist, with his supposed gift for "seeing things whole," ignore the problems of sampling and sampling error? . . . "Old City," Mississippi is not just another collection of native huts on the banks of the river; it is a tremendously complex segment of a culture so vast that one wonders at the audacity. . . . There is a certain bravery in attempts like these, but in science as in war, discretion is the better part of valor. In the long run social scientists will learn more from the modest pursuer of a single spoor, who sharpens his knife as he goes, than from the valorous fellow who hurries out with inadequate weapons to try to capture the whole wolf-pack. (*ASR* 7 [1942]:263)

The third Mississippi volume, *Children of Bondage*, by Davis and Dollard, fared slightly better, though Leonard Cottrell Jr. (*AJS* 47 [1941]:110–15) was unimpressed by the leaps from cases to conclusions, by the uncritical acceptance of Warner's claims about caste, and by the Yale Institute for Human Relations merger of Freud and Hull.

As harsh as the reception of the studies of southern caste was, the Yankee City series called forth still more withering attacks on Warner's model of stratification. Beginning literally where Schmid left off, C. Wright Mills launched a blistering attack that runs an astounding nine pages (the longest featured review was rarely as long as two and a half pages). Although sorting out what sociologists did with and to Warner's conception of class is a fascinating subject, the interest here is only in showing how it was used to call into question the approaches of social anthropology. For this, the most relevant feature of Mills's discussion is the following: "If you define a concept along one line, then you can study other items that vary with it. But if you define it so as to make it a sponge word, letting it absorb a number of variables, then you cannot ask questions with it concerning the relations of analytically isolable items which it miscellaneously harbors" (*ASR* 7 [1942]:265).

Mills criticized Warner's substitution of "many" for any statistical precision and the ahistoricity of such functional studies: "Because it is difficult to obtain 'historical' material on the Murngin of Australia is not a valid reason why we should not have the obvious advantage of easily procurable time-oriented data of Newburyport" (268). Prefiguring his later (1959) polemic against functionalism in *The Sociological Imagination*, Mills (*ASR* 7:263–71) also noted the tautological quality of assertions about functional integration, even for a community initially selected for its lack of conflict and cultural homogeneity.

Warner's claims about caste systems (especially in the North) were roundly rejected, and his posited extension of the importance of skin color gradients to white ethnics was regarded as absurd, based on bad sampling, ignorance of (Chicago School and historical) literature, "hodge-podgy" presentation, and begging questions of how assertions about race and ethnicity were derived from the data gathered (Read Bain, *ASR* 8 [1943]:106). Even Kingsley Davis, who was not only a functionalist but also had been a student of Warner's at Harvard, found "the step from the original observations to the classification adopted imperfectly described. . . . When the results are given, their relation to this abundant material is not always obvious" (*AJS* 48 [1943]:513; also see Everett V. Stonequist, *ASR* 11 [1946]:121; Samuel M. Strong, *ASR* 11 [1946]):240–41). Controversy about Warner's stratification could hardly intensify from such a molten beginning, but it continued at a high temperature, simultaneous with but distinct from the increasingly skeptical views of work by psychological anthropologists. Harold W. Pfautz and Otis Dudley Duncan considered Warner's shortcomings as "in some degrees attributable to the general weakness of the 'anthropological approach' to contemporary complex societies" (1950:215) and faulted him for treating class subcultures "as microscopic societies with distinctive cultures" (212).

Culture and Personality Work: The Other Affront

Just as Warner's work on the United States made sociologists wonder about the reliability of observations and validity of generalizations social anthropologists made about cultures no one else had studied, the extremely reductionist explanations of modal personality in nation states about which there were literatures provoked doubts about psychological anthropologists' reports of nonliterate cultures.

In particular, Margaret Mead's assertions about American culture led sociologists to wonder in print whether her interpretations of alien cultures were as careless and unsound as her ex cathedra pronouncements on American culture. In 1945 Robert Bierstedt wrote of Mead's first book-length account of American culture, *And Keep Your Powder Dry* (1942), that it provided a "stunning example of the inadequacy of anthropological methods in the study of American culture" and added, "This book is full of insights. It is also full of alarums, excitements, and exhortations. In manner and matter it is perhaps the most patriotic journalism ever to pose as a product of the scientific method (1945:291). The reader trained in this method can hardly fail to notice that Miss Mead's assertions are presented with more than a modicum of confidence and less than a suspicion of corroboration. The most basic question in all scientific endeavor—What is the evidence?—received no answer." Mapheus Smith similarly noted that Mead's *And Keep Your Powder Dry* was American propaganda, "not science, either pure or applied" (ASR 8 [1944]:355).

Other sociologists (J. Bernard 1945, 1949; Lindesmith and Strauss 1950) echoed Bierstedt's skepticism about Mead's methods, out of line though it is with Freeman's contentions about the credulity of American social scientists. Other anthropologists venturing to study American communities as if they were historyless islands were also flayed by sociologists. For instance, in 1951 Hortense Powdermaker received barbed critiques (also from Bierstadt) for her Hollywood study: "The notion, for some time suspect, that previous investigation of a primitive tribe uniquely qualifies a person to study a sophisticated society, or any part of it, is now revealed to be absurd. The anthropological method here consists of little more than a series of inane analogies" (ASR 16 [1951]:124).

More gently, David Riesman chided Powdermaker's ignorance of work on professional cultures and, like Bierstadt, looked uneasily beyond the book being reviewed to the limits of an anthropology that "concentrates on the present day and which takes its informants' account of their work relationships as an adequate institutional analysis" (AJS 56 [1951]:592).

As Ralph Beals (1951:4) warned his colleagues in the opening pages of the *American Anthropologist* the same year, "If anthropologists keep on as they have begun in the study of modern culture, they will in time reinvent sociology, but unfortunately it will be at least 50 years behind the rest of the field." From the perspective of having founded at UCLA one of the few joint sociology-anthropology departments in which anthropology was the senior partner, and from trying to make sense of the acculturation of immigrants to Los Angeles, Beals saw that there was no need to reinvent wheels such as sampling.

Conclusion

In subsequent decades some anthropologists have themselves taken up themes initially expressed by sociologists, for example, failing to distinguish norms from behavior, masking intracultural variation behind categorical statements about "the culture" based on the ethnographer's intuitions or favorite informant, and treating fieldwork sites as if they were islands outside history without any urban or state influences. Indeed, by the 1970s anthropological self-consciousness was flowering and some anthropologists even considered the possibility that what was presented as fieldwork might be not merely unreliable but invented outright and not noticed, because of the difficulty of replication for claims about specific peoples at particular historical moments. Although work on a culture by anthropologists remains distinguishable from work on the same culture by sociologists, anthropologists aiming to contribute to a human science have taken up the substance of the critiques of anthropological practices made in sociology journals between 1921 and 1951. By the 1980s anthropologists stressed present and historical connections among cultures (even those on Pacific atolls). Moreover, many studies are now based on more adequate samples than those drawn by earlier generations of anthropologists, and studies of intracultural variability in cultures both large and small in scale are now routinely reported in anthropological journals and monographs. However, there is a very visible belletristic ("postmodernist") movement within anthropology renouncing science and concentrating on the production and analysis of texts that are not expected to reflect anything other than the writer's own consciousness and ambivalences (especially about power). Still, there are continuities with Margaret Mead's vigorous omniscience and Hortense Powdermaker's ad hoc "sampling" to make assertions about complex multiethnic societies on the basis of short and unsystematic observation.

12

The Rights of Research Assistants and the Rhetoric of Political Suppression

Morton Grodzins and the University of California Japanese-American Evacuation and Resettlement Study

In a classic 1938 article Robert Merton described common ownership of the products of science as one of the four institutional norms of science: "The substantive findings of science are a product of social collaboration and are assigned to the community. They constitute a common heritage in which the equity of the individual producer is severely limited. ... The scientist's claim to 'his[/her]' intellectual 'property' is limited to that of recognition and esteem" (1968:610).

A prerequisite to sharing knowledge is access to it. Therefore,

> the institutional conception of science as part of the public domain is linked with the imperative for communication of findings. Secrecy is the antithesis of this norm; full and open communication its enactment. The pressure for diffusion of results is reinforced by the institutional goal of advancing the boundaries of knowledge and by the incentive of recognition which is, of course, contingent upon publication. (611)

> Once he has made his contribution, the scientist no longer has exclusive access to it. It becomes part of the public domain of science. Nor has he the right of regulating its use by others by withholding it unless it is acknowledged as his. In short, property rights in science become whittled down to just this one: the recognition by others of the scientist's distinctive part in having brought the result into being. (Merton 1957:640)

Scientific work that is not publicly available cannot bring recognition and the more tangible rewards of professional advancement to those who have done it. The norm of communism does not, however, solely determine the dissemination of research results. Institutions sponsoring research and publication consider "property rights," whether or not science as an entity does. Moreover, individual scientists may deviate from the ideal norms of the institution of science and also are likely to interpret specific situations in divergent ways in rationalizing their interests.

At the level of characterizing the behavior of individual scientists (i.e., in the context of discovery), several sociologists have vigorously challenged Merton's idealization of science as an institution (e.g., Mulkay 1969; Barnes and Dolby 1970; cf. Stehr 1978). Merton himself applied to the domain of science his theory that anomie produces deviance, including science as "a culture giving emphasis to aspirations for all, aspirations which cannot be realized by many, [which] exerts a pressure for deviant behavior and for cynicism, for rejection of the reigning moralities and the rules of the game" (1957:655–58; for elaboration, see Zuckerman 1977). It seems to me that the norms are invoked within the more public context of justification rather than in the more private context of discovery and that they have been misunderstood in the same way as have post hoc rationalizations of methods, also supposed by many to be descriptions of how research is done. The rules—cognitive and ethical—are better seen as secondary elaborations than as primary processes but are often internalized and have real consequences.

In the case study examined here, one research assistant took data from a large research project that had employed him to gather it. Backed by prominent social scientists at one leading American university he, in effect, accused those who had supervised his research at another leading American university of conduct contrary to one of the fundamental norms of science, communism. His most polemical backer added charges of deviating from another, the norm of disinterestedness, as well. In response, his opponents (former teachers) questioned his own disinterestedness, both personal and political. Their substantive criticisms can be seen as instances of yet another norm of science, organized skepticism.

This case involved a number of the most prominent American social scientists of the late 1940s and early 1950s. More importantly for seeing the operations of science distinct from the behavior of scientists, the administrators and presses of two major American universities asserted their views of what ought to be the rights and obligations of research assistants, those supervising them, and the institutions employing researchers and research assistants. This case study of the contested attempt to publish one PhD dissertation from a large research project on the forced migration and subsequent incarceration of West Coast Japanese Americans during World War II shows one resolution of conflicting institutional norms in actual interuniversity *realpolitik*.

Dorothy Thomas and Research Support

Demographer Dorothy Swaine Thomas, who directed this research, was a student of William F. Ogburn and the wife of W. I. Thomas, two of the central social scientists in the national research councils funded by Rockefeller foundations in the years between the world wars (see chapters 9 and 10). De facto, the Rockefeller monies largely supported W. I. Thomas during the 1920s and 1930s, including a national study of children on which the Thomases first collaborated (D. Thomas 1952a). W. I. Thomas was on the staff of the Social Science Research Council, which was primarily funded by the Rockefeller Foundation, from 1932 to 1933, and the SSRC supported the Swedish research of the Thomases between 1930 and 1936. The Rockefeller Foundation also underwrote the Yale Institute on Human Relations (see Morawski 1986; Darnell 1998b), where Dorothy Thomas directed a series of behavioral studies of children and legal institutions and the Thomases worked with Gunnar and Alva Myrdal on what was intended to be a Swedish sequel to *The Polish Peasant in Europe and America*—partly published as D. Thomas 1941, in which she drew hardly any conclusions from a welter of descriptive statistics (Bannister 1998).

With the support of University of California president Robert Gordon Sproul[1] and Graduate Division dean Charles Lipman, Dorothy Thomas and political science professor Charles Aikin sought and received funding from the university, the Giannini Foundation (Thomas was a Giannini Professor of Rural Sociology), and the Rockefeller Foundation for what became the University of California Japanese-American Evacuation and Resettlement Study (JAERS).[2] The project commenced in February 1942, immediately following President Franklin Roosevelt's issuance of Executive Order 9066, authorizing army commanders to designate and restrict "military areas," and before the "applied anthropology" by those employed by the War Relocation Authority (WRA) aiding the administration of American concentration camps began (on that work see Starn 1986; P. Suzuki 1981; on the history of the roundup and incarceration, Daniels 1993; Okubo 1983).

In May 1942 the Rockefeller Foundation provided $7,500 to support an exploratory study (Joseph Willits:Sproul, May 8, 1942). At the beginning of the 1942–43 fiscal year, Thomas reported to Sproul that she had $3,250 from the Giannini Foundation with another $600 promised, $1,800 for a predoctoral fellowship from the Social Science Research Council (for S. Frank Miyamoto), and $700 from Berkeley's Institute for Social Science. On July 27, 1942 Willits wrote Sproul that he had presented to the Executive Council of the Rockefeller Foundation an application for two more years of support at $7,500 per annum. Total Rockefeller support of the research was $38,750 (including publication subventions of $6,250), supplemented by $30,000 from the Columbia Foundation and $29,554 (plus a matching publication subvention of $6,250) from the university. It bears emphasizing that in 1942–45 dollars JAERS was an extraordinarily heavily funded research project. It also involved the coordination of an exceptionally large number of research assistants, most of whom were simultaneously prisoners in concentration camps.[3] Both the size of the project and the necessity of dealing with the government bureaucracies involved in administering the camps required a project bureaucracy in Berkeley.

The male social scientists involved in the initial planning of JAERS (in addition to Aikin, Robert Lowie, Milton Chernin, and Frank Kidner) took leave from the university for other war work, so Dorothy Thomas was in sole command of the fieldwork. Her own primary interest was in what she considered the unique "migration of a whole population group from the area of primary settlements. . . . [in which] the forces of 'push' and 'pull' could not operate in what we have theoretically conceived of as the normal selective fashion" (D. Thomas 1970:225). She recalled, "I saw the situation initially as just a special case of migration: unselective 'push' at origin (enforced evacuation) and selective 'pull' at destination (voluntary resettlement from camp). . . . I shudder to think of the idiocies I might have perpetrated by way of 'premature quantification' of the essentially 'unquantifiable' had I not been [in] association with W. I. Thomas at the time. In our preparation and interpretation of behavioral data, W. I. Thomas was our counselor and guide" (225).

The first annual report of the study discussed the unusual potential for de-assimilation when assimilated Nisei (born in America of immigrant Japanese parents) were excluded from American society and incarcerated with less-assimilated Issei (Japan-born immigrants who could not become U.S. citizens) and Kibbei (U.S.-born, Japan-educated U.S. citizens). Also, "From the standpoint of political science, interest centers on both national policy and procedures and political life within relocation camps. The first interest involved questions concerning the nature of pressure group activity and the formation of American public opinion as favoring or opposing evacuations, and, more recently, favoring or opposing detention in camps for the duration and permanent exclusion from California; constitutional issues raised in the forced evacuation of American citizens" (JAERS 1942 annual report).

Thomas later asserted that she "could draw upon no systematically accumulated fund of knowledge, and found few realistic 'models' or adequate techniques by which to guide procedures or check conclusions." This led her to supervise what she called a "vacuum-cleaner approach," collecting every kind of documentation that could be found (D. Thomas 1952a:662–63).[4] What was collected in the vacuum cleaner was fiercely guarded from inspection or any use (political or analytical, during the war and after) by anyone other than Dorothy Thomas, even though the paucity of published results, especially when contrasted to the vast amount of unused data, suggests that she did not know what to do with the data collected and the analyses written by staff members.[5] James Sakoda recalled that she tried to avoid theoretical issues by using standard categories such as age, sex, generation, and place of origin but "was uncomfortable with field data, which dealt with behavior, attitudes and values" (Sakoda:author, October 28, 1990).

Ironically, the "theoretical" conceptions that Sakoda, Tamotsu Shibutani, and Frank Miyamoto wanted to use were those such as "attitudes" and "definition of the situation" popularized in earlier work by W. I. Thomas. As argued in chapter 9, by the 1930s W. I. Thomas had largely abandoned the conceptions that influenced later sociologists, and both Thomases were resolute behaviorists. Dorothy Thomas (1929:17), in her review of "Statistics in Social Research," (wrote that "interpretations are the investigator's own business." Her view was that her job was to collect data and do statistics, not to interpret either.

Researching and Writing about the Political Aspects

While the major fieldwork on the adjustment and resistance within the concentration camps was conducted by incarcerated Nisei with social science training and three Anglo graduate students, a political science graduate student, Morton Grodzins, assisted Thomas with administering the study from Berkeley and gathered material on the pressures to round up and imprison Japanese Americans. Grodzins later recalled, "I was first employed for the summer of 1942 only; and my first tasks were largely clerical in nature, e.g., devising a filing system" (Grodzins:University of Chicago Press director William Couch and University of Chicago dean Ralph Tyler, October 7, 1948). According to University of California payroll records, Grodzins was a "research clerk" from May 15, 1942, until June 30, 1942, then a research assistant until March 31, 1945. Grodzins claimed (in the same 1948 memo to Couch and Tyler) to have convinced Dorothy Thomas of the need for a study of the political process that led to the forced migration of Japanese Americans, although such study was planned before his involvement with the project. Grodzins continued,

> I did not resume my teaching fellowship in the Fall of 1942, and devoted my full energies to pursuing the evacuation studies. Soon I was participating as the senior assistant for the study. I worked closely with Mrs. Thomas on every aspect of her work. I drafted for her various applications for foundation grants. I assumed general supervision under Mrs. Thomas's direction, for the study's day-to-day administrative and budgetary problems. I interviewed prospective research assistants and employed clerical help. I aided in securing Selective Service exemptions for various members of the staff. Simultaneously, I was finishing my doctoral examinations and conducting my own field research in Washington, in Los Angeles, and other places. During this entire period, Mrs. Thomas expressed a large measure of satisfaction with my work. My duties became increasingly responsible ones; my salary increased; and Mrs. Thomas made serious efforts to have my status changed from that of a research assistant to that of a research associate.

Research associates, in contrast to research assistants, had clear publication rights (although the JAERS policy might have overridden them).

Both Thomas and Aikin (who remained involved in the political science research) sought such a status for Grodzins in 1943. Aikin had wholeheartedly concurred with Thomas's attempt to promote Grodzins to the rank of research associate (telegram, June 20, 1943). In supporting raising his salary, Thomas wrote of "the distinguished work that Grodzins has done and of his demonstrated capacity to assume responsibility and to carry on an important segment of the Study independently" (Thomas:Robert Sproul, June 23, 1943). Because the status of research associate required a PhD, such promotion was impossible, however, so he remained a research assistant.

In addition to gathering newspaper and magazine articles and texts of speeches advocating punitive actions directed at Japanese Americans after the bombing of Pearl Harbor, Grodzins interviewed public officials and private zealots and gained access to constituent letters sent to U.S. congressmen and to the U.S. Department of Justice.[6] As he was an employee of JAERS, the physical materials he gathered belonged to the study and are in the collection (the vacuum cleaner bag) of the Bancroft Library on the campus of the University of California at Berkeley. Ownership of the physical records was never at issue. Literary rights, specifically the right to decide to publish his own analysis of data (and thereby to receive credit as well as royalties for his work) became an issue, as will be seen below.

Besides coordinating JAERS administration, Grodzins's major task within the study was "preparing descriptive accounts of current [WRA] administrative policies." Although he saw the immediate value of this work for JAERS, Grodzins "believed that the study of why evacuation took place had great importance on its own merits. This feeling—plus the feeling that I should complete my dissertation—led me to work in my free hours on the pre-evacuation study. When this did not lead to sufficient progress, I requested Mrs. Thomas to allow me study-time to complete the pre-evacuation study. She refused. Consequently, in July and Aug. of 1944, I obtained a leave of absence without salary and finished the pre-evacuation manuscript in the form of a doctoral dissertation" (Grodzins:Couch and Tyler, October 7, 1948).

According to Thomas (:Jacobus tenBroek, December 12, 1948), Grodzins dictated drafts of his thesis to the study's secretary, Mrs. Wilson, who also typed "numerous drafts."

There is no break in university payroll records for Grodzins for the summer of 1944. He did take a leave from November 23 until December 8 1944—which seems more like a long Thanksgiving break than a leave of sufficient duration to write an eight-hundred-page dissertation. As of November 4, 1944, Thomas reported to Sproul, "The political and administrative segments are conceived as complete as of Jan. 1945." An annual report dated September 1, 1944 had noted, "The political segment of the Study is virtually complete." Grodzins was paid for one and a half months of work (as a research assistant) in 1945, although his appointment terminated January 1, 1945 (Robert S. Johnson:Sproul, December 6, 1948).

Grodzins's dissertation was defended March 21, 1945—that is, while the war in the Pacific was still going on and before any Japanese Americans could travel to or reside within hundreds of miles of the Pacific Coast. Aikin chaired the committee, which included three other political scientists and Thomas. Access to the dissertation was (and remains) restricted. In its preface Grodzins wrote, "Though in a substantially finished form, the manuscript is still regarded as subject to correction and the addition of further data. It will not be circulated in its present state and may not be quoted for any purpose since it contains material classified confidential by federal administrative agencies."

As director of JAERS, Dorothy Thomas had attached the following restriction, dated September 29, 1944, to the dissertation draft: "This thesis contains confidential information collected by the author as a member of the Evacuation and Resettlement Study. By agreement with the Dean of the Graduate Division, this thesis will be withheld from circulation after its approval for the duration of the war. Its circulation is now restricted to members of the examination committee."

That JAERS owned the dissertation as well as materials used in the dissertation was not claimed at the time. Whether or not the dissertation was written "on company time," it was Grodzins's work in the role of a graduate student, not an official report/product by an employee of JAERS, even though Aikin and Thomas supervised his work in both the student and employee roles. Circulation of Grodzins's manuscript was specifically restricted "for the duration of the war" and "since it contains material classified as confidential by federal administrative agencies." This last assertion is puzzling. "Classified as confidential" is not an official U.S. government category. Moreover, I have been unable to find any demands by any official of the federal government to treat material on the "evacuation" decision as secret.

The war's duration was much less than anyone had expected in March 1945, and by August Grodzins was eager to turn his dissertation into a book. He wrote Thomas a three-page letter outlining "what seem to me sound reasons—social and scientific, personal and for the study as a whole—why immediate plans for publication are both feasible and necessary" (Grodzins:Thomas, August 9, 1945).

The Rockefeller Foundation executives strongly agreed that it was important to publish results of the study at the earliest possible moment (Willits:Sproul, January 25, 1945). As the Rockefeller Foundation had not supported the political and economic studies, Rockefeller publication subventions would not have covered Grodzins's manuscript even if money was left for publishing monographs after the official reports were published. (University of California Press manager Samuel T. Farquhar, in a letter to Dorothy Thomas, August 21, 1945, informed Thomas and Sproul that publication of *The Spoilage* [D. Thomas and Nishimoto 1946] and the not-yet-written *The Salvage* [D. Thomas 1952b] would use up the Rockefeller subvention, matched by the university.)

In reply to Grodzins, Thomas did not comment on any of the reasons he had advanced for moving ahead with publishing his work. Instead she firmly asserted her total discretion over publication of JAERS materials:

Your letter of Aug. 9th makes it apparent that you have a number of misconceptions about the Evacuation and Resettlement Study, and your role in it. You were employed by the University of California as a Research Assistant to prepare reports on one segment of the Study. You were paid for this work. At the same time, you were permitted to prepare a thesis for your Ph.D. Since this thesis was based on data collected in the course of your duties for the Study, I restricted its circulation and any independent use of the materials therein, until the Study's publication plans had matured. Whether or not it will be published as a monograph in our series lies within Mr. Aikin's and my discretion. I have every hope that, when revised, it will be so published. However, I make no commitment as to the form of publication, nor do I release you from any of the restrictions we have made upon you until the Study's publication plans are fully matured. This will be a matter of months.... Determination of the use to which materials collected for the Study, and final revision of anything to be published in our series will be my responsibility. In the case of your manuscripts, it will be Mr. Aikin's and my joint responsibility. We may decide to use parts but not the whole of your thesis and of your other reports. In that case, as I have told you repeatedly, I will release thesis and report for your own use, *after* our publication plans are completed. (Thomas:Grodzins, August 18, 1945, providing very early notice that there was no funding in hand for any of the anticipated subsidiary monographs, including a political science one.)

The rationale for and duration of the restriction of circulation of Grodzins's dissertation in this letter differ from the restrictions Thomas had attached to Grodzins's thesis and Grodzins's statement in the preface of the dissertation (both quoted above). Whatever military necessity was involved in preventing disclosure of materials concerning 1941–42 advocacy of punishing Japanese Americans for the bombing of Pearl Harbor could no longer be used in 1945, when the concentration camps were being dismantled, to justify restriction of Grodzins's research. Dorothy Thomas served her formerly most-trusted lieutenant notice that she might decide to use whatever parts of his work she wished in whatever manner she wished, just as she was doing with fieldworkers' notes and reports in drafting *The Spoilage* (D. Thomas and Nishimoto 1946) at that time. The opening portion of *The Spoilage*, for instance, draws heavily on materials assembled by Grodzins and on Tamotsu Shibutani's field notes from the Tanforan Assembly Center. The remainder of the volume, on events at the Tule Lake Segregation Center, relies almost exclusively on the field notes of Rosalie Hankey. Miyamoto noted the irony that "Thomas granted co-authorship to only one research assistant, namely Richard S. Nishimoto, the only one of the assistants not working toward a graduate degree" (1989a:41). Nishimoto did not make demands for theoretical guidance and imposed his "definition of the situation" of factionalism in concentration camp life on Thomas, in the view of Hirabayashi and Hirabayashi (1989) and Spencer (1989:173).

Grodzins maintained hopes that his dissertation would be published in the series of publications everyone expected to issue—with all deliberate speed[7]—from the JAERS. In prodding Aikin to comment on his revised manuscript, Grodzins expressed his concerns that, for Thomas, his

political science viewpoint is bastard to the sociological viewpoint of the larger study; therefore it is a feasible plan to cut the entire manuscript down until it remains a simple chronology of recorded events immediately germane to the evacuation itself. . . . She has never seen the merit of a study of politics, per se, and it was only because of my own bull-headedness that the political monograph was put into the shape it is now. (Remember my seven[?] weeks "leave of absence"?). . . . I think it would be a grave error to cut down the manuscript as it now stands so as to make it "fit" the sociological preconceptions of Dorothy Thomas. I think it should be judged on its merits as a work of politics. (Grodzins:Aikin, October 12, 1945)

Given that Thomas's PhD was in economics, her lifelong involvement in interdisciplinary research, her radically antitheoretical direction of the JAERS, and her notable lack of commitment to any theoretical perspective within sociology, this particular concern of Grodzins's is difficult to consider as made in good faith. Aikin (:Grodzins, December 15, 1945), whom Grodzins had chosen to chair his doctoral committee, raised serious objections to Grodzins's analyses. He judged the manuscript on its merits *as a work of politics* and found it wanting: "In its present form [it] comes close to being a failure . . . hav[ing] failed to place the study in its proper setting," failing to consider the view of the Japanese Americans themselves, failing to consider their relatively greater ability to succeed in pressure politics in Hawaii than in California, and having a partisan double standard (excoriating Governor Warren and trying to exonerate President Roosevelt for what was a presidential order). In general, Aikin wrote, "In this study you have, consciously or unconsciously, become a propagandist" (Aikin:Grodzins, December 15, 1945). Aikin's major objection was that Grodzins did not demonstrate the causal efficacy of West Coast pressure groups on a federal decision. Sproul's assistant later put the point concisely: "Local luncheon and mothers clubs are lumped with growers associations as 'pressure groups,' which, it is charged, were largely responsible both for arousing mass hysteria and developing the pressures on public officials which caused the evacuation to be made. . . . The luncheon clubs, perhaps unlike the growers associations, only reflected the general hysteria, rather than stimulated it for selfish motives. . . . I suspect that public officials, like us of the public in general, believed that the military forces had intelligence which the rest of us did not possess" (Johnson:Sproul, April 1949).

Especially when a country appears to be losing a war—the situation of the United States in the Pacific in early 1942—civilian officials are unlikely to oppose, or even to examine, claims of military necessity made by military commanders, however ill-founded these claims may be. Jacobus tenBroek (1954) later forcefully stressed the dangers to constitutional government when the magical claim to "military necessity" is made. In times of (life-threatening) crisis, independent (civilian) assessments of the rationale of the "experts" tend not to be made. The official JAERS political monograph is a stern indictment of the misuse of specious claims to the "military necessity" of the forced migration of Japanese Americans and the continued failure of the Supreme Court to assess the military rationale offered in the winter and spring of 1942. In contrast, Grodzins's (1949) long book contains only ten pages on the federal judiciary, generally makes incarceration of Japanese Americans seem like a local (State of California) decision rather than one made by the president of the United States, and at no point takes seriously the possibility that anyone in federal or state government in 1942 believed military claims of danger and of secret intelligence about saboteurs.

The racism and economic motivation of some of those who advocated forced removal of one category of "enemy aliens" and of American citizens from one coast are undeniable, and are bluntly stated in *The Spoilage* (D. Thomas and Nishimoto 1946) and in *Prejudice, War and the Constitution* (tenBroek et al. 1954), as well as in *Americans Betrayed* (Grodzins 1949). What the senior faculty involved in JAERS did not think had been established is that traditional West Coast racism, economic interests, and post–Pearl Harbor hysteria had caused Franklin Roosevelt to act as he did. Subsequent histories based on access to military and presidential documents not available to Grodzins reinforce Aikin's case (as P. Suzuki 1986:198 noted).

Grodzins appears to have been a member of the national FDR cult (although quite impervious to the California Warren cult), unwilling to consider that responsibility for such a reprehensible act could rest with Roosevelt. Thomas saw continuity between the social engineering fervor of the New Deal and the conduct of the WRA. Grodzins did not see— or did not want to see—this. 15. In a January 20, 1944, memorandum about meetings with WRA officials in Washington, Dorothy Thomas described it as a typical New Deal, idealistic agency. They carry the torch for the Japanese people, but always in abstract, idealistic terms without much understanding of the problems that are being faced in the projects, or of what the people themselves want. Policies are formed partly on an opportunistic basis, but partly in terms of their abstract idealism, but almost never in terms of concrete problems met by actual individuals. . . . The Washington group is held together by the attacks they are receiving from the outside, which makes crusaders of them, and by a terrible fear that they will lose their agency, that the Justice Department is about to pull the great double-cross.

Aikin saw a continuity between the advocacy of California's Republican attorney general in 1942 (Earl Warren) and its Democratic governor (Culbert Olson), which Grodzins also did not acknowledge (Aikin:Grodzins, December 15, 1945). I find it hard to imagine anyone reading *Prejudice, War and the Constitution* (1954) as a defense of Earl Warren, but tenBroek, Barnhart, and Matson regarded the cravenness of the federal attorney general (Francis Biddle) in eagerly abrogating the Constitution as being as reprehensible and more effectual than the twisted logic and proposals of one state's attorney general.

In Aikin's view major revisions of Grodzins's dissertation were required: "I am asking for more than a change of a few words and the elimination of a few sentences and the substitution of one adjective for another. There is a big job ahead of you, and I hope you will do it" (Aikin:Grodzins, December 15, 1945).

Thomas also continued "to hope that a revised manuscript will be suitable as one of the monographs of the series" (Thomas:Grodzins, December 6, 1945). A volume each on three categories of inmate "evacuees" were planned. *The Spoilage* (D. Thomas and Nishimoto 1946) dealt with the travesty of determining loyalty and the segregation of those labeled "disloyal" at Tule Lake. *The Salvage* (D. Thomas 1952b) dealt with those resettled from the West Coast to concentration camps and then again to Chicago. A third volume, on those who refused a second relocation, tentatively titled "The Residue," was prepared by James Sakoda. Sakoda (1989a:24) reported that Thomas "once offered to publish my dissertation if I would take out the theoretical section, but I was unwilling to do that and she did not bring up the matter again." In a letter dated October 28, 1990, Professor Sakoda wrote me, "I sent Dorothy a copy of the paper and asked for suggestions as to where it might be published. She did not respond to my question and I let the matter pass and have not made any effort to submit it for publication on my own. . . . In typical Nisei fashion we failed to be assertive." (A portion of it is now available as Sakoda 1989b.) None of the ancillary, more specialized monographs were published, although JAERS material was used in several theses, articles, and books. Thomas reiterated (to Grodzins, December 6, 1945), "(1.) The work you have done for the Study is the property of the Study. (2.) If Mr. Aikin makes a favorable recommendation, and if financing is obtained, we hope to include a radically revised and abridged edition in the monograph series. (3.) Until a decision is made on this matter you are to make no independent use of your materials. 'Independent use' is defined as (a) showing the manuscript around, (b) giving speeches based on the material, and (c) publishing articles, books, pamphlets or anything else."

Aikin added, "You will have to obtain a release from a good many people before a publication can avoid amounting to a breach of faith. Yours is a segment of a University study. The University has made certain commitments, many of them, as I recall, through you. To what degree is your study a breach of confidence? None of it can be made public before that point is settled" (Aikin:Grodzins, December 15, 1945).

Although Grodzins professed not to regard Aikin's ten single-spaced pages of criticisms as "nasty medicine" and said he was willing to try to rework his manuscript to satisfy Aikin's criticisms, he sought assurance that there would not then be an entirely different and contradictory set of demands from Thomas: "I need, in a word, to know exactly what is demanded of me and I need that before I can begin to meet those demands. Unless I have this, I have absolutely no heart for the job. Without it, I face an interminable, messy, and fruitless task" (Grodzins:Thomas, January 2, 1946).

He does not seem to have received any such assurances. Three months later Thomas inquired what progress Grodzins had made in meeting Aikin's criticism, reiterating plans for a series of technical monographs for which she was "counting on using your thesis, if you ever get around to the point of taking seriously the criticisms" (Thomas:Grodzins, May 7, 1946). After another three months' silence, Thomas wrote to inform him that two referees, Forrest LaViolette and Milton Chernin, had delivered negative judgments on the publishability of Grodzins's manuscript, independent of Aikin's critique:

Both felt that your treatment does not always do justice to the material. Both expressed opinions as to the propagandistic nature of your writing, and your tendency to over-dramatization. These, of course, are the same points made by Aikin, whose criticisms have always seemed to be thoroughly sound. You apparently have come to the same conclusion: had you felt that Aikin's criticisms were unsound, you would have replied to them long ago. Charles Aikin and I have had several discussions about ways and means of bringing the preevacuation material into publishable form. We have decided that the only possible solution to the problem is to take your manuscript as the basis of the monograph, but to have it completely rewritten by the most competent scholar we can find here on the campus. This scholar will, of course, appear as joint author with you of the monograph. We have asked Chernin to undertake the job, on a joint authorship basis. (Thomas:Grodzins, July 24, 1946)

Given that the first of the three main volumes of the JAERS was being published very reluctantly by the University of California Press under direct pressure from President Sproul and with $20,000 of subventions for the three volumes (half matched by the University of California to Rockefeller grants) and that there was not then a draft of the second volume, one can wonder why she wrote in the same letter, "The time has come when we must make a decision about the monograph on political aspects of preevacuation."

Grodzins found the proposed solution of having Chernin rewrite his dissertation "neither fair nor justified. . . . I can find nothing in recent events that must so suddenly precipitate a change in plans and leave the revisions to somebody other than myself," since "I see no reason why I cannot meet the criticisms you and Mr. Aikin have raised, and I will bend every effort to that end. Once my revisions are made, I will, of course, expect the manuscript to go through an editing process" (Grodzins:Thomas, July 27, 1946). Thomas reiterated that she—in consultation with Aikin in regard to the political and administrative reports—would make decisions about publication, not Grodzins (Thomas:Grodzins, August 2, 1946), and Aikin also wrote that although he thought that "given unlimited time to reappraise the very foundations of your view and to recast your material, you could turn out a highly creditable manuscript" (Aikin:Grodzins, August 29, 1946), it would take more of his time and energy than Aikin was willing to spend and would in effect constitute coauthorship. Therefore, Aikin was convinced that another coauthor who did have the time was needed. A later Berkeley report provides the following summary of the next, faltering steps:

> In the following twelve months after Chernin had been called in, nothing like collaboration took place. Except for one letter, there was no correspondence between them. They met for one evening early in Jan., 1947. Professor Chernin says that he planned to withdraw from the arrangement if Grodzins produced an acceptable revision. In May, 1947, Grodzins produced a revision which he sent to Chernin with a long letter of explanation. The revision proved wholly unacceptable, not only to Chernin, but also to Professors Thomas and Aikin (Aikin to Thomas, Aug. 1, 1947). It was their opinion that there had been no actual re-writing or re-casting. All that had been done to conform to the extensive criticism was a pastepot and scissors job of deletion. (Jacobus tenBroek and Edward N. Barnhart, "Report on the Grodzins Affair Prepared for the Library Sub-Committee," November 3, 1948)

After Chernin bowed out, Thomas had Richard Nishimoto, the one Japanese American to whom she had granted coauthorship (of *The Spoilage*), attempt to revise Grodzins's manuscript. Feeling that a political scientist needed to be involved, she sent it to Jay Graham, who had studied constitutional law at Berkeley and whose MA had been supervised by Aikin (Thomas:Graham, February 11, March 2, 1948). Graham replied (March 26, 1948) that the best way to handle the "political aspects" material was as she and Nishimoto had done in *The Spoilage*.

The next candidate, Oliver Garceau, turned down an $800 summer stipend, while dismissing the Nishimoto revision as "mere chronology" (Garceau:Thomas, April 4, 1948). Finally, Thomas enlisted Jacobus tenBroek, a prominent authority on constitutional law who was just completing a major study on the history of the fourteenth amendment (tenBroek 1951). He was located in the Berkeley speech department, a rather odd conglomeration of scholars in a university notable for the weakness of departmental organization (see chapter 13). Together with his colleague Edward Barnhart and a graduate student, Floyd Matson, he would write a book using JAERS materials, supplemented by further research and tenBroek's sustained critique of the Supreme Court's failure to reject racially motivated preventive detention of a minority population by the federal government under extraordinarily dubious claims of "military necessity," *Prejudice, War and the Constitution* (1954).

Frozen out of the newly formed sociology department, Thomas left Berkeley and went to the University of Pennsylvania at the end of the summer of 1948. Her ample grounds for bitterness probably exacerbated her feeling of being betrayed by Grodzins. In turning over restricted and unrestricted JAERS materials to a library committee to be appointed by Sproul, Thomas wrote the harshest account to that date of *l'affaire* Grodzins, accusing Grodzins of violating the conditions under which his dissertation was allowed to be written in offering "his copy of the manuscript to at least one commercial publisher," suggesting that her departure might "reactivate Grodzins," and stressing the need "to prevent the virtual destruction of the important and heavily subsidized political segment of the Study by the publication of Grodzins' incompetent work, to make impossible his flagrant abuse of highly confidential materials obtained in the name of the University, to protect members of the University of California faculty who are now preparing a monograph on the subject" (Thomas memorandum to the office of the president, University of California, August 25, 1948).

This definition of the situation has to be regarded as unbalanced. If she and Aikin viewed the dissertation as incompetent, it is not likely that a PhD committee chaired by Aikin and that included her would have granted Grodzins the degree or that the two of them would have written as they did in 1943 when attempting to promote him for the quality of his independent work. If Grodzins's manuscript could be published elsewhere without a subvention and there was no funding at hand for any ancillary manuscripts, publication elsewhere was not a drain on subsidies. Publication would not destroy the data, which were safely housed in Berkeley, and the foundation executives underwriting the original research expected publication of results to commence soon after the end of the war.

Interuniversity Discussions in Late 1948

Unbeknownst to anyone at Berkeley, the University of Chicago Press had been considering Grodzins's manuscript. On the recommendation of Hans Morgenthau, Robert Redfield, and David Riesman, the Social

Science Research Committee of the University of Chicago authorized a $3,500 subsidy for its publication, although expressing concern about the legal status of quoting letters to the Department of Justice and congressmen (Tyler:Couch, April 23, 1948).

A few days after drafting the warning memorandum she was leaving behind, Thomas received confirmation that the University of Chicago Press was preparing to publish Grodzins's manuscript and hastened to inform Chicago that

> the materials on which this manuscript is based are the property of the University of California and that Grodzins had, in effect pirated them.... [that] he gathered the material now offered you for publication as a paid employee of the University of California—most of it on representation that he was so employed and much of it under commitment to secrecy... [and that] the Study has undertaken commitments with members of the University faculty to analyze the data for a monograph to be brought out by the University of California Press. This monograph will utilize materials collected by Grodzins. Its publication is being subsidized in part by the Rockefeller Foundation. The prior and unauthorized publication of Grodzins' manuscript would, of course, constitute an infringement of these commitments. (Tyler:Couch, April 23, 1948)

It is puzzling that Thomas again advanced the Rockefeller subsidy as a reason for Chicago not to publish a book that would not drain any of the resources of that subsidy. Moreover, the Rockefeller subsidy was for the *Spoilage/Salvage/Residue* trilogy. If any money was left, it could be used for other monographs, of which one on the ecology of loyalty had first precedence (it was to be drafted by George Kuznets). A book on pre-evacuation politics was not mentioned in the Rockefeller grant application (Thomas, May 1, 1942) and had been specifically excluded from the application for Rockefeller funding of research. The proposal to support political research was made to the Columbia Foundation. It stipulated that "the study should continue for the duration of the war. Approximately six months after the end of the war will be required for the preparation of the manuscripts." Usual requirements for annual reports were waived, and the foundation's director accepted "the further likelihood of its final report being held until the cessation of the war" in making the grant (Thomas:Marjorie Elkus, July 7, 1942; Elkus:Sproul, August 5, 1942).

I do not think Thomas served her own cause well by writing, "the ERS would have been glad to grant permission for the publication of Grodzins' manuscript, had it been a competent piece of workmanship," and deriding its "unscholarly character." The University of Chicago Press had not sought Thomas's opinion on the quality of the work and had positive evaluations from its own referees (Philip Glick and Eugene V. Rostow) as well as the stellar group of University of Chicago social scientists who had approved a local subvention (Redfield, Riesman, Morgenthau). An unsolicited evaluation so markedly at odds with the approbation of this distinguished quintet drawn from several disciplines must have seemed very strange as well as gratuitous. After all, the University of Chicago had long been the leading American institution in social sciences, and its faculty and press had sufficient experience in judging the value of social science work to reach a decision about a manuscript without the assistance of California faculty. In a September 1948 memorandum to Dean Tyler, Grodzins appealed to what Merton called the norm of communism: "She will, I know, grant our Research Committee and our press the right of forming their own judgments with respect to the merit and scholarly qualities of the MS. Our readers have pronounced the work an excellent and unique contribution to the social sciences. . . . Final judgment on the merit of the work will be the community of scholars. Their judgment should not be forestalled by personal or other reasons."

In the letter that Tyler actually did send, he noted, more briefly, that the University of Chicago Committee on Social Science Research and the University of Chicago Press Board "are satisfied as to the merits of the manuscript and as to the author's competence to deal with a study in this important field. The study reports a highly significant phenomenon about which, six years later, little has been published. Hence, the committees consider the publication a contribution to knowledge and to public policy" (Tyler:Sproul, September 11, 1948).

Grodzins also solicited statements from former JAERS staff at Chicago that verbal agreements not to publish their work done and paid for by JAERS was explicitly "for the duration of the war." Tamotsu Shibutani (letter to Grodzins, September 4, 1948) noted that he had assumed that permission was needed to use data gathered by project colleagues but not data gathered by oneself.[8]

University of Chicago Press director William Couch wrote Jacobus tenBroek, who had been engaged to write the legal/political study and was chairman of a subcommittee of the University of California Library Committee appointed September 7, 1948, to investigate the facts and recommend a course of action to President Sproul, requesting a copy of a contract or letter of understanding between Grodzins and JAERS that would be violated by publication of Grodzins's manuscript (Couch:tenBroek, September 9, 1948).

In reply, tenBroek quoted a September 22, 1948, telegram from the secretary of the American Association of University Professors: "Publication rights of research assistants in universities in absence of specific terms of employment in contract are governed by custom and usage of the institution. In general research assistants do not have rights of independent publication but in published reports based on research projects in which they participated are given credit for participation" (Ralph E. Himstead:tenBroek, telegram, September 22, 1948).

After mentioning that there was no contract or letters from Thomas during the study that established a right to eventual publication, tenBroek reported that the local view was "that a research assistant would not take money of the University and also the data he was paid to collect for the University was simply assumed as so unusual in such employment that it required no express stipulation" (tenBroek:Couch, September 24, 1948). In another letter tenBroek supplied citations from *Corpus Juris* dealing with employer ownership of work done for hire. The University of Chicago's own legal counsel, Howard H. Moore, concurred with tenBroek: "Literary property in data and material collected by a person specifically employed for that purpose vests in the employer unless the contract of employment provides to the contrary. . . . A professor or research assistant in connection with their general employment may write any sort of literary work they see fit and will own the exclusive literary property in such work. Neither a professor nor a Research Assistant, if employed for the specific purpose of *gathering* data and materials with respect to a particular matter in which the employer is interested would own the literary property in the material collected" (Moore:Couch, September 19, 1948)

University of Chicago Law School professor (and future U.S. solicitor general) Edward H. Levi weighed in with his view that "California has stronger legal case than Moore says because of the difficulties of successfully conducting research projects if control over factual material cannot be maintained up to the time of the end of the study" (Levi:Couch, October 25, 1948).

Moore wrote in another letter, "I believe that the legal position of the University of California in this matter is correct and that we have no right to publish this material without its consent. Our publication of the MS would not appear to involve a matter of vital public interest in view of the fact that the original source material presumably is still available for reference" (Moore:Couch, October 1, 1948; neither the project materials nor Grodzins's PhD dissertation were available to anyone at that point, however).

Moore further opined that the burden of proof that material was not gathered as an employee was on Grodzins. Grodzins did nothing to meet this burden of proof but continued to collect affidavits from key former government officials stating that data obtained through their consent could be published and was not given exclusively to the University of California but to public history and/or science.

Throwing Oil on the Flames

Despite instructions not to substitute his legal opinions for the university's legal counsel's, Couch continued to press his own legal judgments—even to the president of the university. Couch wrote President E. C. Doe, "I have not the slightest doubt . . . that the course I have decided to pursue, unless I am ordered not to do so, is legally as well as morally sound" (October 25, 1948). Clearly he had adopted publication of Grodzins's manuscript as a moral imperative. To the manager of the University of California Press, Samuel T. Farquhar, Couch wrote,

> If Mr. Grodzins's study had been made under the auspices of a research committee in the Southern United States, if his subjects had been the Negro, and if he had then had the same experience that he has had with the research committee in California, I think if I were running my own publishing concern I would go ahead and publish his book, and I don't believe anybody anywhere could stop me. There are certain kinds of materials that by their nature belong to the public, and if public or philanthropic funds are spent in the collection of this material, it cannot honestly be kept indefinitely from the public. I would not respect any customs or agreements of

any kind whatever, existing in any southern states, designed to keep information concerning southern white treatment of the Negro from the public at large. If this is a sound position to take with reference to the South, it is a sound one to take with reference to the West. (November 23, 1948)

Couch had headed the University of North Carolina Press before going to Chicago and may have had such experience there, but this inflammatory analogy infuriated the California faculty involved with the study, who had expressed no concern about the public relations of Californians' behavior. This rhetoric of acquiescence to racism was quickly rejected by Grodzins himself, who knew that Thomas, Aikin, and Sproul had opposed evacuation and had not become less critical of the decision over time in deference to the (diminished) feeling of California racists: "I have never, in any way, indicated this ['race prejudice'] as a motive of the people at California; (2) I do not believe this motive has any relevance in explaining your stand; and (3) I have carefully explained this to all concerned. I confess I was a little shocked to hear these statements attributed to me.... After all, the record of Dorothy, President Sproul, and the University of California is very clear with respect to the Japanese evacuation. Why anybody would believe I would spread stories that are clearly inconsistent with that record is beyond my understanding" (Grodzins:tenBroek, October 1948).

A draft of a letter that was apparently not sent, prepared by attorney Jno U. Calkins on November 4, 1948, noted Sproul's "record as Chairman of the Committee on American Principles and Fair Play during the evacuation period, when the feelings of such groups were much more intense than they are now" to intimations of "fear of antagonizing certain powerful political and economic groups."

The issues were more prosaic than the crusade seen by Couch and centered on ownership of materials collected by research assistants and control over publication—something of presumptive shared interest for all research universities. On this subject, also, Couch had inflammatory moralistic rhetoric as his first line of defense. In his summary for the press's editorial board Couch noted that in industry there are written agreements to avoid such misunderstandings and opined that California owned the materials Grodzins had collected but that Grodzins owned his manuscript. These sensible arguments did not suffice for the crusade

Couch was on, however, and he added the kind of inflammatory rhetoric that undercut his own credibility in the same way Dorothy Thomas had, calling *l'affaire* Grodzins "one of the most flagrant cases of abuse of power by scholars controlling research funds" he had ever encountered, adding that "the kind of contract that California insists was made is so irregular that even if written and signed by both parties it is doubtful that it could be maintained if seriously contested in courts" and that "if Chicago acceded to California demands, it would establish a precedent for yellow dog contracts: and the pernicious notion that property claims can control expression of political opinion" (Couch:committee on publications, October 27, 1948). Political "opinion" rather than political "science" is a telling choice of words. Contrary to Couch, this kind of implicit contract providing the faculty member with ownership of work produced by paid subordinates remained regular a quarter of a century later when I was a graduate student research assistant and continues to be. Many graduate students since Grodzins have felt their work was unfairly controlled (indeed, expropriated) by faculty supervisors.

Again, in his statement to the Board of University of Chicago Publications on November 5, 1948, Couch trumpeted his superior legal determination: "The conduct of California displayed an appalling ignorance of the law of literary property [shared by the University of Chicago's lawyer, although not by Couch], as well as disregard of ordinary human rights, an ignorance and disregard unfortunately shared by many people in responsible positions in the academic world." He added that the "precedent of University of Chicago will effect custom and ultimately determine[!] law."

Similarly, in an October 25, 1948, letter to tenBroek that the administration would not let him send, Couch proclaimed that "Mr. Grodzins did not divest himself of the rights common to all persons when he became a RA." Chancellor Robert Hutchins wrote Couch on November 2, 1948, "(1) The protest of the University of California against the publication of Grodzins's MS is not irrelevant to the question whether the University of Chicago should publish it, and (2) the decision whether the MS should be published OVER the protest of the University of California *must* be made in this [the chancellor's] office."

Sproul's Alleged Suppression

There is abundant archival material on Grodzins' and Couch's definition of the situation. There is no evidence that University of California president Sproul ever made any attempt to suppress Grodzins's publication. Unfortunately, there is practically no record of his *personal* view of the matter either. As he was a longtime friend and supporter of Governor Warren (Warren chose Sproul to place his name before the 1948 Republican Convention as a candidate for president of the United States), it is easy to attribute possible political motivation to him, and the opportunity to try to protect Warren and/or other anti-Japanese partisans certainly existed. All that Sproul did, however, was to ask the subcommittee of the library committee that had charge of the JAERS archives to investigate Thomas's charges and to consider what the University of California's position should be. The committee reported back within two months. Sproul then did exactly what Aikin, the subcommittee headed by tenBroek, and also the University of California's counsel, Calkins, Hall, Linforth & Conrad, had recommended he do: make California's case, and "if, after that the University of Chicago is adamant in its position, we then suggest that the University of California should withdraw from the controversy" (Jno U. Calkins:Sproul, November 4, 1948). Calkins made this recommendation even believing that the University of California had a sound legal case:

> I have come to the conclusion, but not with certainty amounting to conviction, that we could enjoin Mr. Grodzins and the University of Chicago from publishing the former's thesis . . . [among other bases] on the ground of unfair competition. . . . The restraining order, if granted, would probably enjoin only such publication as would injure the University of California's economic interest in the material.
>
> The possibility of our enjoining publication on the ground that the thesis quotes from letters and reports obtained in confidence and to a limited extent from what appear at least originally to have been classified government documents seems to be somewhat doubtful. . . . I do not think that the University of California could be held civilly liable in damages to the authors of the letters; neither do I think that it could be held criminally liable for violation of espionage laws, if Mr. Grodzins and the University of Chicago chose to publish the thesis in its present form. I would be practically certain of this conclusion, if the University of California expressly denied permission to publish.

However, extralegal considerations weighed against legal action. These included the necessity of bringing action in Illinois and getting witnesses from both coasts there.

And although this is beyond my field, if the letters from Mr. Couch, the director of the University of Chicago Press, to Mr. Farquhar are a criterion, much talk about suppression of information for political reasons, freedom of speech and press, etc. can be anticipated. Further relationships with the University of Chicago should also be considered. In conclusion, I therefore recommend that you send a letter to Dean Tyler strongly objecting to the proposed publication and pointing out the numerous moral and legal factors involved. Definitely, I do not believe that suit should be threatened. . . . If the University of Chicago should disregard our protest and publish, I believe I would be inclined to let the matter drop. (Calkins:Sproul, November 10, 1948)

Aikin wrote tenBroek on October 11, 1948, "Sproul should be prevailed upon not to file an injunction. I am sure few things would give Morton more pleasure than this sort of action, which he could blazon throughout the so-called liberal elements of the social sciences as a 'dastardly suppression' of a scholar's work in a controversial field." Thus, insofar as "inter-university comity" in the publication of Grodzins's dissertation was involved, this was California not pressing legal action against Chicago, rather than Chicago suppressing a book that may have been uncongenial to the president of the University of California.[9]

Sproul, Tyler, and Grodzins met in Tyler's office on December 7. According to Sproul's notes,

Both Dean Tyler and Mr. Grodzins expressed regret over the intemperate letters which Mr. Couch had written. They explained these on the grounds that Couch is a Southerner, has been deviled in North Carolina and elsewhere for his attitude on race relations, and is disposed to look for censors of publications which are liberal in this regard, where none such exists. . . . Concerning the scholarly integrity of the Study, neither he [Grodzins] nor Dean Tyler seemed able to be able to understand what our people are driving at. (Sproul memorandum on a meeting with Tyler, December 7, 1948)

Both Grodzins and Chicago law school professor Malcolm Sharp had the impression that Sproul was personally more sympathetic to Grodzins's publication than he could officially say. Sharp noted in a December 28, 1948, memorandum to Chancellor Robert Hutchins that Sproul "said that his own opinion did not coincide with that of his board, and emphasized strongly there would be no controversy with California if Chicago should publish. He asked that his remarks be kept strictly confidential but the circumstances indicated plainly that he expected the person who would make the final decision to be informed of his opinion, i.e., that publication by Chicago should cause no further controversy."

Although somewhat impressionistic and uncertain evidence, this indicates that Grodzins and Sharp perceived Sproul to have been on their side and not to have attempted to suppress the book, despite the possible political motivation some have supposed. It also suggests that Sproul telegraphed the intent not to take actions to sustain the objections of the leaders and custodians of the JAERS.

Sproul told Grodzins that California wouldn't formally withdraw objections but that Hutchins would authorize signing a contract,[10] and on December 28, 1948, four months after Thomas raised objections to Chicago, Hutchins authorized publication (Hutchins:Couch, December 30, 1948). The contract was signed January 28, 1949.

Thomas L. Marshall then delivered yet another independent legal opinion to the University of Chicago Press that the repetition of various charges was potentially libelous. He wrote that the book could not be approved as it was, and deletions were made (Marshall:Couch, January 26, 1949). In July 1949 *Americans Betrayed* was published to generally positive reviews. For example, Marc Rivette wrote in the *San Francisco Chronicle*, "If the reading of this study has the effect of making us realize that a democracy never has the need of totalitarian methods, then it will undoubtedly turn out to be one of the most valuable books of the decade" (June 26, 1949, 22). One exception to the favorable reception was a review by someone who had found the manuscript unpublishable: Forrest LaViolette (1949) in *Pacific Affairs*.

On August 25, 1949, Marjorie Elkus, executive director of the Columbia Foundation, which had funded the political part of JAERS, wrote Dorothy Thomas and President Sproul, asking about "the propriety of Mr. Grodzins' action in the publishing of an independent account of the situation, the data of which, according to his own statement, was compiled during his term of employment on the project." Sproul talked to her in person; Thomas wrote Elkus, "The University's record is clear; the Committee and all individuals authorized to speak for the University refused unequivocally to grant permission to the University of Chicago Press to publish the manuscript. Publication was, therefore, entirely unauthorized" (October 21, 1949).

By refusing to grant permission for Grodzins's publication while not attempting any action against the University of Chicago, Sproul succeeded in maintaining amicable relations with foundations and other universities.

Although not without extended difficulties with University of California Press reviewers, the official JAERS book on legal and political aspects of the concentration camps, tenBroek, Barnhart, and Matson's *Prejudice, War and the Constitution*, appeared in 1954. Couch was soon dismissed at Chicago, replaced by none other than Morton Grodzins.[11]

Discussion

The romantic vision of Chicago crusaders for Truth triumphing over Californians cowed by local political consideration into attempting to suppress it has little basis. It does not seem plausible that Robert Sproul, who was willing to oppose vocal racists in the midst of 1942 and who supported a study that was committed to examining pressure by California officials and organizations to trample the constitutional rights of Japanese Americans, was afraid in 1948 of possible negative reactions to a historical book that made arguments similar to those he had made in the heat of wartime hysteria. Nor is there any reason to suppose that Dorothy Thomas or Charles Aikin became sympathetic to California racists after the war. The official JAERS publications are indictments of the rationale for and conduct of American concentration camps.

In addition to substantive dissatisfaction with Grodzins's partial and partisan analysis, the directors of JAERS had legitimate concerns about coordinating a large-scale project. Order could not be maintained on a research project if research assistants could make independent decisions to publish whatever data they chose, before project reports were issued. Although Couch did not evidence any understanding of this concern, Chicago administrators probably did, even before Edward Levi pointed it out (Levi:Couch, October 25, 1948).

That project leaders sought someone else to do the work Grodzins had not and would not do is consistent with routine in team research. Within the JAERS Thomas had had Nishimoto write about Rosalie Hankey's data, George Kuznets analyze Sakoda's, and various people work on Charles Kikuchi's diary (Sakoda:author, October 28, 1990). She felt that she had rightful, complete control of project data, regardless of who had originally collected them. Both the decision to reassign data analysis and intraorganizational conflicts are normal features of ongoing collaborative research projects.[12] If centralization of control over publication decisions is a violation of the First Amendment of the U.S. Constitution, or a "yellow dog contract," as Couch maintained, it is standard operating procedure (and routine trouble) in academic science.

Although less common, cases have been reported to me of graduate students whose advisors agree to grant their degrees and permit them to leave the institution only if the student pledges not to publish research in a particular problem area for a period of some years. "Problem area" has been defined quite broadly in these cases, and no sanctions against such restraint against competition from former students have been invoked against the professors (one of whom holds an endowed chair). The graduated students, even after they have positions elsewhere, felt that they continued to need or might in the future need positive references from their former teachers and suffered through starting new lines of research, honoring what are surely legally unenforceable, unwritten contracts.

In contrast, Grodzins apparently felt he had new patrons at Chicago and that his career would be better advanced by publication of the research he had done than it would be hurt by the attempts of his doctoral mentors to criticize his work. There can be little doubt that this judgment was correct. Thirty years later Grodzins had someone (P. Suzuki 1989) writing of him as practically a martyr because a publication contract was delayed a quarter of a year while conflicting claims were sorted out and adopting the Couch definition of the situation as racially/politically motivated "suppression." As Barnes and Dolby noted, "No scientist is totally in the power of others, sanctions are in fact very limited" (1970:25) against anyone determined to resist social pressure, and especially against anyone with an alternative set of backers, for, as they also noted, "scientists do not typically treat all other scientists as a significant reference group" (20). Grodzins quite clearly cut himself loose from those who had supervised his work at Berkeley and received backing from some prominent Chicagoans—before taking the job of his primary Chicago proponent.

The communications between Thomas and some senior Chicago social scientists suggests a national "invisible college," despite Grodzins's success in disrupting its cohesion and interinstitutional solidarity. Insofar as Thomas and Aikin (correctly, as is now clear) challenged the adequacy of Grodzins's causal inferences, the "technical norms" that Mulkay (1969) argued are the salient norms in scientific conflicts were invoked, although even Grodzins's latter-day advocate (P. Suzuki 1989) does not attempt to claim that *Americans Betrayed* was theoretically or methodologically innovative or that it advanced a new paradigm in political science, or even a paradigm extension. For a genuine challenge to the "normal science" of work on "mass hysteria" in which Grodzins operated, and coincidentally, one that was at least influenced by work on JAERS, see Shibutani (1966).

The delay in publishing Grodzins's book should be weighed against the need of a research project to maintain control of its data and the orderly dissemination of its results. Three years is a very long time for a junior faculty member to wait for his major work to become public. By the time Grodzins's book was under consideration at Chicago other books about the concentration camps for Japanese Americans had already been published (LaViolette 1945; Leighton 1945; Spicer et al. 1946),[13] and the southern branch of the University of California had completed and was about to publish a book based on a study of those Japanese Americans who returned to Los Angeles when they could (Broom and Riemer 1949)— although no study of the decision to remove the Japanese Americans in 1942 had appeared. Only one of the three main books in the JAERS publishing plan had been published by 1948. The official political/administrative report did not appear until 1954, and none of the other ancillary monographs planned (and in some cases written) was ever published at all. Moreover, *The Salvage* was going to exhaust the publication subsidy. (Although Grodzins presumably did not know this, Aikin, Thomas, and Sproul did.) Thomas was separated from the JAERS data after August 1948 and neither she nor anyone else involved with the project apparently knew what to do with the vast amounts of data that had been gathered. In contrast, Grodzins knew what he wanted to do with the data he had gathered and had found a prestigious publisher eager to publish his manuscript. Especially in retrospect, he had good cause to be concerned about both the pace and the extent of JAERS publication.

It is easy to understand Grodzins's desire to get a book out. It is also easy to understand his concern that Thomas and Aikin were attempting to scuttle an academic career they had launched. Sproul was aware of the general pressure to publish that concentrates on academics beginning their careers and of the extraordinary situation Grodzins was in:

> He belongs to the faculty of a university which requires publication of doctoral dissertations. Yet the university which granted him his doctorate not only has prevented publication of his dissertation, his chief work of scholarship to date, but has even refused him permission to show it to his department chairman and college dean, while at the same time a California faculty member [Thomas] has written to Chicago officers denouncing it as unscholarly and incompetent ... [although] the acceptance of his dissertation by the University of California [and, specifically, by the same faculty members then denouncing it as unscholarly] was an implied certification of its publishability. (Johnson:Sproul, October 4, 1948)

As I have already suggested, the spectacle of Aikin and Thomas denouncing a work they had certified and its author, for whom they had written glowing letters of reference, must have puzzled Chicago administrators. It is my impression that Thomas's attacks were written off as the personal animosity of a flighty woman by the administrators of both universities. As Tyler wrote Sproul, "From the exchange of correspondence which I have reviewed, correspondence running for several years, it appears to me that the efforts of Mrs. Thomas to prevent publication of the manuscript has nothing to do with national security, the joint interest of government agencies, the University and the Foundations, but rather with personal biases" (October 4, 1948; also see Johnson:Sproul, October 4, 1948; and TenBroek and Barnhart, "Report on the Grodzins Affair," November 3, 1948, p. 6). The complete break in previously very amicable personal relations between Thomas and Grodzins is striking. Thomas took a very peremptory tone toward Grodzins as a subordinate in the study after he had left, that was quite at odds with her warm and collegial tone toward him when he actually was a direct subordinate and student.

If one were to grant for a moment the sexist expectations that I think were involved in dismissing Thomas's objections, it went unremarked at the time that Aikin, the chair of Grodzins's committee, also had praised Grodzins's independence and judgment during the war, approved Grodzins's dissertation, and attempted to exert control over his scholarship only after Grodzins was beyond the reach of his committee's or the study's control. As tenBroek explained to Grodzins, by 1948, the official California view was that "your study as a factual investigation and collection of vitally important social science data is terrific; that your write-up, integration and handling of the material falls far short of scholarship; and that the University of California has an interest in seeing that the data are handled in a scholarly way" (tenBroek:Grodzins, October 1, 1948). He later added to Sharp, "In varying degrees, practically everybody out here is sympathetic to the major conclusions stated in the manuscript. The University might still have a reasonable interest in maintaining the integrity of its research project and of reasonable standards of scholarship" (tenBroek:Malcolm [Sharp], November 2, 1948).

It is possible that Thomas and Aikin considered the data collection sufficiently impressive original research to grant the degree or to have taken the expedient course of passing Grodzins out. Neither of these rationales would have been unique to PhD examiners, and Grodzins's memorandum for Couch and Tyler (which was not shared with anyone at California) conceded that "she [Thomas] held a number of reservations with respect to its 'unscientific' character at various points" at the time. It is no exaggeration to say that Thomas was compulsively concerned with verification or that she had a strong aversion to speculative conclusions and, indeed, to any linking of research results to existing social science theory. Her comments on staff reports throughout the course of the project are a litany of "How do you know this?" and "Unwarranted speculation!" challenges, and there is no reason to suppose that she had a double standard for Grodzins. Like her husband (and Franz Boas), Dorothy Thomas preferred amassing raw data (notably personal accounts) to generalizing and drawing conclusions from them. Moreover, few publications derived from the massive (for its time) project. Even decades later, JAERS data are closely held. Access to material is restricted in ways that data about American Indians' history of being crowded onto reservations or Mexican Americans being expropriated are not restricted in the same library. Practically nothing from the study has been published,[14] including other dissertations written by JAERS fieldworkers and monographs ready for publication in the 1940s. Little publicly available knowledge resulted from the project.[15]

While it is probably true that no one, including herself, ever met Thomas's standards of proof, it also bears stressing that during the three years between defending his dissertation and submitting a slightly revised version to the University of Chicago Press, Grodzins does not appear to have made any serious efforts to meet or to answer the criticisms made by Charles Aikin, the man he chose to chair the committee that accepted his dissertation, in his ten-page letter of December 15, 1945. The three years—which does not seem unusual, and was far more time than it took administrators at the two universities to sort out myriad legal, moral, and administrative claims—was to a considerable extent an artifact of Grodzins's inaction on the editing demanded by Aikin and endorsed by Thomas, along with some admitted duplicity. By his own admission, Grodzins lied to tenBroek in telling him that his manuscript was not under review (Grodzins:tenBroek, September 1, 1948) and also deliberately misled JAERS directors to believe that he was working on revisions based on Aikin's critique when he was not (Grodzins:Aikin, August 9, 1945, July 27, 1946).

In team research, disputes about credit are routine,[16] but I find it impossible to suppose that either Thomas or Aikin was seeking to have their names listed as coauthors. From what I know of their work and from thorough examination of surviving correspondence, I am certain that they had serious doubts about the "scientific" adequacy of Grodzins's analysis. In terms of the institutional norms of science proposed by Merton, I think it would be fair to say that they felt they were conforming to the demands of organized skepticism, as well as to Mulkay's (1969) "technical norms" of how to do credible "science." Insofar as deviance from the norm of disinterestedness was involved, they saw Grodzins as violating it both in terms of self-aggrandizement and in terms of participating in partisan politics. Since neither Aikin nor Thomas sought to attach their names to publication (including the eventual JAERS product, *Prejudice, War and the Constitution*), they would surely have rejected any charge of self-interest guiding their behavior in opposing publication of Grodzins's manuscript.

In terms of the norms prescribed (for Science, not for individual scientists) by Merton, Thomas exemplified skepticism about claims so thoroughgoing that obligations to share either data or conclusions did not arise in her mind. To express her position within Merton's rhetoric, there was no obligation to share/communicate unverified assertions; Grodzins's conclusions were not (yet) science. Organized skepticism could preempt communism as the guiding norm insofar as only results judged valid need to be released. Thomas and Aikin did not believe that it was "knowledge" or "science" they were holding back from publication. There is no reason to suppose that they would have disagreed with a statement of Merton's norm of communism of scientific findings. Indeed, Thomas attempted to enlist other political scientists to work with the data to bring them into scientific form. Grodzins fervently opposed this kind of sharing of data he had been hired to gather in his job as a research assistant. He clearly felt (and successfully defended) a proprietary interest.

I do think that over the course of the project, with its frequent need to preserve autonomy from mounting demands for access to data made by the army and WRA bureaucracies, Dorothy Thomas developed an excessive concern over the secrecy of project data.[17] It is hard not to speculate that the acute concern about controlling the data was not entirely a function of protecting project workers inside the camps and preventing political uses of reports against the incarcerated population but was also to some degree a compensation for loss of control related to the death of her husband and the successful campaign to keep her outside the sociology department that was founded in Berkeley after the war (the subject of chapter 13).

Whatever the biographical explanations for her extreme concern with secrecy, the rejection of her claims of a continued need to restrict materials by the former officials who had granted the project (in the person of Morton Grodzins) access to material undercut her position as an eminent, reasonable social scientist and helped those with whom she had clashed (especially Dillon Myer, head of the WRA) to portray her as a vindictive, unbalanced woman. I believe that her failed attempt to invoke a need for secrecy distracted officials at both universities from the fundamental question of whether a research assistant could publish data gathered as an employee of a project when the head(s) of the project pressed objections of ownership and the need to coordinate dissemination of results.

Conclusion

Although in my view Dorothy Thomas had exaggerated concerns about the secrecy, reliability, and validity of data and her demands for total, personal control of all data gathered made her reasonableness suspect to the University of Chicago officials seeking to assess University of California claims, it seems to me that the JAERS publication policy established in 1942—in a meeting she did not attend—clearly added some extraordinary restrictions on dissemination of results to those usually necessary for orderly coordination of large-scale projects. The 1940s University of California policy on research assistants' lack of right to independent publication was also clear.[18] *The Spoilage* showed that Thomas would use JAERS project reports and data as she saw fit. It seems to me that Grodzins skillfully misrepresented the independence of his manuscript from the project—and also his financial "sacrifices" to work on the project, as Robert S. Johnson detailed in a December 6, 1948, memorandum to Sproul.

Thomas's scattergun attack, in contrast to the invariably diplomatic tone of Grodzins's letters, helped him convey the appearance that she was on a personal vendetta and was herself manufacturing foundation concerns, even though these actually did arise when Grodzins's book was published. I think that Grodzins succeeded in establishing that WRA, congressional, and Justice Department officials did not grant access exclusively to the University of California and that those who had been involved in negotiating project access wanted the research to be published. On the other hand, Chicago's lawyers were concerned about some issues of ownership that were the real basis of California's case against unauthorized publication of project results. The more peripheral, specific changes demanded by Chicago counsel as well by Aikin and Thomas were made before publication in 1949.

Couch's charges of racism helped Grodzins's cause. Grodzins was in the position of being able to disavow charges made by another, at the same time as the sensitivity about charges inhibited the opposing side. Despite the lack of substantiation of charges about political/racist suppression, and Grodzins's own repudiation of them, California faculty and administrators were sufficiently sensitive about appearances of such motivations as to be reluctant to press their case for control over research assistants' work, a need that they expected Chicagoans to understand.

Out of concern for political fallout and to preserve interuniversity co-mity, President Sproul decided not to seek a legal injunction against the University of Chicago Press. That is, rather than political concerns lead-ing to the suppression of research, they had the opposite effect, leading to the publication by a junior researcher over the objections of senior faculty members administering the research project. The special vul-nerability of women in positions of academic authority in the 1940s and the special sensitivity of the administration of a state university in a state whose officials were criticized in the manuscript for fomenting racially based incarceration inhibit generalization of this case as a precedent for freedom to publish results gathered under contract to a research proj-ect. It does seem that a research assistant who proceeds against the ob-jections of project directors must be independent of their control—and have a secure position beyond their reach and/or new patrons.

   In his tenure as chief editor of the University of Chicago Press, Grodz-ins was confronted with a similar case in which the senior directors of a Chicago research project asserted ownership of all materials from the project and demanded that a work accepted by the press be withheld. Grodzins's zeal for the right of junior scientists to exercise their own judgment about publishing controversial work seems to have waned. The University of Chicago Press did not publish the book, and publica-tion elsewhere was blocked for nine years, in contrast to the precedent of expeditious publication of Grodzins's own book. The case is detailed in James Bennett 1981:219–24.

13

Resistance to Sociology at Berkeley

Around the beginning of the twentieth century in the United States, sociology "was institutionalized before it had a distinctive intellectual content, a distinctive method, or even a point of view," in Anthony Oberschall's (1972:189) characterization. Institutionalization was made possible in part by the zeitgeist of reform of that time. Existing institutions of higher education expanded and new ones were created west of the Eastern seaboard. New programs, particularly graduate studies on the Prussian model, but also new academic departments emerged under the favorable conditions of an expanding system. Another stimulus was that the Christian clergy, whose status was being successfully challenged (Hofstader 1955), were driven to investigate the "modern world" that seemed to be bypassing them. "Social Gospel" inquiry into the lives of urban workers was one response to industrialization, social change, and the isolation of the clergy from the central processes of the day.

In the United States, as in Europe, both Christian and secular reformers set out to collect facts about social disorganization (Oberschall 1965, 1972; T. Clark 1973). The needs of ministers and social workers for vocational training and a theory of the emerging industrial world provided an entrée for university sociology programs. Initially, most academics calling themselves "sociologists" were Protestant ministers or sons of Protestant ministers who were interested in social reform. For the most part, they lacked training in science: many scholars in other longer-established disciplines disdained their education and cultural level.

A "science" of society was desired by some, although this desire prompted schemes of universal historical progress, jargon-coining, and unrealistic programs more often than it led to empirical research or to empirically based theorizing. Nevertheless, as in the simultaneous history of American anthropology (Darnell 1998a) and the somewhat later history of American linguistics (Murray 1984), missionaries and their concerns were ousted by professionally trained advocates of "science," with the scientism of Franz Boas (in anthropology) and Franklin Giddings (in sociology) at Columbia University and the more nebulous science of the social of Albion Small in sociology at the University of Chicago carried in various directions by their students.

Sociology as an academic enterprise flourished in the new universities, most notably at the University of Chicago, where serious research on social disorganization was undertaken by W. I. Thomas and by Robert Park and Park's many students. There were what Mullins (1972) called "intellectual leaders" elsewhere—William Graham Sumner at Yale, E. A. Ross at Wisconsin, Lester Frank Ward at Brown, and Charles Horton Cooley at Michigan (see Hinkle and Hinkle 1954)—but intellectual leadership was supplemented by "organization leadership," primarily at Chicago, first by Albion Small and later by Ernest Burgess. Chicago-trained sociologists were placed in jobs and built sociology departments on the Chicago model, just as Boas-trained anthropologists filled positions (some of which were created for them) and built anthropology departments. Boas placed his students in institutions distant from New York, whereas Chicago school dominance was confined to the Midwest.

Although the University of California was a new and expanding school, no sociology department formed there until much later, even than in elite East Coast universities. To understand the "postmaturity" of the development (see chapter 10) requires examination of the social science fiefdoms established at the university before sociology and the context of the university before the Second World War.

The University of California

University president Benjamin Ide Wheeler was "the sole organ of communication between the faculty and the regents" and made certain that "the President should have sole initiative in appointments and removals of professors" (Stadtman 1967:41). In the two decades of his tenure, Wheeler "planted on his campus a remarkable lot of able men" (Sauer 1951). Wheeler ran the university as he saw fit, but he recruited junior faculty who became distinguished scholars and spent their entire academic careers at Berkeley.

Up until the end of the Second World War, University of California departments had little autonomy in making decisions and professors "saw [it] as part of their mission to maintain the standards of the university," not just of the department that contained them (Kenneth Bock, 1978 interview). They saw themselves not as professors of one discipline but as "professors of the university."

In considering the social science fiefdoms aligned against the introduction of sociology, a discipline that was dismissed as vacuous and/or reformist, it is good to keep in mind that the context of the university was a club of mostly male scholars with wide-ranging intellectual interests and self-confidence akin to President Wheeler's in judging work in research specialties other than their own. At the time that sociology was being considered as a possible addition to the University of California curriculum, professors took very seriously their duty to provide intellectual judgments at a university-wide level and did not confine themselves to relatively autonomous, specialized units such as departments or institutes. Even in much more recent decades, professors have decided to change their departmental location.

The Department of Social Institutions

At the time sociology was diffusing elsewhere, a department labeled "Social Institutions" was created at Berkeley. Its existence made formation of a sociology department difficult, although it was created to house the difficult temperament of one great mind rather than erected as an alternative to sociology.

Frederick J. Teggart was a member of the first class to enter the newly established Stanford University, receiving his AB in 1894. He supported himself by working in the library there until 1900, when he became librarian of the Mechanics-Mercantile Library in San Francisco. During his years as a librarian Teggart was also engaged in historical research, writing a history of civilization that was destroyed along with the original Mechanics-Mercantile Library in the fire following the 1906 San Francisco earthquake.

Also in 1906, "when Hubert Howe Bancroft donated his magnificent collection to the University, it was with the explicit provision that Teggart accompany the collection as its custodian" (Nisbet 1976:3). During the following decade, Teggart taught courses in the history department in addition to serving as curator of the Bancroft Library on the Berkeley campus. His main interests were not in the Bancroft materials, although he guided work using them.

Teggart's "The Circumstance or the Substance of History," published in 1910, challenged the kind of narrative historiography to which most historians of his day were committed. In addition to espousing views considered heretical within the history profession, Teggart wrangled with the historian who made the greatest use of the Bancroft materials, Eugene Bolton, and was deposed as curator of the Bancroft Library in 1916. At the same time Teggart was banished from teaching in the history department, so that his status in the university was acutely insecure: "Unable to get along with conventional historians—arousing their hatred, indeed—he was obliged to get out of the department. . . . Given his temper and enemies, no other department would have him, and the Regents were wise enough to want to hold on to him" (Nisbet:author, March 9, 1977, November 22, 1977).

The solution eventually arrived at was to "create a special department for Teggart, one built exclusively and entirely around his own intellectual interest" (Nisbet 1976:3). Teggart was officially " on leave" from 1917–20 and was reappointed only on condition that he "deposit his resignation with the proper officer, so that in case the Regents in future consider he is unable to work with his associates, the same may be presented and his employment terminated immediately" (November 4, 1919 Regents meeting minutes, repeated May 12, 1921). That his differences with his colleagues in history were not solely theoretical (narrative vs. taxonomic history) received official recognition by the UC regents in the same (1919) document: "The appointment of Frederick J. Teggart as Associate Professor of History has been hitherto terminated because of personal differences which arose between him and his associates in his Department."

A one-man department first appeared in the catalog for 1920 and disappeared the next year, when Teggart was listed as an associate professor of political science, teaching regular political science courses. In 1923 the department was reinstituted (or at least reappeared in the university catalog) with Teggart joined by his protégé Nicholas Spykman, who had written a master's thesis and doctoral dissertation on German sociologist Georg Simmel under Teggart's supervision (published in 1925). Spykman taught introductory sociology and social theory, courses that were taken over by Margaret Hodgen, who had come under Teggart's sway while studying economics and who joined the faculty in 1925.

In 1940, on the eve of Teggart's retirement, a committee convened to recommend what to do with the department noted that "the Department of Social Institutions in the University of California is unique in that it is centered around and largely identified with the interests and activities of a singularly rich and vigorous personality" (Alfred Kroeber:President Gordon Sproul, February 7, 1940). In another report the chair of the committee, Alfred Kroeber, asserted even more specifically that "the department of social institutions was built not around a recognized field of learning but around the rich and influential individuality of Professor Teggart" (Kroeber:Sproul, April 29, 1940).

While a department may be created for a single individual, when it survives for several decades, produces students, and expands in staff, resistance to its dissolution is certain. Tenuous as was the institutionalization, to some degree the charismatic authority of Frederick Teggart had been routinized and supplemented.

Once given a niche and no longer answerable to colleagues, Teggart proceeded with his research. The University of California Press published *Rome and China*, the major exemplification of his (1916) natural history program for cultural history, in 1939.

According to Kenneth Bock (1978 interview), "The kind of research that Hodgen and Teggart carried on having to do with substantive historical materials was never taught in the department. As a department, the concern was with the history of ideas." Hodgen, Teggart's disciple and heir apparent, later claimed, "From 1919 to 1940 or for twenty-one years, the Department of Social Institutions had conducted its work without external or internal effort to alter its course or deflect it from its point of view among the social science[s]" (1971:41). She fought bitterly to maintain the status quo after Teggart's retirement, as will be shown below. (And I will not enumerate the number of misleading assertions in the sentence just quoted!)

Teggart himself evidenced little interest in the fate of his institutional "legacy." He had formed a contemptuous view of sociology early on and it had not changed.

People like Teggart, Kroeber, Robert Lowie, and Margaret Hodgen thought of sociology as it had existed in this country in the early 1900s—that is, as a social reform movement. "Sociology textbooks from that era were mostly arguments for certain reforms. Pick up some textbook from 1939 or 1940 and look at the amount that is devoted to advocacy! They [Teggart et al.] didn't regard sociology as a serious attempt at a science. People like Weber and Durkheim and Marx they did not regard as sociologists. Teggart was a great admirer of W. I. Thomas and Albion Small. These people and [Pitirim] Sorokin were standard fare in the Department of Social Institutions. They may have called themselves 'sociologists,' but they were viewed as being mistaken" (Nisbet:author, November 22, 1977).

What most sociologists today would regard as the intellectual patrimony of the discipline, European social theory and the empirical work from Chicago and Columbia, was not considered "sociology." Hostility was directed not at such work but toward the Chautauqua Assembly and its heirs (e.g., [John L.] Gillin, [John] Gillette, [Edward] Hayes, [James] Lichtenberger). Robert Nisbet (:author, November 22, 1977) recalled that Teggart liked and encouraged the dissertation he wrote on French social thought and that

> he couldn't have much cared what the title of the department was, but the fact is, it was "Social Institutions," well known to be the subject matter of sociology. Moreover, there was an "Introduction to Sociology" taught in the department. All who received PhDs and elected academic careers—Spykman, [Hodgen], Bryson, Frost, Schneider, Foskett, Nisbet—wrote their dissertations on basically sociological subjects, and it was taken for granted that the only possibility of a job would be in a sociology department. Teggart was for years a member of the American Sociological Society, and, starting in 1936, he brought a sociologist from the East of Midwest each year to teach as visiting professor in summer sessions. Among them were Kelsey, Crawford, [Franklin] Hankins, [Floyd] House, [Luther] Bernard, Lynn Smith. (Nisbet:author, November 22, 1977)

Teggart (1929) was distressed by the ahistoricism of American social science and, in his only comment that has been preserved on the possibility of the discipline being introduced to Berkeley, he warned President Sproul of likely evils that I would gloss as license, radicalism, and disruptiveness:

> Under the apparently innocuous caption of the "Family," the discussion of Sex has reached down to almost unimaginable levels in university instruction. As an example of what is going on I send you herewith a copy of an immediately recent number of the official

journal of the American Sociological Society. I owe you an apology for calling your attention to a particular article in it [presumably Riley and White (1940 or 1941) on contraception], but it is imperative that you should be informed as to the matters of discourse which may be expected in university classes when once Sociology is definitely accepted by the administration. If further warning as to possibilities is desired, I might point to the case which has been agitating San Francisco for some weeks [I don't know to what he was referring], a case which is the product of the inspiration of courses in Sociology. Once the subject is recognized, it passes out of the hands of the administration to say what may or may not be taught.

Everywhere, the exponents of Sociology have shown themselves aggressive and intolerant and in more than one institution have not hesitated to bring outside influence to bear upon the university authorities. (Attributed by Hodgen [1971:65] to a Teggart:Sproul communication of April 8, 1941, the original of which is neither signed nor dated)

Teggart's contemporaries in their disciplines shared his contempt for run-of-the-mill American sociology and were not eager to see a sociology department established in their midst. Generally, during "the formative period rivalry for subject matter was keen. American sociologists were quickly repulsed if they encroached on territory already claimed by more mature disciplines, particularly economics. Sociologists were also threatened by competition from the infant disciplines of anthropology and psychology, though these fields appeared later in universities" (Furner 1975:292).

At Berkeley, however, anthropology and psychology were established nearly half a century before sociology was. The internationally known Berkeley anthropologists were more involved in keeping sociology out of the university than was Teggart.

Anthropologists

Alfred Louis Kroeber, who headed anthropology work at the university from the beginning in 1901, guarded anthropology's power and influence jealously and "had absolutely no interest in seeing a sociology department created" (Nisbet:author, March 9, 1977). Robert Lowie shared the distaste for sociology but not Kroeber's interest in campus politics, beyond defending anthropology's place: "Everybody was aware of his eminence, but he was indifferent to University affairs, and let Kroeber run things while he wrote his books. . . . He made slurring references to sociology, its uplift, its strain of evolutionism and its 'consecration to elementary textbooks'" (Nisbet:author, March 9, 1977). Lowie himself authored four textbooks: *Primitive Society*, *Primitive Religion*, *The History of Ethnological Theory*, and *Social Organization*.

According to Kroeber expert Timothy Thoresen, the Berkeley anthropologists greatly admired W. I. Thomas's *Source Book for Social Origins* and shared the general contempt for American sociology: "Kroeber and crew respected—even when they disagreed with—sociology [as it] was practiced by the British and Europeans, but not as practiced by Americans" prior to World War II (Thoresen: author, June 13, 1977). Theodora Kroeber (1978 interview) stressed that while Kroeber held Robert Merton and Talcott Parsons in high regard, he knew them and their work only after his retirement in 1946.

Kroeber's interests in comparative history of civilization and the diffusion of innovations paralleled that of Teggart and Hodgen,[1] but he was little interested in prewar American sociology, whether reformist or empirical. Sociology was not regarded as impinging on anthropology's object of study, which prior to the Second World War was "primitive" cultures, particularly what could be salvaged of memories of prereservation social organizations and languages of California and, to a lesser extent, indigenous South America. When Kroeber and Lowie mused comparatively they were willing to attend to sociologists such as Parsons, Merton, and Nisbet, who were interested in general theory.

Social Welfare

Just as Berkeley was an exception in having anthropology and psychology departments long predating a sociology department, social work there preceded rather than broke off from sociology, moving from melioristic advocacy to positivism.

It was primarily through the interests and efforts of Jessica B. Peixotto, an expert on "social economics" who had practical experience in the charities of Berkeley and on the State Board of Charities and Corrections, that an organized curriculum in social work developed. From 1904 to 1912 she taught courses in Contemporary Theories of Social Reform, Poverty, the Child and the State, Care of Dependents, and Crime as a Social Problem. In 1912 the Department of Economics, stating that "the widespread interest in the control of poverty has given rise, in recent years, to a demand for the services of the trained social worker," announced the inauguration of the Curriculum of Social Economics (Stadtman 1967:76)

Teggart wrote President Sproul that he and Peixotto had pursued a division of labor happily for decades (March 3, 1941; in Hodgen 1971:64), and Nisbet noted, "Her first title was Lecturer in Socialism, then, the following year, Lecturer in Sociology, and then, after that, titles in Economics, her department of many years. . . . [Peixotto had an] unflagging desire to protect her domain. Also, she once told me in conversation, sociology was largely 'uplift' by Protestant ministers in this country, and she would have none of it" (Nisbet:author, March 9, 1977).

"Since [Social Welfare] graduates mostly went into casework, over the years, the psychological component of the curriculum came to be more important than 'social economics'" (Stadtman 1967:76–77). Initially at least, the program was more directly concerned with empirical studies of families, social disorganization, and social movements—considered part of sociology's domain elsewhere.

Cultural/Historical Geography

There is neither recollection nor record of any concerted or open opposition to sociology on the part of Berkeley psychologists or economists, both potential antagonists. The other source of opposition was Carl Sauer, chairman of the geography department, who, like Teggart, was appalled at the ahistoricism of American sociology and with its quantifying mania: "The study of human societies has lost both in breadth and grasp by living apart from the humanistic group. We have come almost to the point where those who call themselves social scientists have eliminated the experience of mankind prior to the present. Many of them have narrowed their horizon to the short span of quantitative series in imitation of experimental science" (Sauer:Nisbet, October 30, 1952).

In planning social science research policy at Berkeley, Sauer wrote his fellow chairmen that the results of large-scale projects "have seemed to continue meagre," wondered whether quantitative data are properly "the province of academic persons," and noted that "to some of us the resultant emphasis on action programs, on 'social engineering,' has been distasteful" (Sauer:Herbert Blumer, November 12, 1953). Sauer further invidiously contrasted his elders Franz Boas, George E, Vincent,[2] William Graham Sumner, and Henry Adams to later generations of social scientists: "They were few, but they had stature. They had wide learning, and the long insights of history. Most of those I knew were detached observers, unconcerned about choosing or directing work in terms of social or political ends. Reform elements came somewhat later. In my Chicago days this intrusion of emotional drive was noticeable only in some of the students of sociology, then already in some numbers refugees from divinity schools, seeking for a new faith in social welfare" (Sauer 1951). Sauer, the youngest of the "old guard" of Berkeley social science potentates, shared the contempt for sociology, explicitly extending it to Chicago sociology.

These learned and powerful scholars lived near each other in North Berkeley, but only the Sauers and the Kroebers socialized together away from campus (T. Kroeber, 1978 interview). "The old titans—Peixotto, Kroeber, Teggart, and Sauer—disliked each other personally, jealousy no doubt entering in," but they were united in their opposition to sociology's establishment on campus, and "only when they were reaching retirement did opposition wane" (Nisbet:author, March 9, 1977).

Dorothy Swaine Thomas

Their solution led to continued conflict, however: "Sauer and one or two others enlisted Kroeber in bringing to the campus [specifically, the College of Agriculture] Dorothy Swaine Thomas, young wife of the great W. I. Thomas. She was brought under the virtual promise that when Teggart retired she would head a department of sociology" (Nisbet:author, March 9, 1977).

As shown in previous chapters, Dorothy Thomas quite clearly represented American scientific sociology at its most positivistic and was backed by sponsors credible at Berkeley or anywhere else. As an undergraduate she became a protégé of William F. Ogburn (E. Lee 1977:12). Ogburn knew practically every social scientist of any import in the world and was a longtime friend of Lowie. Dorothy Thomas coauthored two articles with Ogburn in 1922, then went to the London School of Economics and married W. I. Thomas. Together the Thomases published *The Child in America* (1928) and were ready to collaborate with Gunnar and Alva Myrdal on a Swedish study to parallel *The Polish Peasant in Europe and America* (W. Thomas and Znaniecki 1927). The joint project was not realized because Myrdal studied a group in America other than Swedish immigrants, but Dorothy Thomas produced a major work of descriptive historical demography, *Social and Economic Aspects of Swedish Population Movements, 1759–1933* (Thomas 1941). She also took charge (from Robert Lowie) of the large-scale project to study the forced relocation of West Coast Japanese Americans that became the Japanese-American Evacuation and Resettlement Study (JAERS), discussed in chapter 12.

Given her training by and collaboration with Ogburn and her marriage to W. I. Thomas, Dorothy Thomas was closely connected to major (seminal even) representatives of both kinds of American science-aspiring sociology: quantitative analysis of longitudinal data and case studies using qualitative methods. Her work dealt with dated material (every bit as much as the research of Hodgen, Sauer, and Teggart; more so than that of Kroeber, Lowie, and Pexiotto) and recurrent historical patterns and exemplified a natural science approach to history and a set of problematics congenial to the research done by Hodgen and Teggart. She became anathema at the Department of Social Institutions, for reasons that remain obscure. It is difficult to decide whether Hodgen or Nisbet loathed her more,[3] but it is clear that personality clashes complicated and further delayed the establishment of a sociology department at Berkeley. Both Hodgen and Nisbet were determined to keep Thomas from chairing their department and, if possible, to exclude her from any department with which they would be associated.

The Kroeber Committee

On the eve of Teggart's retirement, a committee chaired by Kroeber was convened to consider what to do about the Department of Social Institutions. The committee recommended maintaining the departmental status quo for the time being—that is, continuing the existing department beyond Teggart's tenure and not inaugurating a full-fledged sociology department (Kroeber:Sproul, February 7, 1940). The committee accepted Hodgen's argument that (1) social institutions was a field of study, and (2) given the social science offerings in existence, sociology was not needed. While there is little doubt that Kroeber believed the second, as his letters to Sproul already quoted evidence, he believed that the Department of Social Institutions *was* Teggart.

Retaining the department was another administrative convenience.

Extirpating the department would have raised the problem of what to do with the remaining staff. Nisbet did not have tenure but was respected and liked by Kroeber and other powerful figures within the university. He might, however, have been absorbed into the Department of History, despite the continued animosity toward Teggart there and his identification with Teggart. Hodgen, in contrast, could not easily return to the department in which she had been trained, economics, because Berkeley economists felt she had betrayed their discipline to become a disciple of Teggart (Bock, 1978 interview). Although her later research dealt with anthropological thought and was published in anthropological outlets, the possibility of absorbing her into Kroeber's department was not mentioned. Theodora Kroeber (1978 interview) told me that her husband had thought highly of Hodgen's work but thought that the idea of incorporating her into his department would not have appealed to her nor to him, because she was to such an extent a disciple of Teggart.

The recommendation that was adopted was to take a "wait and see" attitude toward the post-Teggart Department of Social Institutions. Temporary expedience was clearly the rationale, however much Hodgen would later claim that the decision was intended to settle the question of sociology and the existing program, which she headed following Teggart's retirement, once and for all.

Dorothy Thomas was not deterred by the report. Almost immediately, she and agricultural economist Paul Taylor[4] proposed an interdepartmental major in sociology, and Dean Lipman called for discussion of the idea (Lipman:Hodgen, February 3, 1941). Thomas prepared a memorandum (dated February 24, 1941) offering a detailed comparison of Berkeley's course offerings in sociology with those at the University of Chicago, the acknowledged center of American sociology (even to a Columbia alumna, as she was). She pointed out the lack of training available in cross-sectional (synchronic) methods, sampling, quantitative study of social problems, and European social theory.

Hodgen countered that Thomas's goal "in her own words was 'to try to determine what California hasn't that Chicago has' rather than to determine what California has and evaluate it." Moreover, she contended, Thomas's memorandum was "written by a person had only recently arrived in Berkeley, but who attempted to assess California's facilities for teaching sociology without the slightest investigation of what is actually done here" (Hodgen:Lipman, March 2, 1941).

Lipman appointed a committee consisting of Thomas, Hodgen, Alexander Kidd, and Harold Jones to make recommendations. A majority report outlined an interdepartmental major. A "minority report," signed by half the committee (Hodgen and Kidd), joined by Nisbet and Emily Huntingon, opposed such a major with an argument that strikes me as casuistic and that Nisbet later mocked: "We [Social Institutions] are not sociology, mind you, but no sociology was needed on the campus in any form because we were offering sociology courses and our own department major [Social Institutions] was all that was necessary" (Nisbet:author, November 22, 1977).

The massive disruption of mobilizations for war interrupted reorganization and the majority report was not implemented. Nisbet enlisted in the U.S. Army and Thomas took on administration of the large-scale JAERS, leaving Hodgen to preside of the Department of Social Institutions and whatever wartime students were around.

The Power Struggle Renewed after the War

As the war neared an end, jockeying for position resumed. A committee chaired by philosophy professor George Adams considered the question of sociology (and the Department of Social Institutions) again. Hodgen was annoyed, hoping that the question had been settled and that a few years of old arrangements had made them more secure. The committee's mode of operation annoyed her even more. The administration "sought advice of the most remote and junior member of the Department [of Social Institutions, i.e., Nisbet]. Professor Lehman in his exalted administrative position [head of the University Budget Committee] went over the heads of those in charge of the immediate conduct of the department [i.e., Hodgen] to consult a youthful student of those professors" (Hodgen 1971:100).

Hodgen left ample documentation of her grievances, accusing her former student, former ally, and former intimate of perfidy and opportunism and fulminating at the administration for ignoring duly constituted authority in the department (i.e., herself), placing "professor Teggart [not to mention herself] and all he has stood for at the mercy of a junior in the department" (Hodgen:Nisbet, September 29, 1945).

While leading the opposition to including Thomas, Nisbet was willing to accept sociology in name and in fact. Hodgen regarded this as high treason. She had, she wrote, spent her "life-time contending against certain elements in social thought and inquiry which seemed . . . cheap and dull [and even] obstructive to human welfare" (Hodgen:Nisbet, September 26, 1945), only to find someone whose career she had nurtured aiding in what she conceived to be the demolition of the department she had long served. Sociology's subject matter she regarded as "irredeemably trashy" (Hodgen:Nisbet, September 29, 1945), certain both to drive out the existing tradition (that she and all right-thinking people exalted) and to eclipse the apostolic succession from Teggart's charisma.

Hodgen was inflexibly committed to a science of Teggart; Nisbet was not so sectarian an epigone. He accepted a sociology department as inevitable. His focus was on excluding Thomas while trying to shape the department in ways that excluded areas like criminology and rural sociology, while emphasizing social theory and history.

Hodgen felt betrayed both by Nisbet and by the university she had long served. She bitterly resented her exclusion from the committee planning the fate of the department she chaired. Nor did she take kindly to being passed over as the planners solicited the views of her former student and junior colleague, even after he wrote her that he had assumed everyone in the department had been queried, not just himself (Nisbet:Hodgen, October 8, 1945). Hodgen had excommunicated Nisbet from the sect of keepers of the Teggart flame, and she never forgave him.

Although she was unable to enforce silence on Nisbet, Hodgen did succeed in gaining admittance to the committee. Her report on the committee's deliberations is not exactly dispassionate, but the continued contempt for sociology that she claimed was quite likely accurate:

Mrs. T to a very large extent defeated herself. With a packed committee everything that was said by me . . . fell on deaf ears. But the courses she outlined, the research projects she suggested were so trifling that the opposition, which began with one member, increased to three or four. . . . The reason the psychologists stuck was because they have been trying for years to shed Social Psychology and she obligingly accommodated them. . . . But at the last, when the triviality of . . . sociology courses was exposed (some of the members of the committee actually read several books), a determined opposition to sociology developed. It is true that the minority report favored a compromise, wishing on us the courses they disapproved of, but not one person that I know of expressed anything but contempt for sociology, and they were joined by several members of the majority. (Hodgen:Nisbet, October 17, 1945)

Robert Nisbet's Vision of a Sociology Department

Consulted across the Pacific Ocean, Nisbet suggested an orientation for a Berkeley sociology department. It was not a novel orientation but rather what he would later term "the grand tradition" of sociological theory (Nisbet 1966). The study of disorganization as a historical product of the complex confluences of urbanization, industrialization, capitalism, and bureaucratization was the central raison d'être for sociology at Berkeley, as it had been repeatedly in the institutionalization of sociology throughout the western world. Social groupings intermediate between individual and state, such as kin, neighborhood, church, ethnic group, voluntary associations—what Rousseau and Jacobins sought to extirpate, what Burke, Boland, and Maistre sought to preserve, what Tocqueville saw as the basis for American democracy, and what were independent variables in the macrosociological analyses of Durkheim and Weber—Nisbet proposed as the core of sociological enterprise (see Nisbet 1953, 1966). The weakening of these intermediate groups he saw as a major problem: "I believe that the most menacing fact in America today is the moribund condition of much of that sphere of association that lies intermediate to man and the state. The widespread disorganization of groups which traditionally have been the bases of order and equity in American life presents a problem of the utmost urgency" (Nisbet:Adams, 1946).

History and theory were central to the line of inquiry Nisbet envisioned, but it was still social problems that needed to be investigated in order to be solved that Nisbet suggested as the basis for a sociology department. The rationale was not essentially different from the scientific aspirations of reformers instituting sociology programs earlier and elsewhere.

Hodgen was not impressed. She accused Nisbet of wishing to build a department around his own dissertation topic ("The Social Group in French Social Thought," 1939). "He forgets in his youthful self-absorption that while the fate of the smaller group may well be an appropriate field of investigation for one doctor's candidate, it is not necessarily of departmental magnitude," Hodgen charged to Adams (February 30, 1946).

The Department of Sociology and Social Institutions

After years of bitter and mostly invisible infighting, the provost accepted the recommendations of a committee including Lowie from anthropology and Edward C. Tolman from psychology and concluded that "while certain weaknesses in traditional sociological theories and programs are recognized, nevertheless, it is concluded that such defects must be balanced against merits and accomplishments, and it is decided that the subject justifies a place in the University program" (Provost Deutsch, memorandum, April 2, 1946). I'd like to know which defects and which accomplishments were recognized, but they were not specified. The official definition of the situation, that "social institutions is a descriptive phrase for materials in the field of sociology," must have been a bitter blow to Hodgen, but some consolation was afforded by the exclusion of Dorothy Thomas from the new department. The mandate of the department, as outlined by Deutsch, was to "be concerned in a humanistic spirit with the problem of social disorganization and social change, with the emphasis upon a critical approach to a scientific study of society and a sound conception of history and theory, as the indispensable nucleus [Department of Social Institutions] to be maintained."

Disappointed by blockage of her kind of sociology at Berkeley, Thomas took a position at the University of Pennsylvania (see Bannister 1998 on another large project devoid of explanations or conclusions). Nisbet, who was clearly being groomed as an administrator, was named acting chair of the new department, but upon his return to Berkeley, meeting hostility and noncooperation from Hodgen and George Hildebrand, who had studied with Teggart before earning a PhD at Harvard, he realized the position was untenable. There were no "conventional" sociologists in the department at its inception. Edward Strong, a philosophy professor specializing in social philosophy and the philosophy of history, became chair. In building a department staff, Strong seems to have relied heavily on Nisbet's advice. Reinhard Bendix, Seymour Martin Lipset, and Philip Selznick were brought in from outside and Kenneth Bock from within the Department of Social Institutions as assistant professors.

Although the department rapidly rose to the top of the ranks of sociology programs in the United States, from Hodgen's perspective, her predictions were fulfilled. She believed in a sort of Gresham's Law for ideas and saw bad ideas (sociology) driving out good ones (Teggart's). Conventional sociological subjects swamped traditional Department of Social Institutions concerns; even criminology and demography were added.

Hodgen bitterly complained that the junior faculty made decisions in the new department. Further cause for bitterness against the University of California arose from her discharge in 1951 for refusing to take the loyalty oath forced on faculty. Although she was reinstated two years later, she never returned to teaching at Berkeley. She pursued research on patterns of technical innovation and diffusion using materials at the Huntington Library (Hodgen 1952), retired early (1955) to work on the early history of anthropological speculation (Hodgen 1964, 1974).

In 1953 Nisbet left the Berkeley campus to become dean at the new Riverside campus of the University of California. After a decade of administration, he returned to scholarship and produced the series of books for which he is known, ending his academic career as an Albert Schweitzer Professor of Sociology at Columbia University.

The Berkeley department of sociology grew—and grew away from what its charter specified as its "nucleus." Nevertheless, Hodgen, Nisbet, Bock, and Bock's student Stanford Lyman all published major works in the Teggart tradition, drawing on the history of ideas and attacking neo-Aristotelian conceptions of social change and sociobiology.

Conclusion

While the series of events at the University of California were unique, the low regard for sociology and the competition among social science disciplines certainly were not. In contrast to places where sociology was institutionalized first (see Furner 1975), there was little opposition from economics and much fiercer opposition from disciplines more commonly established elsewhere after sociology (anthropology and social work).

The research produced by members of the Department of Social Institutions took a world-historical comparative perspective, albeit with more concrete data than that of progressive social evolutionist Lester Frank Ward, for example. So did that of Bendix and Lipset. The grab bag of topics unwanted by other disciplines—demography, marriage, the family, poverty, crime, education, religion, and so on—was held together in the American sociology of the 1950s by the general theory of action of Talcott Parsons and by methods imported (as Lipset was) from Columbia University.

The first representative of orthodox American sociology at Berkeley, Thomas, was a productive and by no means ahistorical scholar, but her temperament seems to have alienated some powerful university administrators and the personnel of the existing department that was most sociological. A WASP male of more genial temperament might well have succeeded in 1940. Surely, Ogburn, who was highly esteemed by Kroeber and Lowie and famous for his personal charm as well as for his cultural sociology, would have fared better.

Gender and temperament are personal factors, but as Hodgen (1974) stressed in her account of the spread of innovations, the characteristics of the carriers of alien cultural products are important to their success (acceptance) in a particular locale.

Berkeley was outside the "trade route" of American sociological discourse and personnel—more than three days away from Chicago by train, four from New York City. When a "culture carrier" arrived, she failed to charm or convince the locals. The innovation of a sociology department— already "late" in comparison with other places—was further delayed by personal characteristics of the would-be innovator and by mobilized (and more than a little personalized) opposition.

The University of California accepted a sociology department after the Social Gospel movement had begun to be forgotten and long after sociology was institutionalized in colleges and universities in the U.S. Midwest. The reform movement, frequently an aid to starting sociology programs, was no help at Berkeley, and disdain for it was a hindrance. Another usual aid, expansion of the system, was operative. The expansion of the California population and of the University of California (which became a system with multiple campuses) made establishing a new discipline easier. Once adopted, the innovation of a sociology department at Berkeley flourished: it quickly became a center of American sociology—a fractious one, but that is another story (or twenty or more).

14

Does Editing Core Anthropology and Sociology Journals Increase Citations to the Editor?

Over the course of the twentieth century, formal citations of others' work has become more common in social sciences, including anthropology. Franz Boas and his early students cited others' work rarely in comparison to the numerous citations in a current anthropology journal article. Prominent sociologists such as Robert Park, also German-trained, cited more work than Boas and the Boasians, but Columbia sociologist Frank Giddings did not do so more notably than his Columbia colleague Boas.

Academic administrators (who are often not members of the discipline) increasingly look at quantitative measures of the impact of faculty members' publications—even though there are many motivations for citing a publication other than (or in addition to) recognizing the importance and quality of work that is cited. For the quality—or at least the importance—of work, frequency of citation of published work is increasingly used in evaluating faculty research production.

Not only those seeking tenure or merit pay increases are interested in being cited. Most of us like our work to be recognized. We would prefer that it be cited with approval by someone who seems to understand what we have done, but as Mae West said, it is better to be looked over (critically) than to be overlooked. Generally, grudging and ambivalent recognition seems better than invisibility. Indeed, in more a third of a century of observing anthropologists, sociologists, and linguists, I have yet to encounter anyone who thought his or her work was too well appreciated or too often discussed. An extreme example is Noam Chomsky, one of the most cited authors on the planet, who claimed that hardly anyone has ever been interested in his ideas.

Over the years I have heard various social scientists comment that this or that editor seemed to be getting cited in the journal she or he edited suspiciously often. From what I know of the amount of work that editing a journal requires, undertaking it strikes me as a very labor-intensive and not economically rational way of gaining recognition for one's research. Surely, doing interesting research is a better and more efficient road to citation, and I find it impossible to believe that increasing citations is even a secondary motivation for anyone deciding to edit a journal.

In my personal, extensive experience of the review process, I have never received even indirect pressure to mention or take account of any work by the editor of the journal to which I have submitted a paper. In contrast, I have more than a few times received suggestions amounting to demands from **referees** to discuss their work, even their unpublished work that I could not reasonably be expected to know of. In more than a few instances I have not seen the relevance of the work in obscure or prenatal locations pointedly called to my attention by someone making decisions about publishing mine. (More generally, see Scollon 1995.)

More plausible to me than editors coercing citations to their work is that those who are working in areas (both geographical and specialty areas) close to those in which the editor has worked might expect a more hospitable reception and handling of their work in the journal than when an editor with quite different interests is in charge. For general-interest American sociology journals during the 1970s and 1980s, Richard Wright (1994a, 1994b) found a statistically insignificant decrease in work within the journal editor's primary research specialty and a statistically insignificant increase in citations to work by the editor both in the journal he or she edited and in the two other core sociology journals.

For the *American Anthropologist* and the *American Ethnologist*, citations in the journal that they edited fell during the editor's tenure for slightly more than half the editors, in comparison with rates in the three years preceding their editorship. At the same time, total citations (in the *Social Sciences Citation Index* [*ssci*]) of *American Anthropologist* editors have increased and those of *American Ethnologist* editors have remained more or less constant. (The replacement of the printed *ssci* with its online incarnation would have made extending this analysis very cumbersome.) In the official journal of the Royal Anthropological Institute (*jrai* before and after being titled *Man*), citations to only two of its ten editors between 1965 and 2001 increased during the editor's tenure; the total citations of nine of ten *jrai* journal editors increased. Table 10 shows the number of editors' citations in the journal they edited, the percent-

TABLE 10. Journal Editors' Citations During and After Editing Core Journals

	Number		Percentage		Total		(N)
	During	After	During	After	During	After	
American Anthropologist	40	30	40	10	80	60	(10)
American Ethnologist	50	20	67	20	50	60	(5)
Man/JRAI	22	67	22	89	89	44	(9)
Sociology journal median[a]	67	33	58	36	71	50	(22)

Note: Figures represent number of citations in the journal edited, percentage of editor's citations in the journal edited, and number of overall citations to the journal editor (N).
[a] American Journal of Sociology, American Sociological Review, Social Forces

age of their total citations that were in the journal edited, and the total frequency of citations for editors of the three anthropology journals and three American sociology journals.

Disaggregating these data, however, suggests that there has been a change since the 1960s and 1970s. Four of the most recent (ca. 2001) five American Anthropologist editors (Anthony Woodbury, David Olmstead, Russell Bernard, and Dennis and Barbara Tedlock) were cited more often in the American Anthropologist during their editorial tenure than before it, as were three of the four most recent editors of the American Ethnologist (Norman Whitten, Shirley Lindenbam, Donald Brenneis), in contrast to none of their predecessors in the years covered by the SSCI (or the next one, Michael Herzfeld).

The last editor of the American Anthropologist whose citations in the journal increased after his editorship was George Spindler, and Victoria Bricker, whose work was not cited in American Ethnologist during her tenure, has been the only American Ethnologist editor whose work received more citations in the three years following the end of an editorial term. Total citations to five of the ten post-1965 Man/JRAI journal editors increased following their terms as editor (including four of the last six during the previous millennium).

Short-term Gains in Citations to Editors of Core American Sociology Journals

As figure 2 shows, in the time covered by the SSCI (1956–2001), nine of eleven ASR editors were cited more in ASR during their terms than in the three preceding years. (I did not include William Form's one-year [1981]

TABLE 11. Editors of Core Anthropology and Sociology Journals, 1958–1998

American Anthropologist
Walter Goldschmidt 1956–59
Edward H. Spicer 1960–62
George Spindler 1963–65
Ward H. Goodenough 1966–70
Laura Bohannan 1971–73
Robert A. Manners 1974–75
Richard B. Woodbury 1976–78
David L. Olmsted 1979–81
H. Russell Bernard 1982–90
Janet Dixon Keller 1991–94
Barbara and Dennis Tedlock 1994–98

American Ethnologist
Victoria R. Bricker 1974–76
Richard G. Fox 1977–79
Norman E. Whitten 1980–84
Shirley Lindenbaum 1985–89
Donald L. Brenneis 1990–94
Michael Herzfeld 1995–98

*Man N.S./Journal of the Royal
    Anthropological Institute*
A. C. Mayer 1966–69
I. M. Lewis 1970–73
P. G. Rivière 1974–77
P. Loizos 1978–79
Marilyn Strathern 1980–83
David Turton 1984–86
Ruth Finnegan 1987–89
Tim Ingold 1990–92
Hastings Donnan 1993–95
Simon Harison 1996–98

American Sociological Review
Charles Page 1958–60
Harry Alpert 1961–62
Neal Smelser 1963–65
Norman Ryder 1966–68
Karl Schuessler 1969–71
James Short 1972–74
Morris Zelditch 1975–77
Rita Simon 1978–80
William Form 1981
Sheldon Stryker 1982–86
William Form 1987–89
Gerald Marwell 1990–93
Paula England 1994–96
Glenn Firebaugh 1997–99

American Journal of Sociology
Peter Blau 1960–66
C. Arnold Anderson 1966–73
Charles Bidwell 1973–78
Edward Laumann 1979–84
William Parish 1985–92
Marta Tienda 1993–95
Edward O. Laumann 1996–98

Social Forces (department-edited before
    December 1969)
Richard L. Simpson 1970–72
Everett K. Wilson 1972–82
Richard L. Simpson 1983–2003

FIGURE 1. Percentage of Citations to Editors in the Journal Edited, 1956–1998

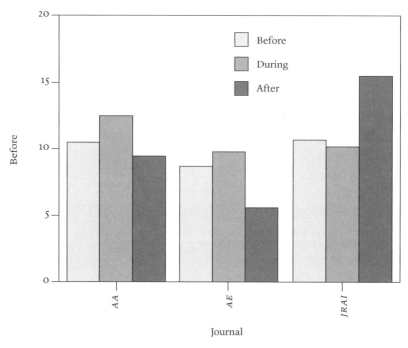

Note: AA = American Anthropologist, AE = American Ethnologist; JRAI = Journal of the Royal Anthropological Institute and Man n.s.

term.) After a slight decrease in the first year, rates of citation to the editor nearly doubled in subsequent years. In the first year of the editor's successor's term, citations in ASR fell back to below the level of citations in the year (and years) preceding his/her term.[1] Four of ten ex-editors of ASR were cited fewer times in ASR during the three years following their terms than in the three years preceding them.

To compare the pattern of citations of ASR editors to those to editors of other core sociology journals who have longer editorial terms, I focused on the three years preceding taking over editing the journal, the first three years in office, and the three years following office. For Social Forces (SF) I found no difference in citations to the three editors before and during editing it, along with an increase afterward for one of the two cases (the third editorship has not ended). For the American Journal of Sociology (AJS) I found no difference in citations in the three years before their terms compared to citations during the first three years for

FIGURE 2. Mean Annual Citations of Sociology Editors in Journal Edited, 1958-1999

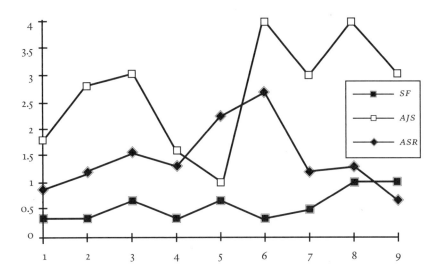

1–3 = three years before editing the journal
4–6 = first three years of editing the journal
7–9 = first three years after ceasing to edit the journal

Note: AJS = American Journal of Sociology, ASR = American Sociological Review, SF = Social Forces

three editors, and a decrease for two. Contrasting citations before and after their terms, two increased and two decreased. On the aggregate, citations in *AJS* to its editors decreased during their terms and returned to previous levels afterward, while citations in *SF* to its editors remained steady during their terms and increased afterward. Figure 2 shows the citations for editors of all three journals in the journal they edited and figure 3 citations in all journals.

The effort of editing a journal takes time from doing one's own research, so the declining rates of citation in the years following an editorial term might be attributed to lower productivity during the years spent editing a journal. Unfortunately, an indicator of productivity is not obvious. By the stage of a professional career at which one is chosen to edit a core journal, a researcher is likely to be receiving invitations to publish work without undergoing anonymous peer review. Generally, with increasing professional age there is a decline in publishing in refereed jour-

FIGURE 3. Mean Citations of Sociology Journal Editors by Year of Office, 1958–1999

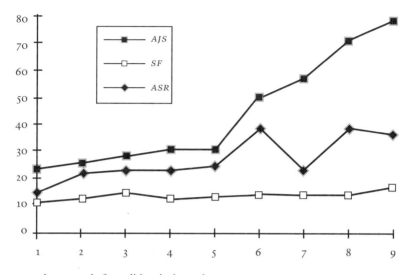

1–3 = three years before editing the journal
4–6 = first three years of editing the journal
7–9 = first three years after ceasing to edit the journal

Note: AJS = American Journal of Sociology, ASR = American Sociological Review, SF = Social Forces

nals that is in no way peculiar to those who serve as journal editors (and thereby have the most experience reading diverging referee reports!).

Book publication seemed a better indication of productivity than article publication. I thought that the experience of having edited a core journal might enhance production of edited books, but there was practically no before/during/after journal editing differences. The eighteen editors edited a total of six books during their tenure as journal editor, in contrast to seven in the preceding equivalent number of years and six in the following years (standardized to account for the years after their terms that have not yet occurred, the rates are 0.389 edited books per editor before, 0.333 during, 0.375 after). There was a more discernible drop in production of books that are not collections of other people's work. The about-to-be editors published a total of thirteen books in the years immediately before becoming editors, eleven while editors, and seven in the three years after being editors.

Productivity interruption is not an adequate explanation for the decrease of citations to former *ASR* editors in *ASR*. Whatever someone published before becoming a journal editor is still out there to be cited, along with whatever she or he published while being the journal editor. Moreover, the decline was only in *ASR* citations, not the former editors' overall citations. I find it hard to imagine that editing *ASR* for three years is more debilitating and distracting from one's own work than editing *AJS* for five-plus years.[2]

A control for any productivity differences is to look at the percentage of an editor's citations that are in the journal she or he edits. Again, with this indicator of visibility, *ASR* editors' proportion of citations in *ASR* was higher in the years they edited it than in the years before they edited it and lower in the years after they ceased editing it than in the years before. The proportion of *AJS* editors' citations that were in *AJS* decreased during the first two years of their regime but shot up during the third. In the years following editing *AJS*, the proportion of their citations that were in *AJS* was higher than in the years before. Similarly, the proportion of *SF* editors' citations in *SF* increased after their tenure (not having changed over the years before and the years during which they edited it). And, as figure 3 shows, for former editors of all three journals, total citations to their work were more frequent after their term of office than before it (in the aggregate and in thirteen of sixteen instances—including seven of ten former *ASR* editors).

The growth of the field and an increase in the total number of citations in the journals also cannot account for the difference in the visibility of *ASR* editors in *ASR* compared to *AJS* and *SF*. A possibly important difference between *ASR* and the other two journals is that the *ASR* editor appoints an editorial board of his or her own choice, whereas the other two journals are products of particular departments, with external editorial boards chosen less by the editor than is the case for *ASR*. In tailoring an article for *ASR* the question Who is the editor? may be more salient to authors (before they submit an article as well as in dealing with suggestions for revisions from referees and editors). The extent to which citations are conscious choices is far from certain, and I have no means of differentiating citations that were anticipatory (i.e., in the draft submitted for review) from those that were acquiescent (i.e., added after suggestions about revisions were received).

The increased recognition within *ASR* of the *ASR* editor's reputation during his or her term in office does not persist. No such intrajournal increase occurs in *AJS* or *SF*. In the long run, recognition of an individual's research does not appear to be affected by the visibility or by the demands of the office.

Conclusion

Editing a journal takes considerable time and energy; whatever the residual prestige of having held the position, undertaking it does not increase citations very much or for very long. Gains in citations within American anthropology and sociology journals to work by editors are reversed in the immediately following years. This pattern does not hold for the official Royal Anthropological Institute journal. For overall citations, roughly half of the editors of both the English and American core anthropology (and sociology) journals experienced declines in the three years following their term. Thus, the answer to the question posed in the title is: a bit (for recent editors of American journals), for a short time, with a fall afterward for recent editors of American anthropology journals but not for English ones.

Conclusion

Doing History of Anthropology

Those who have come along through explorations of the historical connections I have made in the preceding chapters are unlikely to expect a
conclusion that proclaims the Truth that anthropology or human sciences more generally should be pursuing or has discovered. Instead, I
want to draw on my experience of questioning "just-so" stories about
intellectual connections in the past to offer some suggestions about how
not to do history of a field. I have given some thought of late to my own
intellectual genealogy and—if that is not narcissistic enough a topic to
contemplate—the history of the history of anthropology.

The title of my PhD dissertation was "Social Science Networks." Robert Redfield once said that an academic discipline is at once a group of
people in persisting social relations and a method of investigation. He
further noted that "the two kinds of relations, social and methodological, are mutually influential, but neither determines the other" (1953:728).
I think that I began with a focus on the social and drifted to focus increasingly on shared practices—methods rather than methodologies—
and on shared assumptions about what should be studied how. Trying
to make sense of where the history of anthropology in general and my
work in particular came from, it seems to me that there are two streams
of what I would call emic history of anthropology. I want to say something about these streams both as social groupings and as methods of
investigation.

What I see as the first serious work on the history of anthropology that
aimed to understand the past in its own terms rather than to promote the
author's position or positions in the present and tried to contextualize
ideas from the past as something other than building blocks of current
models was done by students trained in Frederick Teggart's Department

of Social Institutions at Berkeley. Teggart taught a course on the history of the idea of progress during the 1930s that aimed to make sense of the concept *progress* in the intellectual contexts of different times in western history.

One of his protégés—who later became my first graduate school mentor in social theory—Robert Nisbet eventually crystallized that into a book, *History of the Idea of Progress*, published in 1980, that should be—but has not has been—of interest to historians of anthropology. Two of Teggart's other students more directly examined the interrelations of social theory and the accounts by explorers, travelers, and missionaries of the beliefs, institutions, and physical characteristics of the peoples encountered and subjugated by Europeans between the fifteenth and nineteenth centuries. Katherine Oakes completed a dissertation in 1944 on the shifting representations of Africans. Under her married name, Katherine George, she published a synopsis of this in *Isis* in 1958. Margaret T. Hodgen, who had been a student of Teggart's and became his colleague, wrote what remains the standard and thus far definitive book *Early Anthropology in the Sixteenth and Seventeenth Centuries*, published in 1964. Back in 1936 she had published a history of the idea of "survivals." In 1952, in an anthropological monograph series, she published an exemplification of how to examine cultural innovation and diffusion across time and space, *Change and History*, and she followed that book and *Early Anthropology in the Sixteenth and Seventeenth Centuries* with a book that attempted to tell anthropologists how to do history, titled *Anthropology, History, and Social Change*, in 1974.

There is certainly a Teggartian tradition with a catastrophist rather than a gradualist view of cultural change. This tradition also includes repeated criticisms of the use of the comparative method and of unilinear cultural evolution (while recommending comparisons). In addition to Nisbet, Kenneth Bock continued this tradition, not least in criticizing sociobiology. Both as a student of a student of both Teggart and Hodgen (Robert Nisbet) and as the author of a history of the Berkeley Department of Social Institutions based heavily on the views of Hodgen, Bock, and Nisbet (chapter 13), I can readily claim a legitimate academic genealogical connection to this tradition of intellectual history of social science.

However, although I certainly share some assumptions—in particular catastrophism in its Kuhnian form as "scientific revolutions" (punctuating Brownian motion of professors' theoretical and methodological approaches)—I don't think that my work is very much like that of Teggart's students. I am interested in the institutions and less formal social networks of twentieth-century American social science(s), whereas they examined the texts and memes (what they called "unit-ideas") of pre-academic science, generally over the course of centuries and generally not into the twentieth century. Moreover, in common with Arthur Lovejoy, Teggartians focused on unit-ideas like progress or community rather than on individual thinkers or schools of thought. I very much admire Robert Nisbet's (1966) *Sociological Tradition*, but I am unlikely to emulate his approach, even if I were to make *tradition* plural. I think that there are anthropological traditions, but I associate them with prototype individuals rather than with unit-ideas. Or perhaps I simply failed to learn how to do what Teggart and Hodgen and (sometimes) Nisbet did, despite the genealogical place I could claim.

Although I am not done with my own genealogy yet, I want to point out the first lesson for historical inference from this self-analysis. This is, don't jump to the conclusion that because B studied with A, B is doing what A did—even if B reveres A and even if B calls himself or herself an A-ian. I admire the Teggartian tradition and wouldn't reject the label *Teggartian* if anyone tagged me with it, but I don't think it predicts or explains much of what I do.

For the traditions I do feel myself within, 1962 was a watershed year. In 1962 Thomas Kuhn published *The Structure of Scientific Revolutions*, a book that significantly increased interest in social history of science and one that challenged the conception of progress in science as smooth and incremental and turned at least some attention to social processes in accepting or rejecting old and new ideas and methods. Also in 1962 the Social Science Research Council (SSRC) sponsored a conference on the history of anthropology that legitimated the emerging historicist approach with which I identify my own work. I see this as a Pennsylvania tradition, not least because the prime mover for the conference was A. Irving Hallowell, whose "The History of Anthropology as an Anthropological Problem" appeared in 1965 in the first issue of the *Journal of the History of the Behavioral Sciences*, a major outlet for my work and that of others trying to make sense out of past work in psychology and in social sciences.

Also in the first volume of that journal was George Stocking's paper

"On the Limits of Presentism and Historicism in the Historiography." I thought that the paper was given at the 1962 conference, but the version in Stocking's 1968 book *Race, Culture, and Evolution* doesn't indicate any provenance, so the connection of publication may have given me the illusion that the two papers were presented at the same meeting. Not only that, but looking again at Hallowell's "The History of Anthropology as an Anthropological Problem" I found that it only drew on the ssrc presentation and was actually more directly based on a paper presented at the 1962 American Anthropological Association meetings. Stocking, and also Dell Hymes, whose work constructing a tradition of American linguistic anthropology heavily influenced my work, were both at that point at Berkeley. Both took up positions at the University of Pennsylvania, and Stocking had taken courses from Hallowell there earlier. Regna Darnell, who as the external examiner of my dissertation defended it from the ad hoc committee that included none of the three professors with whom I had worked on the dissertation research (all three were on sabbatical), was a student at Penn not only of Hymes and Stocking but of Hallowell and as an undergraduate was a student of Fredrica de Laguna, who was a student of Franz Boas.

Before characterizing what I see as essential to the tradition I think I work in, I want to draw a second lesson for doing history from my too-facile Pennsylvania tradition; namely, keep track of the dates, of who was where when, especially when reminiscences are flowing. In my experience interviewing our elders, chronology is not remembered well, and what seems to them to fit together often has been put together in recollection. Actual historical connections are rarely so neat. The unity of a Pennsylvania tradition in my memory probably owed more to knowing that Darnell was a student of Hallowell and Stocking and Hymes at Pennsylvania during the 1960s and that she considers the 1962 ssrc meeting the start of professional history of anthropology than to ever having given any thought to where those three were in 1962. In this case, Hymes was not yet at Pennsylvania and was probably not at all influenced by Hallowell. Hymes and Stocking were at Berkeley after Teggart's death and the departure of both Hodgen and Nisbet, but I know from Hodgen's papers in the Bancroft Library that she and Stocking were in correspondence about how to do history of anthropology. Moreover, Hallowell's article cites Hodgen, Teggart, Bock, and Oakes-George, and I suspect that Hallowell had some part in the publication of Hodgen's book by the University of Pennsylvania Press. I know that he was the editor of the Viking Fund Publications in Anthropology series in which her *Change and History* was published in 1952, so there were Berkeley connections to this Pennsylvania tradition, along with teacher-student ties like those between Hallowell and Stocking and both to Darnell.

I don't want to draw the methodological moral "seek and ye shall find," although that is very often true. The lesson that I would rather draw is to look for connections beyond those based on propinquity. Geography is not the only basis for social ties and intellectual influence, especially in the development of sciences, including social. It is dangerous to assume that because C and D were in the same institution, say department, at the same time, there was any real interchange of ideas between them.[1] Professor E across the continent may have been a more important source of ideas and support to C or D than they were to each other (or they may not have had links to the same person located elsewhere or to each other).

Breaking out of that tangle of social connections, I will finally say something about the content of the "Pennsylvania tradition" in the history of anthropology. Hallowell approached historical research in the same way he approached fieldwork, with respect for difference and a wish to understand alien assumptions, beliefs, institutions, and so on. "The past is a different country" is the formula for this approach. Just as anthropologists are supposed to suspend a commitment to their own culture's ways in order to try to understand those of another, contemporary culture, Hallowell (and Hodgen) sought to understand why earlier anthropologists thought what they did and how what they thought made sense by their own cultural logic. He did not search for precursors or attack the follies of the past. He did not scorn ideas that differed from those to which he subscribed, nor did he condemn past writers for failing to understand cultures the way he did. He sought to make sense of chronologically alien worldviews of anthropologists in the same way he tried to make sense of Ojibwe cultural assumptions and cosmology (Hallowell 2010).

In his 1965 paper, Hallowell made what I would like to make my third point for doing history of anthropology (or of any other discourse): don't assume that the same word means the same thing in older texts. Hallowell uses *nature* as an example. In my own work, I have had to deal with quite different senses of *phonology*, *etymology*, *revolution*, and *per-*

sonality, all words in current discourse. I think of these historically variable meanings of "the same word" as equivalent to false cognates across languages. That is, the familiar word only looks the same across time and may have been used quite differently in the old text one is reading.

Hallowell and Hodgen also touched on the question of reliability of reports. Both recalled the spectacular example of the *monopoli*, headless men with faces on their chests supposedly seen by John Mandeville in his travels—travels that didn't take place. Rather, Mandeville took the *monopoli* from Pliny, just as Carlos Castaneda constructed the teachings of "Don Juan" out of the books in the UCLA library. It took centuries, with many editions and translations, before Mandeville's nontravels and nonobservations were established, and the Library of Congress continued to classify Castaneda novels in the part of the E99 cataloging for work about Yaquis. Reports of observation can be faked, and no one knows how many more plausible accounts passing as observations are hearsay or outright invention. I suppose that my second lesson, know who was where when, applies. Even for "modern, professional" observers, field notes and letters from the field are important for interpreting what anthropologists did and the basis for what anthropologists have written (see Sanjek 1990).

For instance, I think that it is important for understanding Edward Sapir's Southern Paiute work to know that the data were elicited from one person, Tony Tillohash, far from any Paiute world. Sapir encountered him at the Carlisle School in Pennsylvania and carried him off to Philadelphia, where almost all the material on Paiute language and culture Sapir ever published was gathered in 1910 (see Fowler and Fowler 1986). For sorting out who discovered phonemic analysis, it is important to know that what Sapir published in 1930–31 was written before 1917. In a 1916 letter to Alfred Kroeber, Sapir already communicated what would be the prime example in his 1933 paper on the psychological reality of the phoneme. This seems to me to eliminate the possibility that either Saussure or gestalt psychologists sparked Sapir's "discovery" of phonemic analysis (Murray 1981b). That Sapir relied on Tillohash's feelings and even analyses of the forms of his own language is important for understanding classic publications, and, I think, the great remove from the speech community is important for understanding how little linkage there is between Sapir's linguistic methods and the ethnography of speaking or other sociolinguistic traditions (a topic considered at length in chapter 10). Sapir largely avoided ethnography and naturally occurring speech. When he spent some time in a functioning native speech community, among the Navajos, he was perplexed by individual differences and fled from participant observation, preferring the controlled elicitation that is sometimes called "white room ethnography."

I suppose Joseph Casagrande's (1965) book *In the Company of Man* deserves some credit for moving toward a focus on the natives on whom anthropologists' pronouncements about alien cultures rest. My reservation about that book is that it is again the anthropologists speaking of (and for) the natives. What I think would be really interesting is for the natives to speak for themselves about how the ethnographers behaved, what sort of weird questions they asked, and how they regard the quality of the representations eventually published. I wish that someone in Chan Kom or Tepoztlán would write the history of American anthropologists' involvement there. I read a manuscript autobiography of Alfonso Villa Rojas, but aside from his not being a native of Chan Kom, that he wrote it for Redfield makes it suspect for documenting how Redfield was perceived in that "village that chose progress."

Similarly, I'd like to know what Balinese and Javanese villagers recall about Clifford Geertz's fieldwork, as well as their interpretations of cockfights. I think that close reading of his famous 1972 article on the Balinese cockfight suffices to show a lack of Balinese support for his interpretations, but it is impossible from the text of his 1966 monograph on the lack of a conception of personhood in Bali to know how much came from observation, how much from native testimony, and how much from preconceptions based on earlier representations by Gregory Bateson and Margaret Mead (1942), which in turn were facilitated by and to some degree based on the interpretations of Walter Spies and other Dutch romanticizers (see Vickers 1997). I'd like to know what Balinese who were photographed as children for *Balinese Character* say as they examine Bateson's photos and try to make sense of what was—and wasn't—photographed as well as what was and wasn't published. Of course, these are interpretive endeavors, and even if I had Geertz's field notes, I am sure that I would still have questions about how he framed whatever questions he asked. Even if Mark Hobart (1986) and Unni Wikan (1990) are right that Geertz's account is totally wrong, a serious historian of anthropology has to ask why he thought what he did in fashioning his model of the Balinese. The extent to which the Balinese with whom

Geertz lived wanted the Balinese to be as he portrayed them needs to be distinguished from his own wishes to accentuate cultural differences, and what he recorded needs to be distinguished from what he "knew" in advance from reading Bateson and Mead (1942).

Winkin (1988), Daubenmier (2008), and Migliore et al. (2009) provide exemplars of what I would like to see explored more often in field sites: eliciting memories from the "natives" and their views on how their culture was represented by the alien observer.

Somewhat surprisingly, the rabid critic of Mead's first fieldwork report, Derek Freeman (1991b, 1999), eventually set out to reconstruct where Mead was and what she did in Samoa in 1925.[2] He documented, though not seeming to notice, that she spent a great deal of time on problems other than the one he maintains that Boas "set" her—that is, showing that adolescent turmoil didn't exist. It is very interesting to me that after that research Freeman could still attack what I published in *Current Anthropology* (Murray 1990, 1991), which asserted that throughout her life she did what she thought was interesting and was too inner-directed to be "set" a task she didn't want to do. To my mind, as a historian Freeman didn't know what he was doing. Freeman remained so eager to undercut what Mead wrote about Samoan adolescence that he failed to see that his showing how much she worked on other topics in her Samoan fieldwork undercut his own representation of her as Boas's puppet. Although he did it for the wrong reasons, I think that Freeman finally contributed to understanding what a "Boasian anthropologist" did in one field setting at one time. (This does not redeem his account of Boasian theory!) I think that some sympathetic attempt to understand what Mead was doing would enhance understanding of his chronicling of what she did, but relating what she wrote to what she did seems to me more revealing than labeling her work "Boasian," as if that label were an explanation.

In recent years Jennifer Brown has done some of this with descendants of Hallowell's Ojibwe sources, as have Sally Cole (2009) with descendants of those with whom Ruth Landes worked and Judith Daubenmier (2008) with those with whom University of Chicago anthropologists worked on the "Fox Project" in rural Iowa in the years after World War II. Although I know less about archaeology and nothing about physical anthropology, I am relatively confident that to understand the contributions of past practitioners of those to me arcane subdisciplines also requires examining what they actually did—that is, their practices rather than their pronouncements about methodology (fascinatingly exemplified by Pykles 2009).

Describing practices differing from current standards risks being interpreted as criticizing the past for not being the present and for doing things differently then and there. I think that even marginal outsiders—like Hodgen, Stocking, and I, none of whom hold anthropology degrees[3]—have presentist concerns and sometimes at least implicitly criticize those about whom we write. Certainly Hodgen aimed to discredit the "age and area hypothesis." In writing my dissertation—at least consciously—I thought that I could criticize lines of work with still-active proponents, such as conversation analysis, but not how Boas or Gallatin or Morgan went about studying and writing about Native Peoples. In the decades since then I have vacillated between thinking that it is impossible not to judge theoretical and methodological approaches past or present and thinking that I should attempt sympathetic understanding from within even (or especially) what I regard as ludicrous. Kuhn wrote somewhere that the historian of science should try to understand what it felt like to believe in phlogiston. Some historians of anthropology try to understand what it was like to conceive of Caribs or Iroquois as lost tribes of Israel. Others of us grapple with concepts like kinship and structure, the Kwagiutl culture inscribed by a half-Tlingit, half-white trader named George Hunt, and the southern Paiute language that Edward Sapir and Tony Tillohash constructed from their sense of patterning of sound and sense.

I think that we can no more recover the past than we can enter into the full native sense of cultures other than those in which we were raised. Again, searching across time is similar to reaching across space or across social/cultural distances within a place to so-called subcultures. Nonetheless, I think that these ultimately impossible goals are ones we should reach for and try to approximate. I do not approve of jettisoning attempts at sympathetic understanding of other cultures or of other anthropologies. Berating those who came before us for not seeing things the way we see them is equivalent to berating other peoples for not doing things the way we do them or patronizing them for what seem to be similarities to "our way," the "right way," the way we should be in some imagined future, or the way we were in some imagined golden past age.

It seems to me that some emic anthropology has achieved wide circulation, along with such etic anthropology as Marvin Harris's popular books or Margaret Mead's (1928) quite etic *Coming of Age in Samoa*. When it comes to the history of anthropology, the emic writings are known only to other historians of anthropology, and to some extent to anthropologists, not to the public. The three most widely disseminated books dealing with anthropology in the past and/or anthropology over time, in chronological order of their publication, are H. R. Hays's (1958) *From Ape to Angel*, which no one reads anymore; Marvin Harris's (1968) *The Rise of Anthropological Theory*, which perhaps some anthropologists read, though I doubt anyone else does; and Derek Freeman's (1983) *Margaret Mead and Samoa*. All three of these books are resolutely presentist. Hays's book is a longer version of a typical introductory textbook's review of the progress of the field. The other two books explore what went wrong; specifically, how did the bad guys—and in Freeman's case a fallen woman as well—go wrong. Harris and Freeman both had what they considered a proper and more than adequate understanding of humankind. They each revealed this understanding and what they consider the proper program for the science of humankind. Puzzled that not all anthropologists march under their banner, angry and resentful that most anthropologists persist in what they see as error, both turned toward the past to explore the sources of error. Although I think that Harris was rather grudging in giving credit to forerunners of his own cultural materialism, there is in his account some interest in developments leading up to his theory. For Freeman, anthropology, particularly American cultural anthropology, was benighted, fundamentally rested on Mead's claims about Samoa, and persists in its folly.

The popular histories and textbook histories of all sciences are what Herbert Butterfield called "presentist," which is to say that in writing about the past their primary purpose is making sense of the present, legitimating present preoccupations with some sort of tradition and development, and lauding those who made contributions that are either accepted in the present or believed to have led to present understandings of whatever phenomena are of concern to science, or would be if only others would value the proposed progenitor as the author does. Popular accounts of all sciences are "presentist" and what Thomas Kuhn called "textbook history"—and more properly could have called textbook substitutes for history. These do not aim to make sense of scientists in their own world with their own assumptions but as prefiguring "what we know now." Generally the past is presented as a glorious march or fitful but heroic advance to present understanding. Although Harris and Freeman had positive visions, these are more visions of what anthropology should be than visions of what it is. Not just the past but most of the present of the discipline, in their view, is lost in error.[4] Ancestors were not groping toward the truth as now properly understood by Harris or Freeman, but building intellectual structures to keep human self-understanding in the dark. Franz Boas, who is cast as the king of darkness by both Harris and Freeman and earlier by Leslie White, has had plenty of hagiographers. Earlier books, including Robert Lowie's (1937) *History of Ethnological Theory*, Margaret Mead's (1972) autobiography and her book on Ruth Benedict (1959a), and Melville Herskovits's (1953) book on Boas, portrayed Boas as a Culture Hero, dispelling the racist darkness of nineteenth-century unilinear evolutionism, building science on its wreckage. Boas's admirers were every bit as much presentist as his detractors have been.

Well, perhaps one or more of these authors really does have the truth. My own view of anthropology probably colors my view that etic history is spurious. I am certain that it is bad history, but I am not certain that anthropology or any science needs good history or that bad history is harmful to it. If someone today has a completely adequate understanding of our species, it doesn't matter whether she or he distorts the history of anthropology either as a path to the present or a bog from which his or her revelation will rescue us. Those of us less confident that we hold the final truth should be aware that what we do and think may seem as stupid or inexplicable from the perspective of the future as some of what our predecessors did and thought seems to us. And perhaps some of what we know will be forgotten, just as some of what our predecessors knew has been forgotten. What has been forgotten is not necessarily what was wrong. Lines of inquiry are dropped. New paradigms ask new questions, as Kuhn said; they do not necessarily offer new answers to the old questions, and the old questions may arise again—or keep nagging in the background.

• • •

I am not sure why anyone should try the ultimately impossible task of making sense across time or across space, but for those so inclined, I have made some suggestions about how to do history of anthropology better, applying, I think, to history of ideas as well as to history of institutions. Recapitulating the maxims, drawn from my experiences in trying to understand the history of social science:

1. Don't jump to the conclusion that because B studies with A, B is doing what A did—even if others, or even B, call B an A-ian.

2. Keep track of the dates, of who was where when, especially when using material elicited from informants or from public recollections. When working with published texts, it is important to ascertain when the texts were written, not just when they were published. In making inferences based on chronology, it is often important to find out whether a work circulated before publication. It's great to know that B had a copy of A's work, but in the absence of citation or a dated inventory of B's library the historian often has to assess the probability that A sent her work to B before B wrote whatever work the historian is trying to place and make sense of.

   It's also nice to know what the persons you are trying to understand were doing, especially when they were "in the field." *Fieldwork* would be another good example of a term that means different things to different people at different times, which brings us to:

3. Don't assume that the same word means the same thing in older texts as it means when you use the word. Indeed, don't assume that the same word means the same thing to people writing at the same time. Meanings are constantly shifting, and one person may use an older sense of a word after someone else used it with a newer meaning.

4. A subsidiary fourth point is that geography isn't destiny. Action at a distance occurs in anthropology and other sciences, while inaction at proximity also recurs. Supposedly the fathers of ethnoscience, Harold Conklin, Ward Goodenough, and Floyd Lounsbury, all studied with George Peter Murdock at Yale after World War II, yet they developed emic componential analysis independently of each other—and with only vague and general encouragement from Murdock, whose assumptions that the same etic domains can be coded in all cultures are institutionalized in the Human Relations Area Files. Similarly, Edward Sapir seems to have had precious little interchange

with his urban ethnographer colleagues in the University of Chicago Sociology and Anthropology Department, and he was on better terms with the positivist, quantitativist William Ogburn and his students than with the urban ethnographers and symbolic interactionists. Don't assume important contact from proximity or exclude it on the basis of geographical distance.

5. My fifth and final maxim is to treat "schools" as possibly useful fictions, not as explanations. That Ruth Bunzel or Ruth Underhill or Gladys Reichard wrote down texts as the natives dictated them because she was a Boasian is a pseudo-explanation. They may have been Boasians because they understood the point of collecting native texts—as Radcliffe-Brown did not—and Boas may even have been the one to suggest the activity to them, but whomever we have in mind as the paradigmatic Boasian woman, you can be sure that there were other influences on her and that being a Boasian was not the beginning and end of her self-understanding. There are some shared assumptions between, say, Benedict and Mead, and Kroeber and Sapir. They certainly knew each other, and all been influenced by Franz Boas, but there are considerable differences in what each of them did and substantial shifts of interest over the life course of each. I don't think that Kroeber's views on kinship changed much between 1909 and his death in 1960, but I think that his views on evolution changed markedly, as Mead's views on the extent of biological constraints on cultural difference did. Sapir gave up hypothesizing historical linguistic connections, and all four of them gave up tabulating trait distributions, albeit at different times.

When I looked closely at much written-about named traditions in American social science—the Chicago school of sociology, functionalism, ethnoscience, Boasian anthropology, so on—they didn't so much dissolve as shatter into smaller molecules. Not atoms, but smaller molecules—three simultaneous Chicago schools, four ethnoscience groupings plus a residue of fellow travelers not very connected to each other, and at least two sets of Boasians, with Papa Franz himself turning against the historical inferences of the first generation of his students, such as Alfred Kroeber and Edward Sapir.

I now think of theory groups as loose amalgams of individuals pursuing often-differing objectives, held together more by a common labeling by outsiders than by allegiance to such a label from inside. Often, as with Boasian anthropologists, those viewed as a school deny that they are a school and emphasize intragroup differences, even though these may strike outsiders as narcissism of small differences among those with distinctive shared assumptions and practices.

There are purposes for which similarities are salient, but theoretical traditions within anthropology—or within any other discipline—are not homogeneous. And they are very fuzzily bounded. In some senses Boas became anti-Boasian, so even prototypes can get fuzzy. Whether trying to make sense of what one person did or what a number of people with some link (like having studied with Boas) did, first one needs to examine what they actually did. Perhaps their practices were sufficiently similar that a label condenses the practices and is heuristic. The danger for history as for anthropology is, I think, inordinate haste in applying etic labels—this is a "shaman," that is a "structuralist."

I am Sapirian enough to think that we need to understand how various influences come together in an individual culture carrier, whether the culture being carried is that of Samoans or of Oceanist social anthropologists. In this ego-centered chapter, I have linked my own assumptions to Sapirian, Teggartian, and University of Pennsylvania traditions.[5] I must think that such labels make some sense and, specifically, make some sense about what I do. I don't think that my cravings to be viewed as legitimate are so keen that I need so many families, and what has been transmitted through the genealogy I have made visible in this chapter is open to question. More generally, although there are obviously concentrations of social and intellectual ties, boundaries between clusters within social networks are fuzzy. I've at least hinted at connections between Teggartian and Hallowellian historians of anthropology traditions—both personal and the intellectual connections—but I can't imagine anyone claiming they formed a group.

Like Hallowell, I think that trying to understand across time takes the same effort to suspend judgment and to make sense of others in their own frame of reference as understanding across space does. Depending on how far back one goes, the possibility of natives rejecting one's interpretations disappears. Personally, I have preferred to risk the wrath of the living, which constitutes interesting if not necessarily privileged insight on the past. When the natives are literate—as most anthropologists are (even if they tend to eschew reading what others wrote about their fieldwork sites)—and combative—as many are—a dialogue of interpretation can occur and does not have to be imagined. What people think they are doing or think that they did and what they think they meant provide interesting data, and through criticism by peers and by natives one may make better sense of cultures, including historical professional cultures. For me, making sense of the ways of others is the raison d'être of social science, including history and anthropology, and history of anthropology.

Acknowledgments

Revisiting these works on particular historical subjects reminds me of many debts of gratitude. One that jumps out at me is to journal editors who encouraged my historical work by accepting multiple pieces for publication: Jonathan Benthall (*Anthropology Today*), Russ Bernard (*American Anthropologist*), Konrad Koerner (*Historiographia Linguistica* and the John Benjamins monograph series), Barbara Ross (*Journal of the History of the Behavioral Sciences*), and Florence Voegelin (*Anthropological Linguistics*). I have an even deeper debt to Regna Darnell, for defending my dissertation to an ad hoc group of University of Toronto sociologists and for decades of discussions about anthropology and its history, and more recently, joining the first list (as coeditor of the *Histories of Anthropology Annual* and of the University of Nebraska Press's Critical Studies in the History of Anthropology monograph series).

Reaching further back, I remain grateful for the education in ancient and modern (socio)political theory I received at James Madison College from Peter Lyman, Bruce Miller, Lewis Zerby, and Dick Zinman (and to my introductions to the sociology of knowledge and Freudian metapsychology from Peter Lyman, and the opportunity to explore the Rousseau-Lévi-Strauss tradition provided by an independent study with my undergraduate academic advisor, Dick Zinman). Neither they nor I had any idea I was being prepared to perform on Robert Nisbet's pretest in a way that impressed him and further "primed the pump" to move from Lévi-Strauss's theories to Boasian and structuralist practices. I learned much about history, culture, and society from my anthropological linguistics mentors, Keith Basso, William Samarin, and John Gumperz (in chronological order). Dennis Magill ran interference for me and directed my dissertation research and writing, though his own primary interest was in the history of Canadian sociology, a field to which I have contributed nothing.

William Samarin introduced me to ethnohistory in general and Jan Vansina's work in particular (a byproduct of which was "Historical Inferences from Ethnohistorical Data" in the *Journal of the History of the Behavioral Sciences* 19 [1983]: 335–40) and also to thinking about dictation of texts affecting how informants spoke (in an unnaturally slow and formal register). He, Richard de Mille, Victor Golla, and John Gumperz made helpful comments on earlier drafts of "The Manufacture of Linguistic Structure," which appeared in the *American Anthropologist* 85 (1983): 356–62, though agreement with my interpretations should not be inferred. From Alaska, Ron Scollon and Michael Krauss both provided me information I gratefully used.

I wrote a paper about "Margaret Mead and the Professional Unpopularity of Popularizers" before Freeman's 1983 book—with an inexplicable assist from George Stocking, who usually delighted in blocking publication of anything he had not initiated—polluted the waters of discourse about Mead. Showing that Mead's influence (and fan base among professional anthropologists) was grossly exaggerated (as Stocking knew and Freeman resolutely did not want to know) and that there were strong disagreements among those classed as "Boasians" took on urgency. There is a ripple of this in the third chapter of this book and in a series of attempts to correct Freeman's misrepresentations that are not reprinted here. The revival and revision of the popularizer paper that is included here draws heavily on "Margaret Mead and Paradigm Shifts within Anthropology during the 1920s" (Murray and Darnell 2000), solicited by James Côte for a special issue of the *Journal of Youth and Adolescence* 29 (2005): 557–73. The only comments on the original paper that I recall came from Richard de Mille.

The chapter on late-blooming anthropology of peasants draws heavily on collections (Redfield, Tax, Burgess, Park, press) in the Regenstein Library of the University of Chicago, on the Kroeber and anthropology department archives in the Bancroft Library of the University of California, and on the Spicer collection of the Arizona State Museum in Tucson. My thoughts about the people and ideas discussed herein have been shaped in ways that are not always obvious by tape-recorded interviews of George Foster, Theodora Kroeber, and Rosamond Spicer and by untaped conversations with Raymond Fogelson, Everett Hughes, Edward Spicer, Sol Tax, and Yves Winkin. I am also grateful for comments on an earlier draft provided by Paul Kutsche and Clifford Wilcox and to Sol

Tax for allowing me access to his papers before they were officially open to researchers. A slightly different version of the chapter appeared in *Histories of Anthropology Annual* 3 (2005): 61–98.

I am grateful to Regna Darnell and Lisa Philips Valentine for inviting me to a conference at the University of Western Ontario on theorizing the Americanist tradition, papers from which appeared in a volume of that name published in 1999 by the University of Toronto Press. The discussion following my presentation was quite heated (though, I think, misunderstandings were resolved, and they were not about the principal thesis). In addition to the organizers, Ellen Basso, Ray DeMallie, Raymond Fogelson, Jane Hill, Dell Hymes, Bill Leap, Doug Park, and Blair Rudes provided comments (and/or encouragement) that were useful for revising the paper. (The second two figures in the original publication were mislabeled; see the third and fourth columns of table 5.1 herein.)

A longer version of the Devereux-Kroeber chapter was published in *Histories of Anthropology Annual* 5 (2009): 12–27. I am grateful to Karl Kroeber for permission to quote his father's unpublished words, to Regna Darnell and Will Roscoe for editorial suggestions, and to correspondence with Devereux from the early 1980s.

The heretofore unpublished chapter on Berkeley anthropology during the 1950s was presented at the 2002 centennial meeting of the American Anthropological Association in a session organized by Regna Darnell. Interesting comments there were made by Harold Conklin, Fred Gleach, Ira Jacknis, and Murray Leaf. Obviously, I drew heavily on the memories from being a graduate student there and then of Jeffrey Dickemann.

Much of "American Anthropologists Looking through Taiwanese Culture" appeared in *Dialectical Anthropology* 16 (1991): 273–99. Donald Nonini, Judith Farquhar, Claude Lévi-Strauss, and Li Khîn-Hôa made helpful comments. The "aftermath" section derives from *Looking through Taiwan* (University of Nebraska Press, 2005). The impetus for this line of work was definitely Keelung Hong's dismay with the invisiblization of Taiwanese in the cultural anthropological research done on Taiwan (see, especially, Hong 1994). We are grateful to the Yen Family Foundation for some support for this work.

"W. I. Thomas, Behaviorist Ethnologist" appeared in the *Journal of the History of the Behavioral Sciences* 24 (1988): 381–91. Evan Thomas and Robert Faris shared insights about Thomas with me.

An earlier version of "The Postmaturity of Sociolinguistics" appeared in *History of Sociology* 6(2) (1986): 75–108, a variant of my Sapir centenary conference paper presented in Ottawa in 1984, published as Murray (1986a). The original impetus for this investigation was discussion with William Samarin about the tardy and marginal institutionalization of the study of language within sociology. In addition to the published literature, this research drew on the Kroeber and Lowie collections preserved in the Bancroft Library of the University of California at Berkeley, on the Sapir papers at the National Museum of Man in Ottawa, and on the Ogburn, Park, Redfield, Wirth, and anthropology department archives in the Regenstein Library of the University of Chicago. It also greatly benefited from patient answers to the author's numerous queries by Herbert Blumer, Martin Bulmer, Bingham Dai, Regna Darnell, Fred Eggan, Murray Emeneau, Robert Faris, William Fenton, Paul Friedrich, Mary Haas, Philip Hauser, Everett Hughes, Theodora Kroeber, Weston LaBarre, Barbara Laslett, David Mandelbaum, Kenneth Pike, Stanley S. Newman, Edward Shils, Anthony F. C. Wallace, and Ellen Black Winston. The text was clarified and otherwise improved by comments from Regna Darnell, Fred Eggan, Wendy Leeds-Hurwitz, Yakov Malkiel, James Nyce, and Michael Silverstein and by close editorial scrutiny from the father of the sociology of science, Robert K. Merton.

An earlier version of "The Reception of Anthropological work in American Sociology, 1921–1951" appeared in *Journal of the History of the Behavioral Sciences* 24 (1988): 135–51. I appreciate answers to my queries from Jessie Bernard, Robert Bierstedt, Samuel Bloom, Robert Faris, Erving Goffman, and Robert Nisbet.

An earlier, even longer version of "The Rights of Research Assistants and the Rhetoric of Political Suppression" appeared in the *Journal of the History of the Behavioral Sciences* 27 (1991): 130–56. It drew on the presidential papers of Robert Gordon Sproul, materials on the foundation of the sociology department at Berkeley, and the archives of the Japanese-American Evacuation and Resettlement Study in the Bancroft Library at the University of California, Berkeley; the University of Chicago Press archives in the Regenstein Library of the University of Chicago; observation of a 1987 conference on the project held in Berkeley; a 1990 interview of Tamotsu Shibutani; supportive comments on my interpretations by him, S. Frank Miyamoto, and Edward Shils; information from Evan A. Thomas and James M. Sakoda; and withering criticisms (of varying plausibilities) of the study and of the conduct of Berkeley social scientists and administrators by Peter T. Suzuki.

An earlier version of "Resistance to Sociology at Berkeley" appeared in the *Journal of the History of Sociology* 2 (1980): 61–84. It obviously draws on Margaret Hodgen's collection of documents in the Bancroft Library, and those in the Kroeber and Sauer collections and Board of Regents minutes there and answers to questions I posed to Kenneth Bock, Theodora Kroeber, and Robert Nisbet. In addition to Bock and Nisbet, Mary Jo Deegan, Mary Furner, and Timothy Thoresen also made helpful comments on earlier drafts.

The anthropology part of "Does Editing Core Anthropology and Sociology Journals Increase Citations to the Editor?" appeared in *Anthropology News* 42(2) (2001): 16–17. The sociology part appears for the first time here.

An earlier version of the concluding essay was presented to an anthropology department colloquium at the University of California, Davis, April 29, 1991. I appreciate encouraging and helpful comments by Bill Skinner, Aram Yengoyan, and anthropology graduate students at UCD.

Regna Darnell, Fred Gleach, and Sean O'Neil commented helpfully on a draft of the entire book. Matthew Bokovoy and Elisabeth Chretien shepherded it through the *very* long evaluation process; Joy Margheim pointed out and/or corrected many lapses in my manuscript.

Notes

Information about archival collections consulted and cited can be found in the acknowledgments.

Introduction

1. Some archaeologists are employed to do archaeology rather than to teach about it, though they seem to me to lack autonomy and to be employees (on the other hand, many physicians these days are employees and find their autonomy in deciding what to do for patients highly constrained by bureaucracies, whether insurance companies in the United States or governmental healthcare bureaucracies elsewhere).
2. I use "Americanist" here as a site of research (mostly in the restricted sense of Native North America; "First Nations" in Canadianese) not as a theory, method, or approach (cf. Hymes 1983:116; Darnell 1995, 1999).
3. Though much of my work is "internalist" in following internal developments in disciplines, the choice of subject matter clearly is and has been affected by external stimuli, most notably herein in the instance of the forced relocation and prolonged incarceration of Japanese Americans from the West Coast of the United States (and Canada) but also in increasing interest in "acculturation" replacing attempts to factor out nonaboriginal influences on contemporary peoples. Also, looking beyond aboriginal North American peoples was influenced by the expanding military and imperial reach of the United States.

Part 1 Introduction

1. Even within the monogenist paradigm, Gallatin had to contend with the belief that American Indians had degenerated in the adverse environment of the Americas.
2. As governor of the Territory of Michigan Cass circulated questionnaires gathering information on Native American cultures and languages. C. C. Trowbridge compiled reports based on these data.
3. If Ward is remembered at all, it is as a sociologist and ideologist of social

planning (see Commager 1967; Hinkle and Hinkle 1954), but Powell hired
him as a paleontologist in the Geological Survey.

4. Powell combated the ideological claims of powerful vested interests and
popular fantasies. Because western land speculation was based on such
fantasies, Powell's science clashed with powerful popular views. Similarly,
he opposed the view that Native Peoples were destined to be exterminat-
ed. See Stegner 1954.

5. On his formative years, see D. Cole 1999.

1. Historical Inferences from Ethnohistorical Data

1. Lowie (1959:133) did not include Dixon or Swanton or Kroeber with Sapir,
Radin, Ruth Benedict, and Goldenweiser, and there seems to me at least a
hint of contempt for Swanton in a letter from Lowie to Kroeber dated
March 13, 1917: "Swanton's most recent effusion adds zero."

2. "Methodological asceticism" is how Karl Mannheim (1945) characterized
American social science's eschewal of any knowledge not derived from
replicable methods. One later Boasian, Leslie Spier (1929:142), characterized Roland Dixon as "stoutly conservative in his use of inferential methods" with "an almost Puritanical adherence to evidence and logic," a view
shared by Cole (1952:164).

3. Margaret Mead and the Unpopularity of Popularizers

1. Mead's single encounter with fieldwork among Native Americans took
place after her Samoan fieldwork. She and her second husband, Reo Fortune, spent the summer of 1930 on the Omaha Reservation, where Mead
in particular was appalled by what she considered the disintegration of
culture. She did not compare it to the rapid culture change occurring in the
Pacific and failed to acknowledge linguistic complexity (and her own reliance on interpreters) as one reason for the thinness of her Omaha work.

2. Her attraction to this non-Boasian school may owe something to the
greater expertise on Pacific societies of non-American anthropologists, as
well as to the intense intellectual ferment of her initial collaboration with
Fortune.

4. American Anthropologists Discover Peasants

1. Godoy stresses that Redfield studied the early Spanish texts about Mexico
and considers that "the chapter [of *Tepoztlán*] on material culture, like the
appendix on kinship nomenclature, shows Redfield's sensitivity to the
historical background" (1978:75n9; cf. the peculiar explaining away of use
of historical records in M. Singer 1991:177). To ignore the revolutionary
violence that led him to evacuate his family and commute from the capital

rather than continue to live in Tepoztlán does not seem to me to differ from the general ignoring of events and the colonial, neocolonial, or other authoritarian settings of the peoples studied by anthropologists.

2. As Redfield summarized Gamio's findings on U.S.-to-Mexico money orders, "the heaviest immigration comes from the States at the west end of the south central plateau, Jalisco, Guanajato, and Michoacán" (1929a:435), not from south of the capital. That is, Redfield did not choose to study a village generating emigrants, such as Tzintzuntzan, Michoacán, studied later and over the course of decades by George M. Foster. Proximity to the capital and acquaintances there must have been part of the reason Redfield chose to work in Tepoztlán.

3. Although many Americans would and did read "the road to light" as unremarkable recognition of the superiority of U.S. culture and prosperity, Redfield's recurrent romanticizing of folk solidarity makes it seem likely that he was at least ambivalent and possibly being ironic in this designation and in labeling what Chan Kom people chose as "progress."

4. Apparently the Illinois Institute for Juvenile Research rather than the Local Community Research Committee funded Gower's Chicago fieldwork. Burgess was the key gatekeeper of research funds for both (Bulmer 1984:123-25; also see James Bennett 1981 on the Illinois Institute for Juvenile Research).

5. Another instance of a peasant community study followed by research on emigrants from the community to a metropolis is provided by Bernard and Rita Gallin (1974a, 1974b).

6. Embree had already placed the state rather than the city as the decisive entity: "Each little peasant group is part of a larger nation which controls its economic life, enforces a code of law from above, and, more recently requires education in national schools. . . . The farmer's crop is adjusted to the needs of the state" (1939:xvi). Yet, as late as 1953, Redfield claimed that it took the city to bring into existence the "human type" peasant, and that "there were no peasants before the first cities" (31; also see ix). Ironically, still later, Oscar Lewis asserted that "peasant communities came into existence only after the rise of cities" (1970:253).

7. And not just of rural communities: Aasel Hansen, who was responsible for the urban pole of the folk-urban continuum (i.e., Merida) recalled that "Redfield criticized me for spending too much time on Merida history" (1974:179).

5. The Non-eclipse of Americanist Anthropology

My primary focus in this chapter is on cultural anthropology. My 1994 book, especially pages 174-76, discusses the relative decline of Americanist research in American linguistics and linguistic anthropology.

1. Radcliffe-Brown's "fieldwork" on Andamanese people and Australians was primarily "white room ethnography" rather than observation of functioning aboriginal cultures (Langham 1981). Much of Mead's Samoan research consisted of questioning Samoans on the verandah of a colonial government house where she lived. Redfield lived in Tepoztlán seventy-six days (minus two stays in Mexico City) and commuted in for interviews during some of the three remaining months before his earlier-than-scheduled return to Chicago (Godoy 1978). The length of Malinowski's Trobriand stay was mostly a result of his being stranded as an enemy alien during World War I.

2. Mead claimed that "unawareness was essential to the successful prosecution of a study involving intimate details of contemporary life" (1965:xxi). "Prosecution" is a particularly apt choice of words. As Thorne (1980:287) noted, many fieldworkers prefer misrepresenting what they are doing over trying to see how much can be studied and written about with informed consent. Also see M. Wax 1991:451.

3. Also see Mead (1959a:313–17, 1965:xv). She recalled that, after her Omaha fieldwork, she and Reo Fortune "explained that we would like to work among the Navaho, as an American Indian group whose culture was still alive and intact," but "Boas told us that the Navaho 'belonged' to Gladys Reichard" (1972:193).

4. "I was responsible for having brought him to Chicago," Sapir wrote Louis Wirth in a November 25, 1931 letter (in the Regenstein Library at the University of Chicago). Sapir had been acting chair of the anthropology department the previous year, while Fay-Cooper Cole was in Washington DC, and I do not think he would have made this assertion if his role had been only titular. It was primarily Radcliffe-Brown's ill-disguised contempt for previous Americanist work (in particular, publishing native texts—see the Sapir-Cole letters of May 2, 1932, and June 2, 1932, quoted in Darnell 1990a:250–51) that antagonized Boasians. The Benedict:Mead letter of December 28, 1932, (in Mead 1959a:326–27) is typical of the irritation at the combination of arrogance, pretentiousness, ignorance, and cultism that non-Chicago anthropologists saw. Before Brown's arrival on the American scene, Lowie sympathized with Brown's "attempt to explain the parts of Andamanese culture not as isolated fragments but as parts of an organic unity" (1923:575), even while demurring from making the discovery of general laws the sole purpose of anthropology. There was plenty of American skepticism toward followers of W. H. R. Rivers, both the "Children of the Sun" diffusionist branch and the functionalists. Kroeber had crossed swords with Rivers in 1909, and many American anthropologists in the interwar years remained skeptical of British anthropologists'

psychological, historical, and sociological views. Lowie (1915) expressed criticism even of earlier, more restrained Rivers methods of inference, and he unequivocally objected to the wilder later inferences (Lowie 1937:156–66). Brown could have made common cause with them, since it was the conjectures (and "method") of William Perry, Grafton Elliott-Smith, and Rivers himself (after the time he trained Brown), not the more cautious reconstructions of Boasians, that Brown originally rejected (publicly, only after Rivers's 1922 death), and there was at least an implicit sense that there was a whole under the details of Boas's particularistic data. In response to Murdock's (1951) blistering attack on the narrowness of British social anthropology (as the kind of antiquated sociology from which Murdock with great effort had freed himself), Radcliffe-Brown (1952a:276) provided a mythical history, tracing the ethnology–social anthropology division of labor to the contrast of A. C. Haddon and James G. Frazer, with no mention of Rivers, the dead Laius of the story, or of the evolutionist focus of Frazer, Herbert Spencer, and E. B. Tylor that underlay Brown's interrogations of Andamanese prisoners.

5. I fail to see American anthropological "isolationism" in the interbellum years as a "revolution against the destructive and immoral First World War" or as "an unavoidable consequence of the Great Depression," as Goldschmidt (1985:165) does. I recall Murray Emeneau (ca. 1981) telling me that it was cheaper for his sponsors to support him in India than in America during the late 1930s. Boas and Sapir elicited information from Africans resident in the United States, and Leonard Bloomfield's descriptions of Tagalog and Ilocano were based on work in the United States with native speakers. Both linguistic and psychological anthropological work done during World War II relied on natives of other societies resident in the United States.

6. Besides Mead, another exception was Cora Du Bois, who had earlier done Wintu fieldwork, collaborated with Dorothy Lee, and wrote a standard work on the 1870 ghost dance before Abraham Kardiner financed her psychological anthropology of Alor. John and Beatrice Whiting did Paiute fieldwork before going to New Guinea or Africa. The flow was not entirely out from North America to Pacific islands; see, e.g., Felix Keesing's (1939) monograph on Menomini-white contact and Laura Thompson's work on the Indian Personality, Education, and Administration Research Project during the 1940s (Thompson and Joseph 1944; Joseph, Spicer, and Chesky 1949; Thompson 1951).

7. Lloyd Warner, Brown's first American protégé, had studied at Berkeley with Kroeber and Lowie before going to Australia, and then he studied European Americans. (Warner supervised some New Deal studies of Native American personality and education; see Thompson 1951).

8. Raymond DeMallie (letter to author, July 2, 1995) suggested the points in the preceding two sentences. Paul Kutsche suggested that "the heyday of [anthropologists'] interest in Native Americans was pretty much isomorphic with the height of interest in comparative kinship studies" (letter to author, July 6, 1995) and declined with them in a combination of paradigm exhaustion and exogenous political processes, not least of which was availability of funding for anthropological research outside the United States.

9. See M. Wax (1956), heavily influenced by Redfield's impatience with Boasian particularism.

10. Kroeber (1936:341) had already published his view that what Brown's method had produced was (to date) sterile, after noting that "determinants are multiple and variable" (340) and that the fit between kinship terms and social usage is partial, not exact (339; retreating from his 1909 total rejection of **any** fit).

11. The first criticism clearly does not apply to Fred Eggan, who sought whatever historical documentation existed. A chapter about "change" was tacked on to many functionalist books on the supposed equilibrium of what was treated as a closed system (or, occasionally, as one disrupted by European agency).

12. Foster identified an earlier period in which theorizing was done by armchair ethnologists reading secondary sources and/or querying missionaries and colonial officials. After the community study period he saw a "longitudinal, repeat-visit" period, pioneered by Clyde Kluckhohn among the Navajos. The periodization fits Foster's ontogeny from graduate student to supervisor of ongoing observation of Tzintzuntzan, Michoacán, very well but also seems more plausible to me for the phylogeny of American anthropology than other periodizations not based on fieldwork practices.

13. The oft-repeated folklore of anthropologists is that American anthropologists outside the University of Chicago preferred no funding to funding directed by Brown. Not having examined the internal Rockefeller Foundation documents, I suspect that the worldwide economic depression was a more important factor and that lack of agreement among anthropologists was at most a minor factor in the foundation's decision to refocus on health-related issues.

14. Leaving aside the propriety of trampling the sensitivities of subordinated peoples to gather materials (of all sorts, including religious secrets and plundering burial sites) for science, I find it hard to imagine the payoff for governments of elicitation by Harrington and colleagues of memories and lexicons from the last survivors of a California people, and so on. I do not

think that utility for dominating regimes was either the goal or the result of Boasian work. Kroeber was especially skeptical of government employment of anthropology/anthropologists, and Boasians did not advertise useful application of their knowledge as Malinowski and Radcliffe-Brown tried to do (Asad 1973; Kuper 1983:100–120).

15. Reorganization of the reservations imposed a romantic sense of primitive communism along with liberal assumptions about leadership and engineering of people and of land (see E. Hall 1994). As Murray Wax stressed to me, legal recognition of Indian land was important and there were severe (Congressional/popular) limits on what the executive branch could do about empowering Native people. Collier and anthropologists who became bureaucrats thought they were defending the interests of Native people while trying to guide them.

16. Murray (1994b:162) contains a more detailed breakdown of Bloch's (1950:16) official report. I have excluded the 10.5 percent (in both periods) of articles he coded as being about "general topics" rather than dealing with a particular language or family.

17. No final report of the Southwest Project appeared (see Murray 1994b: 195–96). In some sense all the linguistic eggs for the anthropological market were put in the Whorfian basket. (This image is from Hymes 1983:175.) The basket was then fumbled, although other linguistic eggs were hatched and carried by Lévi-Strauss and by cognitive scientists.

18. There is certainly some sense to saying that British and French social anthropology were dominated by Africanists.

19. "Theory" is not as distinct a field (separate specialty) in anthropology as it is in sociology, though some distinction between those who gather empirical data and those who theorize goes far back—before John Wesley Powell and Daniel Garrison Brinton (toward the end of the nineteenth century), at least to Albert Gallatin or, arguably, to Thomas Jefferson (see introduction to part one here).

20. R. Murphy (1976:13) considered structural functionalism to have climaxed and been exhausted (in Kroeber's sense of both climax and pattern exhaustion) in 1963, though it continued, zombielike, to stalk the earth after its demise. Elsewhere he wrote that functionalism had reached an intellectual dead end in 1955 (Murphy introduction to Steward 1977:35). I do not know why he chose that date and would myself date the climax to Radcliffe-Brown and Forde 1950, followed quickly by the onslaught of Murdock 1951 and the apostasies of Evans-Pritchard 1951, with Firth 1954 and Leach 1954 constituting major (if incomplete) turns against the assumption of synchronic equilibrium of (what were treated as) closed systems.

21. Expansion seems to have been more gradual (or later) in Canada. See Burridge 1983 and Preston 1983, the latter markedly uneasy about overspecialization.

22. Sinologist anthropologists who worked on Taiwan (see chapter 8) are, I hope, extreme in ideological service to contemporary domination by a neocolonial regime. I have endeavored not to overgeneralize from them and from Nancy Scheper-Hughes's various apologias for Cuban HIV-positive concentration camps but am aware that their work and anthropologists' refusal to address criticism of them may have colored (jaundiced) my view of contemporary American anthropological praxis overseas.

23. As Ellen Basso (1999) shows, such narratives differ from "life histories" but portray individual characters, not schematic types.

24. I consider Eggan (1950, 1966) and Steward (1955, 1977) as having supplied exemplars of controlled comparison of aboriginal patterns; Spicer (1962), Dozier (1970), and M. Wax (1971) of more recent and/or long-term "acculturations." I also think that what Leach (1961:1) wrote continues to apply: anthropologists "are giving up the attempt to make comparative generalizations; instead they have begun to write impeccably detailed historical ethnographies of particular peoples."

25. In my view, the stories anthropologists tell about themselves in various locales threaten to drown out the stories that other people tell them. Geertz (1995:120) suggested that they misrepresent what is very public activity as introspection and provide little insight into how "knowledge" is constructed in fieldwork.

6. Pre-Freudian Devereux, Post-Freudian Kroeber

1. The very elaborate *alyhâ* initiation rite Devereux (1937) detailed is not mentioned in the dissertation, which has a test of vocation involving dancing to an *alyhâ* song. The *alyhâ's* simulated menstruation and pregnancy were reported in the dissertation. Drucker (1937:27) alluded to an initiation rite for Quechan *elxa*, a transgendered role for natal males in another Yuman-language-family Southern California people. Roscoe (1995:149) noted that "Devereux's only source of information on *alyhâ* pregnancies appears to have been Hivsû Tupôma, who was repeating the stories of his friend Kuwal, a Mohave from Parker who in the late nineteenth century married a series of *alyhâ*" (1998:152). Only one of whom was Mohave, the rest being from the neighboring Quechan.

7. University of California, Berkeley, Anthropology during the 1950s

1. After noting that the Parsonian synthesis was "a far more sophisticated brand than that of Radcliffe-Brown," Murphy opined that functionalism

"failed not because it was proven wrong but because it had exhausted its possibilities" (R. Murphy 1976:13), an echo of Kroeber's notion of "pattern exhaustion" filtered through Thomas Kuhn.

2. Berreman reported that he was shunned by the "young Turks" as an appointee of the "old guard," while the "old guard" thought him one of the "young Turks." The son of a sociologist, Berreman, like Murphy and Schneider, was interested in some sociological theory. On Foster's intervention to prevent Berreman being elected president of the American Anthropological Association, see Berreman 1980:143.

3. Geertz (1995:114) said that his salary for his first five years at Chicago came entirely from the committee's budget. After that he was supported by an NIMH Senior Research Career Fellowship that lasted until he went off to the Institute of Advanced Studies at Princeton. The year before he taught at Berkeley, the only year during his career that he had a regular appointment in an anthropology department, he was at the Center for Advanced Studies in Palo Alto. His account of his career in *Available Light* (Geertz 2000) skips from Harvard to Chicago. The account in *After the Fact* skips from the Palo Alto Center to Chicago and characterizes himself as "arriving [at Chicago] an unformed assistant professor in the fall of 1960" (1995:110). Fallers was recruited by David Apter for the same committee, in Geertz's account, and was a protégé of Talcott Parsons and Edward Shils from the "general theory of social action" days, as Schneider (1995:174) recalled.

4. In justifying a merit increase for Norbeck, Mandelbaum wrote that "in the two years that Dr. Norbeck has been with the Department he has gained our respect and confidence. He is an excellent teacher and has successfully given the larger courses in the departmental curriculum" and was "also one of the principal faculty advisors for lower-division students" (letter dated March 5, 1956). Mandelbaum judged Norbeck "a good colleague, an effective teacher, and [an] able anthropologist."

5. After a long hiatus, William Hanks was hired in 2000, so there is one linguistic anthropologist in the department now.

8. American Anthropologists Looking through Taiwan

1. See the bibliography in Herbert Passin 1947. For an overview of work published in Chinese, see the special issue of *Bulletin of the Institute of Ethnology, Academica Sinica* ""Symposium on Taiwan Aborigines: Retrospect and Prospect," volume 40, 1975.

2. Pressures and cultural expectations for early family division are a central concern in Margery Wolf's (1972) *Women and the Family in Rural Taiwan*. In contrast, another pioneer American ethnographer of rural Taiwan, Ber-

nard Gallin, explicitly distinguished Taiwanese and Chinese practices in the first American ethnography of a Taiwanese village, *Hsin Hsing, Taiwan*, in 1966.

3. Although few anthropologists today are as determined to sort out the sources of cultural traits as Boasians and diffusionists were in the first third of the twentieth century, there is still an equation of *genuine* with *original*, a distaste for historical complexity, and a continuing quest for at least relative "purity" of "tradition." See Fichte 1985:285; Murray 1981a, 1999.

4. The sense of some Taiwanese that their religion is related to Hinduism and the borrowing and transformation of Hindu deities might stimulate research to investigate a "folk brahman complex" carried with Buddhism, as in its diffusion to Thailand—see Kirsch 1977:252; Tambiah 1970.

5. For a very Durkheimian view of the primacy of social accommodation over imaginable doctrinal conflicts, see Reischauer 1981:138–45; also see R. Smith 1983:16, 29, 110–14.

6. Similarly, in using Japanese colonial records Barrett (1990) attributed a similarity between colonial Japanese and Taiwanese seasonality of birth to climate rather than to culture, without considering the possible importance of Japanese culture, in an article the title of which purports that it is about "traditional Chinese."

7. In the same preface Wolf (1985:x) mentioned that data from land title registers and land tax registers was being culled to collate with the household registry data, so perhaps "yet" should be added, even nearly three decades after he wrote this statement. Given the frequency of land transactions, the noncontiguity of holdings, and the variations in grade of land, estimating the value or yield of property owned by families in Japanese Taiwan is not at all an easy task.

8. We consider insider views of Taiwanese religion in "A Taiwanese Woman Who Became a Spirit Medium" (Hong and Murray 2005: chapter 8). Here, we are dealing only with external, "rational" explanations of religious phenomena.

9. For cautions that "authenticity is not a function of antiquity and recency is not evidence of triviality" in cultural patterning, see R. Smith 1989:722. Native concerns with such analyses were sensitively considered by J. Jackson 1989.

10. Interestingly, the title of the first sustained discourse on Taiwan in English, the entirely fraudulent George Psalmanazar's 1704 *An Historical and Geographical Description of Formosa, an Island Subject to the Emperor of Japan*, shows how little established in European views was the subordination of the island to Qing emperors. In discussing this book, Rodney

Needham (1985:90) noted that there was an 1896 reprinting (by Kegan Paul in London) of that curious piece of ethnographic fiction that included no indication that it was fictitious and had been retracted in a posthumous publication by its author.

11. Chen Chi Lu (1971:64) made a similar claim.

12. Donald Nonini reminded us of this.

13. Julian Steward (1950) made a searing, pioneering critique of the application of simplistic anthropological assumptions about cultural homogeneity. Rather, a lot of anthropological assertions have come from atypical and very "marginal natives." See Kluckhohn 1943, 1945:99, 138–45; Cannizzo 1983; Murray 1983a (chapter 2 herein).

14. E.g., Wallace 1952; Hart 1954. Compare the more mainstream homogeneity of each of the five cultures in longtime contact that were contrasted in Clyde Kluckhohn's study of values (eventually edited and published as Vogt and Albert 1966).

15. On the complicated partial Sinification and (after communist takeover) retribalization of those Hsu studied, see D. Wu (1990). Hsu noted that some traits considered outside China as typical of "traditional China" have become part of self-identification as non-Chinese in Yunnan (as in Taiwan in opposition to another modernizing regime opposed to "feudal superstitions"). Hsu recurrently dismissed variance within a very broad conception of Chinese essence (see Murray 2002).

16. Aside from the un-Taiwaneseness of "Hsin Hsing" as a place name, the Chinese characters on the cover of the book skip from "Hsin Hsing" to the subtitle without including the characters for Taiwan. Rita Gallin (personal communication, 1992) told KH that Xin Xing was a name, though not a usually used official name, of the village.

17. There are also examples from Taiwan in Kleinman's (1988) later paradigm's exemplar, *The Illness Narratives*. We have not found any Kleinman publication with *Taiwan* or *Taiwanese* in the title, including the chapter titles in Kleinman 1980, but—within his work and that of other medical anthropologists—it is much easier to tell when data from Taiwan is being discussed than in the literature on "Chinese religion" based on fieldwork on Taiwan.

18. On the dangers of essentializing "Chinese medicine" and "patient," see Farquhar 1987.

19. However, Kleinman and his colleagues forced Taiwanese data into the dubious etic domain of "medicine." We find it hard to believe the claim by Kleinman that Taiwanese *dang-gi* "use the term 'client,' *k'e-jen*, literally, 'guest'" (1980:219). Aside from *k'e-jen* being a Beijinghua term (rather than the Hokkien *lang-kheh*), it is too mercantile and not sufficiently reverent.

Inquiries to devotees of a Dailam *dang-gi* from across Taiwan in 1992 confirmed that my skepticism was justified, that *k'e-jen* is irreverent, and that the proper term is *sin-tô* (follower). Bruce Holbrook (1977) challenged *dang-gi* being considered part of the same domain as *se-I-sian* (western-style doctor) and *diong-I-sian* (Chinese-style doctor). He also rejected Kleinman's folk/professional dichotomy, arguing that "there are no native terms for these mystically cognized categories" (151; criticizing specifically Kleinman 1975). On the problematic conceptual status of *professional* more generally, see Roth 1974.

It bears noting that Holbrook did not satisfactorily establish the emic salience of his own favored domain of "Chinese medicine," including "real" and "fake" Chinese doctors, either. Just as, despite the preoccupation of anthropologists with kinship, the full set of Taiwanese kinship terms has not been published, there is no emically warranted typology of whatever the emic domain closest to the etic domain "medicine" may be, despite the volume of work on Taiwanese healers and clients. This is elaborated later in this chapter.

20. Emphasizing intracultural diversity, Kleinman and his followers rejected the quest for the formal native taxonomies of mutually exclusive, tightly integrated, hierarchically arranged categories and for uniquely derivable native diagnoses in the ethnoscience tradition exemplified by Frake (1961). Kleinman (1975) launched an all-out attack on one attempt at ethnoscientific analysis of healers on Taiwan (Holbrook 1974) but blandly absorbed some ethnoscientific work in the background to his synthesis of clinical and cultural analysis (see, e.g., Kleinman 1980:30). In general, as Murray 1982 suggested, ethnoscience dissolved into various cognitive anthropologies rather than being destroyed by criticism.

21. See, e.g., Williams 1988; Mueller 1977; J. Fei et al. 1979; Kuo et al. 1981; Barrett and Whyte 1982. There is one mention of Taipei pollution in the generally laudatory account of urbanization in Speare et al. 1988:192. Ho noted that air pollution doubled in residential areas of Daiba between 1959 and 1965 and commented, "For those living in Daiba and its vicinity the quality of life has been adversely affected by this development—a change not taken into account by the per capita consumption indicator" (or other conventional indicators of development) (1978:230). Cheng (1989:499) noted the increasing salience of environmental concerns in Taiwan; Kim (2000a) noted the greater tie to dissident politics of the environmental movement in Taiwan in contrast to that in South Korea. Also see Williams 1989; Bello and Rosenfeld 1990; Weller 2000:111–25; and the massive Academia Sinica steering committee's report *Taiwan 2000: Balancing Economic Growth and Environmental Protection*.

22. E.g., M. Brown 1996, 2001, 2004; Chu 2000; Chun 2000, 2002; Corcuff 2002; Kuo 2002; Simon 2003a; F. Wang 1994; Wong 2001; D. Wu 1997; You 1994; N. Wu 2002, among others. The only anthropologist in this now-licit discourse (M. Brown) has been investigating the Hanification of aborigines, mostly in the Japanese colonial era, while the rest address cultural and political meanings of Taiwanese/mainlander contrasts. Wang Fu-Chang (2002b) found that the highest amount of ethnic consciousness typified the mainlanders (early generations of whom made a Chinese/Taiwanese distinction extremely salient for those in the latter, disprivileged group). Using data collected from several sets of nationwide house interview surveys, Wu Nai-Teh (2002) showed that for ethnic politics there is not a cleavage between Hakka and Holo speakers but only one between mainlanders and Taiwanese (the latter including mainlander progeny identifying as "new Taiwanese" rather than as "Chinese"; also see M. Li 2003).

Part 2 Introduction

1. Boas frequently claimed that anthropology was a historical endeavor (while eschewing any documentary evidence that might exist, preferring to map distributions of "traits" he or his students recorded). Though Boas's work carried the Romantic "genius of the folk" tradition of Herder to North America, his rejection of general theory (Hegel's in particular) frustrated some, just as Boas's focus on primary sources (natives rather than documents) and allergy to general concepts annoyed Edward Sapir (and Sapir's student Leslie White [1963] and Robert Redfield's student Murray Wax [1956]) in ways that the methodological and theoretical asceticism of Leopold von Ranke (1795–1886) had. Boas was trained in physics; the American sociologists studied history in Germany. (Park, who studied sociology in Berlin with Georg Simmel, also became famous for mapping "traits" within Chicago, while diffusion, the great subject of German anthropology before Hitler came to power, was a major fascination of Sumner.)

9. W. I. Thomas, Behaviorist Ethnologist

1. The proceedings of the 1938 conference and the critique in Blumer 1979 were originally published as *Social Science Research Council Bulletin* 44 (1939). See E. Thomas 1978.

2. Janowitz 1966:xiv–xvii discussed the complex political motivations for FBI action that led to Thomas's firing. The charges were thrown out of court, but publicity, especially in the *Chicago Tribune*, led the University of Chicago to fire him before this, without any proof of actual wrongdoing.

Thomas lectured part time at the New School for Social Research between 1923 and 1928 and was a visiting lecturer at Harvard during the 1936-37 academic year. He did obtain research funds from various sources, not always openly in his own name.

3. Park was never formally a student of Thomas, having studied at Harvard and Heidelberg. Thomas did most of the work on the Carnegie Americanization study. When the results were published as *Old World Traits Transplanted* (1921), the authorship was listed as Robert E. Park and Herbert A. Miller, although it is unclear how much work either of the credited authors did or whether there was any genuine collaboration with Thomas. See Janowitz 1966:xvi.

4. On the lack of continuity in Thomas's thought, see Volkart 1953. Volkart (1968) argued that his later behaviorism was accompanied by a shift from expecting social science laws to probabilistic, statistical statement. The contention of John Petras that a method of sympathetic introspection "gradually led him to emphasize the societal factor in the individual and society relationship" (1970:79) is untenable, perhaps because Petras ignores what Thomas wrote and thought in the last thirty years of his life, instead making the astonishing claim that "undoubtedly [!], the finest single source for understanding the later theories of Thomas is the monumental study of the Polish peasant" (78). In my opinion, much of what is superindividual in *The Polish Peasant* comes from Znaniecki. Thomas was never focused on the "societal" level, even before the behaviorist conversion that underlies his "later theories." Moreover, a "method of sympathetic introspection" is a distortion even of the method of *The Polish Peasant*, which relied on documents, particularly letters and life history produced by Polish immigrants, not on attribution by analysts (sympathetically taking the role of others). See Leeds-Hurwitz and Nyce 1986; and Platt 1983.

5. Lowie regarded Meyer "as doing the very sort of reformative work my intellectual guides, Franz Boas and Ernst Mach were attempting in their respective fields—a quasi-methodological critique that swept away catchwords and facile classifications in the search for what phenomena really were like" (1945:140-41).

6. Adler spent some time in the United States, contributed an article to the Chicago sociology department's journal, the *American Journal of Sociology*, and was discussed by John Dollard in his *Criteria for the Life History* and by Radcliffe-Brown and Ogburn (Fred Eggan, personal communication, 1984).

7. W. I. Thomas was funded by Rockefeller money for the *Child in America* work, 1926-28, and at least his 1932-33 position with the Social Science Research Council was indirectly funded by Rockefeller money.

8. It bears repeating that Thomas's brand of symbolic interactionism was realist and objectivist, not nominalist and subjectivist like that of Herbert Blumer. See Cottrell 1980; J. Lewis and Smith 1980.

10. The Postmaturity of Sociolinguistics

1. An oral presentation of this paper led to Faris's call to the vacancy at Chicago created by Thomas's departure (R. Faris 1967:31).

2. Faris rejected my surmise that he was testing Sullivan's etiological theory (outlined in a Social Science Research Council/American Psychiatric Association personality colloquium), cautioned me against interpreting the title, because it was given by Louis Wirth, and added, "if I pretended to state a theory of schizophrenia, I was much too far ahead of my data." As for any influence from Sapir, Faris reported, "I hardly knew Sapir. I don't remember that I ever conversed with him . . . and did not think of him in connection with social psychology topics. . . . I believe that the overwhelming majority of my thoughts [on such topics] must have come from my rich association with my father," who taught the social psychology courses at Chicago (Faris:author, May 13, 1984).

3. It must be admitted that for all their sharing in the tradition of German romanticism, neither Boas nor Lowie had any training in sensitivity to philology or sympathy with it.

4. Although accepting the probability of some influence of Durkheim on Saussure mediated by Meillet, Koerner (1973:59–62, 69) categorically rejects the possibility of any influence of Tarde on Saussure. According to Koerner (74ff.), what has been mistakenly viewed as Tarde's influence was really that of the great nineteenth-century Yale philologist William Dwight Whitney. What makes the recurrence of Tarde in linguistic theorizing particularly jarring is that Hanns Oertel was a philologist at Yale in the years between Whitney's and Sapir's tenure there. Interestingly, Kroeber (1956:154) asserted that Boas "was definitely influenced by Tarde" and noted that Elsie Clews Parsons translated Tarde, so Tarde's influence on American scholars in diverse fields was probably more pervasive than is remembered.

5. See Murdock 1943:136; Eggan 1974:7. Like Radcliffe-Brown, Redfield was interested in European sociological theory (see chapter 4). Even though many prominent Boasian anthropologists were European-born, they looked at European theorizing only to scorn it as insufficiently based speculations for invidious contrast to their own "scientific" study, which substituted counterexamples for every proposed law (or even generalization). This peculiar kind of nativism was alien to Ogburn, Park, and Faris, all of whom had personal ties to leading European sociologists and/or assigned

their students French and German treatises. Durkheim, Simmel, and Mannheim (if not Weber) were introduced to American sociologists by Chicagoans prior to the advent of Talcott Parsons. Boasians may have been interested in European psychoanalyses (though quite critical of any claims about "primitives" or equations of children and the stages of "primitive" cultures), but they were boosters of only their own work as worthwhile anthropology and little interested in Weber and Simmel, or even Durkheim and Mauss. Michael Silverstein helped me to focus on this curious lack of cosmopolitanism, which I have also discussed in analyzing Kroeber's opposition to the establishment of a sociology department at Berkeley (chapter 13).

6. David Mandelbaum, personal communication, October 23, 1981; Weston La Barre, personal communication, May 19, 1984; Fred Eggan, personal communication, May 15, 1984. From obviously later contact, David Schneider spoke of a general anti-Semitic climate at Yale but saw Murdock as more pro-Yankee than anti-Semitic (1995:34–37).

11. Reception of Anthropological Work, 1921–1951

1. C. W. M. Hart, *AJS* 45 (1940):138–39; R. Redfield, *AJS* 34 (1929):394–95, 728–30; W. F. Ogburn, *AJS* 40 (1936):897; E. Mannheim, *AJS* 43 (1937):344. Also see E. Reuter on Mead, *AJS* 41 (1936):523.

2. See W. Jackson 1986; Gershenhorn 2004. Herskovits published seven papers in *SF*, was located in a sociology department (Northwestern), and coauthored a number of papers with sociologist Malcolm Willey.

3. Hankins's views were closer to those of Clark Wissler than to Ruth Benedict's; see Freed and Freed 1983. Bernhard J. Stern, who was trained by Boas and Ogburn at Columbia and wrote an ethnography, *The Lummi Indians of Washington State* (published by Columbia University Press in 1934), wrote an important paper in *SF* arguing that "culture" is an entity distinct from individual psychology and social forms of association (Stern 1929). The views expressed in it on race and on the value of Boasian anthropology are completely orthodox. An excellent account of Stern's institutional career is contained in a paper by Samuel W. Bloom, "The Intellectual in a Time of Crisis," presented at the 1984 meetings of the American Sociological Association in San Antonio.

4. See Madge 1962:199; Homans 1984:161. Along with W. Allison Davis, who was his and Malinowksi's student, psychiatrist Harry Stack Sullivan did some fieldwork in Greenville, Mississippi, although "Frazier and Johnson had difficulties in obtaining final reports from Sullivan after his field visits" (S. Smith 1974:179). Sullivan crosscut many interdisciplinary endeavors, influencing Edward Sapir in particular.

12. Research Assistants and Political Suppression

1. Sproul evidenced great concern about ensuring that students of Japanese descent would be able to pursue their studies. Those who were to graduate in the spring of 1942 received their degrees. After the "evacuation," which he publicly opposed, he proposed federal scholarships for Japanese American students, according to Morton Grodzins ("History of Relocation," 1948 typescript). Over intense local opposition Sproul insisted that the International House, of which he was a longtime trustee, be racially integrated, and those who knew him are shocked that anyone would accuse him of racism.

2. Charles Aikin, Milton Chernin, Frank Kidner, and Dorothy Thomas, "The Mechanism and Consequences of the Civilian Wartime Control Program for the Evacuation and Resettlement of Classes of the Population," unpublished manuscript, March 26, 1942. Five "governmental" research topics, three "economic," and two "sociological" ones were listed. Dorothy Thomas drafted and submitted to the Rockefeller Foundation a proposal dated May 1, 1942, that specifically "omitted the governmental and administrative aspects, including analysis of the pressures of various sorts that led to the formulation of evacuation policies, the constitutional and legal issues raised by evacuation, and the role played by the various branches of the government" and "the economic aspects, including economic conditions predisposing the formation of policies" (3). That is, the Rockefeller grant was for the sociological and anthropological study of the consequences for individual behavior and social institutions of forced migration, specially focused on those incarcerated at the Tanforan racetrack and then moved to the Tule Lake concentration camp.

3. Fairgrounds and the stables of racetracks were used as "assembly camps" for those being "evacuated" from the West Coast of the United States to be "resettled" behind barbed wire with armed guards in "planned communities" set in barren interior locales. Although "concentration camp" may connote death camps to some, the "assembly centers" and "resettlement communities" were quite literally concentration camps for one ethnic group. German Americans and Italian Americans were not similarly extirpated from the East Coast, despite evidence of sabotage and spying there and a total lack of examples of such by Japanese Americans on the West Coast. President Roosevelt, whose order established them, himself used the term "concentration camp."

4. In discussing the recurrent battles between the camp staff and Dorothy Thomas, Tamotsu Shibutani (personal communications, 1987, 1990) recalled that at one point S. Frank Miyamoto had outlined the particular

kinds of stress involved in the forced migration of a population as a basis for collecting data on reactions to such stress. Even this was judged by Thomas to be too a priori theorizing. In response to doubts expressed by a University of California Press referee (presumed by Thomas to be Alexander Leighton) about "the absence of conceptualization" in a draft of the first official report, she wrote, "There is at present no body of sociological theory which might be used as a foundation for studies of this sort. There is a great deal of loose speculation and armchair philosophizing out of which almost no hypotheses capable of testing have emerged" (Thomas:August Fruge, June 24, 1946).

5. See P. Suzuki 1986. Although delivering less-blanket condemnations than Suzuki, the participant observers from the project still alive in the late 1980s remained perplexed about what they were supposed to have done and frustrated at the lack of theoretical guidance. Frank Miyamoto wrote that Thomas "never discussed the problem under study, the research design, or methodological procedures" (1989a:40; also see 59, 148-49; Spencer 1989:160, 167, 173; and Sakoda 1989a:223-24). Ichioka (1989:9-11) quoted a number of 1942-43 statements of concern about lack of guidance.

6. In the correspondence to California attorney general Earl Warren I have examined, Grodzins invoked "faculty members of the University of California" and Rockefeller Foundation funding. The approach to California's congressional delegation was made by jurisprudence professor Max Radin (August 19, 1942) to Congressman John A. Tolan, chairman of the House Committee Investigating National Defense Migration, also mentioning Rockefeller funding. Tolan wrote a generic letter of introduction for Grodzins, September 23, 1942, noting that "I have made available to him all records, hearings, and correspondence" for a study "financed by the Rockefeller Foundation and sponsored by the University of California."

7. Six months after the cessation of hostilities was the goal for wartime reports.

8. Shibutani confirmed this understanding in a July 1990 interview, as had Rosalie Hankey (letter to Grodzins, September 8, 1948). Miyamoto wrote Grodzins (October 4, 1948) that he thought JAERS project staff needed explicit permission to quote JAERS material for the duration of the war to protect informants and JAERS neutrality. James M. Sakoda wrote that "it was understood that we could use the material for a doctoral dissertation, but it was not clear whether the dissertation itself could be published" (Sakoda:author, October 28, 1990). Not until the summer of 1945 (when the Grodzins dispute was already building) did the Nisei researchers learn

that Thomas expected to exercise continued control of material. Miyamo-to explained that Thomas "had relatively little direct contact with the field research, and from the standpoint of the field staff, gave minimal supervisory guidance to the data collection. Because of the critical role that fieldworkers played in the data-gathering process, they tended to develop a strong proprietary sense with regard to the data they collected" (1989a:41).

In contrast, Grodzins and Thomas were in frequent contact in Berkeley, and unlike the fieldworkers in the concentration camp, Grodzins did not risk his life to record data for the project. Moreover, Grodzins used the legitimacy of the University of California to gain access to data, whereas the Japanese American fieldworkers had to rely entirely on their own skills and contacts to obtain data. All in all, it seems that Grodzins had less claim to independently gathered data than anyone else on the project.

9. By overidentifying with Couch (to whom his paper is dedicated), Peter T. Suzuki (1989) reversed this.

10. FW:WC[ouch] note, December 30, 1948; Sproul:Tyler, December 27, 1948; Grodzins:Hutchins, December 28, 1948.

11. A faculty committee of inquiry concluded that the immediate stimulus for Couch's dismissal was a pretext and took seriously Couch's suggestion that his championing freedom of speech may have been the real reason. The faculty members of the Board of University Publications (including Malcolm Sharp), in a letter to University of Chicago president Ernest C. Colwell dated November 23, 1950, protested the dismissal, noting, "Couch evidently lost the confidence of the Central Administration some two years ago. The immediate issues on the basis of which the director was relieved of his duty, while typical of operational difficulties of the Press, do not seem to have been serious; they were an occasion rather than the cause." They did not state what they believed to be the cause. I would suggest that it was the form and not the substance of Couch's 1948 offensives on behalf of Grodzins's manuscript. Not surprisingly, Couch himself (letter to the Council of the University of Chicago Senate, March 7, 1951) believed that the reason was because he kept the university from suppressing *Americans Betrayed*. As Peter Suzuki noted, Grodzins's "only previous experience in book publishing had been with the student publications while at the University of Louisville" (1989:123). Given Grodzins's lack of experience or qualifications to head a major university press, Suzuki's inference that muting criticism of Couch's dismissal must have been at least part of the basis for the choice seems very likely. If Grodzins shared this definition of the situation, he was not restrained by loyalty for past support from taking the job that had been Couch's.

12. In the laboratory of a major research university that I observed intermittently for more than a decade, the director frequently assigned projects that had not been completed to his satisfaction to a new worker. Thirteen out of fifteen scientists who joined the lab in that span took over projects in this manner. In most cases the scientist who began the project was senior to the one taking it over. A new postdoctoral fellow routinely was given data from an existing project started but not carried through the full course of experiments viewed as needed to support a scientific paper by someone who usually still remained in the lab. The new worker was told to finish the project. Quite often the person who had worked first on the project, like Grodzins, did not concede any lack of appropriate progress and was unenthusiastic about sharing data as ordered from above. Getting work done this way has a considerable cost in anger, bitterness, and resentment. These feelings frequently surfaced when decisions were made about whose names appeared and in what order on published results. Roughly half the papers judged by the primary drafter to be ready to be sent out were held up (for weeks or months) by one or another of the senior members of the laboratory, either to manage the order of publication of results or to contest authorship (inclusion and order of names).

13. On the ways in which paternalistic anthropologists employed by the WRA legitimated concentration camps as "communities" and represented resistance as "pathological," see Starn 1986 and P. Suzuki 1981.

14. Two chapters (Miyamoto 1989b, Sakoda 1989b) in the book deriving from the 1987 conference reviewing JAERS (Ichioka 1989) present material heretofore available only in dissertations. Miyamoto (1996) recast some materials in generalizing about a dialectic between intergroup and intragroup factionalism.

15. Peter Suzuki (1986) rightly criticized this irresponsibility in communicating the results of research. It might, nonetheless, be noted that failure to publish results is not uncommon in relatively large-scale social science research. On the lack of final reports from the Southwest Project and the Chiapas Drinking Project, see Murray 1982:168–69; 1998:22–23, 202–3.

16. To continue comparison to my observations of the aforementioned lab, no papers were held back more than four months there; demands for revisions prior to submitting a work for publication in some cases continued for years rather than the weeks it takes to work out authorship conflicts.

17. By "excessive" I certainly do not mean to imply that there were no grounds for concern. There were serious dangers to fieldworkers who might have been labeled as "spies" if their work became known, and WRA officials were very eager to gain access to JAERS data, as Ichioka (1989:13–16) reviews. James Sakoda, in a October 28, 1990, letter to the author, and

Tamotsu Shibutani, in a July 13, 1990, interview, also stressed the dangers of being denounced as government spies that Nisei researchers within the concentration camps felt.

18. There can be some doubt about its dissemination, since the directive was not immediately invoked when the controversy began. It is, however, impossible to imagine the project's particular policy being unknown to the person who initially organized project material and was actively involved in recruiting other research assistants.

13. Resistance to Sociology at Berkeley

1. There was no priority dispute while either was alive. Hodgen (1971) claimed priority for Teggart to Kroeber's (1944) monumental *Configurations of Cultural Growth*. Theodora Kroeber (1970 interview) noted that the work her husband reported in that book had been in process for decades.

2. I find inclusion of Vincent as an exception puzzling. Sociology at the University of Minnesota (see Martindale 1976) would seem particularly to embody what Sauer and others condemned in American sociology. It should also be noted that while Sauer may have found their politics congenial, none of the four he melded into a past "golden age" were apolitical.

3. Nisbet accorded stronger feeling to Hodgen, but his own were expressed with greater frequency in correspondence from the 1940s. (When he read the prepublication version of this chapter, he did not comment on this observation of mine.)

4. Taylor worked with and married photographer Dorothea Lange. Their works of advocacy for Dust Bowl emigrants, along with Thomas's research on demonized and removed Japanese Americans, likely supported suspicions that sociology was inevitably committed to social reform and valorization of stigmatized populations (especially populations stigmatized within California).

14. Does Editing Increase Citations to the Editor?

1. Since editors almost never publish articles in the journals they edit, self-citation in the journal disappears during their tenure as editor. One might, therefore, expect citations to their work to decrease during their tenure in comparison to the time preceding it, during which some published in the journal they were later going to edit.

2. There is no one who has done both to ask, alas. Perhaps the best counter-example of decreased productivity while editing a core journal is provided by Peter Blau. While editing *AJS* between mid-1960 and mid-1966, he published (and presumably wrote) *Exchange and Power in Social Life* (1964). In the year following the end of his tenure as *AJS* editor, he published an even

more-heavily-cited book, for which he was the first author (the one picked up in citation indexing), *The American Occupational Structure* (1967).

Conclusion

1. During my last year in residence in Toronto, I had an office just down the hall at St. Michael's from Marshall McLuhan. I saw another University of Toronto celebrity, novelist Robertson Davies, master of Massey College, several times a week but never saw, let alone talked to, McLuhan. (I also never saw Lewis Feuer, whom Robert Nisbet sent me to work with at Toronto: Feuer was on sabbatical when I arrived and then left the University of Toronto.)

2. I was naïve to think Freeman's modus operandi of cherry-picking quotations and ignoring explicit rejection of what he wanted to argue had changed for his second Mea/Samoa book. In a paper presented at the 2012 American Anthropological Association meetings (published in *Current Anthropology* [February 2013]), Paul Shankman showed that Freeman's hoaxing claims were based on flagrant misrepresentation of what his prime informant, Fa'apua'a Fa'amū, had said: "An analysis of Mead's relationship with Fa'apua'a demonstrates that she was not an informant for Mead on adolescent sex, and an examination of the three interviews used by Freeman does not support his interpretation of them. In fact, responding to direct questioning during the interviews, Fa'apua'a stated that Mead did not ask her questions about her own sexual conduct or about adolescent sexual conduct. Nor did she provide Mead with information on this subject" (quote from the abstract; also see Shankman and Boyer 200).

3. Having taken postgraduate courses in anthropology for four years at three universities, I "went native" to some extent, joined the American Anthropological Association, presented research and served as a discussant at sessions of its annual meetings (on subjects other than the history of anthropology), and have published research that is not history of the fields in anthropological and linguistic anthropology journals.

4. More properly, since both are now dead, in the views propounded in their books.

5. Each of my successive anthropological linguistic mentors provide a link to Sapir: Keith Basso through Clyde Kluckhohn, William Samarin through Mary Haas and Murray Emeneau, John Gumperz through Kenneth Pike. I also consider myself a "Weberian" comparativist more than a little influenced by Alexis de Tocqueville. I was introduced to their ideas as an undergraduate student at James Madison College by Peter Lyman, Bruce Miller, and Richard Zinman (before being a graduate student of Robert Nisbet and Irving Zeitlin, both of whom wrote books about Tocqueville).

References

Abbreviations

AA   *American Anthropologist*
AJS   *American Journal of Sociology*
ASR   *American Sociological Review*
CA   *Current Anthropology*
IJAL   *International Journal of American Linguistics*
SF   *Social Forces*
Univ. University

Abel, Theodore. 1930. "Is a Cultural Sociology Possible?" *AJS* 35:739–52.
Ahern, Emily M., and Hill Gates, eds. 1981. *The Anthropology of Taiwanese Society*. Stanford CA: Stanford Univ. Press.
Allen, J. S. 1989. "Franz Boas's Physical Anthropology." *CA* 30:79–84.
Alpert, Harry. 1941. Review of Redfield 1941. *ASR* 6:896–98.
APA (Committee on the Relations of Psychiatry and the Social Sciences of the American Psychiatric Association and the Social Science Research Council). 1928. *First Colloquium on Personality Investigation*. Baltimore: Johns Hopkins Univ. Press.
———. 1930. *Second Colloquium on Personality*. Baltimore: Johns Hopkins Univ. Press.
Arensberg, Conrad M. 1937. *The Irish Countryman: An Anthropological Study*. New York: Macmillan.
———. 1961. "The Community as Object and Sample." *AA* 63:41–64.
Asad, Talal. 1973. *Anthropology and the Colonial Encounter*. London: Ithaca Press.
Baity, Philip C. 1975. *Religion in a Chinese Town*. Taipei: Orient Culture Service.
Bannister, Robert C. 1998. "Dorothy Swain Thomas: The Hard Way in the Profession." www.swarthmore.edu/SocSci/rbannis1/DST.html.
Barclay, George W. 1954. *Colonial Development and Population in Taiwan*. Princeton NJ: Princeton Univ. Press.

Barnes, S. Barry. 1972. *Sociology of Science*. Baltimore: Penguin.

Barnes, S. Barry, and R. G. A. Dolby. 1970. "The Scientific Ethos." *Archives Européennes de Sociologie* 11:3–25.

Barrett, Richard E. 1990. "Seasonality in Vital Processes in a Traditional Chinese Population: Births, Deaths and Marriages in Colonial Taiwan, 1906–1942." *Modern China* 16:190–225.

Barrett, Richard E., and Martin K. Whyte. 1982. "Dependency Theory and Taiwan: A Deviant Case Analysis." *AJS* 87:1064–89.

Barth, Fredrik. 1993. *Balinese Worlds*. Chicago: Univ. of Chicago Press.

Bashkow, Ira. 1991. "The Dynamics of Rapport in a Colonial Situation: David Schneider's Fieldwork on the Islands of Yap." *History of Anthropology* 7:170–242.

Basso, Ellen B. 1999. "'Interpersonal Relations' in a Kalapalo Shaman's Narratives." In Valentine and Darnell 1999:315–29.

Basso, Keith H. 1979. *Portraits of "The Whiteman": Linguistic Play and Cultural Symbols among the Western Apache*. New York: Cambridge Univ. Press.

Bateson, Gregory. 1936. *Naven*. Cambridge: Cambridge Univ. Press.

Bateson, Gregory, and Margaret Mead. 1942. *Balinese Character*. New York: New York Academy of Sciences.

Beals, Ralph L. 1930. *The Comparative Ethnology of Northern Mexico before 1750*. PhD diss., Univ. of California.

———. 1946. *Cherán: A Sierra Tarascan Village*. Smithsonian Institution Institute of Social Anthropology, Contribution 2. (Reprinted by the Univ. of Oklahoma Press, 1998.)

———. 1951. "Urbanism, Urbanization, and Acculturation. *AA* 53:1–10.

———. 1954. Review of Miner 1953. *AA* 56:307–8.

———. 1961. "Community Typologies in Latin America." *Anthropological Linguistics* 3:8–16.

———. 1975. *The Peasant Marketing System of Oaxaca, Mexico*. Berkeley: Univ. of California Press.

———. 1978. "Anthropologist and Educator." Oral history manuscript, Bancroft Library, Univ. of California, Berkeley.

Beals, Ralph, and Harry Hoijer. 1953. *An Introduction to Anthropology*. New York: Macmillan.

Beardsley, Richard K. 1954. "Community Studies in Japan." *Far Eastern Quarterly* 14:37–55.

Becker, Howard, and Harry Elmer Barnes. 1938. *Social Theory from Lore to Science*. Washington DC: Harren.

Bello, Walden, and Stephanie Rosenfeld. 1990. *Dragons in Distress: Asia's Miracle Economies in Crisis*. San Francisco: Institute for Food and Development Policy.

Benedict, Ruth. 1930. Review of Redfield 1930. *New York Herald Tribune*, 2 November 2: 24.

———. 1934. *Patterns of Culture*. Boston: Houghton-Mifflin.

Benet, Francisco. 1963. "Sociology Uncertain: The Ideology of the Rural-Urban Continuum." *Comparative Studies in Society and History* 6:1–23.

Bennett, James. 1981. *Oral History and Delinquency*. Chicago: Univ. of Chicago Press.

Bennett, John W. 1943. "Some Problems of Status and Solidarity in a Rural Society." *Rural Sociology* 8:396–408.

———. 1948. "The Study of Cultures: A Survey of Technique and Methodology in Field Work." *ASR* 13:672–89.

———. 1988. "Anthropology and the Development Process: The Ambiguous Engagement." In *Production and Autonomy: Anthropological Studies and Critiques of Development*, ed. John W. Bennett and John Bowed, 1–29. Lanham MD: Univ. Press of America.

———. 1998. *Classic Anthropology*. New Brunswick NJ: Transaction.

Bernard, H. Russell. 1992. "Preserving Language Diversity." *Human Organization* 51:82–89.

Bernard, Jessie. 1945. "Observation and Generalization in Cultural Anthropology." *AJS* 50:284–91.

———. 1949. "Sociological Mirror for Cultural Anthropologists." *AA* 51:671–77.

Bernard, Luther, and Jessie Bernard. 1943. *The Origins of American Sociology*. New York: Crowell.

Bernstein, Jay H. 1985. "The Perils of Laura Watson Benedict." *Philippine Quarterly of Culture and Society* 13:171–97.

Berreman, Gerald D. 1980. *The Politics of Truth*. Berkeley: Univ. of California Press.

Berreman, Gerald, Murray B. Emeneau, and George M. Foster. 1987. "David Mandelbaum." Unpublished manuscript, Bancroft Library, Univ. of California, Berkeley.

Bieder, Robert E. 1986. *Science Encounters the Indian, 1820–1880: The Early Years of American Ethnology*. Norman: Univ. of Oklahoma Press.

Bieder, Robert E., and Thomas G. Tax. 1974. "From Ethnologists to Anthropologists: A Brief History of the American Ethnological Society." In Murra 1974:11–21.

Bierstedt, Robert. 1945. "Limitations of Anthropological Methods in American Society." *AJS* 51:671–77.

Blackwell, James E. 1975. *Black Sociologists: Historical and Contemporary Perspectives*. Chicago: Univ. of Chicago Press.

Bloch, Bernard. 1950. "Publication Committee Report." *Linguistic Society of America Bulletin* 23:12–17.

Blom, Jan-Petter, and John J. Gumperz. 1972. "Social Meaning in Linguistic Structure: Code-Switching in Norway." In *Directions on Sociolinguistics*, ed. John Gumperz and Dell Hymes, 407–34. New York: Holt, Rinehart and Winston.

Bloomfield, Leonard. 1933. *Language*. New York: Rinehart.

Blumer, Herbert. 1937. "Social Psychology." In *Man and Society*, ed. E. Schmidt, 144–98. New York: Prentice-Hall.

———. 1979. *An Appraisal of Thomas and Znaniecki's "The Polish Peasant in Europe and America."* New Brunswick NJ: Transaction Books.

Boas, Franz. 1903. Heredity in Head Form. *AA* 5:530–38.

———. 1911. *Handbook of American Indian Languages*. Washington DC: Bureau of American Ethnology.

———. 1912. "Changes in Bodily Form of Descendants of Immigrants." 61st Congress, Senate Document 208. Washington DC.

———. 1940. *Race, Language, and Culture*. New York: Free Press.

Bock, Kenneth E. 1956. *The Acceptance of Histories: Toward a Perspective for Social Sciences*. Berkeley: Univ. of California Press.

———. 1963. "Evolution, Function, and Change." *ASR* 28:229–37.

Bock, Philip K. 1999. *Rethinking Psychological Anthropology*. New York: W. H. Freeman.

Bougainville, Louis Antoine de. 1982[1771]. *Le voyage autour du monde, par la frégate La Boudeuse, et la flûte L'Étoile*. Paris: Gallimard.

Bourguignon, Erika. 1973. *Religion, Altered States of Consciousness, and Social Change*. Columbus: Ohio State Univ. Press.

Bressler, Marvin. 1952. "Selected Family Patterns in W. I. Thomas' Unfinished Study of the Bintl Brief." *ASR* 17:563–71.

Broom, Leonard, and Ruth Riemer. 1949. *Removal and Return*. Berkeley: Univ. of California Press.

Brown, Kenneth, and Michael Roberts. 1980. "Using Oral Sources." *Social Analysis* 4.

Brown, Melissa J. 1996. *Negotiating Ethnicities in China and Taiwan*. China Research Monograph 46. Berkeley CA: Center for Chinese Studies.

———. 2001. "Reconstructing Ethnicity: Recorded and Remembered Identity in Taiwan." *Ethnology* 40:153–64.

———. 2004. *Is Taiwan Chinese? The Impact of Culture, Power, and Migration on Changing Identities*. Berkeley Series in Interdisciplinary Studies of China 2. Berkeley: University of California Press.

Bulmer, Martin. 1984. *The Chicago School of Sociology*. Chicago: Univ. of Chicago Press.

Bulmer, Martin, and Joan Bulmer. 1981. "Beardsley Ruml and the Laura Spelman Rockefeller Memorial." *Minerva* 19:370–90.

Bunker, Stephen G. 1982. "Latin American Migration and Migrants." *Contemporary Sociology* 10:222–23.

Burgess, Ernest W., and Harvey J. Locke. 1945. *The Family: From Institution to Companionship*. New York: American Book Company.

Burridge, Kenelm. 1983. "An Ethnology of Canadian Ethnology." In *Consciousness and Inquiry: Ethnology and Canadian Realities*, ed. Frank Manning, 306–20. Mercury Series 89E. Ottawa: National Museums of Canada.

Calhoun, Craig. 2007. *Sociology in America: A History*. Chicago: Univ. of Chicago Press.

Cannizzo, Jeanne. 1983. "George Hunt and the Invention of Kwakiutl Culture." *Canadian Review of Sociology and Anthropology* 20:44–58.

Caplow, Theodore. 1949. "The Social Ecology of Guatemala City." *SF* 28:113–33.

Cappanari, Stephen. 1973. Review of Chapman 1971. *AA* 75:327–28.

Carey, James T. 1975. *Sociology and Public Affairs: The Chicago School*. Beverly Hills: Sage.

Carneiro, Robert L. 1981. "Leslie A. White." In *Totems and Teachers*, ed. S. Silverman, 209–54. New York: Columbia Univ. Press.

Casagrande, Joseph. 1965. *In the Company of Man*. New York: Harpers.

Cass, Lewis. 1826. "Indians of North America." *North American Review* 22:53–93.

Cavan, Ruth Shonle. 1926. "Suicide." PhD diss., Univ. of Chicago.

Chang Chin-Fen. 2002. "Bringing the Culture Back In: The Gendered Processes within Institutions and Structures in Taiwanese Labor Markets." *Taiwanese Journal of Sociology* 29:97–125.

Chapman, Charlotte Gower. 1971[1930]. *Milocca: A Sicilian Village*. Cambridge MA: Schenkman.

Chen Chi Lu. 1971. "The Taiwanese Family." *Journal of the China Society* 7:64–69.

Cheng Tun-Jen. 1989. "Democratizing the Quasi-Leninist Regime in Taiwan." *World Politics* 41:471–99.

Ching, Leo T. 2001. *Becoming "Japanese": Colonial Taiwan and the Politics of Identity Formation*. Berkeley: Univ. of California Press.

Cho, Sungnam. 1989. "The Emergence of a Health Insurance System in a Developing Country." *Journal of Health and Social Behavior* 30:467–71.

Chomsky, Noam. 1965. *Aspects of the Theory of Syntax*. The Hague: Mouton.

Chu Jou-Juo. 2000. "Nationalism and Self-Determination: The Identity Politics in Taiwan." *Journal of Asian and African Studies* 35:303–21.

Chuang Ying-Chang. 1987. "Ching Dynasty Chinese Immigration to Taiwan." *Bulletin of the Institute of Ethnology, Academia Sinica* 64:179–203.

———. 1989. "Settlement Patterns of the Hakka Migration to Taiwan." *Bulletin of the Institute of Ethnology, Academia Sinica* 36:85–98.

Chugerman, Samuel. 1939. *Lester F. Ward: The American Aristotle*. Durham NC: Duke Univ. Press.

Chun, Allen. 2000. "Democracy as Hegemony, Globalization as Indigenization, or the 'Culture' in Taiwanese National Politics." *Journal of Asian and African Studies* 35:7–27.

———. 2002. "The Coming Crisis of Multiculturalism in 'Transnational' Taiwan." *Social Analysis* 46:102–22.

Clark, Cal. 1989. *Taiwan's Development: Implications for Contending Political Economy Paradigms*. New York: Greenwood.

Clark, Terry N. 1973. *Prophets and Patrons: The French University and the Emergence of the Social Sciences*. Cambridge MA: Harvard Univ. Press.

Cline, Howard. 1952. "Mexican Community Studies." *Hispanic American Historical Review* 32:212–42.

Coedès, George. 1968[1944]. *The Indianized States of Southeast Asia*. Honolulu: East-West Center Press.

Cohen, Myron L. 1990. "Being Chinese: The Peripheralization of Traditional Identity." *Dædalus* 120(2):113–35.

Cole, Douglas. 1973. "The Origins of Canadian Anthropology." *Journal of Canadian Studies* 8:33–45.

———. 1999. *Franz Boas: The Early Years, 1858–1906*. Seattle: Univ. of Washington Press.

Cole, Fay-Cooper. 1952. "Eminent Personalities of the Half Century." *American Anthropologist* 54:157–67.

Cole, Jonathan, and Harriet Zuckerman. 1975. "The Emergence of a Scientific Specialty." In *The Idea of Social Structure*, ed. L. Coser, 139–74. New York: Harcourt.

Cole, Sally. 2003. *Ruth Landes*. Lincoln: Univ. of Nebraska Press.

———. 2009. *Rainy River Lives: Stories Told by Maggie Wilson*. Lincoln: Univ. of Nebraska Press.

Collins, Randall. 1975. *Conflict Sociology*. San Francisco: Academic Press.

Colson, Elizabeth. 1985. "Defining American Ethnology." In Helm 1985:177–84.

Commager, Henry Steele. 1967. *Lester Frank Ward and the Welfare State*. Indianapolis: Bobbs-Merrill.

Corcuff, Stéphane. 2002. *Memories of the Future: National Identity Issues and the Search for a New Taiwan*. Armonk NY: M. E. Sharpe.

Cornford, F. M. 1908. *Microcosmographia Academica*. London: Bowes and Bowes.

Côté, James E. 1992. "Was Mead Wrong about Coming of Age in Samoa?" *Journal of Youth and Adolescence* 21:499–527.

———. 1994. *Adolescent Storm and Stress*. Hillsdale NJ: Erlbaum.

———. 2000. "Was *Coming of Age in Samoa* Based on a 'Fateful Hoaxing'"? CA 41:617–22.

Coser, Lewis A. 1977. *Masters of Sociological Thought: Ideas in Historical and Social Context.* New York: Harcourt Brace Jovanovich.

Cottrell, Leonard S., Jr. "George Herbert Mead." In *Sociological Traditions from Generation to Generation*, ed. Robert K. Merton and Mathilda W. Riley, 45–65. Norwood NJ: Ablex.

Cressman, Luther S. 1988. *A Golden Journey.* Salt Lake City: Univ. of Utah Press.

Cronin, Constance. 1973. Review of Chapman 1971. CA 14:515.

Dai, Bingham (Bing-Hen). 1932. "Speaking with Tongues or Glossalalia." MA thesis, Univ. of Chicago.

———. 1941. "Personality Problems in Chinese Culture." ASR 6:88–96.

———. 1944. "Divided Loyalty in War." *Psychiatry* 7:327–40.

———. 1952. "A Socio-psychiatric Approach to Personality." ASR 17:44–49.

———. 1970[1937]. *Opium Addiction in China.* Montclair NJ: Patterson Smith.

Daniels, Roger. 1993. *Prisoners without Trial: Japanese Americans in World War II.* New York: Hill and Wang.

Darnell, Regna. 1969. "The Development of American Anthropology, 1880–1920." PhD diss., Univ. of Pennsylvania.

———. 1970. "The Emergence of Academic Anthropology at the University of Pennsylvania." *Journal of the History of the Behavioral Sciences* 6:80–92.

———. 1971. "The Revision of the Powell Classification." *Papers in Linguistics* 4:70–110.

———. 1977. "Hallowell's *Bear Ceremonialism* and the Emergence of Boasian Anthropology." *Ethos* 5:13–30.

———. 1986. "Personality and Culture." *History of Anthropology* 4:156–83.

———. 1990a. *Edward Sapir.* Berkeley: Univ. of California Press.

———. 1990b. "Franz Boas, Edward Sapir, and the Americanist Text Tradition." *Historiographia Linguistica* 17:129–44.

———. 1995. "Continuities in Americanist Anthropology." Presidential address, North American Association for the History of the Linguistic Sciences annual meeting, New Orleans.

———. 1998a. *. . . And Along Came Boas.* Amsterdam: John Benjamins.

———. 1998b. "Camelot at Yale: The Construction and Dismantling of the Sapirian Synthesis, 1931–39." AA 100:361–72.

———. 1999. "Theorizing American Anthropology: Continuities from the B.A.E. to the Boasians." In Valentine and Darnell 1999:38–51.

———. 2001. *Invisible Genealogies.* Lincoln: Univ. of Nebraska Press.

———. 2004. Review of *History of Anthropology* 9. *Ethnohistory* 51:827–29.

Darnell, Regna, and Frederic W. Gleach. 2002. *Celebrating a Century of the American Anthropological Association: Presidential Portraits.* Lincoln: Univ. of Nebraska Press.

Daubenmier, Judith. 2008. *The Meskwaki and Anthropologists*. Lincoln: Univ. of Nebraska Press.

Davis, Allison, Burleigh Gardner, and Mary Gardner. 1941. *Deep South*. Chicago: Univ. of Chicago Press.

De Glopper, Donald R. 1974. "Religion and Ritual in Lukang." In *Religion and Ritual in Chinese Society*, ed. A. Wolf, 43–69. Stanford CA: Stanford Univ. Press.

——. 1977. "Old Medicine in a New Bottle." *Reviews in Anthropology* 4:349–59.

de la Cruz, Alicia. 1996. *The Two Milpas of Chan Kom*. Albany: State Univ. of New York Press.

DeMallie, Raymond. 1994. "Fred Eggan and American Indian Anthropology." In *North American Indian Anthropology*, ed. R. DeMallie and A. Ortiz, 3–22. Norman: Univ. of Oklahoma Press.

de Mille, Richard. 1978. *Castaneda's Journey*. Santa Barbara: Capricorn.

——. 1980. *The Don Juan Papers*. Santa Barbara: Ross-Erikson.

Devereux, Georges. 1935. "Sexual Life of the Mohave Indians." Ph.D. diss., Univ. of California, Berkeley.

——. 1937. "Institutionalized Homosexuality of the Mohave Indians." *Human Biology* 9:498–527.

——. 1953. "Why Oedipus Killed Laius." *International Journal of Psychoanalysis* 34:132–41.

——. 1956. "Normal and Abnormal: The Key Problem of Psychiatric Anthropology." In *Some Uses of Anthropology: Theoretical and Applied*, ed. Joseph B. Casagrande and Thomas Gladwin, 23–48. Washington DC: Anthropological Society of Washington.

——. 1961. *Mohave Ethnopsychiatry and Suicide*. Bureau of American Ethnology Bulletin 175. Washington DC: U.S. Government Printing Office.

——. 1976. *Dreams in Greek Tragedy: An Ethno-Psycho-Analytical Study*. Berkeley: Univ. of California Press.

——. 1978. "The Works of Georges Devereux." In *The Makings of Psychological Anthropology*, ed. G. Spindler, 361–406. Berkeley: Univ. of California Press.

Dexter, Ralph W. 1989. "The Putnam-Kroeber Relation in the Development of American Anthropology." *Journal of California and Great Basin Anthropology* 11:91–96.

Diamond, Norma. 1969. *K'un Shen, a Taiwan Village*. New York: Holt, Rinehart and Winston.

——. 1979. "Women in Industry in Taiwan." *Modern China* 5:317–40.

Dickemann, Mildred. 1997. *Coming to Cal, 1950: An Interview Conducted by William Benemann in 1996*. Berkeley CA: Univ. Archives, Bancroft Library.

Dixon, Roland B. 1915. "Reply." *AA* 17:599–600.

———. 1916. *The Mythology of All Races*, vol. 9: *Polynesia*. New York: Marshall Jones.

———. 1928. *The Building of Culture*. New York: Scribner's.

Dollard, John. 1931. "The Changing Function of the American Family." Ph.D. diss., Univ. of Chicago.

———. 1934. "The Psychotic Person Seen Culturally." *AJS* 39:637–48.

———. 1935. *Criteria for the Life History*. New Haven CT: Yale Univ. Press.

———. 1937. *Caste and Class in a Southern Town*. New Haven CT: Yale Univ. Press.

———. 1938. "The Life History in Community Studies." *ASR* 3:724–37.

Dorsey, George. 1925. *Why We Behave Like Human Beings*. New York: Harper.

Dozier, Edward P. 1970. *The Pueblo Indians of North America*. New York: Holt, Rinehart and Winston.

Drucker, Philip. 1937. "Cultural Elements Distribution 5: Southern California." *Univ. of California Anthropological Records* 1:1–52.

Duncan, Otis Dudley. 1984. *Notes on Social Measurement*. New York: Russell Sage Foundation.

Duncan, Otis Dudley, and Albert J. Reiss Jr. 1956. *Social Characteristics of Urban and Rural Communities, 1950*. New York: John Wiley.

Durkheim, Émile. 1893. *De la division du travail social*. Paris: F. Alcan.

———. 1897. *Le suicide*. Paris: F. Alcan.

———. 1910. *Les formes élémentaires de la vie religeuse*. Paris: F. Alcan.

Ebihara, May. 1985. "American Ethnology in the 1930s." In Helm 1985:101–21.

Eggan, Fred. 1937, 1955. *Social Organization of North American Tribes*. Chicago: Univ. of Chicago Press.

———. 1950[1933]. *Social Organization of the Western Pueblos*. Chicago: Univ. of Chicago Press.

———. 1966. *The American Indian: Perspectives for the Study of Social Change*. Chicago: Aldine.

———. 1974. "Among the Anthropologists." *Annual Review of Anthropology* 3:1–20.

Embree, John F. 1937. *Suye Mura*. Chicago: Univ. of Chicago Press.

———. 1939. "New Local and Kin Groups among the Japanese Farmers of Kona, Hawaii." *AA* 41:400–407.

———. 1941. *Acculturation among the Japanese of Kona, Hawaii*. Memoirs of the American Anthropological Association 59. Menasha WI: American Anthropological Association.

———. 1950a. "A Note on Ethnocentrism in Anthropology." *AA* 52:430–32.

———. 1950b. "Thailand: A Loosely-Structured Social System." *AA* 52:181–93.

Evans-Pritchard, E. E. 1951. *Social Anthropology*. New York: Free Press.

———. 1962. *Social Anthropology*. London: Free Press.

Evers, Hans-Dieter. 1969. *Loosely Structured Social Systems: Thailand in Comparative Perspective*. New Haven CT: Yale Univ. Southeast Asia Studies Center.

Faris, Ellsworth. 1918. "The Mental Capacity of Savages," AJS 23: 609–19.

———. 1922. "Are Instincts Data or Hypotheses?" AJS 27:184–96.

———. 1925. "Pre-literate Peoples." AJS 30:710–12.

———. 1937a. *The Nature of Human Nature*. Chicago: Univ. of Chicago Press.

———. 1937b. Review of W. Thomas 1937. AJS 43:169–70.

———. 1951. Review of *Social Behavior and Personality*, by W. I. Thomas. ASR 16:877.

Faris, Robert E. L. 1934. "Cultural Isolation and the Schizophrenic Personality." AJS 40:155–64.

———. 1938. "Demography of Urban Psychotics with Special Reference to Schizophrenia." ASR 3:203–9.

———. 1944. "Reflections of Social Disorganization in the Behavior of a Schizophrenic Patient." AJS 50:134–41.

———. 1967. *Chicago Sociology, 1920–1932*. San Francisco: Chandler.

Farquhar, Judith. 1987. "Problems of Knowledge in Contemporary Chinese Medical Discourse." *Social Science and Medicine* 24:1013–21.

Fei, John C. H. Gustav Ranis, and Shirley W. Y. Kuo. 1979. *Growth with Equity: The Taiwan Case*. Washington DC: World Bank.

Fei Hsiao-Tung [Xiaotong]. 1939. *Peasant Life in China: A Field Study of Country Life in the Yangtze Valley*. London: Kegan Paul.

Fei Hsiao-Tung and Chang Chih-I [Zang Zhiyi]. 1945. *Earthbound China: A Study of Rural Economy in Yunnan*. Chicago: Univ. of Chicago Press.

Feuchtwang, Stephan. 1992. *The Imperial Metaphor: Popular Religion in China*. London: Routledge.

Fichte, Hubert. 1985. *Lazarus und die Waschmaschine*. Frankfurt: Fischer.

Firth, Raymond. 1954. "Social Organization and Social Change." *Journal of the Royal Anthropological Institute* 84:1–20.

Foerstel, Lenora, and Angela Gilliam. 1992. *Confronting the Margaret Mead Legacy: Scholarship, Empire, and the South Pacific*. Philadelphia: Temple Univ. Press.

Forde, C. Daryll. 1931. "Ethnography of the Yuma Indians." *Univ. of California Publications in American Archeology and Ethnology* 28:83–278.

Foster, George M. 1942. "A Primitive Mexican Economy." PhD diss., Univ. of California Berkeley. (Published, Seattle: American Ethnological Society, 1966.)

———. 1948. *Empire's Children: The People of Tzintzuntzan*. Smithsonian Institution Institute of Social Anthropology Publication 6. Washington DC: Smithsonian Institution.

———. 1952. Review of O. Lewis 1951. *AA* 54:239–40.

———. 1953. "What Is Folk Culture?" *AA* 55:159–73.

———. 1961. "Interpersonal Relations in Peasant Society." *Human Organization* 19:174–78.

———. 1965. "Peasant Society and the Image of Limited Good." *AA* 67:293–315.

———. 1967a. *Tzintzuntzan: Mexican Peasants in a Changing World*. Boston: Little, Brown.

———. 1967b. "What Is a Peasant?" In *Peasant Society: A Reader*, ed. Jack M. Potter, May N. Diaz, and George M. Foster, 2–14. Boston: Little Brown.

———. 1976. "Graduate Study at Berkeley, 1935–1941." *Anthropology UCLA* 8:9–18.

———. 1979. "Fieldwork in Tzintzuntzan: The First Thirty Years." In *Long-Term Field Research in Social Anthropology*, ed. George Foster et al., 165–84. New York: Academic Press.

———. 1982. "Relationships between Anthropological Field Research and Theory." In *Crisis in Anthropology: Views from Spring Hill, 1980*, ed. E. A. Hoebel, R. Currier, and S. Kaiser, 141–53. New York: Garland.

———. 2002. "A Half Century of Field Research in Tzintzuntzan, Mexico: A Personal View." In *Chronicling Cultures: Long-Term Field Research in Anthropology*, ed. Robert Kemper and Anya Royce, 252–83. Walnut Creek, CA: AltaMira Press.

Fowler, Catherine S., and Don D. Fowler. 1986. "Edward Sapir, Tony Tillohash and Southern Paiute Studies." In *New Perspectives in Language, Culture, and Personality: Proc. of the Edward Sapir Centenary Conference*, ed. William Cowan, Michael Foster, and Konrad Koerner, 41–65. Amsterdam: John Benjamins.

Frake, Charles O. 1961. "Diagnosis of Disease among the Subanun of Mindanao." *AA* 63:113–32.

Frantz, Charles. 1985. "Relevance: American Ethnology and Wider Society, 1900–1940." In Helm 1985:83–100.

Freed, A. Stanley, and S. Ruth Freed. 1983. "Clark Wissler and the Development of Anthropology in the United States." *AA* 85:800–825.

Freeman, Derek. 1983. *Margaret Mead and Samoa*. Cambridge MA: Harvard Univ. Press.

———. 1987. Review of *Quest for the Real Samoa*, by L. Holmes. *Journal of the Polynesian Society* 96:392–400.

———. 1991a. "Franz Boas and the Samoan Researches of Margaret Mead." *CA* 32:322–30.

———. 1991b. "'There's trick i' th' world': An Historical Analysis of the Samoan Researches of Margaret Mead." *Visual Anthropology Review* 7:103–28.

——. 1999. *The Fateful Hoaxing of Margaret Mead: A Historical Analysis of Her Samoan Research*. New York: Basic Books.

Freud, Sigmund. 1913. *Totem und Tabu: Einige Übereinstimmungen im Seelenleben der Wilden und der Neurotiker*. Leipzig: Internationaler Psychoanalytischer Verlag.

——. 1916. *Leonardo da Vinci*. New York: Knopf.

Fried, Morton. 1954. "Community Studies: China." *Far Eastern Quarterly* 14:11–36.

Friedman, Edward. 1993. "A Failed Chinese Modernity." *Dædalus* 122(2):1–17.

Fry, Peter. 1976. *Spirits of Protest*. Cambridge: Cambridge Univ. Press.

Furner, Mary O. 1975. *Advocacy and Objectivity*. Lexington: Univ. Press of Kentucky.

Gallin, Bernard. 1963. "Land Reform in Taiwan: Its Effect on Rural Social Organization and Leadership." *Human Organization* 22:109–22.

——. 1964. "Rural Development in Taiwan: The Role of the Government." *Rural Sociology* 29:313–23.

——. 1966. *Hsin Hsing, Taiwan*. Berkeley: Univ. of California Press.

——. 1975. "Comments on Contemporary Sociocultural Studies of Medicine in Chinese Societies." In *Medicine in Chinese Cultures*, ed. Arthur Kleinman et al., 273–80. Washington DC: U.S. Government Printing Office.

——. 1985. "Development and Change in Taiwan and Hong Kong." In *The Future of Hong Kong and Taiwan*, ed. Jack Williams, 47–65. East Lansing MI: Asian Studies Center.

Gallin, Bernard, and Rita S. Gallin. 1974a. "The Integration of Village Migrants in Taipei." In *The Chinese City between Two Worlds*, ed. M. Elvin and G. Skinner, 331–58. Stanford CA: Stanford Univ. Press.

——. 1974b. "The Rural-to-Urban Migration of Anthropologists in Taiwan." In *Anthropologists in Cities*, ed. G. Foster and R. Kemper, 223–48. Boston: Little Brown.

Gallin, Rita S. 1983. "Women at Work in Hsin Hsing." *Taiwan Review* (Spring):12–15.

——. 1984. "The Entry of Chinese Women into the Rural Labor Force: A Case Study from Taiwan." *Signs* 9:383–98.

——. 1989. "Women and Work in Rural Taiwan." *Journal of Health and Social Behavior* 30:374–85.

——. 1992. "Wife Abuse in the Context of Development and Change: A Chinese (Taiwanese) Case," In *Sanctions and Sanctuary: Cultural Perspectives on the Beating of Wives*, ed. D. Counts, J. Brown, and J. Campbell, 219–27. Boulder: Westview Press.

Gamio, Manuel. 1922. *La población del Valle de Teotihuacán: El medio que se ha desarrollado, su evolución ethnica y social*. Mexico City: Dirrecíon de Talleres Gráficos.

———. 1930. *Mexican Immigration to the United States: A Study of Human Migration and Adjustment.* Chicago: Univ. of Chicago Press.

———. 1931. *The Mexican Immigrant: Autobiographic Documents.* Chicago: Univ. of Chicago Press.

Gates, Hill. 1979. "Dependency and the Part-Time Proletariat in Taiwan." *Modern China* 5:381–407.

———. 1981. "Ethnicity and Social Class." In Ahern and Gates 1981:241–81.

———. 1987. *Chinese Working-Class Lives.* Ithaca NY: Cornell Univ. Press.

———. 1997. *China's Motor: A Thousand Years of Petty Capitalism.* Ithaca NY: Cornell Univ. Press.

———. 1999. *Looking for Chengdu: A Woman's Adventures in China.* Ithaca NY: Cornell Univ. Press.

Geertz, Clifford. 1959. "Form and Variation in Balinese Village Structure." *AA* 61:991–1012.

———. 1962. "Studies of Peasant Life: Community and Society." *Biennial Review of Anthropology* 1961:1–41.

———. 1966. *Person, Time, and Conduct in Bali: An Essay in Cultural Analysis.* Cultural Report series, no. 14. New Haven CT: Yale Southeast Asia Program.

———. 1972. "Deep Play: Notes on the Balinese Cockfight." *Daedalus* 101:1–37.

———. 1995. *After the Fact: Two Countries, Four Decades, One Anthropologist.* Cambridge MA: Harvard Univ. Press.

———. 2000. *Available Light: Anthropological Reflections on Philosophical Topics.* Princeton NJ: Princeton Univ. Press.

George, Katherine. 1958. "The Civilized West Looks at Primitive Africa: 1400–1800; Study in Ethnocentrism." *Isis* 49:62–72.

Gershenhorn, Jerry. 2004. *Melville J. Herskovits and the Racial Politics of Knowledge.* Lincoln: Univ. of Nebraska Press.

Gleach, Frederic W. 2009. "Sociology, Progressivism, and the Undergraduate Training of Anthropologists at the Univ. of Wisconsin, 1925–30." *Histories of Anthropology Annual* 5:229–50.

Goddard, Pliny E. 1912. "Analysis of Cold Water Dialect Chipewyan." *Anthropological Papers of the American Museum of National History* 10:69–165.

Godoy, Ricardo. 1978. "The Background and Context of Redfield's *Tepoztlán.*" *Journal of the Steward Anthropological Society* 10:47–79.

Gold, Thomas B. 1986. *State and Society in the Taiwan Miracle.* Armonk NY: M. E. Sharpe.

Goldenweiser, Alexander A. 1915. "The Heuristic Value of Traditional Records." *AA* 17:763–64.

———. 1917. "The Autonomy of the Social." *AA* 19:441–47.

———. 1925. "Diffusionism and the American School of Ethnology." *AJS* 31:19–38.

———. 1933. *History, Psychology and Culture*. New York: Knopf.

Goldfrank, Esther S. 1978. *Notes on an Undirected Life*. Flushing NY: Queens College Press.

Goldkind, Victor. 1965. "Social Stratification in the Peasant Community: Redfield's Chan Kom Reinterpreted." *AA* 67:863–84.

———. 1966. "Class Conflict and Cacique in Chan Kom." *Southwestern Journal of Anthropology* 22:325–45.

Goldschmidt, Walter R. 1942. "Social Structure of a California Rural Community." PhD diss., Univ. of California, Berkeley.

———. 1946. *Small Business and the Community: A Study in the Central Valley of California on Effects of Scale of Farm Operations*. Washington DC: U.S. Government Printing Office.

———. 1947. *As You Sow: Three Studies in the Social Consequences of Agribusiness*. New York: Harcourt, Brace.

———. 1985. "The Cultural Paradigm in the Post-War World." In Helm 1985:164–76.

———. 1986. "Ralph Leon Beals." *AA* 88:947–53.

———. 1997. "Foreword: The End of peasantry." In *Farewell to Peasant China*, ed. G. Guldin, vii–xv. Armonk NY: M. E. Sharpe.

Goldschmidt, Walter R., and Evalyn Kunkel. 1971. "The Structure of the Peasant Family." *AA* 73:1058–76.

Gould, Stephen Jay. 1977. *Ontogeny and Phylogeny*. Cambridge MA: Harvard Univ. Press.

Gouldner, Alvin W. 1965. *Enter Plato: Classical Greece and the Origins of Social Theory*. New York: Basic Books.

Gower, Charlotte Day. 1928. "The Supernatural Patron in Sicilian Life." PhD diss., Univ. of Chicago.

Gregg, Dorothy, and Elgin Williams. 1948. "The Dismal Science of Functionalism." *AA* 50:594–611.

Guindon, Hubert. 1988. *Quebec Society: Tradition, Modernity and Nationhood*. Toronto: Univ. of Toronto Press.

Graebner, Fritz. 1911. *Methode der Ethnologie*. Heidelberg: C. Winter.

Grajdanzev, Andrew J. 1942. *Formosa Today*. New York: Institute of Pacific Research.

Grayson, Benjamin Lee. 1979. *The American Image of China*. New York: Ungar.

Griaule, Marcel. 1965. *Conversations with Ogotemmêli*. London: International African Institute.

Grodzins, Morton. 1945. "Political Aspects of the Japanese Evacuation." PhD thesis, Univ. of California, Berkeley.

———. 1949. *Americans Betrayed: Politics and the Japanese Evacuation*. Chicago: Univ. of Chicago Press.

Guldin, Gregory E. 1994. *The Saga of Anthropology in China: From Malinowski to Moscow to Mao*. Armonk NY: M. E. Sharpe.

Gumperz, John J. 1962. "Types of Linguistic Communities." *Anthropological Linguistics* 4(1):28–40. (Reprinted in Gumperz 1971:97–113.)

———. 1971. *Language in Social Groups*. Stanford CA: Stanford Univ. Press.

Gumperz, John J., and Robert Wilson. 1971. "Convergence and Creolization." In *Language in Social Groups*, by John J. Gumperz, 251–73. Stanford CA: Stanford Univ. Press.

Guttman, Bruno. 1926. *Das Recht der Dschagga*. Munich: Beck.

Hagstrom, Warren. 1965. *The Scientific Community*. New York: Basic Books.

Halbwachs, Maurice. 1930. *Les causes du suicide*. Paris: F. Alcan.

Hall, Edward T. 1992. *An Anthropology of Everyday Life: An Autobiography*. New York: Doubleday.

———. 1994. *West of the Thirties: Discoveries among the Navajo and Hopi*. New York: Doubleday.

Haller, Dietrich. 2001. "Reflections on the Merits and Perils of Insider Anthropology." *Zietschrift für Kulturwissenschaften* 14:113–46.

Hallowell, A. Irving. 1934. "Culture and Mental Disorder." *Journal of Abnormal and Social Psychology* 29:1–9.

———. 1954. "Southwestern Studies of Culture and Personality." AA 56:700–703.

———. 1955. *Culture and Experience*. Philadelphia: Univ. Pennsylvania Press.

———. 1960. "The Beginnings of Anthropology in America." In *Selected Papers from the American Anthropologist, 1888–1920*, ed. Frederica de Laguna, 1–104. Washington DC: American Anthropological Association.

———. 1965. "The History of Anthropology as an Anthropological Problem." *Journal of the History of the Behavioral Sciences* 1:24–38.

———. 2010. *Contributions to Ojibwe Studies: Essays 1934–1972*, ed. Jennifer S. H. Brown and Susan Elaine Gray. Lincoln: Univ. of Nebraska Press.

Handy, E. S. C. 1923. *The Native Culture of the Marquesas*. Honolulu: Bishop Museum.

Hankins, Frank H. 1926. *The Racial Basis of Civilization*. New York: Macmillan.

———. 1927. "The Social Sciences and Biology." In *The Social Sciences and Their Interrelations*, ed. W. Ogburn and A. Goldenweiser, 41–54. Boston: Houghton-Mifflin.

Hansen, Aasel T. 1954. Review of Miner 1953. AJS 59:501–2.

———. 1974. "Robert Redfield, the Yucatán Project, and I." In Murra 1974:167–86.

Harris, Marvin. 1968. *The Rise of Anthropological Theory*. New York: Crowell.

Hart, C. W. M. 1954. "The Sons of Turimpi." AA 56:242–61.

Hartland, Edwin Sidney. 1914. "On the Evidential Value of the Historical Traditions of the Baganda and Bushongo." *Journal of American Folklore* 25:428–56.

———. 1917. *Matrilinial [sic.] Kinship, and the Question of its Priority*. Memoirs
of the American Anthropological Association 4. Lancaster PA: American
Anthropological Association.

Hays, Hoffman Reynolds. 1958. *From Ape to Angel: An Informal History of Social Anthropology*. New York: Knopf.

Hays, T. E. 1997. "Sacred Texts and Introductory Texts: The Case of Margaret
Mead's Samoa." *Pacific Studies* 20(3):81–103.

Heims, Steven. 1977. "Gregory Bateson and the Mathematicians." *Journal of
the History of the Behavioral Sciences* 13:141–59.

Heizer, Robert F., and Alma Almquist. 1971. *The Other Californians*. Berkeley:
Univ. of California Press.

Helm, June. 1985. *Social Contexts of American Ethnology, 1840–1984*. Washington DC: American Ethnological Society.

Herdt, Gilbert H. 1991. "Representations of Homosexuality: An Essay on Cultural Ontology and Historical Comparison." *Journal of the History of Sexuality* 1:481–504.

Herskovits, Melville J. 1940. *The Economic Life of Primitive Peoples*. New York:
Knopf.

———. 1941. *The Myth of the Negro Past*. New York: Harper and Brothers.

———. 1953. *Franz Boas: The Science of Man in the Making*. New York: Charles
Scribner's Sons.

Hewitt de Alcántara, Cynthia. 1984. *Anthropological Perspectives on Rural Mexico*. London: Routledge and Kegan Paul.

Hinkle, Roscoe C. 1980. *Founding Theory of American Sociology, 1881–1915*.
Boston: Routledge and Kegan Paul.

Hinkle, Roscoe C., and Gisela J. Hinkle. 1954. *The Development of Modern Sociology, 1881–1915*. New York: Random House.

Hinsley, Curtis M., Jr. 1981. *Savages and Scientists: The Smithsonian Institution
and the Development of American Anthropology, 1846–1910*. Washington
DC: Smithsonian Institution Press.

Hirabayashi, Lane Ryo, and James Hirabayashi. 1989. "The 'Credible' Wit-
ness: The Central Role of Richard S. Nishimoto in *JERS*." In Ichioka
1989:65–94.

Ho, Samuel P. S. 1978. *The Economic Development of Taiwan, 1860–1970*. New
Haven CT: Yale Univ. Press.

Ho Szu-Yin and Liu I-Chou. 2002. "The Chinese/Taiwanese Identity of the
Taiwan People in the 1990s." *American Asian Review* 20(2):29–74.

Hobart, Mark. 1986. "Thinker, Thespian, Soldier, Slave? Assumptions about
Human Nature in the Study of Balinese Society." In *Context, Meaning and*

Power in Southeast Asia, ed. M. Hobart and R. H. Taylor, 131–56. Ithaca NY: Cornell Southeast Asia Program.

Hodge, Frederick W. 1955. "Frederick William Hodge, Ethnologist." Manuscript interview, Bancroft Library, Univ. of California, Berkeley.

Hodgen, Margaret T. 1933. The Doctrine of Survivals: A History of Scientific Method in the Study of Man. London: Allenson.

———. 1939. The Doctrine of Survivals: A Chapter in the History of Scientific Method in the Study of Man. London: Allenson.

———. 1945. "Glass and Paper: An Historical Study of Acculturation." Southwestern Journal of Anthropology 1:445–65.

———. 1952. Change and History: A Study of Dated Distributions of Technological Innovations in England. New York: Wenner-Gren.

———. 1964. Early Anthropology in the Sixteenth and Seventeenth Centuries. Philadelphia: Univ. of Pennsylvania Press.

———. 1968. "Frederick J. Teggart." International Encyclopedia of Social Science 15:598–99.

———. 1971. "The Department of Social Institutions, 1919–1946." Unpublished manuscript, Bancroft Library, Univ. of California, Berkeley.

———. 1974. Anthropology, History, and Social Change. Tucson: Univ. of Arizona Press.

Hofstader, Richard. 1944. Social Darwinism in American Thought. Philadelphia: Univ. of Pennsylvania Press.

———. 1955. The Progressive Era. New York: Vintage.

Holbrook, Bruce. 1974. "Chinese Psycho-social Medicine: Doctor and Tang-ki, an Inter-Cultural Analysis." Bulletin of the Institute of Ethnology, Academia Sinica 37:85–112.

———. 1977. "Ethnoscience and Chinese Medicine, Genuine and Spurious." Bulletin of the Institute of Ethnology, Academia Sinica 43:129–80.

Holder, Preston. 1966. Preface to Introduction to Handbook of American Indian Languages, by Franz Boas, and Indian Linguistic Families of american North of America, by J. W. Powell. Lincoln: Univ. of Nebraska Press.

Homans, George C. 1961. Social Behavior. New York: Harcourt.

———. 1984. Coming to My Senses. New Brunswick NJ: Transaction Books.

Hong, Keelung. 1994. "Experiences of Being a 'Native' Observing Anthropology." Anthropology Today 10(3):6–9.

Hong, Keelung, and Stephen O. Murray. 1989. "Complicity with Domination." AA 91:1028–80.

———. 2005. Looking through Taiwan: American Anthropologists' Collusion with Ethnic Domination. Lincoln: Univ. of Nebraska Press.

Horsman, Reginald. 1975. "Scientific Racism and the American Indian in the Mid-nineteenth Century." American Quarterly 27:152–68.

Householder, Fred W., Jr. 1951. Review of *Structural Linguistics*, by Zellig Harris. *IJAL* 18:99–105.

Hsieh Jih-Chang and Chuang Ying-Chang, eds. 1985. *The Chinese Family and Its Ritual Behavior*. Daiba, Taiwan: Institute of Ethnology, Academia Sinica.

Hsiung Ping-Chun. 1996. *Living Rooms as Factories: Class, Gender, and the Satellite Factory System in Taiwan*. Philadelphia: Temple Univ. Press.

Hsu, Francis L. K. 1948. *Under the Ancestors' Shadow*. New York: Columbia Univ. Press.

Huff, Toby. 1973. "Theoretical Innovation in Science." *AJS* 79:261–77.

Hughes, Everett C. 1974. "American Ethnology: The Role of Redfield." In Murra 1974:139–44.

Hughes, Helen M. 1959. "William F. Ogburn." *SF* 8:1–2.

Hymes, Dell H. 1972. *Reinventing Anthropology*. New York: Random House.

———. 1974. *Studies in the History of Linguistics: Traditions and Paradigms*. Bloomington: Indiana Univ. Press.

———. 1981. *In Vain I Tried to Tell You: Essays in Native American Ethnopoetics*. Philadelphia: Univ. of Pennsylvania Press.

———. 1983. *Essays in the History of Linguistic Anthropology*. Amsterdam: John Benjamins.

Ichioka. Yuji. 1989. *Views from Within: The Japanese American Evacuation and Resettlement Study*. Los Angeles: Asian American Studies Center.

Jacknis, Ira. 1993a. "Alfred Kroeber as a Museum Anthropologist." *Museum Anthropology* 17(2):27–33.

———. 1993b. "Museum Anthropology in California, 1899–1939. *Museum Anthropology* 17(2):3–6.

———. 2000. "A Museum Prehistory: Phoebe Hearst and the Founding of the Museum of Anthropology, 1891–1901." *Chronicle of the University of California* 4:47–77.

———. 2002. "The First Boasian: Alfred Kroeber and Franz Boas, 1896–1905." *American Anthropologist* 104:520–32.

Jackson, Jean. 1989. "Is There a Way to Talk about Making Culture without Making Enemies?" *Dialectical Anthropology* 14:127–43.

Jackson, Walter. 1986. "Melville Herskovits and the Search for Afro-American Culture." *History of Anthropology* 4:72–94.

Janowitz, Morris. 1966. *W. I. Thomas on Social Organization and Social Personality*. Chicago: Univ. of Chicago Press.

Joseph, Alice, Rosamond B. Spicer, and Jane Chesky. 1949. *The Desert People: A Study of the Papago Indians*. Chicago: Univ. of Chicago Press.

Keesing, Felix M. 1939. *The Menomini Indians of Wisconsin: A Study of Three Centuries of Cultural Contact and Change*. Memoir 10. Philadelphia: American Philosophical Society.

Kelly, Lawrence C. 1985. "Why Applied Anthropology Developed When It Did." In Helm 1985:122–38.

Kemper, Robert V. 1977[1971]. *Migration and Adaptation: Tzintzuntzan Peasants in Mexico City*. Beverly Hills CA: Sage.

———. 1979. "Fieldwork among Tzintzuntzan Migrants in Mexico City: Retrospect and Prospect." In *Long-Term Field Research in Social Anthropology*, ed. George Foster et al., 189–207. New York: Academic Press.

———. 2002. "From Student to Steward: Tzintzuntzan as Extended Community." In *Chronicling Cultures: Long-Term Field Research in Anthropology*, ed. Robert V. Kemper and Anya Peterson Royce, 284–312. Walnut Creek CA: AltaMira Press.

Kerr, Clark. 2001. *The Gold and the Blue: A Personal History of the University of California, 1949–1967*. Berkeley: Univ. of California Press.

Kilborne, Benjamin. 1987. "In Memoriam: George Devereux." *Psychoanalytic Study of Society* 11:1–14.

Kim Sunhyuk. 2000a. "Democratization and Environmentalism: South Korea and Taiwan in Comparative Perspective." *Journal of Asian and African Studies* 35:287–302.

———. 2000b. *The Politics of Democratization in Korea: The Role of Civil Society*. Pittsburgh: Univ. of Pittsburgh Press.

King, Russell, and Guy Patterson. 1991. "Charlotte Gower Chapman." In *International Dictionary of Anthropologists*, ed. Christopher Winter, 105–6. New York: Garland Publishing.

Kirsch, A. T. 1977. "Complexity in the Thai Religious System." *Journal of Asian Studies* 36:241–66.

Kitsuse, John I., and Aaron V. Cicourel. 1963. "A Note on the Use of Official Statistics." *Social Problems* 11:131–38.

Kleinman, Arthur. 1975. "Medical and Psychiatric Anthropology and the Study of Traditional Forms of Medicine in Modern Chinese Culture." *Bulletin of the Institute of Ethnology, Academia Sinica* 39:107–23.

———. 1980. *Patients and Healers in the Context of Culture*. Berkeley: Univ. of California Press.

———. 1986. *Social Origins of Distress and Disease: Depression, Neurasthenia, and Pain in Modern China*. New Haven CT: Yale Univ. Press.

———. 1988. *The Illness Narratives: Suffering, Healing, and the Human Condition*. New York: Basic Books.

———. 1991. "Suffering and Its Professional Transformation." *Culture, Medicine and Psychiatry* 15:275–301.

Kleinman, Arthur, and James L. Gale. 1982. "Patients Treated by Physicians and Folk Healers in Taiwan." *Culture, Medicine, and Psychiatry* 6:405–23.

Kluckhohn, Clyde. 1943. Review of *Sun Chief*, by Leo Simmons. *AA* 45:267–70.

———. 1945. "The Personal Document in Anthropological Science." *Social Science Research Council Bulletin* 53:79–173.

Kluckhohn, Clyde, and Henry A. Murray. 1948. *Personality*. New York: Knopf.

Kluckhohn, Clyde, and Olaf Prufer. 1959. "Influences during the Formative Years." *American Anthropological Association Memoir* 89:4–28.

Koerner, E. F. K. 1973. *Ferdinand de Saussure*. Braunshweig: Vieweg.

Koffka, K. 1928. *The Unconscious: A Symposium*. New York: Knopf.

Krauss, Michael. 1978. "Athabaskan Tone." Unpublished manuscript.

———. 1980. "On the History and Use of Comparative Athabaskan Linguistics." Unpublished manuscript.

Kroeber, Alfred L. 1905. *The Department of Anthropology at the University of California*. Berkeley CA: Univ. Press.

———. 1909. "Classificatory Systems of Relationship." *Journal of the Royal Anthropological Institute* 39:77–84.

———. 1915a. "Eighteen Professions." *AA* 17:283–88.

———. 1915b. "Frederic Ward Putnam [obituary]." *AA* 17:138–44.

———. 1917. "The Superorganic." *AA* 19:441–47.

———. 1918. "The Possibility of a Social Psychology." *AJS* 23:633–50.

———. 1920. "Totem and Taboo: An Ethnologic Psychoanalysis." *AA* 22:8–55.

———. 1923a. "Roland Burrage Dixon [obituary]." *AA*, 25:294–97.

———. 1923b, 1933, 1948. *Anthropology*. New York: Harcourt, Brace.

———. 1925. *Handbook of the Indians of California*. Bureau of American Ethnology Bulletin 8. Washington DC: U.S. Government Printing Office.

———. 1929. "Pliny Earle Goddard [obituary.]" *AA* 31:1–8.

———. 1931a. Review of *Growing up in New Guinea*, by Margaret Mead. *AA* 33:248–50.

———. 1931b. Review of Redfield 1930. *AA* 33:236–38.

———. 1936. "Kinship and History." *AA* 38:338–41.

———. 1939. "An Outline of American Indian Linguistics." *ACLS Bulletin* 29:116–20.

———. 1943. "Franz Boas [obituary]." *AA* 45:5–26.

———. 1944. *Configurations of Culture Growth*. Berkeley: Univ. of California Press.

———. 1948. *Anthropology*. 2nd ed. New York: Harcourt, Brace.

———. 1955. "Linguistic Time Depth Results So Far and Their Meaning. *IJAL* 21:95–104.

———. 1956. "The Place of Boas in Anthropology." *AA* 58:151–59.

———. 1960. "Powell and Henshaw: An Episode in the History of Ethnolinguistics." *Anthropological Linguistics* 2(3):1–5.

———. 1961. Semantic Contributions of Lexicostatistics. *IJAL* 27:1–8.

———. 1967. "Goddard's California Athabaskan Texts. *IJAL* 33:269–75.

Kroeber, Alfred L., and Thomas T. Waterman. 1931. *Source Book in Anthropology*. New York: Harcourt, Brace.

Kroeber, Clifton. 1973. Introduction. In *A Mohave War Reminiscence, 1854–1880*, by A. L. and C. B. Kroeber, 1–6. *Univ. of California Publications in Anthropology* 10.

Krueger, Ernst T. 1925. "Autobiographical Documents and Personality." PhD diss., Univ. of Chicago.

Kuhn, Thomas S. 1962. *The Structure of Scientific Revolutions*. Chicago: Univ. of Chicago Press. (Rev. ed. 1970.)

———. 1977[1959]. *The Essential Tension*. Chicago: Univ. of Chicago Press.

Kuklick, Henrika. 1973. "A 'Scientific Revolution': Sociological Theory in the United States, 1930–1945." *Sociological Inquiry* 32:3–22.

———. 1980. "Boundary Maintenance in American Sociology." *Journal of the History of the Behavioral Sciences* 16:201–19.

Kung, Lydia. 1984. *Factory Women in Taiwan*. Ann Arbor MI: UMI Research Press. (2nd ed., Columbia Univ. Press, 1994.)

Kuo, Shirley W. Y., Gustav Ranis, and John C. Fei. 1981. *The Taiwan Success Story*. Boulder CO: Westview.

Kuper, Adam. 1983. *Anthropology and Anthropologists: The Modern British School*. London: Routledge and Kegan Paul.

Kurtz, Lester. 1984. *Evaluating Chicago Sociology*. Chicago: Univ. of Chicago Press.

LaBarre, Weston. 1958. "The Influence of Freud on Anthropology." *American Imago* 15:275–328.

Labov, William. 1972. *Sociolinguistic Patterns*. Philadelphia: Univ. of Pennsylvania Press.

Lamb, F. Bruce. 1971. *Wizard of the Upper Amazon*. Boston: Houghton Mifflin.

Langham, Ian. 1981. *The Building of British Social Anthropology*. Dordrecht, Netherlands: Reidel.

Latour, Bruno. 1987. *Science in Action*. Cambridge MA: Harvard Univ. Press.

LaViolette, Forrest. 1945. *Americans of Japanese Descent*. Toronto: Canadian Institute of International Affairs.

———. 1949. Review of Grodzins 1949. *Pacific Affairs* 22:442.

Leach, Edmund. 1954. *Political Systems of Highland Burma*. Cambridge MA: Harvard Univ. Press.

———. 1961. *Rethinking Anthropology*. London: Athlone Press.

Leaf, Murray J. 1979. *Man, Mind and Science: A History of Anthropology*. New York: Columbia Univ. Press.

Lee, Anru. 2000. "Stand by the Family: Gender and Taiwan's Small-Scale Industry in the Global Context." *Anthropology of Work Review* 21(3):5–9.

Lee, Everett S. 1977. "Dorothy Swaine Thomas, 1900–1977." *ASA Footnotes* (August):12.

Leeds-Hurwitz, Wendy. 1985. "The Committee on Research in Native American Languages." *Papers of the American Philosophical Society* 129:129–60.

Leeds-Hurwitz, Wendy, and James M. Nyce. 1986. "Linguistic Text Collection and the Development of Life History in the Work of Edward Sapir." In *New Perspectives on Language, Culture and Personality: Proceedings of the Sapir Centenary Conference*, ed. W. Cowan, M. Fox, and K. Koerner, 495–531. Amsterdam: John Benjamin.

Leighton, Alexander. 1945. *The Governing of Men*. Princeton NJ: Princeton Univ. Press.

Lengermann, Patricia M. 1979. "The Founding of the *American Sociological Review*." *ASR* 44:185–98.

Lepowsky, Maria. 2000. "Charlotte Gower and the Subterranean History of Anthropology." *History of Anthropology* 9:123–70.

Leslie, Charles. 1974. "The Hedgehog and the Fox in Robert Redfield's Work." In Murra 1974:146–66.

Lévi-Strauss, Claude. 1963. *Structural Anthropology*. New York: Basic Books.

Lewis, I. M. 1971. *Ecstatic Religion: An Anthropological Study of Spirit Possession and Shamanism*. Baltimore: Penguin.

Lewis, J. David, and Richard L. Smith. 1980. *American Sociology and Pragmatism: Mead, Chicago Sociology and Symbolic Interaction*. Chicago: Univ. of Chicago Press.

Lewis, Oscar. 1944. "Social and Economic Changes in a Mexican Village: Tepoztlán 1926–44." *América Indígena* 4:281–314.

———. 1946. "Bumper Crops in the Desert." *Harper's Magazine* 1159 (December):525–28. (Reprinted in O. Lewis 1970:232–42.)

———. 1947. "Wealth Differences in a Mexican Village." *Scientific Monthly* 65:127–32. (Reprinted in O. Lewis 1970:269–76.)

———. 1948a. *On the Edge of the Black Waxy: A Cultural Survey of Bell County, Texas*. Washington Univ. Studies 7. St. Louis: Washington University.

———. 1948b. "Rural Cross Section." *Scientific Monthly* 66:327–34. (Reprinted in O. Lewis 1970:243–48.)

———. 1951. *Life in a Mexican Village: Tepoztlán Re-studied*. Urbana: Univ. of Illinois Press.

———. 1952. "Urbanization without Breakdown: A Case Study." *Scientific Monthly* 75:31–41. (Reprinted in O. Lewis 1970:413–26.)

———. 1953. "Tepoztlán Restudied: A Critique of the Folk-Urban Conceptualization of Social Change." *Rural Sociology* 18:121–36. (Reprinted in O. Lewis 1970:35–52.)

———. 1960. "Some of My Best Friends Are Peasants." *Human Organization* 19:179–80.

———. 1970. *Anthropological Essays*. New York: Random House.

Li Fang-Kuei. 1930a. "A Study of Sarcee Verb Stems." *IJAL* 6:3–27.

———. 1930b. *Mattole, an Athabaskan Language*. Univ. of Chicago Publications in Anthropology. Chicago: Univ. of Chicago Press.

———. 1933a. "Chipewyan Consonants." *Bulletin of the Institute of History and Philology of the Academica Sinica* 1:429–67.

———. 1933b. "A List of Chipewyan Stems." *IJAL*: 7:122–51.

———. 1946. "Chipewyan." In *Linguistic Structures of Native America*, ed. Harry Hoijer et al., 398–423. New York: Wenner-Gren Foundation.

Li Hung Chang. 1913. *Memoirs*. Boston: Houghton-Mifflin.

Li Mei-Chih. 2003. "Bases of Ethnic Identification in Taiwan." *Asian Journal of Social Psychology* 6:229–37.

Lindesmith, Alfred, and Anselm Strauss. 1950. "A Critique of Culture and Personality Writings." *ASR* 15:587–600.

Linton, Adelin, and Charles Wagley. 1971. *Ralph Linton*. New York: Columbia Univ. Press.

Linton, Ralph. 1936. *The Study of Man*. New York: D. Appleton-Century.

———. 1940. *Acculturation in Seven American Indian Tribes*. New York: D. Appleton-Century.

Lin Yueh Hwa [Yaohua]. 1948. *The Golden Wing: A Sociological Study of Chinese Familism*. London: Kegan Paul.

Lo Ming-Cheng. 1994. "Crafting the Collective Identity: The Origin and Transformation of Taiwanese Nationalism." *Journal of Historical Sociology* 7:198–223.

Lowie, Robert H. 1913. "On the Principle of Convergence in Ethnology." *Journal of American Folk-Lore* 25:24–32.

———. 1915. "Oral Tradition and History." *AA* 17:597–99.

———. 1918. "Survivals and the Historical Method." *AJS* 21:529–33.

———. 1919. Review of Sapir 1916. *AA* 19:75–77.

———. 1923. Review of *The Adaman Islanders*, by A. R. Brown. *AA* 25:572–75.

———. 1929. Review of M. Mead 1928. *AA* 31:532–34.

———. 1930. *History of Ethnological Theory*. New York: Rinehart.

———. 1937. *The History of Ethnological Theory*. New York: Holt.

———. 1940. "Native Languages as Ethnographic Tools." *AA* 42:81–89.

———. 1945. "The Psychiatry-Anthropology Relation." *American Journal of Psychiatry* 102:414–16.

———. 1948. *Social Organization*. New York: Holt and Rinehart.

———. 1954. *Toward Understanding Germany*. Chicago: Univ. of Chicago Press.

———. 1955. "Contemporary Trends in American Cultural Anthropology." *Sociologus* 5:113-21. (Reprinted in *Lowie's Selected Papers in Ethnology*, ed. Cora DuBois, 461-71 [Berkeley: Univ. of California Press, 1960].)

———. 1959. *Robert Lowie, Ethnologist*. Berkeley: Univ. of California Press.

———. 1960[1917]. "Oral Tradition and History." In *Lowie's Selected Papers in Ethnology*, ed. Cora DuBois, 202-10 (Berkeley: Univ. of California Press, 1960). (Originally published in *Journal of American Folk-Lore* 30:161-67.)

Lucas, George R., Jr. 2009. *Anthropologists in Arms*. Lanham MD: AltaMira Press.

Lu Hsin-Yi. 2002. *The Politics of Locality: Making a Nation of Communities in Taiwan*. New York: Routledge.

Luo Zhufeng. 1991. *Religion under Socialism in China*. Armonk NY: M. E. Sharpe.

Lu Yu-Hsia. 2001. "The 'Boss's Wife' and Taiwanese Small Family Business." In *Women's Working Lives in East Asia*, ed. Mary Brinton, 263-97. Stanford CA: Stanford Univ. Press.

Lyman, Stanford M. 1972. *The Black American in Sociological Thought*. New York: Putnam.

———. 1978. *Structure, Consciousness, and History*. New York: Cambridge Univ. Press.

Lynd, Robert S. 1931. Review of Redfield 1930. *AJS* 36:823-24.

Lynd, Robert S., and Helen M. Lynd. 1929. *Middletown: A Study in Contemporary American Culture*. New York: Harcourt, Brace.

Lyons, Andrew P., and Harriet D. Lyons. 2004. *Irregular Connections: A History of Anthropology and Sexuality*. Lincoln: Univ. of Nebraska Press.

Madge, John. 1962. *The Origins of Scientific Sociology*. New York: Free Press.

Malinowski, Bronislaw. 1922. *Argonauts of the Western Pacific*. New York: E.P. Dutton.

———. 1924. "Psycho-analysis and Anthropology." *Psyche* 4:293-326.

———. 1929. *The Sexual Life of Savages in North-Western Melanesia*. London: G. Routledge and Sons.

———. 1954. *Magic, Science, and Religion*. Toronto: Doubleday.

Mandelbaum, David. 1949. *Selected Writings of Edward Sapir in Language, Culture, Personality*. Berkeley: Univ. of California Press.

———. 1953. "On the Study of National Character." *AA* 55:174-87.

———. 1973. "The Study of Life History." *CA* 14:177-206.

Mannheim, Karl. 1945. "American Sociology." In *Twentieth Century Sociology*, ed. George Gruvitch and W. E. Moore, 503-37. New York: Philosophical Library.

Mariott, McKim. 1955. *Village India: Studies of the Little Community*. Chicago: Univ. of Chicago Press.

Martindale, Don. 1976. *The Romance of a Profession: A Case History in the Sociology of Sociology*. St. Paul MN: Windflower.

Massey, Douglas, Rafael Alarcón, Jorge Durand, and Humberto González. 1987. *Return to Aztlan: The Social Process of International Migration from Western Mexico*. Berkeley: Univ. of California Press.

Mauss, Marcel. 1904. *L'origine des pouvoirs magiques dans les societes australiennes*. Rapport 190. Paris: École Pratique des Hautes Études, Section des Sciences Religieuses.

———. 1979[1938]. "A Category of the Human Mind: The Notion of Person, the Notion of 'Self.'" In *Sociology and Psychology*, 57-94. Boston: Routledge and Kegan Paul.

McDowell, Nancy. 1984. Review of Freeman 1983. *Pacific Studies* 7:99-140.

McKee, James B. 1993. *Sociology and the Race Problem: The Failure of a Perspective*. Champaign IL: Univ. of Illinois Press.

Mead, George Herbert. 1913. "The Social Self." *Journal of Philosophy* 10:374-80.

———. 1924. "The Genesis of the Self and Social Control." *International Journal of Ethics* 35:251-77.

Mead, Margaret. 1928. *Coming of Age in Samoa*. New York: Morrow.

———. 1930. *Social Organization of Manu'a*. Honolulu: Bishop Museum.

———. 1935. *Sex and Temperament*. New York: Morrow.

———. 1939. "Native Languages as Fieldwork Tools." *AA* 41:189-205.

———. 1942. *And Keep Your Powder Dry*. New York: Morrow.

———. 1949. *Male and Female*. New York: Morrow.

———. 1959a. *An Anthropologist at Work*. Boston: Houghton-Mifflin.

———. 1959b. "Apprenticeship under Boas." *American Anthropological Association Memoir* 61:29-45.

———. 1965[1932]. *The Changing Culture of an Indian Tribe*. New York: Capricorn Books.

———. 1972. *Blackberry Winter: My Earlier Years*. New York: Simon and Schuster.

Mendel, Douglas. 1970. *The Politics of Formosan Nationalism*. Berkeley: Univ. of California Press.

Merton, Robert K. 1941. "Karl Mannheim and the Sociology of Knowledge." *Journal of Liberal Religion* 2:125-47.

———. 1945. "Sociology of Knowledge." In *Twentieth Century Sociology*, ed. G. Gurvitch and W. Moore, 366-405. New York: Philosophical Library.

———. 1957. "Priorities in Scientific Discovery." *ASR* 22:635-59.

———. 1961. "Singletons and Multiples in Scientific Discovery." *Proceedings of the American Philosophical Society* 105:470-86.

———. 1963. "Resistance to the Systematic Study of Multiple Discoveries in Science." *European Journal of Sociology* 4:237-82.

———. 1968. *Social Theory and Social Structure*. 3rd ed. New York: Free Press.

Michelson, Truman. 1938. "Sol Tax on the Social Organization of the Fox Indians." *AA* 40:177–79.

Migliore, Sam, Margaret Dorazio-Migliore, and Vincenzo Ingrascì. 2009. "Living Memory: Milocca's Charlotte Gower Chapman." *Histories of Anthropology Annual* 5:110–51.

Miller, R. Berkeley. 1975. "Anthropology and Institutionalization." *Kroeber Anthropological Society Papers* 51:49–60.

Mills, C. Wright. 1959. *The Sociological Imagination*. New York: Oxford Univ. Press.

Miner, Horace M. 1939[1963]. *Saint Denis: A French-Canadian Parish*. Chicago: Univ. of Chicago Press.

———. 1949. *Culture and Agriculture: An Anthropological Study of a Corn Belt County*. Ann Arbor: Univ. of Michigan Press.

———. 1950. "A New Epoch in Rural Quebec." *AJS* 56:1–10. (Incorporated as a postscript to the 1963 reprinting of *Saint Denis*.)

———. 1952. "The Folk-Urban Continuum." *ASR* 17:529–36.

———. 1953. *The Primitive City of Timbuctoo*. Memoirs of the American Philosophical Society, 32. Princeton NJ: Princeton Univ. Press.

———. 1968. "Community-Society Continua." *International Encyclopedia of Social Science* 1:174–80.

Miner, Horace M., and George De Vos. 1960. *Oasis and Casbah: Algerian Culture and Personality in Change*. Ann Arbor: Univ. of Michigan Museum of Anthropology.

Mintz, Sydney. 1953. "The Folk-Urban Continuum and the Rural Proletarian Community." *AJS* 59:136–43.

———. 1981. Afterword. In Ahern and Gates 1981:427–42.

Miyamoto, Shotaro Frank. 1939. *Social Solidarity among the Japanese in Seattle*. Seattle: Univ. of Washington Press.

———. 1989a. "Dorothy Swaine Thomas as Director of JERS." In Ichioka 1989:31–63.

———. 1989b. "Resentment, Distrust and Insecurity at Tule Lake." In Ichioka 1989:127–40.

———. 1996. "Intergroup Conflict and Intragroup Factionalism." In *Individuality and Social Control*, ed. Kian Kwan, 271–93. Greenwich CT: JAI Press.

Morawski, Jill G. 1986. "Organizing Knowledge and Behavior at Yale's Institute of Human Relations." *Isis* 77:219–42.

Morgan, Lewis Henry. 1877. *Ancient Society*. New York: Henry Holt.

Morice, A. G. 1907. "The Units of Speech among the Northern and Southern Dené." *AA* 9:721–37.

Moskowitz, Marc L. 2001. *The Haunting Fetus: Abortion, Sexuality, and the Spirit World in Taiwan*. Honolulu: Univ. of Hawai'i Press.

Mueller, Eva. 1977. "The Impact of Demographic Factors on Economic Development in Taiwan." *Population and Development Review* 3:1–23.

Mulkay, Michael. 1969. "Some Aspects of Cultural Growth in the Natural Sciences." *Social Research* 36:22–52.

Mullins, Nicholas C. 1972. *Theories and Theory Groups in American Sociology*. New York: Harper and Row.

———. 1975. "A Sociological Theory of Scientific Revolutions." In *Determinants and Controls of Scientific Development*, ed. K. Knorr et al., 185–203. Dordrecht, Netherlands: Reidel.

Murdock, George P. 1940. Review of Miner 1939. *AA* 42:323–24.

———. 1943. Review of Redfield 1940. *AA* 45:133–36.

———. 1949. *Social Structure*. Glencoe IL: Free Press.

———. 1951. "British Social Anthropology." *AA* 53:465–73.

———. 1959. *Africa*. New York: McGraw-Hill.

———. 1971. "Anthropology's Mythology." *Proceedings of the Royal Anthropological Institute* 7:17–26.

Murphy, H. B. M. 1982. Review of *Normal and Abnormal Behavior in Chinese Culture*, by A. Kleinman and T. Y Lin. *Transcultural Psychiatric Research* 14:37–40.

Murphy, Robert F. 1967. "Tuareg Kinship." *AA* 69:159–70.

———. 1972. *Robert H. Lowie*. New York: Columbia Univ. Press.

———. 1976. Introduction. In *Selected Papers from the "American Anthropologist," 1946–1970*, 1–22. Washington DC: American Anthropological Association.

———. 1981. "Julian Steward." In *Totems and Teachers: Perspectives on the History of Anthropology*, ed. Sydel Silverman, 171–208. New York: Columbia Univ. Press.

———. 1990[1987]. *The Body Silent*. New York: Holt.

Murra, John V. 1974. *American Anthropology: The Early Years*. Proceedings of the American Ethnological Society 1974. St. Paul: West.

Murray, Stephen O. 1980a. "Gatekeepers and the 'Chomskian Revolution.'" *Journal of the History of the Behavioral Sciences* 16:73–88.

———. 1980b. "The Invisibility of Scientific Scorn." In *The Don Juan Papers*, ed. R. de Mille, 188–202. Santa Barbara CA: Ross-Erikson.

———. 1980c. "Resistance to Sociology at Berkeley." *Journal of the History of Sociology* 2:61–84.

———. 1980d. "The Scientific Reception of Castaneda." *Contemporary Sociology* 8:189–92.

——. 1981a. "Die ethnoromantische Versuchung." In *Der Wissenschaftler und das Irrationale*, ed. Hans-Peter Duerr, 1:377–85. Frankfurt: Syndikat.

——. 1981b. "Sapir's Gestalt." *Anthropological Linguistics* 23:8–12.

——. 1982. "The Dissolution of Classical Ethnoscience." *Journal of the History of the Behavioral Sciences* 18:163–75.

——. 1983a. "The Creation of Linguistic Structure." AA 85:356–62.

——. 1983b. "Historical Inferences from Ethnohistorical Data." *Journal of the History of the Behavioral Sciences* 19:335–40.

——. 1984. "Fauler Zauber in der Südsee." *Psychologie Heute* 3(11):68–72.

——. 1986a. "Edward Sapir in the 'Chicago School of Sociology.'" In *New Perspectives on Language, Culture and Personality: Proceedings of the Sapir Centenary Conference*, ed. W. Cowan, M. Fox, and K. Koerner et al., 241–91. Amsterdam: John Benjamin.

——. 1986b. "The Postmaturity of Sociolinguistics." *History of Sociology* 6(2):75–108.

——. 1987. "Ein homoerotisches Phantásien-Ethnographisch mißdeutet. In *Authentizität und Betrug in der Ethnologie*, ed. H-P. Duerr, 58–62. Frankfurt/m: Suhrkamp. (English version in *Ethnographic Studies of Homosexuality*, ed. by Wayne Dynes and Stephen Donaldson, 353–56. New York: Garland, 1992.)

——. 1988a. "The Reception of Anthropological Work in American Sociology Journals, 1921–1951." *Journal of the History of the Behavioral Sciences* 24:121–38.

——. 1988b. "W. I. Thomas, Behaviorist Ethnologist." *Journal of the History of the Behavioral Sciences* 24: 381–91.

——. 1989. "The Poverty of 'Popperian' History of Anthropology." CA 31:401–7.

——. 1991. "Boasians and Margaret Mead." CA 32:448–52.

——. 1994a. "Subordinating Native Cosmologies to the Empire of Gender." CA 35:59–61.

——. 1994b. *Theory Groups in the Study of Language in North America: A Social History*. Amsterdam: John Benjamin.

——. 1998. *American Sociolinguistics*. Amsterdam: John Benjamins.

——. 1999. "The Non-eclipse of Americanist Anthropology during the 1930s and 40s." In Valentine and Darnell 1999:52–74.

——. 2002. "Francis L. K. Hsu." In *Celebrating a Century of the American Anthropological Association: Presidential Portraits*, ed. Regna Darnell and Frederic W. Gleach, 245–48. Lincoln: Univ. of Nebraska Press.

——. 2009. "The Pre-Freudian Georges Devereux, the Post-Freudian Alfred Kroeber, and Mohave Sexuality." *Histories of Anthropology Annual* 5:12–27.

Murray, Stephen O., and Regna Darnell. 2000. "Margaret Mead and Paradigm Shifts within Anthropology during the 1920s." *Journal of Youth and Adolescence* 29:557-73.

Murray, Stephen O., and Keelung Hong. 1988. "Taiwan, China, and the 'Objectivity' of Dictatorial Elites." *AA* 90:976-78.

———. 1991. "American Anthropologists Looking through Taiwanese Culture." *Dialectical Anthropology* 16:273-99.

———. 1994. *Taiwanese Culture, Taiwanese Society*. Lanham MD: Univ. Press of America.

Myrdal, Gunnar. 1944. *An American Dilemma*. New York: Harper and Brothers.

Nash, Dennison, and Ronald Wintrob. 1972. "The Emergence of Self-Consciousness in Ethnography." *CA* 13:527-42.

Nash, Philleo. 1979. "Anthropologist in the White House." *Practicing Anthropology* 1(3):3, 23-24.

Needham, Rodney. 1985. *Exemplars*. Berkeley: Univ. of California Press.

Newman, Stanley S. 1955. "Vocabulary Levels." *Southwestern Journal of Anthropology* 11:345-54.

Nisbet, Robert A. 1943. "The French Revolution and the Rise of Sociology in France." *American Journal of Sociology* 49:156-64.

———. 1953. *The Quest for Community*. New York: Oxford Univ. Press.

———. 1966. *The Sociological Tradition*. New York: Basic Books.

———. 1969. *Social Change and History*. New York: Oxford Univ. Press.

———. 1976. "An Eruption of Genius: Frederick J. Teggart at Berkeley." *California Monthly* 66(6):3-7.

———. 1979. "Teggart and Berkeley." *American Scholar* 48:71-82.

———. 1980. *History of the Idea of Progress*. New York: Basic Books.

Oakes, Katherine B. 1944. "Social Theory in the Early Literature of Voyage and Exploration in Africa." PhD diss., Univ. of California, Berkeley.

Oberschall, Anthony. 1965. *Empirical Sociology in Germany*. The Hague: Mouton.

———. 1972. *The Establishment of Empirical Sociology*. New York: Harper and Row.

Odum, Howard. 1951. *American Sociology*. New York: Longman and Green.

Oertel, Hanns. 1904. "Some Present Problems and Tendencies in Comparative Philology." *Congress of Arts and Science, Universal Exposition, St. Louis* 3:53-58.

Ogburn, William F. 1922. "Bias, Psychoanalysis and the Subjective in Relation to the Social Sciences." *Publications of the American Sociological Society* 17:62-74.

———. 1927. "The Contribution of Psychiatry to Social Psychology." *Publications of the American Sociological Society* 11:82-91.

———. 1928. *Family Life Today*. Boston: Houghton Mifflin.

———. 1955. *Technology and the Changing Family*. Boston: Houghton Mifflin.

———. 1959. "Influences Affecting the Future of Sociology." *SF* 51:3-7.

Ogburn, William F., and Dorothy S. Thomas. 1922a. "Are Inventions Inevitable?" *Political Science Quarterly* 37:83-98.

———. 1922b. "The Influence of Business Cycles on Certain Social Conditions." *Quarterly Publications of the American Statistical Association* 18:324-40.

Ogburn, William F., and Ellen Winston. 1929. "The Frequency and Probability of Insanity." *AJS* 34:822-31.

Ogden, Laura A. 2011. *Swamplife*. Minneapolis: Univ. of Minnesota Press.

Okubo, Miné, 1983. *Citizen 13660*. Seattle: Univ. of Washington Press.

Orans, Martin. 1996. *Not Even Wrong: Margaret Mead, Derek Freeman, and the Samoans*. Novato CA: Chandler and Sharp.

Paddock, John. 1961. "Oscar Lewis's Mexico." *Anthropological Quarterly* 34:129-49.

Palmer, Vivien M. 1928. *Field Studies in Sociology: A Student's Manual*. Chicago: Univ. of Chicago Press.

Park, Robert E. 1920[1952]. "The Foreign Language Press." In *The Collected Papers of Robert Park*, ed. E. Hughes, 3:165-75. Glencoe IL: Free Press.

———. 1924. "Experience and Race Relations." *Journal of Applied Sociology* 9:18-24.

———. 1925[1952]. "Immigrant Community and Immigrant Press." In *The Collected Papers of Robert Park*, ed. E. Hughes, 3:152-645. Glencoe IL: Free Press.

———. 1928. "Migration and the Marginal Man." *AJS* 33:881-93.

———. 1973[1927]. "Life History." *AJS* 79:251-60.

Park, Robert E., and Ernest W. Burgess. 1921[1924, 1970]. *Introduction to the Science of Society*. Chicago: Univ. Chicago Press.

Park, Robert E., and Herbert A. Miller. 1921. *Old World Traits Transplanted*. New York: Harper.

Parsons, Elsie Clews. 1936. *Mitla*. Chicago: Univ. of Chicago Press.

Passin, Herbert. 1947. "A Note on Japanese Research in Formosa." *American Anthropologist* 49:514-18.

———. 1982. *Encounter with Japan*. Tokyo: Kodansha.

Passin, Herbert, and John W. Bennett. 1943. "Changing Agricultural Magic in Southern Illinois: A Systematic Analysis of Folk-Urban Transition." *SF* 22:98-106.

Pasternak, Burton. 1972. *Kinship and Community in Two Chinese Villages*. Stanford CA: Stanford Univ. Press.

———. 1983. "Sociology and Anthropology in China: Revitalization and Its

Constraints." In *The Social Sciences and Fieldwork in China: Views from the Field*, ed. A. Thurston and B. Pasternak, 37–62. Boulder CO: Westview.

———. 1989. "Age at First Marriage in a Taiwanese Locality, 1916–1945." *Journal of Family History* 14:91–117.

Peace, William J. 2004. *Leslie A. White: Evolution and Revolution in Anthropology*. Lincoln: Univ. of Nebraska Press.

Perry, Helen S. 1982. *The Psychiatrist in America*. Cambridge MA: Harvard Univ. Press.

Petras. John W. 1970. "Changes of Emphasis in the Sociology of W. I. Thomas." *Journal of the History of the Behavioral Sciences* 6:70–79.

Pfautz, Harold W., and Otis Dudley Duncan. 1950. "A Critical Evaluation of Warner's Work in Community Stratification." *ASR* 15:205–15.

Phillips, Herbert P. 1973. "Some Premises of American Scholarship on Thailand." In *Western Values and Southeast Asian Scholarship*, ed. J. Fischer, 446–66. Berkeley: Center for South and Southeast Asian Studies.

Platt, Jennifer. 1983. "The Development of the 'Participant Observation' Method in Sociology." *Journal of the History of the Behavioral Sciences* 19:379–93.

———. 1992. "Mrs. Ethel Sturges Dummer's Role in Sociology." *American Sociologist* 23:23–26.

Potter, Jack M., May N. Diaz, and George M. Foster, eds. 1967. *Peasant Society: A Reader*. Boston: Little Brown.

Powell, John Wesley. 1881. *First Annual Report of the Bureau of Ethnology*. Washington DC: U.S. Government Printing Office.

———. 1891. "Indian Linguistic Families of America North of Mexico." *Bureau of Ethnology Annual Report* 7:1–142.

Preston, Richard J. 1983. "The Social Structure of an Unorganized Society: Beyond Intentions and Peripheral Boasians." In *Consciousness and Inquiry: Ethnology and Canadian Realities*, ed. Frank Manning, 286–305. Mercury Series 89E. Ottawa: National Museums of Canada.

Price, David H. 1998. "Cold War Anthropology: Collaborators and Victims of the National Security State." *Identities* 4:389–430.

———. 2002a. "Interlopers and Invited Guests: On Anthropology's Witting and Unwitting Links to Intelligence Agencies." *Anthropology Today* 18(6):16–21.

———. 2002b. "Lessons from Second World War Anthropology." *Anthropology Today* 18(3):14–20.

———. 2008. *Anthropological Intelligence: The Deployment and Neglect of American Anthropology in the Second World War*. Durham NC: Duke Univ. Press.

Punch, Maurice. 1986. *The Politics and Ethics of Fieldwork*. Qualitative Research Methods, 3. Beverly Hills CA: Sage.

Pykles, Benjamin C. 2009. *"The Archaeology of the Mormons Themselves": The Restoration of Nauvoo and the Rise of Historical Archaeology in America*. Lincoln: Univ. of Nebraska Press.

Radcliffe-Brown, A. R. 1922. *The Andaman Islanders*. Cambridge: Univ. Press.

———. 1952a. "Historical Note on British Social Anthropology." *American Anthropologist* 54:275–77.

———. 1952b. *Structure and Function in Primitive Society*. Glencoe IL: Free Press.

Radcliffe-Brown, A. R., and Daryll Forde. 1950. *African Systems of Kinship and Marriage*. New York: Oxford Univ. Press.

Rapaport, Roy. 1986. "Desecrating the Holy Woman." *American Scholar* 55:313–47.

Rauschenbush, Winifred. 1979. *Robert E. Park*. Durham NC: Duke Univ. Press.

Redfield, Robert. 1928a. "Among the Middle Americans: A Chicago Family's Adventures as Adopted Citizens of a Mexican Village." *Univ. of Chicago Magazine* 20:242–47.

———. 1928b. "A Plan for a Study of Tepoztlán, Morelos." PhD diss., Univ. of Chicago.

———. 1929a. "The Antecedents of Mexican Immigration to the United States." *AJS* 35:433–38.

———. 1929b. Review of M. Mead 1928. *AJS* 34:728–30.

———. 1930. *Tepoztlán, a Mexican Village: A Study of Folk Life*. Chicago: Univ. of Chicago Press.

———. 1931. Introduction. In *The Mexican Immigrant: Autobiographic Documents*, by Manuel Gamio, xi–xv. Chicago: Univ. of Chicago Press.

———. 1939a. "Culture Contact without Conflict." *AA* 41:514–17.

———. 1939b. "Primitive Merchants of Guatemala." *Quarterly Journal of Inter-American Relations* 1:42–56. (Reprinted in Redfield 1962:200–210.)

———. 1940. "The Folk Society and Culture." In *Eleven Twenty-Sex*, ed. Louis Wirth, 731–42. Chicago: Univ. of Chicago Press.

———. 1941. *The Folk Culture of the Yucatan*. Chicago: Univ. of Chicago Press.

———. 1950a. *The Primitive World and Its Transformation*. Chicago: Univ. of Chicago Press.

———. 1950b. *A Village that Chose Progress: Chan Kom Revisited*. Chicago: Univ. of Chicago Press.

———. 1953. "Relations of Anthropology to the Social Sciences and to the Humanities." In *Anthropology Today*, ed. A. Kroeber, 728–38. Chicago: Univ. Chicago Press.

———. 1954a. "Community Studies in Japan and China." *Far Eastern Quarterly* 14:3–10.

———. 1954b. Methods in Cultural Anthropology. (Anthropology 340 syllabus.)

———. 1954c. "The Peasant's View of the Good Life." Lecture included in Redfield 1962:310–26.

———. 1955a. *The Little Community*. Chicago: Univ. of Chicago Press.

———. 1955b. "The Social Organization of Tradition." *Far Eastern Quarterly* 15:13–21. (Reprinted in Redfield 1962:302–10.)

———. 1956a. *Peasant Society and Culture: An Anthropological Approach to Civilization*. Chicago: Univ. of Chicago Press.

———. 1956b. "The Relations between Indians and Ladinos in Agua Escondida, Guatemala." *América Indígena* 16:253–76. (Reprinted in Redfield 1962:210–30.)

———. 1957. "Thinker and Intellectual in Primitive Society." In Redfield 1962:350–63.

———. 1960. *The Little Community and Peasant Society and Culture*. Chicago: Univ. of Chicago Press.

———. 1962. *Human Nature and the Study of Society*. Edited by Margaret Park. Chicago: Univ. of Chicago Press.

Redfield, Robert, Ralph Linton, and Melville J. Herskovits. 1936. "Memorandum for the Study of Acculturation." *AA* 38:149–52.

Redfield, Robert, and Alfonso Villa Rojas. 1934. *Chan Kom: A Maya Village*. Chicago: Univ. of Chicago Press.

Reischauer, Edwin O. 1981. *The Japanese*. Cambridge MA: Harvard Univ. Press.

Rhoades, Lawrence J. 1981. *A History of the American Sociological Association, 1905–1980*. Washington DC: American Sociological Association.

Riess, Suzanne. 1999. *An Anthropologist's Life in the Twentieth Century: Theory and Practice at UC Berkeley, the Smithsonian, in Mexico, and with the World Health Organization of George M. Foster*. Berkeley CA: Regional Oral History Office. http://ark.cdlib.org/ark:/13030/kt7s2005ng.

Rigdon, Susan M. 1988. *The Culture Façade: Art, Science, and Politics in the Work of Oscar Lewis*. Urbana: Univ. of Illinois Press.

Riley, John, and Matilda White. 1940. "The Uses of Various Methods of Contraception." *ASR* 5:890–93.

———. 1941. "Actual and Preferred Sources of Contraceptive Information." *ASR* 6:33–36.

Róheim, Géza. 1932. "Psychoanalysis of Primitive Cultural Types." *International Journal of Psychoanalysis* 13:1–224.

Rohsenow, Hill Gates. 1973a. Review of *Gods, Ghosts and Ancestors*, by David Jordan. *Journal of Asian Studies* 33:478–80.

———. 1973b. Review of *Kinship and Community in Two Chinese Villages*, by Burton Pasternak. *Journal of Asian Studies* 33:476–78.

———. 1975. Review of *Religion in Chinese Society*, ed. Arthur P. Wolf. *Journal of Asian Studies* 35:487–99.

Rosaldo, Renato. 1976. "The Story of Tukbaw." In *The Biographical Process*, ed. F. Reynolds and D. Capp, 121–51. The Hague: Mouton.

Roscoe, Will. 1998. *Changing Ones: Third and Fourth Genders in Native North America*. New York: St. Martin's Press.

Roth, Julius A. 1974. "Professionalism: The Sociologist's Decoy." *Work and Occupations* 1:6–23.

Rubinstein, Robert A. 1991. *Doing Fieldwork: The Correspondence of Robert Redfield and Sol Tax*. Boulder CO: Westview.

Ruitenbeek, Hendrik M. 1963. *The Problem of Homosexuality in Modern Society*. New York: Dutton.

Sahlins, Marshall. 1981. *Historical Metaphors and Mystical Realities*. Ann Arbor: Univ. of Michigan Press.

Said, Edward. 1978. *Orientalism*. New York: Vintage.

Sakoda, James Ma. 1989a. "Reminiscences of a Participant Observer." In Ichioka 1989:219–45.

———. 1989b. "The 'Residue': Unsettled Minidokans, 1943–1945." In Ichioka 1989:247–81.

Samarin, William J. 1967. *Field Linguistics*. New York: Holt, Rinehart and Winston.

———. 1972. *Tongues of Men and Angels: The Religious Language of Pentecostalism*. New York: Macmillan.

———. 1980. "Theory of Order with Disorderly Data." In *Linguistics and Anthropology*, ed. Dale Kinkade, 505–19. Lisse: Ridder.

Samelson, Franz. 1981. "Struggle for Scientific Authority: The Reception of Watson's Behaviorism, 1913–1920." *Journal of the History of the Behavioral Sciences* 17:399–425.

———. 1985. "Organizing the Kingdom of Behavior: Academic Battles and Organization Policies in the Twenties." *Journal of the History of the Behavioral Sciences* 21:33–47.

Sandel, Todd L. 2003. "Linguistic Capital in Taiwan: The KMT's Mandarin Language Policy and Its Perceived Impact on Language Practices of Bilingual Mandarin and Tai-gi Speakers." *Language in Society* 32:523–51.

Sangren, P. Steven. 1987. *History and Magical Power in a Chinese Community*. Stanford CA: Stanford Univ. Press.

———. 2001. *Chinese Sociologics: An Anthropological Account of the Role of Alienation in Social Reproduction*. London: Athlone.

Sanjek, Roger. 1990. *Fieldnotes: The Makings of Anthropology*. Ithaca NY: Cornell Univ. Press.

Sapir, Edward. 1916. *Time Perspective in Aboriginal American Culture*. Canadian Geological Survey Memoir 90. Ottawa: Government Printing Bureau.

———. 1917. "Do We Need a 'Superorganic'?" *AA* 18:327–37.

———. 1921a. "A Bird's Eye View of American Languages North of Mexico." *Science* 54:408.

———. 1921b. *Language*. New York: Harcourt Brace.

———. 1922. "Athabaskan Tone." *AA* 24:390–91.

———. 1924. "Culture, Genuine and Spurious." *AJS* 29:401–29.

———. 1925. "Sound Patterns in Language." *Language* 1:37–51.

———. 1927a. "Anthropology and Sociology." In *The Social Sciences and Their Interrelations*, ed. W. F. Ogburn and A. A. Goldenweiser, 97–113. Boston: Little, Brown.

———. 1927b. Review of *Crashing Thunder*, by Paul Radin. *AJS* 33:303–4.

———. 1927c. "Speech as a Personality Trait." *AJS* 32:892–905.

———. 1929. "The Discipline of Sex." *American Mercury* 16:413–20.

———. 1930. "What Is the Family Still Good For?" *American Mercury* 19:145–51.

———. 1931. "The Concept of Phonetic Law as Tested in Primitive Languages by Leonard Bloomfield." In *Methods in Social Science*, ed. Stuart Rice, 297–306. Chicago: Univ. of Chicago Press.

———. 1930–31. "The Southern Paiute Language." *Proceedings of the American Academy of Arts and Sciences* 65:1–730.

———. 1937. "The Contribution of Psychiatry to an Understanding of Behavior in Society." *AJS* 42:862–70.

———. 1938a. Foreword. In *Son of Old Man Hat*, by Walter Dyk, v–x. New York: Harcourt.

———. 1938b. "Why Cultural Anthropology Needs the Psychiatrist." *Psychiatry* 1:7–12.

Sauer, Carl O. 1936. "American Agricultural Origins: A Consideration of Nature and Culture." In *Essays in Anthropology Presented to A. L. Kroeber in Celebration of His Sixtieth Birthday*, 279–97. Berkeley: Univ. of California Press.

———. 1951. "Folkways of Social Science." Mimeographed address for the dedication of Ford Hall at the Univ. of Minnesota. Sauer Collection, Bancroft Library, Univ. of California, Berkeley.

Scarpaci, J. 1973. Review of Chapman 1971. *International Migration Review* 7:212–13.

Schneebaum, Tobias. 1969. *Keep the River on Your Right*. New York: Grove Press.

Schneider, David M. 1968[1980]. *American Kinship: A Cultural Account*. Chicago: Univ. of Chicago Press.

———. 1995. *Schneider on Schneider*. Durham NC: Duke Univ. Press.

Scollon, Ronald. 1979. "236 Years of Variability in Chipewyan." *IJAL* 45:332–42.

———. 1995. "Coercive Citation." *Anthropology Newsletter*, April:5.

Scollon, Ronald, and Suzanne Scollon. 1979. *Linguistic Convergence: An Ethnography of Speaking at Fort Chipewyan, Alberta*. San Francisco: Academic Press.

Scott, Clifford H. 1976. *Lester Frank Ward*. Boston: Twayne.

Shankman, Paul. 1996. "The History of Samoan Sexual Conduct and the Mead-Freeman Controversy." *AA* 98:555-67.

———. 1998. "All Things Considered." *AA* 97:977-79.

———. 2000. "Culture, Biology, and Evolution: The Mead–Freeman Controversy Revisited." *Journal of Youth and Adolescence* 29:539-56.

———. 2013. "The 'Fateful Hoaxing' of Margaret Mead: A Cautionary Tale." *Current Anthropology* 54:51-70.

Shankman, Paul, and Paul S. Boyer. 2009. *The Trashing of Margaret Mead: Anatomy of an Anthropological Controversy*. Madison: Univ. of Wisconsin Press.

Shaw, Clifford R. 1930. *The Jack-Roller: A Delinquent Boy's Own Story*. Chicago: Univ. Chicago Press.

———. 1931. *The Natural History of a Delinquent Career*. Chicago: Univ. Chicago Press.

Shibutani, Tamotsu. 1941. Fieldnotes. JERS Archives, Bancroft Library, Univ. of California, Berkeley.

———. 1966. *Improvised News*. Indianapolis: Boobs-Merrill.

Sica, Alan. 2007. "Defining Disciplinary Identity: The Historiography of U.S. Sociology." In *Sociology in America: A History*, ed. Craig Calhoun, 713-31. Chicago: Univ. of Chicago Press.

Simon, Scott. 2000. "Entrepreneurship and Empowerment: Experiences of Taiwanese Businesswomen." *Anthropology of Work Review* 21(3):19-24.

———. 2003a. "Contesting Formosa: Tragic Remembrance, Urban Space, and National Identity in Taipak." *Identities* 10:109-31.

———. 2003b. *Sweet and Sour: Life Worlds of Taipei Women Entrepreneurs*. Lanham MD: Rowman and Littlefield.

Singer, Milton. 1991. *Semiotics of Cities, Selves, and Cultures*. Berlin: Mouton de Gruyter.

Singer, Philip, and Kate W. Ankenbrandt. 1980. "The Ethnography of the Paranormal." *Phoenix: New Directions in the Study of Man* 4:19-34.

Siu, Helen F. 1993. "Cultural Identity and the Politics of Difference in South China." *Dædalus* 122(2):19-43.

Siu, Paul Chan Pang. 1952. "The Sojourner." *AJS* 58:34-44.

———. 1987[1953]. *The Chinese Laundryman: A Study of Social Isolation*. New York: New York Univ. Press.

Skinner, G. William. 1954. "A Study of Chinese Community Leadership in Bangkok Together with an Historical Survey of Chinese Society in Thailand." PhD diss., Cornell Univ. (Revised version published in 1958 by Cornell Univ. Press.)

———. 1964. "Marketing and Social Structure in Rural China." *Journal of Asian Studies* 24:3-23.

Skolnick, Jerome H. 1967. *Justice without Trial—Law Enforcement in Democratic Society*. New York: Wiley.

Small, Albion W. 1916. "Fifty Years of Sociology in the United States." *AJS* 21:721-864.

———. 1924. *The Origins of Sociology*. Chicago: Univ. of Chicago Press.

———. 1926. "Sociology and Plato's *Republic*." *AJS* 32:49-58.

Smith, Robert J. 1961. "The Japanese Rural Community: Norm, Sanction, and Ostracism." *AA* 63:241-64.

———. 1983. *Japanese Society*. Cambridge: Cambridge Univ. Press.

———. 1989. "Something Old, Something New: Tradition and Culture in the Study of Japan." *Journal of Asian Studies* 48:715-23.

Smith, Robert J., and John B. Cornell. 1956. *Two Japanese Villages*. Ann Arbor MI: Center for Japanese Studies.

Smith, Robert J., and Ella Lury Wiswell. 1982. *The Women of Suye Mura*. Chicago: Univ. of Chicago Press.

Smith, Stanley H. 1974. "Sociological Fieldwork and Fisk University." In *Black Sociologists*, ed. J. Blackwell and M. Janowitz, 164-90. Chicago: Univ. of Chicago Press.

Smith, Zadie. 2009. "Speaking in Tongues." *New York Review*, February 26: 41-44.

Solovey, Mark. 2001. "Project Camelot and the 1960s Epistemological Revolution: Rethinking the Politics-Patronage-Social Science Nexus." *Social Studies of Science* 31:171-206.

Sorokin, Pitirim, Carle Zimmerman, and Charles Galpin. 1931. *Source Book in Rural Sociology*. Minneapolis: Univ. of Minnesota Press.

Sorokin, Pitirim A., and Robert K. Merton.

———. 1937. "Social Time." *AJS* 42:615-29.

Speare, Alden Jr., Paul Liu, and Ching-Lung Tsay. 1988. *Urbanization and Development: The Rural-Urban Transition in Taiwan*. Boulder CO: Westview.

Spencer, Robert F. 1989. "Gila in Retrospect." In Ichioka 1989:157-75.

Spicer, Edward H. 1940. *Pascua*. Chicago: Univ. of Chicago Press.

———. 1954. *Potam*. American Anthropological Association Memoir 77. Menasha WI: American Anthropological Association.

———. 1962. *Cycles of Conquest: The Impact of Spain, Mexico and the United States on the Indians of the Southwest*. Tucson: Univ. of Arizona Press.

———. 1980. *The Yaquis: A Cultural History*. Tucson: Univ. of Arizona Press.

———. 1988[1941–42]. *People of Pascua*, ed. Kathleen Sands and Rosamond Spicer. Tucson: Univ. of Arizona Press.

Spicer, Edward H., Asael T. Hansen, Katherine Luomala, and Marvin K. Opler. 1946. *Impounded People*. Washington DC: Department of the Interior.

Spier, Leslie. 1929. Review of *The Building of Culture,* by Roland Dixon. *American Anthropologist* 31:140–45.

Spindler, George D. 1978. *The Makings of Psychological Anthropology*. Berkeley: Univ. of California Press.

Spykman, Nicholas J. 1925. *The Social Theories of Georg Simmel*. Chicago: Univ. of Chicago Press.

Stadtman, Verne A. 1967. *Centennial Record of the University of California*. Berkeley: Univ. of California Printing Dept.

Stafford, Charles. 1992. "Good Sons and Virtuous Mothers: Kinship and Chinese Nationalism in Taiwan." *Man* 27:363–78.

———. 1995. *The Roads of Chinese Childhood: Learning and Identification in Angang*. Cambridge: Cambridge Univ. Press.

———. 2000. *Separation and Religion in Modern China*. Cambridge: Cambridge Univ. Press.

Starn, Orin. 1986. "Engineering Internment: Anthropologists and the War Relocation Authority." *American Ethnologist* 13:700–720.

Stegner, Wallace E. 1954. *Beyond the 100th Meridian: John Wesley Powell and the Second Opening of the West*. Boston: Houghton-Mifflin.

Stehr, Nico. 1978. "The Ethos of Science Revisited." In *The Sociology of Science*, ed. Jerry Gaston, 178–85. San Francisco: Jossey-Bass.

Stekel, Wilhelm. 1933[1917]. *Bisexual Love: The Homosexual Neurosis*. Boston: Badger.

Stern, Bernhard J. 1929. "Concerning the Distinction between the Social and the Cultural." *SF* 8:264–71.

———. 1934. *The Lummi Indians of Washington State*. New York: Columbia Univ. Press.

Steward, Julian. 1937. "Ecological Aspects of Southwestern Society." *Anthropos* 32:87–104.

———. 1938. Review of Eggan 1937. *AA* 40:720–22.

———. 1950. *Area Research*. Bulletin 63. New York: Social Science Research Council.

———. 1955. *Theory of Culture Change: The Methodology of Multilinear Evolution*. Urbana: Univ. of Illinois Press.

———. 1956. *The People of Puerto Rico: A Study in Social Anthropology*. Urbana: Univ. of Illinois Press.

———. 1960. "John Reed Swanton." *National Academy of Sciences Biographical Memoirs* 34:328–49.

———. 1967. *Contemporary Change in Traditional Societies*. 3 vols. Urbana: Univ. of Illinois Press.

———. 1977. *Evolution and Ecology*. Urbana: Univ. of Illinois Press.

Stocking, George W., Jr. 1968. *Race, Culture and Evolution*. New York: Free Press.

———. 1974a. "The Boas Plan for the Study of American Indian Languages." In *Traditions and Paradigms*, ed. Dell Hymes, 454-83. Bloomington: Indiana Univ. Press.

———. 1974b. *The Shaping of American Anthropology, 1883-1911: A Franz Boas Reader*. New York: Basic Books.

———. 1979. "Anthropology at Chicago" (pamphlet). Chicago: Regenstein Library.

Strathern, Marilyn. 1983. "The Punishment of Margaret Mead." *Canberra Anthropology* 6:70-79.

Sugimoto, Y. 1971. "Japanese in Taiwan." *Current Trends in Linguistics* 8:969-95.

Sullivan, Gerald. 1999. *Margaret Mead, Gregory Bateson, and Highland Bali*. Chicago: Univ. of Chicago Press.

Sullivan, Paul. 1989. *Unfinished Conversations: Mayas and Foreigners between Two Wars*. New York: Knopf.

Suzuki, Mitsuo. 1976. "The Shamanistic Element in Taiwanese Folk Religion." In *The Realm of the Extra-Human: Agents and Audiences*, ed. Agehananda Bharati, 253-60. The Hague: Mouton.

Suzuki, Peter T. 1981. "Anthropologists in the Wartime Camps for Japanese Americans." *Dialectical Anthropology* 6:23-60.

———. 1986. "The University of California Japanese Evacuation and Resettlement Study: A Prolegomenon." *Dialectical Anthropology* 10:189-213.

———. 1989. "For the Sake of 'Inter-university Comity': The Attempted Suppression by the University of California of Morton Grodzins' *Americans Betrayed*." In Ichioka 1989:95-123.

Swanton, John R. 1915. "Reply." *AA* 17:600-601.

———. 1930. "Some Neglected Data Bearing on Cheyenne, Chippewa and Dakota History." *AA* 32:155-60.

———. 1932. "Ethnological Value of de Soto Narratives." *AA* 34:570-90.

———. 1942. *Source Materials on the History and Ethnology of the Caddo Indians*. Bureau of American Ethnology Bulletin 132. Washington DC: U.S. Government Printing Office.

———. 1952. *Indians of the Southeastern United States*. Bureau of American Ethnology Bulletin 145. Washington DC: U.S. Government Printing Office.

Swanton, John R., and Roland B. Dixon. 1914. "Primitive American History." *AA* 16:376-412.

Taeuber, Irene B. 1974. "Migrants and Cities in Japan, Taiwan, and Northeastern China." In *The Chinese City between Two Worlds*, ed. Mark Elvin and G. W. Skinner, 359–84. Stanford CA: Stanford Univ. Press.

Tambiah, Stanley J. 1970. *Buddhism and the Spirit Cults in Northeast Thailand*. Cambridge: Cambridge Univ. Press.

Tan, Shao-Hwa. 1925. "Chinese Characters: Their Nature, Origin and Development." MA diss., Univ. of Chicago.

Tang Mei Chun. 1978. *Urban Chinese Families: An Anthropological Field Study in Taipei City, Taiwan*. Taipei: National Taiwan Univ. Press.

Tanner, J. M., and Bärbel Inhelder. 1956. *Discussions on Child Development*. London: Tavistock.

Tax, Sol. 1937a. "The *Municipios* of the Midwestern Highlands of Guatemala." AA 39:423–44.

Tax, Sol. 1937b. "Some Problems of Social Organization." In Eggan 1937:3–32.

———. 1941. "World View and Social Relations in Indian Guatemala." AA 43:27–42.

———. 1952. *Penny Capitalism: A Guatemalan-Indian Economy*. Smithsonian Institution Publication in Social Anthropology 16. Washington DC: U.S. Government Printing Office.

Tedlock, Dennis. 1993. *Breath on the Mirror: Mythic Voices and Visions of the Living Maya*. San Francisco: HarperCollins.

Teggart, Frederick J. 1910. "The Circumstance or the Substance of History." *American Historical Review* 15:709–19.

———. 1916. *Prolegomena to History*. Berkeley: Univ. of California Press.

———. 1918. *The Processes of History*. New Haven CT: Yale Univ. Press.

———. 1929. "Note on Timeless Sociology." SF 7:362–65.

———. 1939. *Rome and China*. Berkeley: Univ. of California Press.

———. 1941. *Theory and Processes of History*. Berkeley: Univ. of California Press.

tenBroek, Jacobus. 1951. *The Antislavery Origins of the Fourteenth Amendment*. Berkeley: Univ. of California Press.

tenBroek, Jacobus, Edward Barnhart, and Floyd Matson. 1954. *Prejudice, War and the Constitution*. Berkeley: Univ. of California Press.

Thelin, Mark. 1977. *Two Taiwanese Villages*. Daidiong, Taiwan: Dunghai Univ.

Thomas, Dorothy Swaine. 1929. "Statistics in Social Research." *American Journal of Sociology* 35:1–17.

———. 1941. *Social and Economic Aspects of Swedish Population Movements, 1750–1933*. New York: Macmillan.

———. 1952a. "Experiences in Interdisciplinary Research." ASR 17: 663–69.

———. 1952b. *The Salvage*. Berkeley: Univ. of California Press.

———. 1970. "Contribution." In *Scientists at Work: Festchrift in Honour of Her-*

man *Wold*, ed. T. Dalenius, G. Karlson, and S. Malmquist, 206–27. Stockholm: Almquist and Wiksell.

Thomas, Dorothy Swaine, and Richard S. Nishimoto, with contributions by Rosalie A. Hankey, James Sakoda, Morton Grodzins, and Frank Miyamoto. 1946. *The Spoilage : Japanese-American Evacuation and Resettlement during World War II*. Berkeley: Univ. of California Press.

Thomas, Evan A. 1978b. "Herbert Blumer's Critique of *The Polish Peasant*: A Post Mortem on the Life History Approach in Sociology." *Journal of the History of the Behavioral Sciences* 14:124–31.

———. 1986. "The Sociology of William I. Thomas in Relation to *The Polish Peasant*." Ph.D. diss., Univ. of Iowa.

Thomas, W. I. 1909. *Source Book for Social Origins*. Chicago: Univ. of Chicago Press.

———. 1923. *The Unadjusted Girl*. Boston: Criminal Science Monographs.

———. 1925. "The Problem of Personality in the Urban Environment." *Publications of the American Sociological Society* 22: 1–13.

———. 1927. "The Configurations of Personality." In *The Unconscious: A Symposium*, ed. H. Koffka, 143–77. New York: Knopf.

———. 1928. *The Unadjusted Girl*. Boston: Little, Brown.

———. 1933. *Outline of a Program for the Study of Personality and Culture*. New York: Social Science Research Council.

———. 1937. *Primitive Behavior*. New York: McGraw-Hill.

———. 1973[1927]. "Life History." *AJS* 79:245–50.

Thomas, W. I., and Dorothy Swaine Thomas. 1928. *The Child in America*. New York: A. A. Knopf.

Thomas, W. I., and Florian Znaniecki. 1927[1918–20]. *The Polish Peasant in Europe and America*. 2 vols. New York: Knopf.

Thompson, Laura. 1951. *Personality and Government: Findings and Recommendations of the Indian Administration Research*. Mexico City: Ediciones del Instituto Indigenista Interamericano.

Thompson, Laura, and Alice Joseph. 1944. *The Hopi Way*. Chicago: Univ. of Chicago Press.

Thoresen, Timothy H. H. 1975. "Paying the Piper and Calling the Tune." *Journal of the History of the Behavioral Sciences* 11:157–75.

Thorne, Barrie. 1980. "'You Still Takin' Notes?': Fieldwork and Problems of Informed Consent." *Social Problems* 27:284–97.

Tozzer, A. M., and A .L. Kroeber. 1945. "Roland Burrage Dixon [obituary]." *AA* 47:104–18.

Tumin, Melvin M. 1945. "Culture, Genuine and Spurious: A Re-evaluation." *ASR* 10:199–207.

———. 1952. *Caste in a Peasant Society*. Princeton NJ: Princeton Univ. Press.

Valentine, L., and R. Darnell, eds. 1999. *Theorizing the Americanist Tradition.* Toronto: Univ. of Toronto Press.

Vansina, Jan. 1965. *Oral Tradition: A Study in Historical Methodology.* London: Routledge and Kegan Paul.

———. 1985. *Oral Tradition as History.* Madison: Univ. of Wisconsin Press.

Vickers, Adrian H. 1997. *Bali: A Paradise Created.* Singapore: Periplus.

Villa Rojas, Alfonso. 1945. *The Maya of East Central Quintana Roo.* Carnegie Institution of Washington Publication 559. Washington DC: Carnegie Institution.

———. 1979. "Fieldwork in the Mayan Region of Mexico." In *Long-Term Field Research in Social Anthropology*, ed. G. Foster et al., 45–64. New York: Academic Press.

Vogt, Evan Z., and Ethel M. Albert. 1966. *People of Rimrock: A Study of Values in Five Cultures.* Cambridge MA: Harvard Univ. Press.

Volkart, Edmund H. 1953. "Aspects of the Theories of W. I. Thomas." *Social Research* 20:345–57.

———. 1968. "W. I. Thomas." In *International Encyclopedia of Social Science*, 16:5. New York: Macmillan.

Wallace, Anthony F. C. 1952. "Individual Differences and Cultural Uniformities." *ASR* 17:747–50.

———. 1956. "Revitalization Movements." *American Anthropologist* 58:274–81.

———. 1970. *The Death and Rebirth of the Seneca.* New York: Knopf.

———. 2001. *Jefferson and the Indians: The Tragic Fate of the First Americans.* Cambridge MA: Harvard Univ. Press.

———. 2003. *Revitalization and Mazeways.* Lincoln: Univ. of Nebraska Press.

Wallace, Anthony F. C., and John Atkins. 1960. "The Meaning of Kinship Terms." *AA* 62:58–80.

Warner, W. Lloyd. 1937. *A Black Civilization.* New York: Harper and Row.

Warner, W. Lloyd, and Paul S. Lunt. 1941. *The Social Life of a Modern Community.* New Haven CT: Yale Univ. Press.

Wang Fu-Chang. 1994. "Ethnic Assimilation and Mobilization." *Bulletin of the Institute of Ethnology, Academia Sinica* 77:1–34

Watson, James L. 1976. Review of *Religion and Ritual in Chinese Society*, by Arthur Wolf. *China Quarterly* 66:355–64.

Wax, Dustin M. 2008. *Anthropology at the Dawn of the Cold War.* London: Pluto Press.

Wax, Murray L. 1956. "The Limitations of Boas' Anthropology." *AA* 58:63–74.

———. 1971. *Indian Americans.* Toronto: Prentice-Hall.

———. 1991. "The Ethics of Research in American Indian Communities." *American Indian Quarterly* 15:431–56.

Wax, Rosalie H. 1971. *Doing Fieldwork*. Chicago: Univ. of Chicago Press.

Weiner, Annette. 1983. "Ethnographic Determinism." *AA* 85:909-18.

Weller, Robert P. 1987. *Unities and Diversities in Chinese Religion*. Seattle: Univ. of Washington Press.

———. 1994. *Resistance, Chaos and Control in China: Taiping Rebels, Taiwanese Ghosts and Tiananmen*. Seattle: Univ. of Washington Press.

———. 1999. *Alternate Civilities: Democracy and Culture in China and Taiwan*. Boulder CO: Westview.

———. 2000. "Living at the Edge: Religion, Capitalism, and the End of the Nation-State in Taiwan." *Public Culture* 12:477-98.

Wen, Lily. 2000. "Colonialism, Gender and Work: A Voice from the People of the Lily and the Leopard." *Anthropology of Work Review* 21(3):24-27.

Westrum, Ron. 1982. "Social Intelligence about Hidden Events." *Knowledge: Creation, Diffusion, Utilization* 3:381-400.

White, Leslie A. 1963. *The Ethnography and Ethnology of Franz Boas*. Austin: Texas Memorial Museum.

Whiting, John, and Beatrice Whiting. 1978. "A Strategy for Psychocultural Research." In *The Makings of Psychological Anthropology*, ed. G. Spindler, 41-61. Berkeley: Univ. of California Press.

Wikan, Unni. 1990. *Managing Turbulent Hearts: A Balinese Formula for Living*. Chicago: Univ. of Chicago Press.

Wilen, Tracey. 1995. *Asia for Women on Business: Hong Kong, Taiwan, Singapore, and South Korea*. Berkeley CA: Stone Bridge Press.

Willey, Malcolm M. 1929. "The Validity of the Culture Concept." *AJS* 35: 204-19.

Williams, Jack F. 1988. "Urban and Regional Planning in Taiwan: The Quest for Balanced Regional Development." *Tijdschrift voor economische en sociale geografie* 79:175-81.

———. 1989. "Paying the Price of Economic Development in Taiwan: Environmental Degradation." *Journal of Oriental Studies* 27:58-78.

Winckler, Edwin A., and Susan M. Greenhalgh. 1988. *Contending Approaches to the Political Economy of Taiwan*. Armonk NY: M. E. Sharpe.

Winkin, Yves. 1988. "Goffman à Baltasound." *Politex* 3/4:66-70.

Winks, Robin W. 1987. *Cloak and Gown: Scholars in the Secret War, 1939-1961*. New York: Morrow.

Winston, Ellen Black. 1934. "The Alleged Lack of Mental Diseases among Primitive Groups." *AA* 36: 234-38.

———. 1935. "The Assumed Increase of Mental Illness." *AJS* 40:427-39.

Winter, Jürgen. 1979. *Bruno Gutmann, 1876-1966*. Oxford: Clarendon Press.

Wirth, Louis. 1938. "Urbanism as a Way of Life." *AJS* 44:1-24.

Wissler, Clark. 1927. "The Culture Area Concept in Social Anthropology." *AJS* 32:881-91.

Wittfogel, Karl A. 1957. *Oriental Despotism: A Comparative Study of Total Pow-er*. New Haven CT: Yale Univ. Press.

Wolf, Arthur P., ed. 1974. *Religion and Ritual in Chinese Society*. Stanford CA: Stanford Univ. Press.

———. 1981. "Domestic Organization." In Ahern and Gates 1981:341–60.

———. 1985. "The Study of Chinese Society on Taiwan." In *The Chinese Family and Its Ritual Behavior*, ed. Hsieh Jih-Chang and Chuang Ying-Chang, 3–26. Daiba, Taiwan: Institute of Ethnology, Academia Sinica.

———. 1995. *Sexual Attraction and Childhood Association: A Chinese Brief for Edward Westermarck*. Stanford CA: Stanford Univ. Press.

Wolf, Arthur P., and Chieh-shan Huang. 1980. *Marriage and Adoption in Chi-na*. Stanford CA: Stanford Univ. Press.

Wolf, Eric R. 1955. "Types of Latin American Peasantry." *AA* 57:452–71.

———. 1957. "Closed Corporate Peasant Communities in Mesoamerica and Central Java." *Southwestern Journal of Anthropology* 13:1–18.

———. 1966. *Peasants*. Toronto: Prentice-Hall.

———. 1969. *Peasant Wars of the Twentieth Century*. New York: Harper and Row.

———. 1982. *Europe and the People without History*. Berkeley: Univ. of Califor-nia Press.

———. 1999. *Envisioning Power: Ideologies of Dominance and Power*. Berkeley: Univ. of California Press.

Wolf, Margery. 1968. *The House of Lim*. London: Prentice-Hall.

———. 1972. *Women and the Family in Rural Taiwan*. Stanford CA: Stanford Univ. Press.

———. 1990. "The Woman Who Didn't Become a Shaman." *American Ethnol-ogist* 17:419–30.

———. 1992. *A Thrice-Told Tale: Feminism, Postmodernism, and Ethnographic Responsibility*. Stanford CA: Stanford Univ. Press.

Wright, Arthur F. 1953. *Studies in Chinese Thought*. American Anthropological Association Memoir 75. Menasha WI: American Anthropological Association.

Wright, Earl II. 2010. "The Tradition of Sociology at Fisk University." *Journal of African American Studies* 14:44–60.

Wright, Richard A. 1994a. "Does an Editorial Appointment Affect the Num-ber of Articles Appearing in the Editor's Primary Research Specializa-tion?" *Footnotes* (American Sociological Association) 27(3):3.

———. 1994b. "The Effect of Editorial Appointments on the Citations of Soci-ology Journal Editors, 1970–1989." *American Sociologist* 25:40–46.

Wu, David Yen-Ho. 1990. "Chinese Minority Policy and the Meaning of Minority Culture: The Example of the Bai in Yunnan, China." *Human Organization* 49:1-13.

——. 1997. "McDonald's in Taipei: Hamburgers, Betel Nuts, and National Identity." In *Golden Arches East: McDonald's in East Asia*, ed. James L. Watson, 110-35. Stanford CA: Stanford Univ. Press.

Wu Nai-Teh. 1992. "Party Support and National Identities: Social Cleavages and Party Competition in Taiwan." *Bulletin of the Institute of Ethnology, Academia Sinica* 74:33-61.

——. 2002. "Identity Conflict and Political Trust: Ethnic Politics in Contemporary Taiwan." *Taiwanese Sociology* 4:75-118.

Yang, Martin M. C. 1945. *A Chinese Village: Taitou, Shangtung Province*. New York: Columbia Univ. Press.

——. 1970. *Socio-economic Results of Land Reform in Taiwan*. Honolulu: East-West Center Press.

Yi Chin-Chun and Chien Wen-Yin. 2001. "The Continual Employment Patterns of Married Women in Taiwan: A Compromise between Family and Work." *Taiwanese Sociology* 1:149-82.

Yoshino, I[kuro] Roger. 1954. "Selected Social Changes in a Japanese Village, 1935-1953." PhD diss., Univ. of Southern California.

You Ying-Lung. 1994. "Party Image, Ideology, and Secular Realignment in Taiwan." *Bulletin of the Institute of Ethnology, Academia Sinica* 78:61-99.

Yu Wei-Hsin. 2001. "Taking Informality into Account: Women's Work in the Formal and Informal Sectors in Taiwan." In *Women's Working Lives in East Asia*, ed. Mary Brinton, 233-62. Stanford CA: Stanford Univ. Press.

Znaniecki, Florian. 1938. "Social Groups as Products of Participating Individuals." *AJS* 44:799-811.

——. 1942. Review of *An Apache Life Way*, by Morris Opler. *ASR* 7:724-26.

——. 1948. "W. I. Thomas as a Collaborator." *Sociology and Social Research* 32:765-67.

Zuckerman, Harriet. 1974. "Postmaturity of Scientific Discoveries." Paper presented at American Sociological Association meetings, Montreal.

——. 1977. "Deviant Behavior and Social Control in Science." In *Deviance and Social Change*, ed. Edward Sagarin, 87-138. Beverly Hills CA: Sage.

Zuckerman, Harriet, and Joshua Lederberg. 1986. "The Postmature Scientific Discovery." *Nature*, 18 December: 629-31.

Index

Abel, Theodore, 178
acculturation, 174
Adams, George, 258
Agassiz, Louis, 7–8
Ahern, Emily, 144
Aikin, Charles, xxiv, 213, 217, 220–21, 223, 224–47, 232–34, 235, 237, 239–42, 244, 311
Alpert, Harry, 64–65, 200
alyhâ, 104–5, 107–8
American Anthropologist, 265–67
American culture, xxiii, 205–10
American Ethnologist, 265–65
Americanist, 295
American Journal of Sociology, 194–99, 267–71
American Sociological Review, 199–201, 266–71
Anthropological Society of Washington, 9, 11
Arendt, Hannah, 50
Arensberg, Conrad, 83, 86, 205
Aristotle, 157
Athabaskan, 25–30

Bacon, Francis, 22
Bain, Read, 201
Barclay, George, 123
Baron, Salo, 196, 203
Barrows, David, 163
Bascom, William, 117, 118
Basso, Keith, xv, 98, 289

Beals, Ralph, 46, 55, 60, 79–80, 114, 299
Beardesley, Richard, 127
Beijinghua ("Mandarin"), 124, 130, 133, 150
Bendix, Reinhard, 261
Benedict, Laura, 90, 163
Benedict, Ruth, 34–36, 40, 47, 91, 96, 198, 203, 283
Bennett, John, 78–79, 84
Bernard, Luther, 165, 202, 204, 251
Bernard, Jessie, 209
Berremann, Gerald, 117, 118, 303
Biddle, Francis, 233
Bierstedt, Robert, 209
Blau, Peter, 315–16
Bloomfield, Leonard, 22, 23, 27, 189, 299
Blumer, Herbert, 165, 176, 181, 191, 193, 195, 197, 198, 201
Boas, Franz, xxi, 8–9, 12–13, 15, 17, 21, 23–24, 27, 33–48, 96, 158, 163–65, 178, 197, 200, 241, 254, 264, 281, 285, 307, 309
Bock, Kenneth, 250, 257, 261, 274
Bolton, Eugene, 249
Briggs, Jean, 98
Brown, Jennifer, 280
Brown, Melissa, 127, 152, 307
Bunzel, Ruth, 94, 196, 285
Bureau of American Ethnology (BAE), 9

Hokkien (Holo), 122, 127–29, 147, 150, 307

Holbrook, Bruce, 306

Hong, Keelung, xxii, 122–54

Honigman, John, 204

Hooton, E. A., 32, 205

Hopi, 179

Householder, Fred, 23

Hsu, Francis, 141–42, 305

Huang, Chiehshan, 123–29

Huff, Toby, 178

Hughes, Everett, xx, 50–52, 53, 173, 191, 195, 198

Hull, Clark, 180, 200

Human Relations Area Files (HRAF), 100, 284

Hunt, George, 281

Hurston, Zora, 89

hwamê, 104–8

Hymes, Dell, 88–89, 114, 115, 119, 276

immigrants, 181

James Madison College, xix, 289, 316

Japan, 70–73; household registry, 127, 304; occupation of Taiwan, 122, 124, 126–29, 134–38, 304

Japanese Evacuation and Resettlement Study (JERS), xxiv, 213–45, 256, 311–15

Jefferson, Thomas, 3–4

Johnson, Charles, 159

Johnson, Guy, 203

Johnson, Jane, 6

Johnson, Robert, 240, 244

Jones, William, 90

Journal of the Royal Anthropological Institute (JRAI), 265–66

Kardiner, Abraham, 200

Keller, Alfred, 189

Kelly, Lawrence, 89

Kemper, Robert, 83

Kerr, Clark, 116

Kidd, Arthur, 203

Kidder, A. V., 41

kinship, 129–30, 166, 300

Kirsch, A. T., 125, 304

Kleinman, Arthur, 144–47, 305

Kluckhohn, Clyde, 116, 119, 185, 200, 203, 300

Koffka, Kurt, 167

Kona, 73

Korea, 127, 150, 306

Krauss, Michael, 25–26, 29

Kroeber, Alfred, xvi, xxiii, 8–9, 12–13, 16, 20–21, 24, 35–37, 42–44, 46, 79–106, 108–12, 119, 165, 176, 177, 197, 202, 203, 215, 250, 252, 255, 283, 298, 300–301, 309

Kroeber, Clifton, 108

Kroeber, Theodora, 257, 313

Krogman, Wilton, 188, 191, 197

Kuhn, Thomas, xv, 31, 36, 274–75, 282, 283

Kung, Lydia, 148, 153

Kuomintang (KMT), 122–23, 125–26, 133–35, 145, 150, 153–54

Kuznets, George, 228, 238

Landes, Ruth, 280

La Violette, Forrest, 224–25, 236

Lazarus, Moritz, 162

Leach, Edmund, 141, 302

Lee, Dorothy, 98

Leighton, Alexander, 95–96, 312

Leslie, Charles, 53

Levi, Edward, 230–31, 237

Lévi-Strauss, Claude, xviii, 289, 301

Lévy-Bruhl, Lucien, 102, 177, 202, 203

Lewis, Oscar, 50, 51, 53, 58, 65, 82–83, 85–87, 297

Oedipus complex, 177
Ogburn, William, xx, xxiii, 35, 158, 168, 170, 174, 178–80, 182, 188, 192–93, 195–97, 255, 256, 263, 285, 309
Olson, Culbert, 223
Omaha, 88, 296
Opler, Morris, 186, 196, 198, 204
Oral traditions, 15–21
Orientalism, 139–40

Park, Robert, 52–53, 159, 169, 174, 176, 179, 181–82, 188, 192–93, 195–97, 255, 256, 263, 285, 309
Parsons, Elsie Clews, 80, 302, 303, 309
Parsons, Talcott, 253, 263
Pascua, 68–70
Passin, Herbert, 78
Pasternak, Burton, 135, 152
Peace, William, 107
peasants, xvi, 62–87
Peixotto, Jessica, 253–54
personality, 35–36, 42, 91, 157–71, 173–76, 183–85
Pfautz, Harold, 206
Philippines, 163
Phillips, Herbert, 125
phylogeny, 105
Plato, 157
pollution, 306
Popper, Karl, 42
popularization, 31–32, 49–51
postmaturity, xv–xvi, 172–73, 193
Potam, 69–70
Powdermaker, Hortense, 209, 210
Powell, John, 9–12, 24, 158, 296
Psmalmanzar, George, 304–5
Pueblo cultures, 110
Putnam, Frederic, 7–8, 21, 114, 163

Qing Dynasty, 129–30, 135–37, 304

racism, 27, 231–34, 244
Radcliffe-Brown, Alfred, 196, 199, 204–6
Radin, Paul, 30, 44, 109, 184, 185
Ratzel, Friedrich, 164
Redfield, Robert, xvi, xxi, 13, 52–79, 81–88, 91–93, 133, 159, 172, 190, 192–93, 195, 198, 264, 296, 297, 308, 309
Reichard, Gladys, 98, 298
Replication, 28, 72–73, 100
Republic of China. See Kuomintang (KMT)
Riesman, David, 209, 227, 229
Riley, John, 252
Rivers, W. H., 165, 187, 200, 202, 204, 298–99
Rivet, Paul, 102
Rockefeller Foundation(s), 55, 94, 100, 102, 107, 157, 171, 214, 219, 224, 228, 308, 311
Róheim, Géza, 203, 204
Roosevelt, Franklin, 213, 220, 311
Rosaldo, Renato, 185
Roscoe, Will, 103, 107–8
Rostow, Eugene, 229
Rousseau, Jean-Jacques, 85, 289
Rowe, John, 116

Sagan, Carl, 50
Said, Edward, 139
Saint Denis de Karmouraska, 74–75
Sakoda, James, 223–24, 238, 312–14
Salisbury, Richard, 117, 118
Samarin, William, xv, 23, 30, 289, 290
Samoa, 35–50
Sapir, Edward, 173–93, 196, 199, 281, 284–85
Sauer, Carl, 254, 313
Sawyer, Jesse, 20
Schmid, Robert, 206–7
Schneider, David, 116, 118, 119, 310

Excavating Nauvoo: The Mormons and the Rise of Historical Archaeology in America
Benjamin C. Pykles
Foreword by Robert L. Schuyler

Cultural Negotiations: The Role of Women in the Founding of Americanist Archaeology
David L. Browman

Homo Imperii: A History of Physical Anthropology in Russia
Marina Mogilner

American Anthropology and Company: Historical Explorations
Stephen O. Murray

Racial Science in Hitler's New Europe, 1939–1945
Edited by Anton Weiss-Wendt and Rory Yeomans

To order or obtain more information on these or other University of Nebraska Press titles, visit www.nebraskapress.unl.edu.